GHOST HUNT

4

MANGA BY SHIHO INADA

STORY BY FUYUMI ONO

TRANSLATED BY AKIRA TSUBASA

ADAPTED BY DAVID WALSH

LETTERED BY FOLTZ DESIGN

DEL
REY

BALLANTINE BOOKS · NEW YORK

A Del Rey Trade Paperback Original

Ghost Hunt copyright © 2000 by Fuyumi Ono and Shiho Inada
English translation copyright © 2006 by Fuyumi Ono and Shiho Inada

Published in the United States by Del Rey Books, an imprint of The Random House Publishing Group, a division of Random House, Inc., New York.

DEL REY is a registered trademark and the Del Rey colophon is a trademark of Random House, Inc.

Publication rights arranged through Kodansha Ltd.

First published in Japan in 2000 by Kodansha Ltd., Tokyo

ISBN 0-345-48680-3

Printed in the United States of America

www.delreymanga.com

1 2 3 4 5 6 7 8 9

Translator—Akira Tsubasa
Adaptor—David Walsh
Lettering and Text Design—Foltz Design
Cover Design—David Stevenson

CONTENTS

Honorifics Explained

Throughout the Del Rey Manga books, you will find Japanese honorifics left intact in the translations. For those not familiar with how the Japanese use honorifics, and, more important, how they differ from American honorifics, we present this brief overview.

Politeness has always been a critical facet of Japanese culture. Ever since the feudal era, when Japan was a highly stratified society, use of honorifics—which can be defined as polite speech that indicates relationship or status—has played an essential role in the Japanese language. When addressing someone in Japanese, an honorific usually takes the form of a suffix attached to one's name (example: "Asuna-san"), as a title at the end of one's name, or in place of the name itself (example: "Negi-sensei" or simply "Sensei!").

Honorifics can be expressions of respect or endearment. In the context of manga and anime, honorifics give insight into the nature of the relationship between characters. Many translations into English leave out these important honorifics, and therefore distort the feel of the original Japanese. Because Japanese honorifics contain nuances that English honorifics lack, it is our policy at Del Rey not to translate them. Here, instead, is a guide to some of the honorifics you may encounter in Del Rey Manga.

-san: This is the most common honorific and is equivalent to Mr., Miss, Ms., Mrs., etc. It is the all-purpose honorific and can be used in any situation where politeness is required.

-sama: This is one level higher than "-san." It is used to confer great respect.

-dono: This comes from the word "tono," which means "lord." It is an even higher level than "-sama" and confers utmost respect.

-kun: This suffix is used at the end of boys' names to express familiarity or endearment. It is also sometimes used by men among friends, or when addressing someone younger or of a lower station.

-chan: This is used to express endearment, mostly toward girls. It is also used for little boys, pets, and between lovers. It gives a sense of childish cuteness.

Bozu: This is an informal way to refer to a boy, similar to the English terms "kid" or "squirt."

Sempai/ Senpai: This title suggests that the addressee is one's senior in a group or organization. It is most often used in a school setting, where underclassmen refer to their upperclassmen as "sempai." It can also be used in the workplace, such as when a newer employee addresses an employee who has seniority in the company.

Kohai: This is the opposite of "-sempai," and is used toward underclassmen in school or newcomers in the workplace. It connotes that the addressee is of a lower station.

Sensei: Literally meaning "one who has come before," this title is used for teachers, doctors, or masters of any profession or art.

-[blank]: This is usually forgotten on these lists, but is perhaps the most significant difference between Japanese and English. The lack of honorific means that the speaker has permission to address the person in a very intimate way. Usually, only family, spouses, or very close friends have this kind of license. Known as *yobisute*, it can be gratifying when someone who has earned the intimacy starts to call one by one's name without an honorific. But when that intimacy hasn't been earned, it can also be insulting.

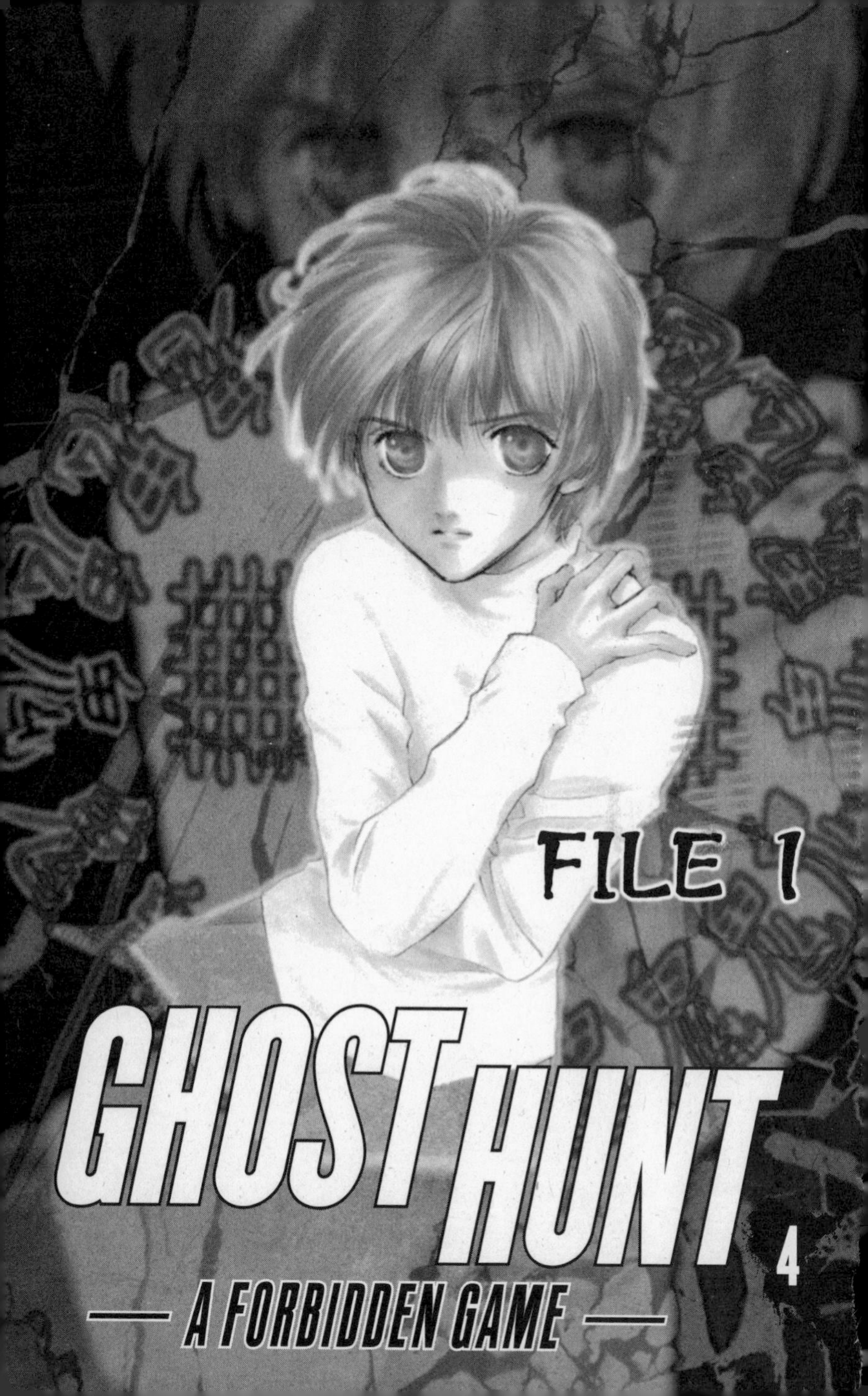
FILE 1
GHOST HUNT
4
— A FORBIDDEN GAME —

GHOST HUNT

THIS IS WHAT SPR IS ALL ABOUT!

CASES SO FAR AT SPR:

WE PLAY AN ACTIVE ROLE IN SOLVING VARIOUS PSYCHIC PHENOMENA. FOR EXAMPLE, WE RECENTLY WORKED ON A CASE AT AN OLD MANSION WHERE WE HAD TO PERFORM AN EXORCISM ON THE EVIL SPIRIT CAUSING THE POLTERGEIST THERE. WE'VE ALSO FOUND THE CAUSE OF PSYCHIC PHENOMENA AT A SCHOOL WHERE EVERYONE WAS IN A MAJOR PANIC OVER MYSTERIOUS EVENTS THAT HAD BEEN HAPPENING!!

SPR MEMBERS ARE...

BELOW ARE SPR MEMBERS WHO WERE ORIGINALLY HIRED TO PERFORM AN EXORCISM TO GET RID OF A SPIRIT AT MAI'S SCHOOL.

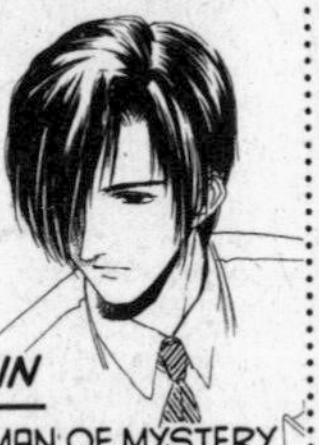

LIN

HE'S A MAN OF MYSTERY WHO WORKS CLOSELY WITH NARU.

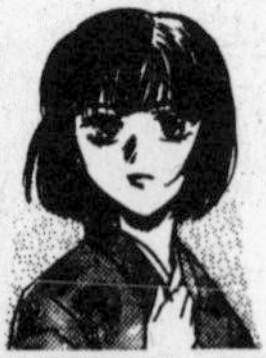

MASAKO HARA

A PSYCHIC MEDIUM. SHE IS WELL KNOWN IN THE PSYCHIC INDUSTRY.

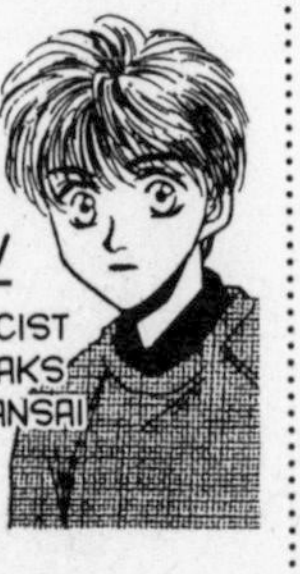

JOHN BROWN

AN EXORCIST WHO SPEAKS WITH A KANSAI DIALECT.

AYAKO MATSUZAKI

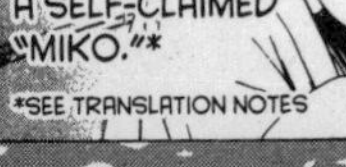

A SELF-CLAIMED "MIKO."*

HOUSHOU TAKIGAWA

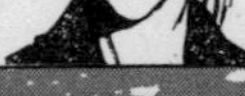

FORMERLY A MONK AT MT. KOYA.

*SEE TRANSLATION NOTES

SHIBUYA PSYCHIC RESEARCH (SPR)

AVAILABLE FOR HIRE TO SCIENTIFICALLY RESEARCH AND SUBDUE UNEXPLAINABLE PHENOMENA THAT OCCUR AROUND THEIR CLIENTS.

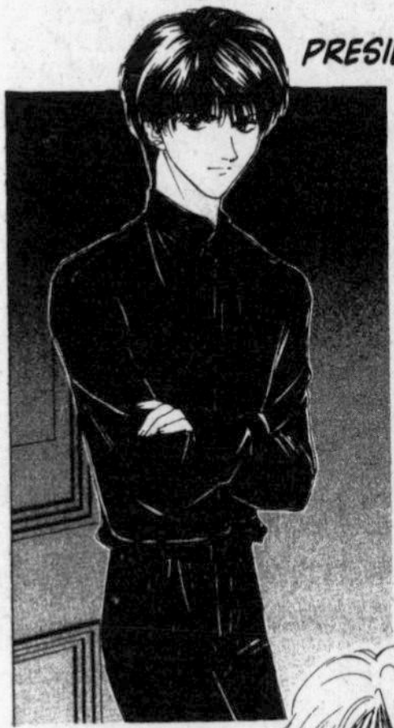

PRESIDENT OF SPR: KAZUYA SHIBUYA (AKA NARU)

17 YEARS OLD. HE'S COOL-HEADED, GOOD LOOKING AND SMART, BUT HE'S A SUPER NARCISSIST. SO HE HAS BEEN NICKNAMED NARU (SHORT FOR NARCISSIST).

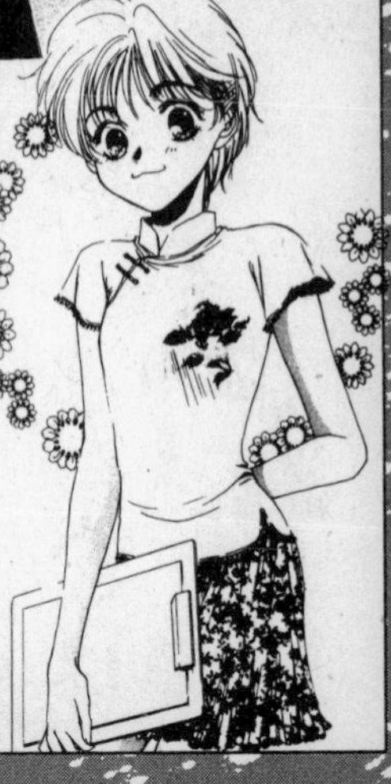

MAI TANIYAMA

A LIVELY 16-YEAR-OLD STUDENT WHO WORKS PART-TIME AT SPR. SHE'S ENTHUSIASTIC, THOUGH NARU ALWAYS GIVES HER A HARD TIME. (SHE'S ONLY SEEN NARU SMILE IN HER DREAMS!) BUT SHE MAY SECRETLY BE IN LOVE WITH HIM♡!

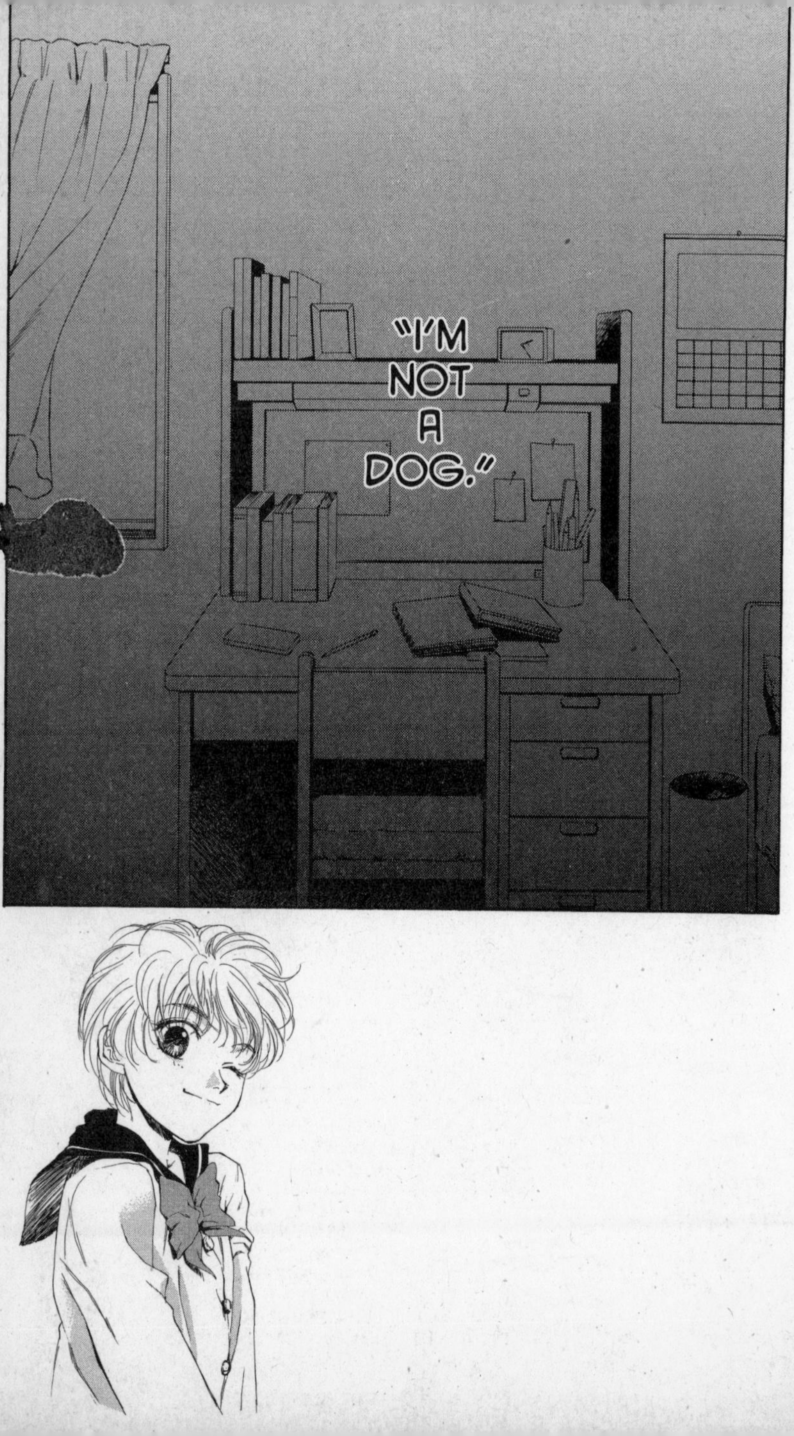
"I'M NOT A DOG."

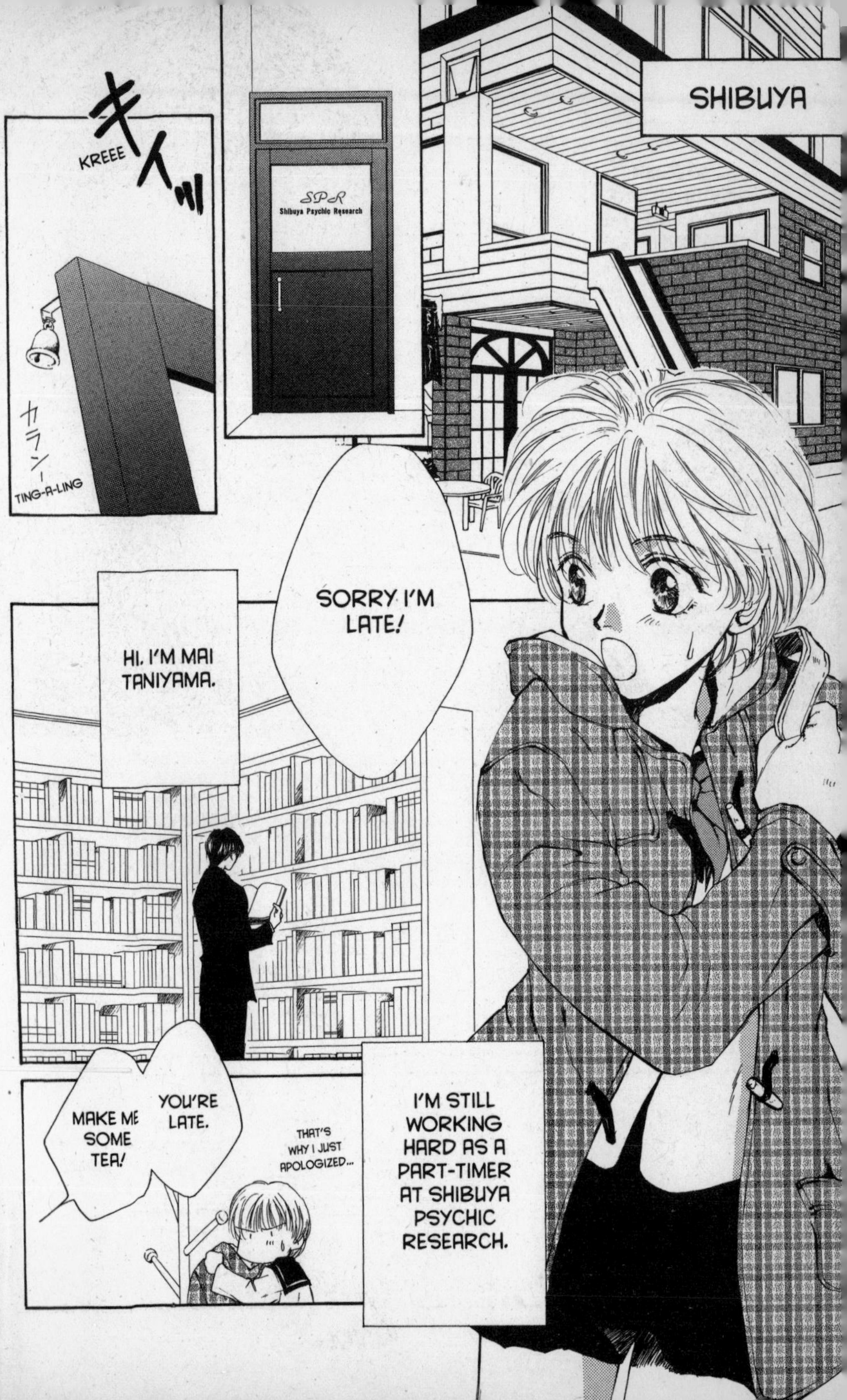
SHIBUYA
SPR
Shibuya Psychic Research
キイッ
KREEE
カラン
TING-A-LING
SORRY I'M LATE!
HI, I'M MAI TANIYAMA.
I'M STILL WORKING HARD AS A PART-TIMER AT SHIBUYA PSYCHIC RESEARCH.
YOU'RE LATE.
MAKE ME SOME TEA!
THAT'S WHY I JUST APOLOGIZED...

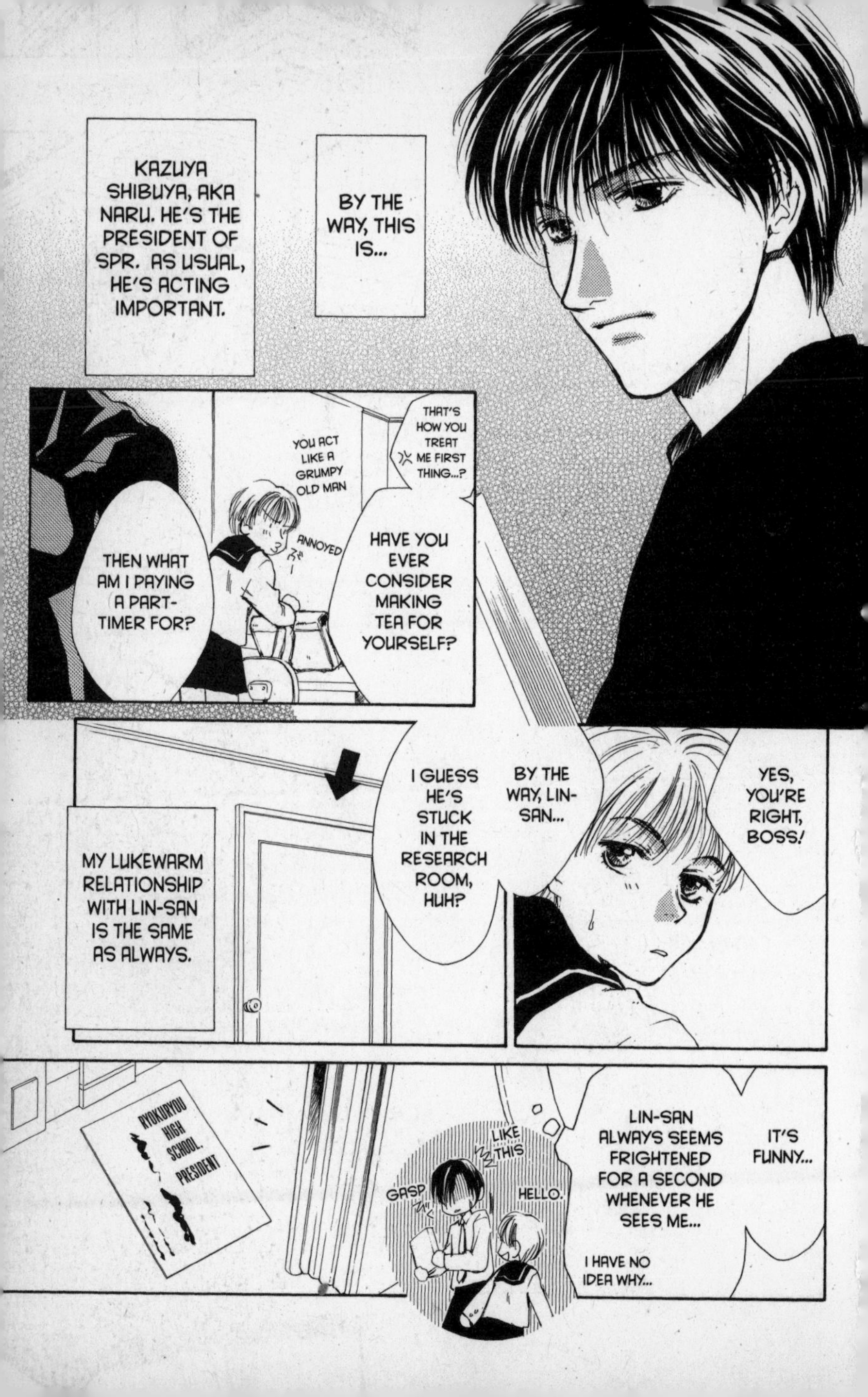
BY THE WAY, THIS IS...
KAZUYA SHIBUYA, AKA NARU. HE'S THE PRESIDENT OF SPR. AS USUAL, HE'S ACTING IMPORTANT.
THAT'S HOW YOU TREAT ME FIRST THING...?
HAVE YOU EVER CONSIDER MAKING TEA FOR YOURSELF?
YOU ACT LIKE A GRUMPY OLD MAN
ANNOYED
THEN WHAT AM I PAYING A PART-TIMER FOR?
YES, YOU'RE RIGHT, BOSS!
BY THE WAY, LIN-SAN...
I GUESS HE'S STUCK IN THE RESEARCH ROOM, HUH?
MY LUKEWARM RELATIONSHIP WITH LIN-SAN IS THE SAME AS ALWAYS.
IT'S FUNNY...
LIN-SAN ALWAYS SEEMS FRIGHTENED FOR A SECOND WHENEVER HE SEES ME...
I HAVE NO IDEA WHY...
HELLO.
LIKE THIS
GASP
RYOKURYOU HIGH SCHOOL PRESIDENT

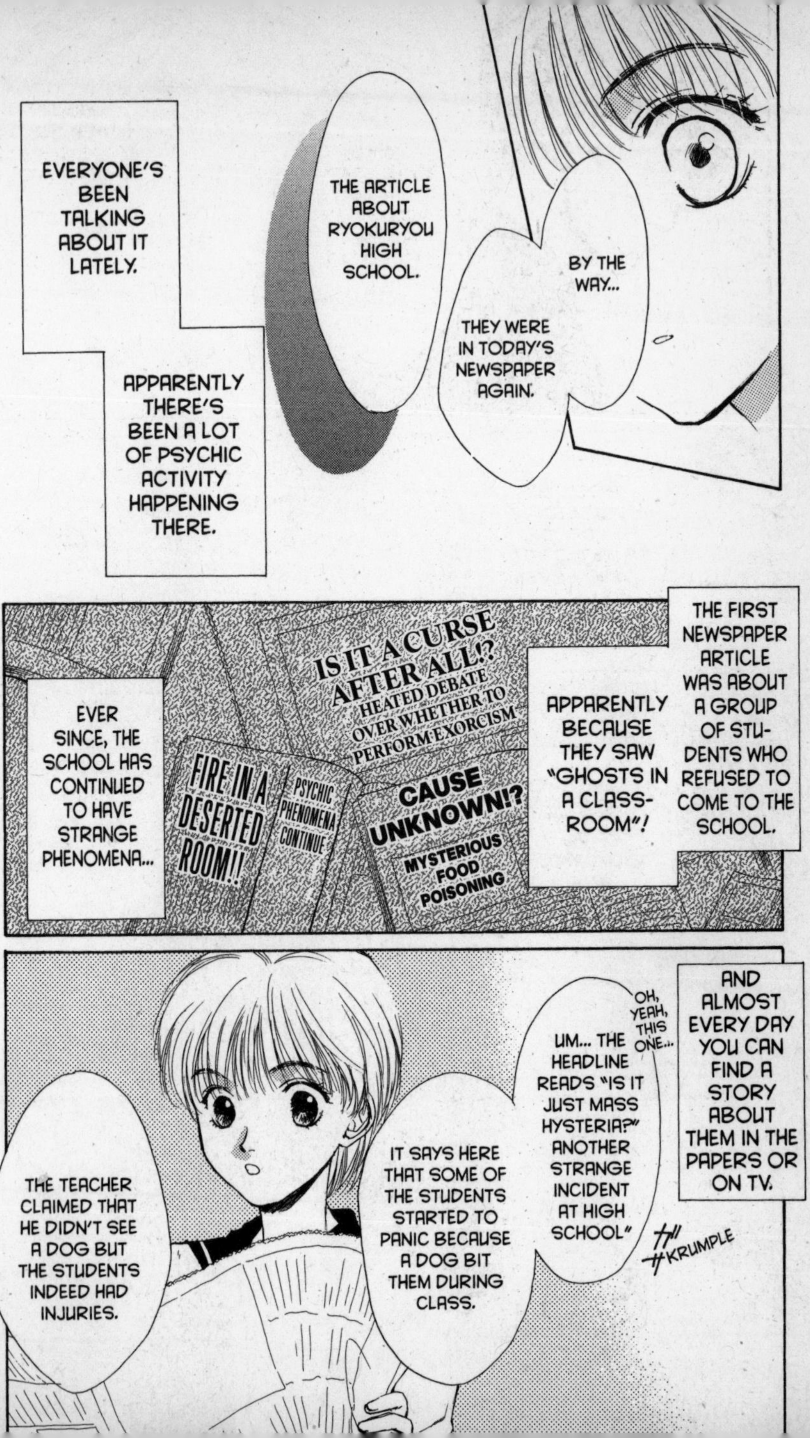
BY THE WAY...
THEY WERE IN TODAY'S NEWSPAPER AGAIN.
THE ARTICLE ABOUT RYOKURYOU HIGH SCHOOL.
EVERYONE'S BEEN TALKING ABOUT IT LATELY.
APPARENTLY THERE'S BEEN A LOT OF PSYCHIC ACTIVITY HAPPENING THERE.
THE FIRST NEWSPAPER ARTICLE WAS ABOUT A GROUP OF STUDENTS WHO REFUSED TO COME TO THE SCHOOL.
APPARENTLY BECAUSE THEY SAW "GHOSTS IN A CLASSROOM"!
IS IT A CURSE AFTER ALL!? HEATED DEBATE OVER WHETHER TO PERFORM EXORCISM
CAUSE UNKNOWN!? MYSTERIOUS FOOD POISONING
PSYCHIC PHENOMENA CONTINUE
FIRE IN A DESERTED ROOM!!
EVER SINCE, THE SCHOOL HAS CONTINUED TO HAVE STRANGE PHENOMENA...
AND ALMOST EVERY DAY YOU CAN FIND A STORY ABOUT THEM IN THE PAPERS OR ON TV.
OH, YEAH, THIS ONE...
UM... THE HEADLINE READS "IS IT JUST MASS HYSTERIA?" ANOTHER STRANGE INCIDENT AT HIGH SCHOOL"
KRUMPLE
IT SAYS HERE THAT SOME OF THE STUDENTS STARTED TO PANIC BECAUSE A DOG BIT THEM DURING CLASS.
THE TEACHER CLAIMED THAT HE DIDN'T SEE A DOG BUT THE STUDENTS INDEED HAD INJURIES.

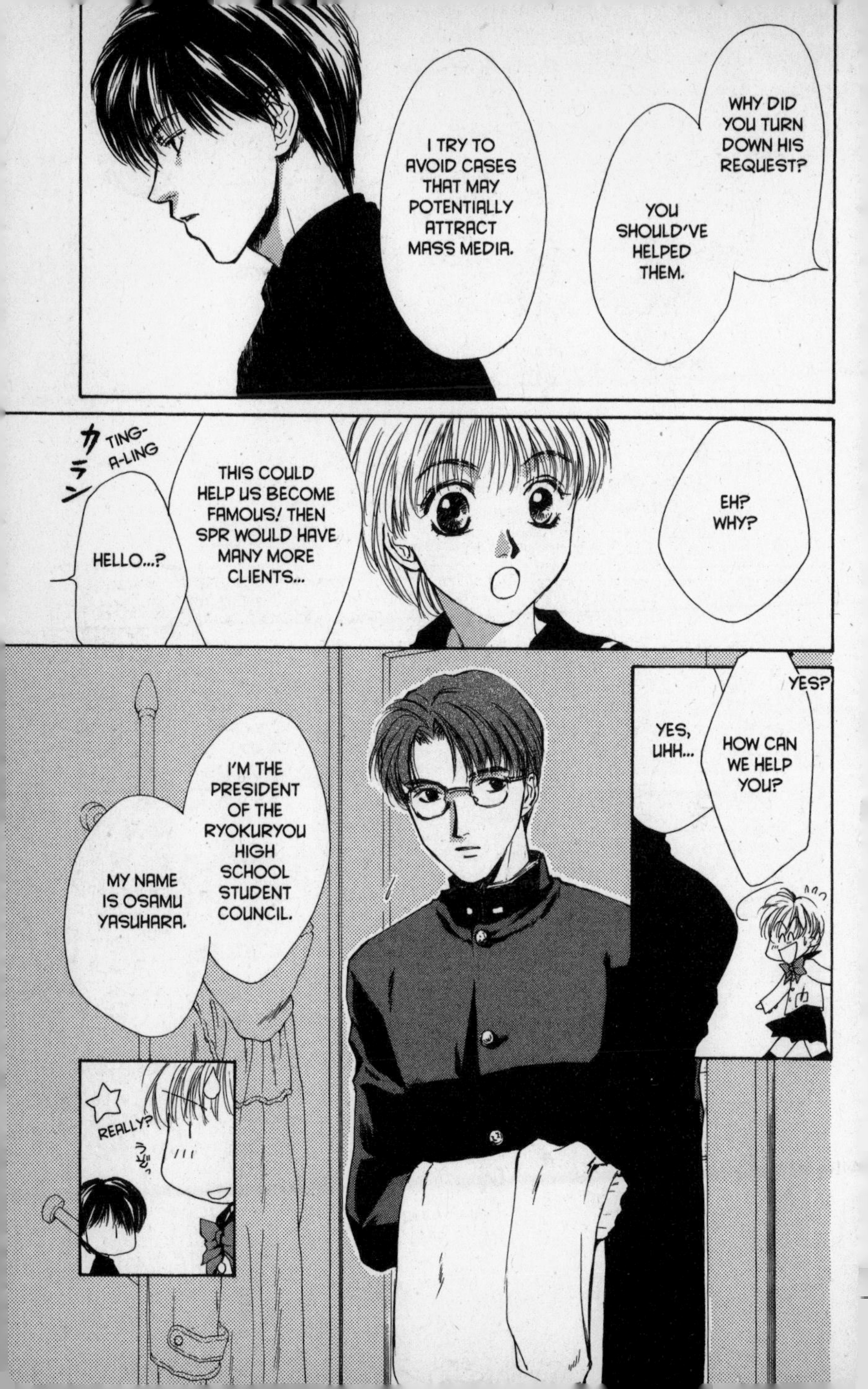
WHY DID YOU TURN DOWN HIS REQUEST?
YOU SHOULD'VE HELPED THEM.
I TRY TO AVOID CASES THAT MAY POTENTIALLY ATTRACT MASS MEDIA.
EH? WHY?
THIS COULD HELP US BECOME FAMOUS! THEN SPR WOULD HAVE MANY MORE CLIENTS...
カラン TING-A-LING
HELLO...?
YES?
HOW CAN WE HELP YOU?
YES, UHH...
I'M THE PRESIDENT OF THE RYOKURYOU HIGH SCHOOL STUDENT COUNCIL.
MY NAME IS OSAMU YASUHARA.
REALLY?

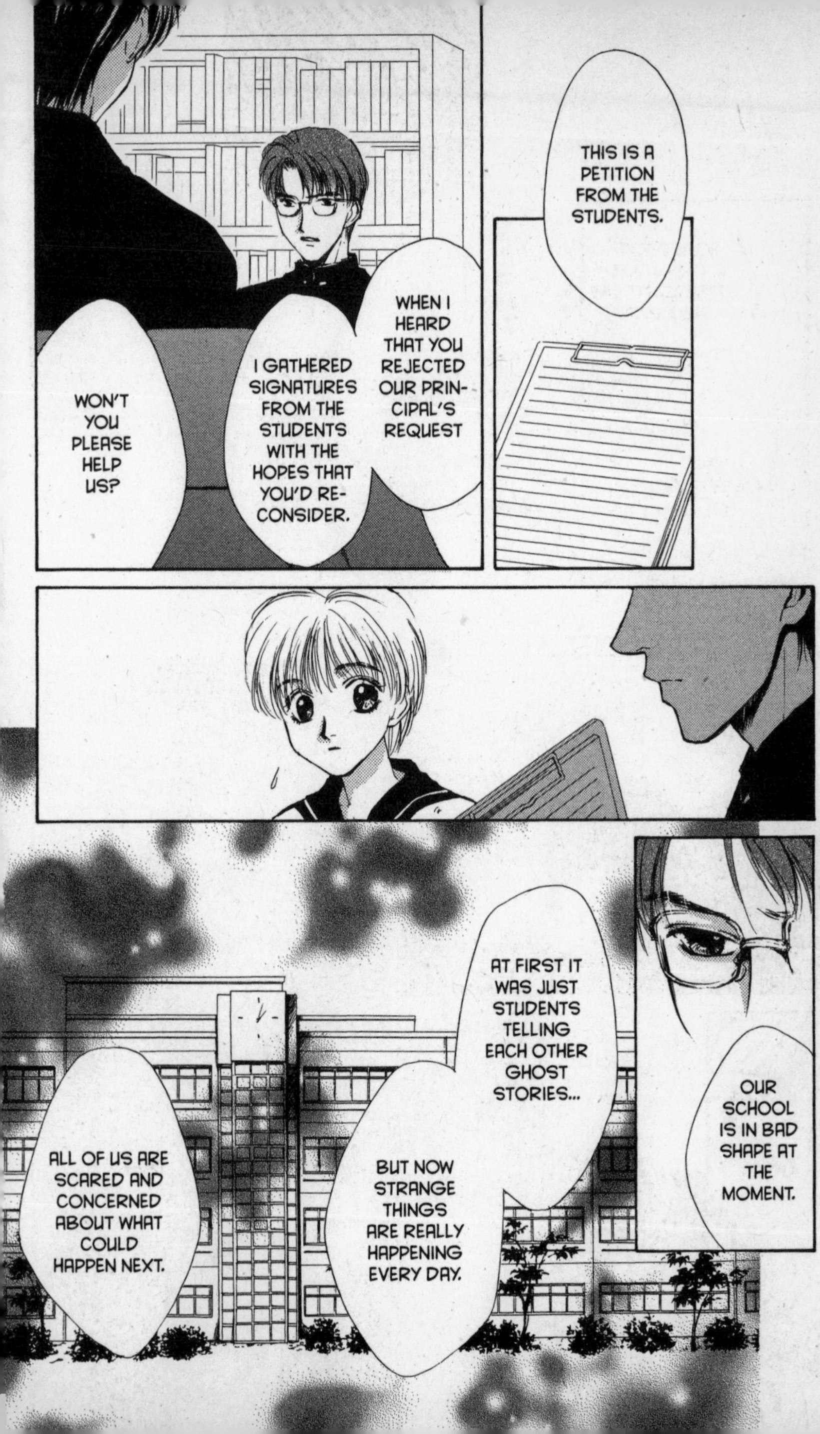
THIS IS A PETITION FROM THE STUDENTS.
WHEN I HEARD THAT YOU REJECTED OUR PRIN-CIPAL'S REQUEST
I GATHERED SIGNATURES FROM THE STUDENTS WITH THE HOPES THAT YOU'D RE-CONSIDER.
WON'T YOU PLEASE HELP US?
OUR SCHOOL IS IN BAD SHAPE AT THE MOMENT.
AT FIRST IT WAS JUST STUDENTS TELLING EACH OTHER GHOST STORIES...
BUT NOW STRANGE THINGS ARE REALLY HAPPENING EVERY DAY.
ALL OF US ARE SCARED AND CONCERNED ABOUT WHAT COULD HAPPEN NEXT.

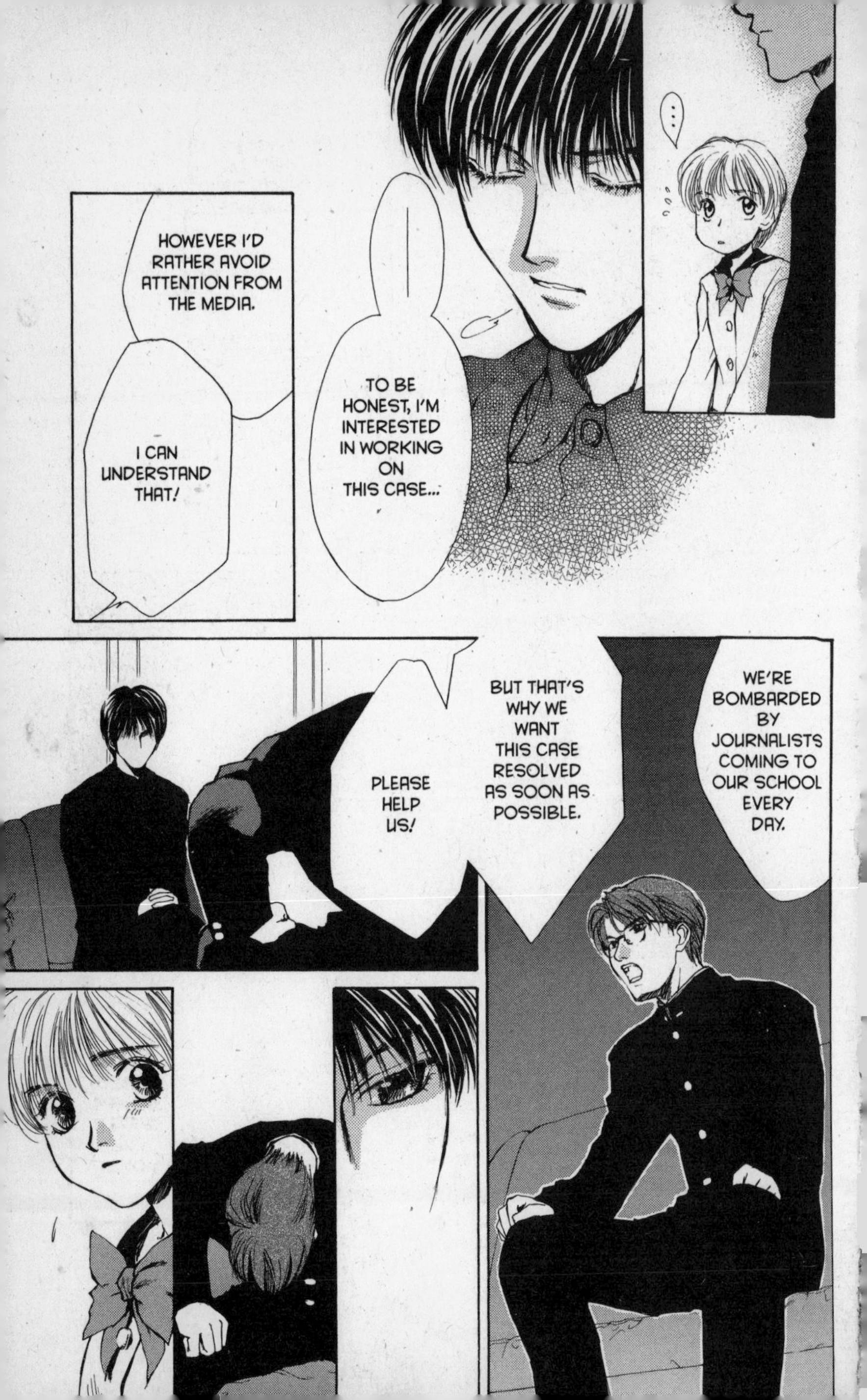
...
TO BE HONEST, I'M INTERESTED IN WORKING ON THIS CASE...
HOWEVER I'D RATHER AVOID ATTENTION FROM THE MEDIA.
I CAN UNDERSTAND THAT!
WE'RE BOMBARDED BY JOURNALISTS COMING TO OUR SCHOOL EVERY DAY.
BUT THAT'S WHY WE WANT THIS CASE RESOLVED AS SOON AS POSSIBLE.
PLEASE HELP US!

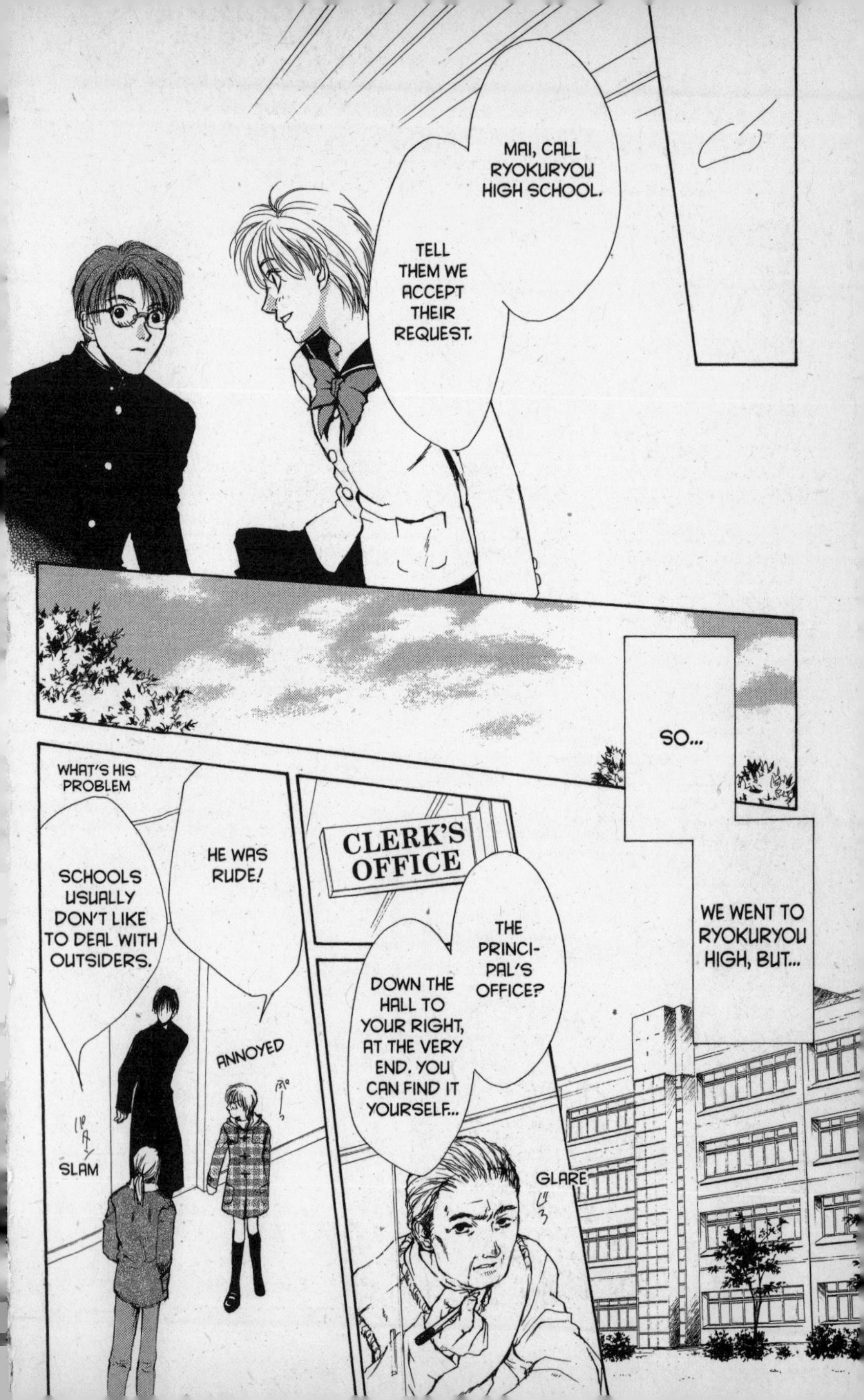
MAI, CALL RYOKURYOU HIGH SCHOOL.
TELL THEM WE ACCEPT THEIR REQUEST.
SO...
WE WENT TO RYOKURYOU HIGH, BUT...
CLERK'S OFFICE
THE PRINCI-PAL'S OFFICE?
DOWN THE HALL TO YOUR RIGHT, AT THE VERY END. YOU CAN FIND IT YOURSELF...
GLARE
HE WAS RUDE!
WHAT'S HIS PROBLEM
SCHOOLS USUALLY DON'T LIKE TO DEAL WITH OUTSIDERS.
ANNOYED
SLAM

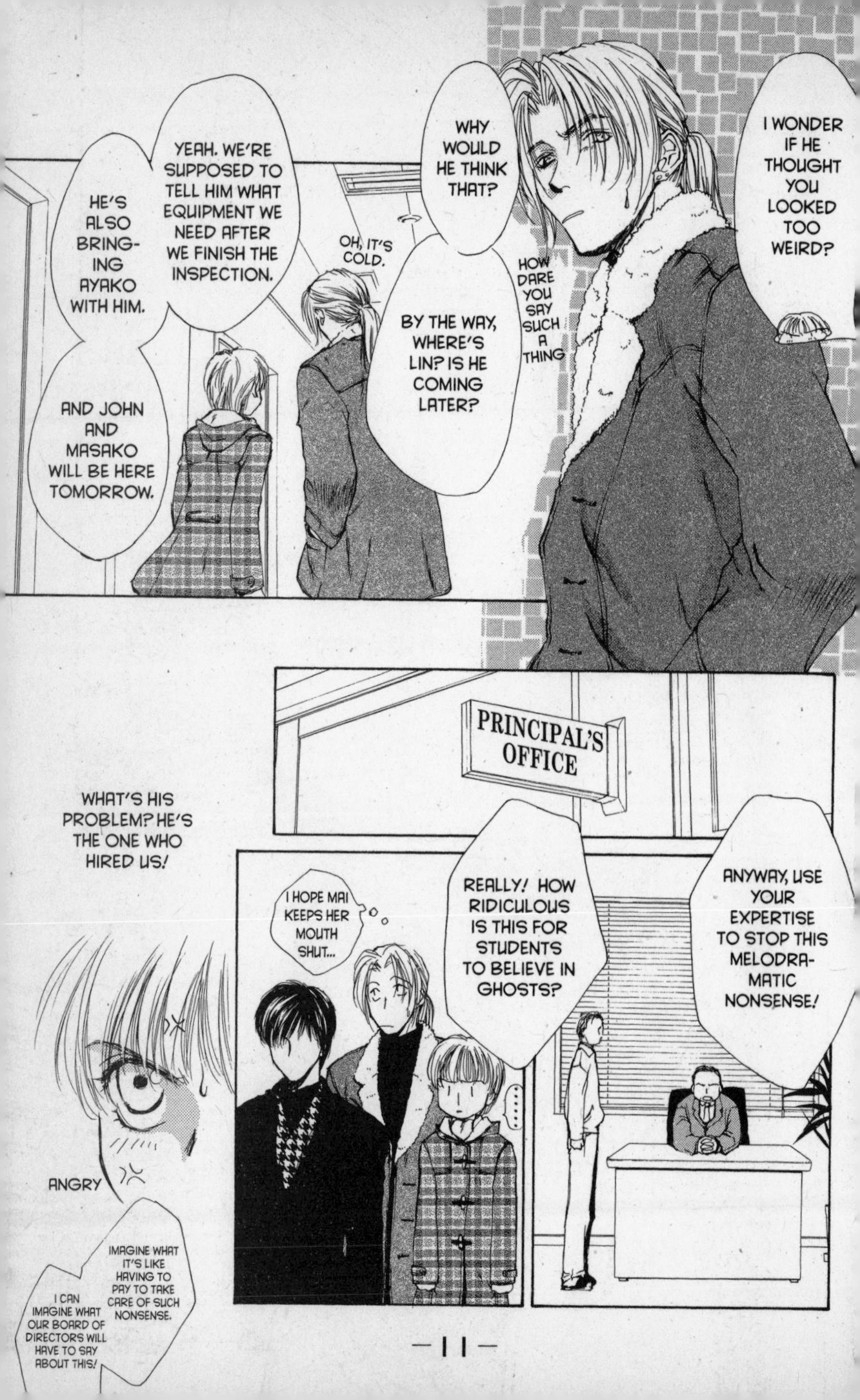
I WONDER IF HE THOUGHT YOU LOOKED TOO WEIRD?
WHY WOULD HE THINK THAT?
HOW DARE YOU SAY SUCH A THING
BY THE WAY, WHERE'S LIN? IS HE COMING LATER?
OH, IT'S COLD.
YEAH. WE'RE SUPPOSED TO TELL HIM WHAT EQUIPMENT WE NEED AFTER WE FINISH THE INSPECTION.
HE'S ALSO BRING-ING AYAKO WITH HIM.
AND JOHN AND MASAKO WILL BE HERE TOMORROW.
PRINCIPAL'S OFFICE
REALLY! HOW RIDICULOUS IS THIS FOR STUDENTS TO BELIEVE IN GHOSTS?
ANYWAY, USE YOUR EXPERTISE TO STOP THIS MELODRA-MATIC NONSENSE!
I HOPE MAI KEEPS HER MOUTH SHUT...
......
WHAT'S HIS PROBLEM? HE'S THE ONE WHO HIRED US!
ANGRY
IMAGINE WHAT IT'S LIKE HAVING TO PAY TO TAKE CARE OF SUCH NONSENSE.
I CAN IMAGINE WHAT OUR BOARD OF DIRECTORS WILL HAVE TO SAY ABOUT THIS!

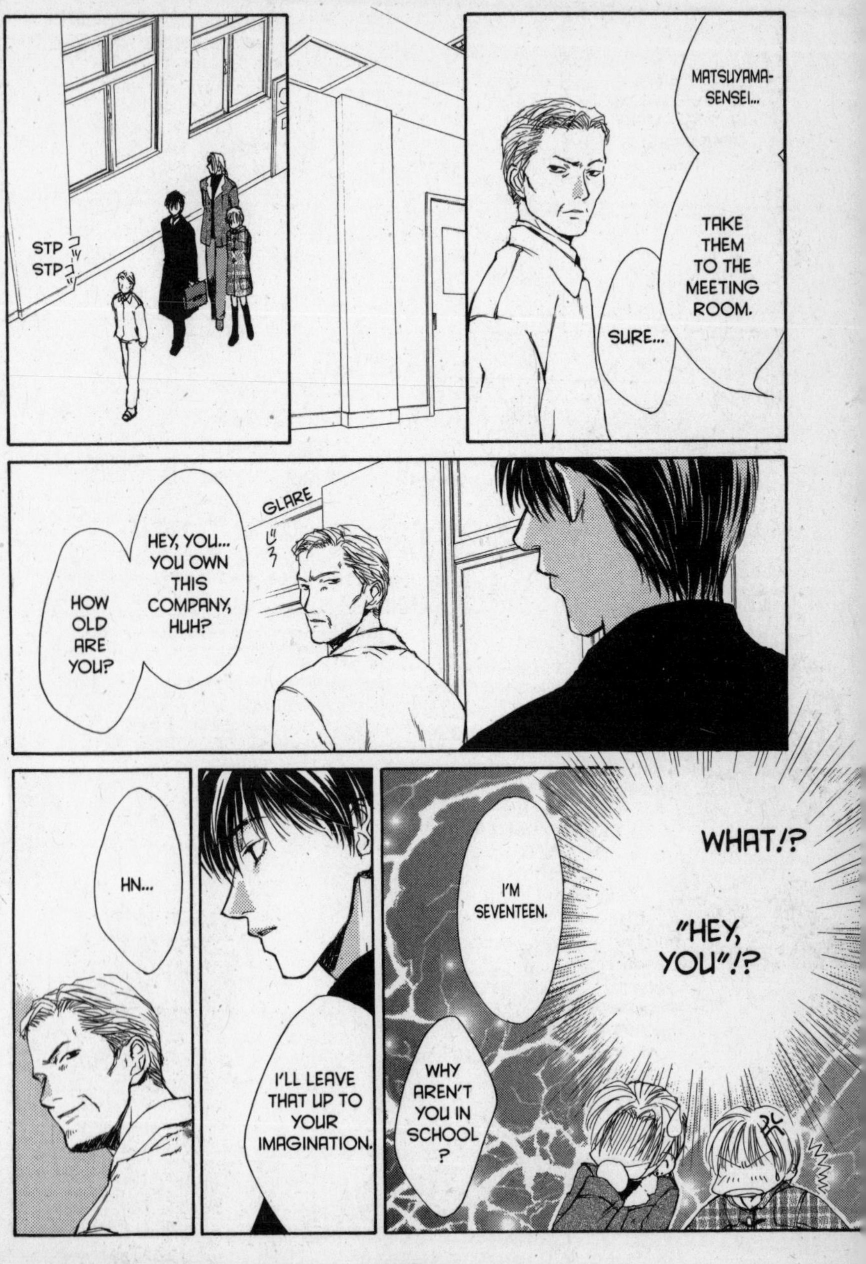
MATSUYAMA-SENSEI...
TAKE THEM TO THE MEETING ROOM.
SURE...
STP
STP
GLARE
HEY, YOU... YOU OWN THIS COMPANY, HUH?
HOW OLD ARE YOU?
WHAT!?
"HEY, YOU"!?
I'M SEVENTEEN.
WHY AREN'T YOU IN SCHOOL?
I'LL LEAVE THAT UP TO YOUR IMAGINATION.
HN...

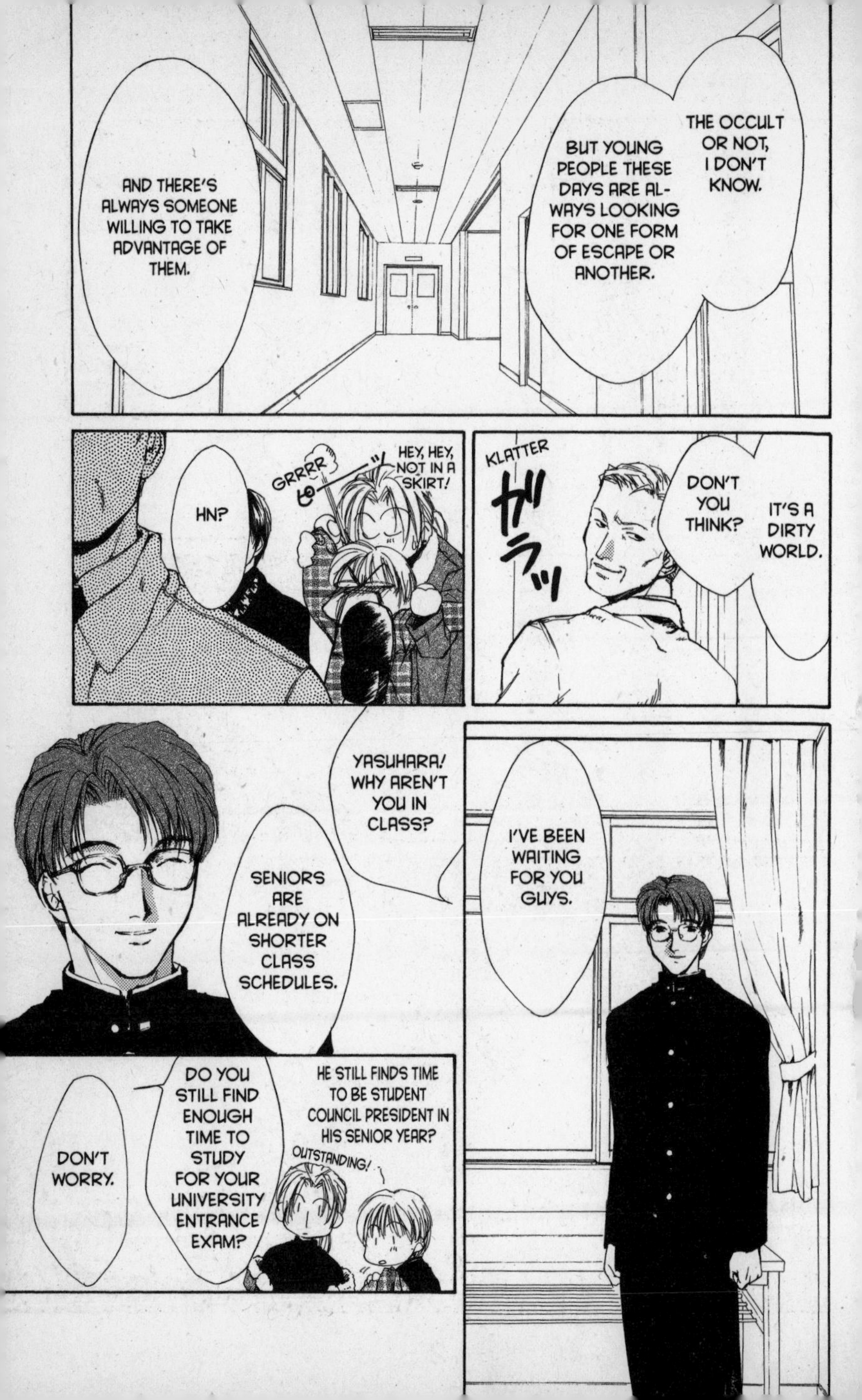
THE OCCULT OR NOT, I DON'T KNOW.
BUT YOUNG PEOPLE THESE DAYS ARE AL-WAYS LOOKING FOR ONE FORM OF ESCAPE OR ANOTHER.
AND THERE'S ALWAYS SOMEONE WILLING TO TAKE ADVANTAGE OF THEM.
IT'S A DIRTY WORLD.
DON'T YOU THINK?
KLATTER
ガラッ
HEY, HEY, NOT IN A SKIRT!
GRRRR
HN?
I'VE BEEN WAITING FOR YOU GUYS.
YASUHARA! WHY AREN'T YOU IN CLASS?
SENIORS ARE ALREADY ON SHORTER CLASS SCHEDULES.
HE STILL FINDS TIME TO BE STUDENT COUNCIL PRESIDENT IN HIS SENIOR YEAR?
OUTSTANDING!
DO YOU STILL FIND ENOUGH TIME TO STUDY FOR YOUR UNIVERSITY ENTRANCE EXAM?
DON'T WORRY.

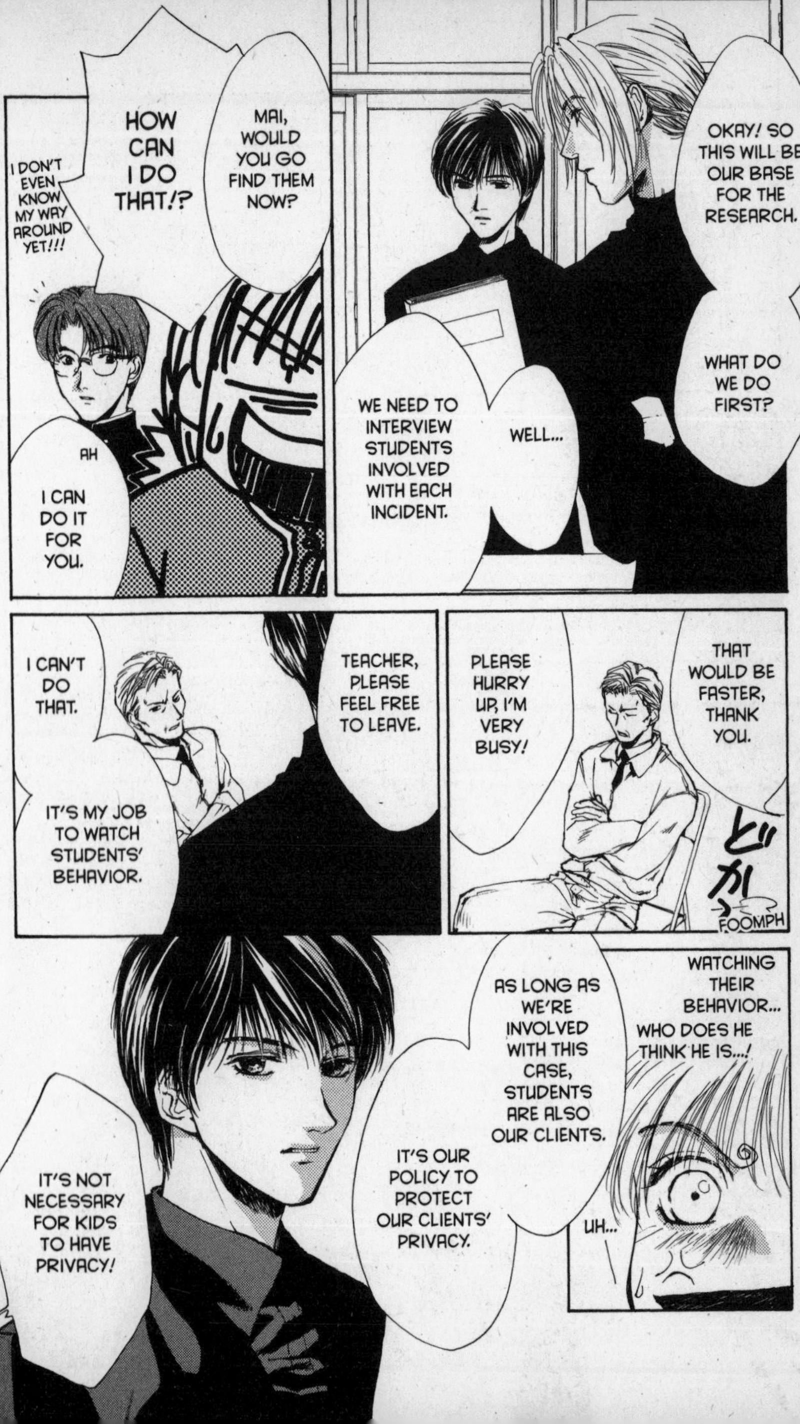
OKAY! SO THIS WILL BE OUR BASE FOR THE RESEARCH.
WHAT DO WE DO FIRST?
WELL...
WE NEED TO INTERVIEW STUDENTS INVOLVED WITH EACH INCIDENT.
MAI, WOULD YOU GO FIND THEM NOW?
HOW CAN I DO THAT!?
I DON'T EVEN KNOW MY WAY AROUND YET!!!
AH
I CAN DO IT FOR YOU.
THAT WOULD BE FASTER, THANK YOU.
どかっ
FOOMPH
PLEASE HURRY UP, I'M VERY BUSY!
TEACHER, PLEASE FEEL FREE TO LEAVE.
I CAN'T DO THAT.
IT'S MY JOB TO WATCH STUDENTS' BEHAVIOR.
WATCHING THEIR BEHAVIOR... WHO DOES HE THINK HE IS...!
UH...
AS LONG AS WE'RE INVOLVED WITH THIS CASE, STUDENTS ARE ALSO OUR CLIENTS.
IT'S OUR POLICY TO PROTECT OUR CLIENTS' PRIVACY.
IT'S NOT NECESSARY FOR KIDS TO HAVE PRIVACY!

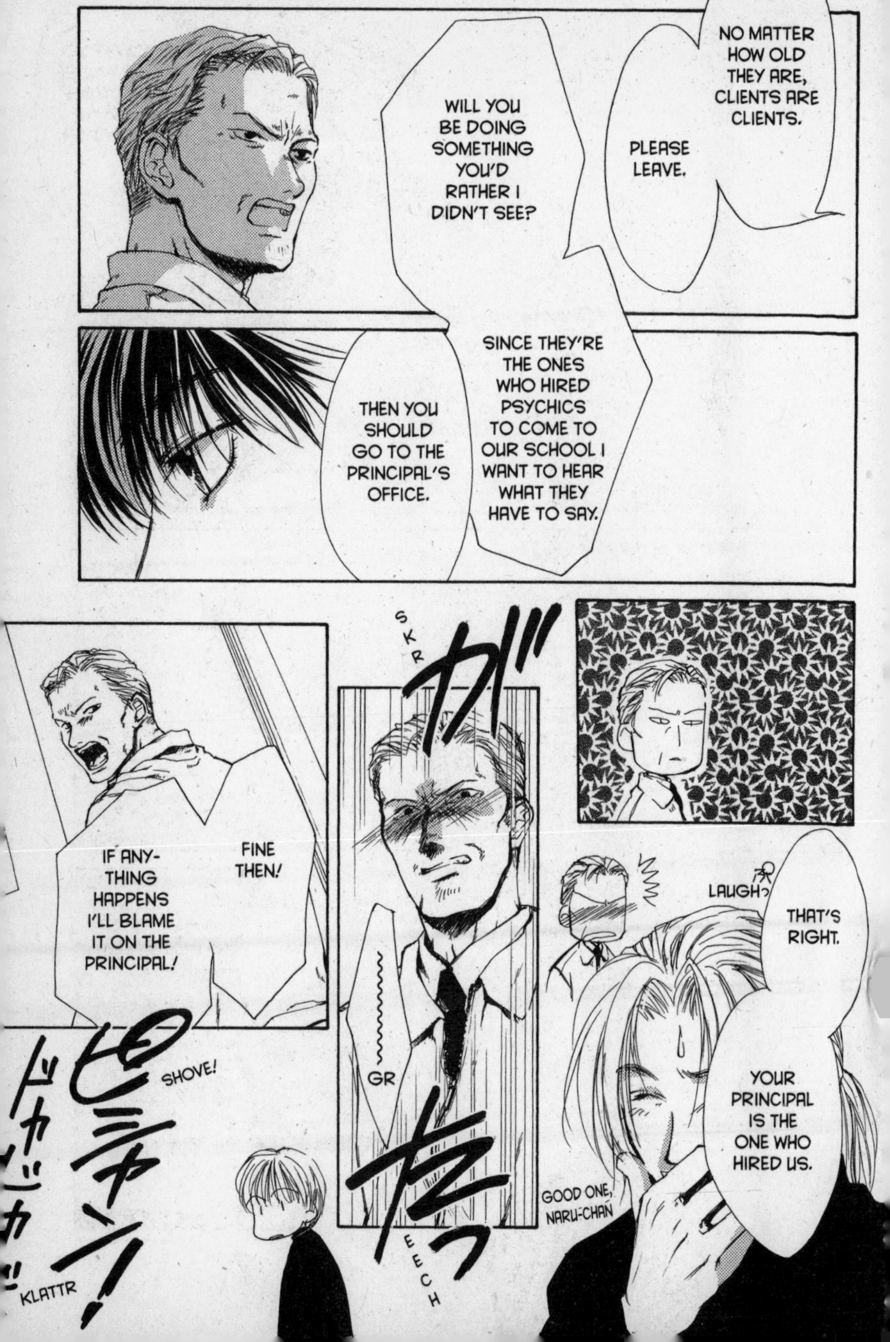
NO MATTER HOW OLD THEY ARE, CLIENTS ARE CLIENTS.
PLEASE LEAVE.
WILL YOU BE DOING SOMETHING YOU'D RATHER I DIDN'T SEE?
SINCE THEY'RE THE ONES WHO HIRED PSYCHICS TO COME TO OUR SCHOOL I WANT TO HEAR WHAT THEY HAVE TO SAY.
THEN YOU SHOULD GO TO THE PRINCIPAL'S OFFICE.
LAUGH
THAT'S RIGHT.
YOUR PRINCIPAL IS THE ONE WHO HIRED US.
GOOD ONE, NARU-CHAN
SKR
GR
EECH
FINE THEN!
IF ANY-THING HAPPENS I'LL BLAME IT ON THE PRINCIPAL!
SHOVE!
KLATTR

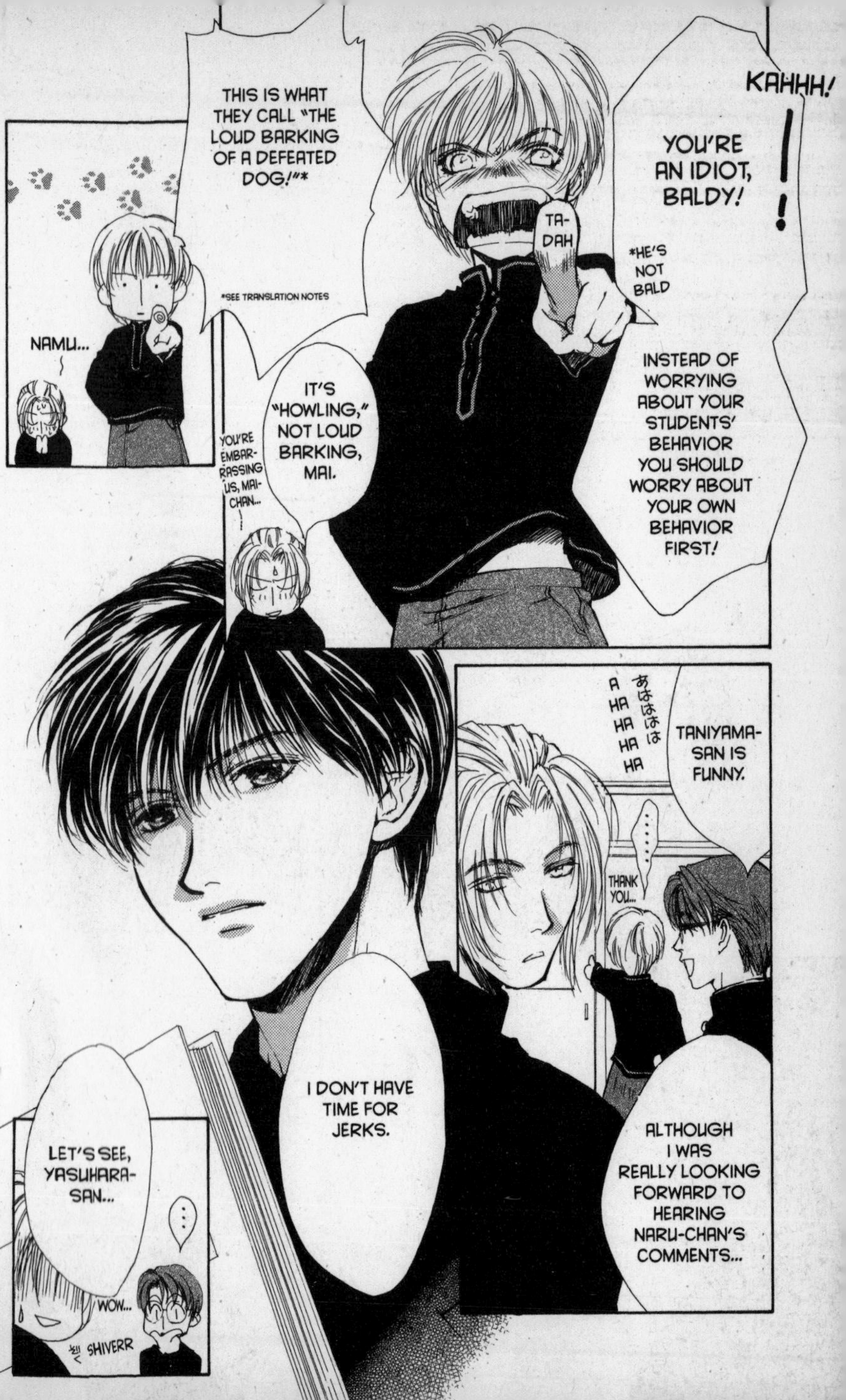
KAHHH!
YOU'RE AN IDIOT, BALDY!
TA-DAH
*HE'S NOT BALD
INSTEAD OF WORRYING ABOUT YOUR STUDENTS' BEHAVIOR YOU SHOULD WORRY ABOUT YOUR OWN BEHAVIOR FIRST!
IT'S "HOWLING," NOT LOUD BARKING, MAI.
YOU'RE EMBARRASSING US, MAI-CHAN...
THIS IS WHAT THEY CALL "THE LOUD BARKING OF A DEFEATED DOG!"*
*SEE TRANSLATION NOTES
NAMU...
あははは
A HA HA HA HA
TANIYAMA-SAN IS FUNNY.
......
THANK YOU...
ALTHOUGH I WAS REALLY LOOKING FORWARD TO HEARING NARU-CHAN'S COMMENTS...
I DON'T HAVE TIME FOR JERKS.
LET'S SEE, YASUHARA-SAN...
...
WOW...
SHIVERR

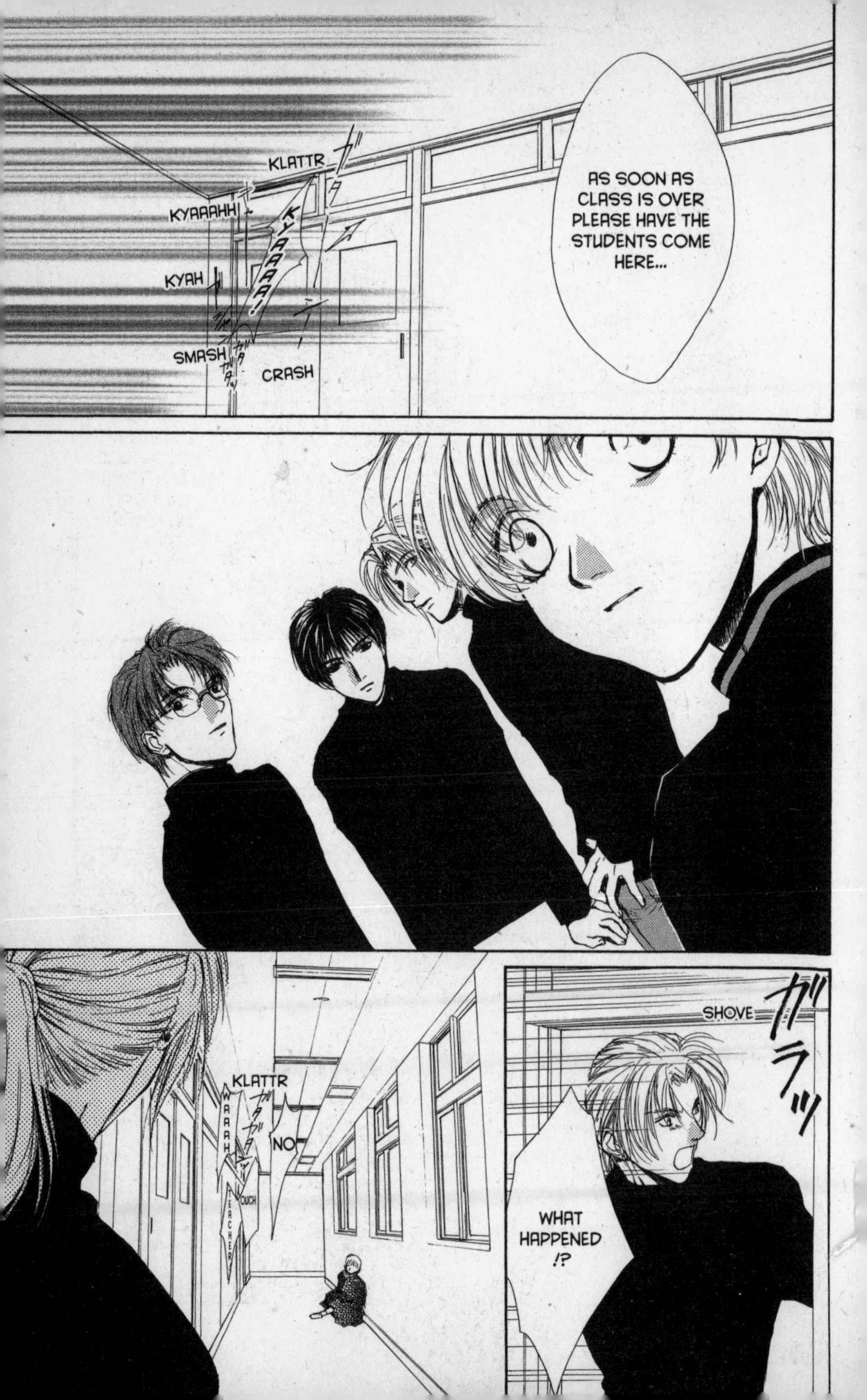
AS SOON AS CLASS IS OVER PLEASE HAVE THE STUDENTS COME HERE...
KLATTR
KYAAAAA!
KYAAAHH
KYAH
SMASH
CRASH
SHOVE
WHAT HAPPENED !?
KLATTR
NO
WAAAH
OUCH
TEACHER

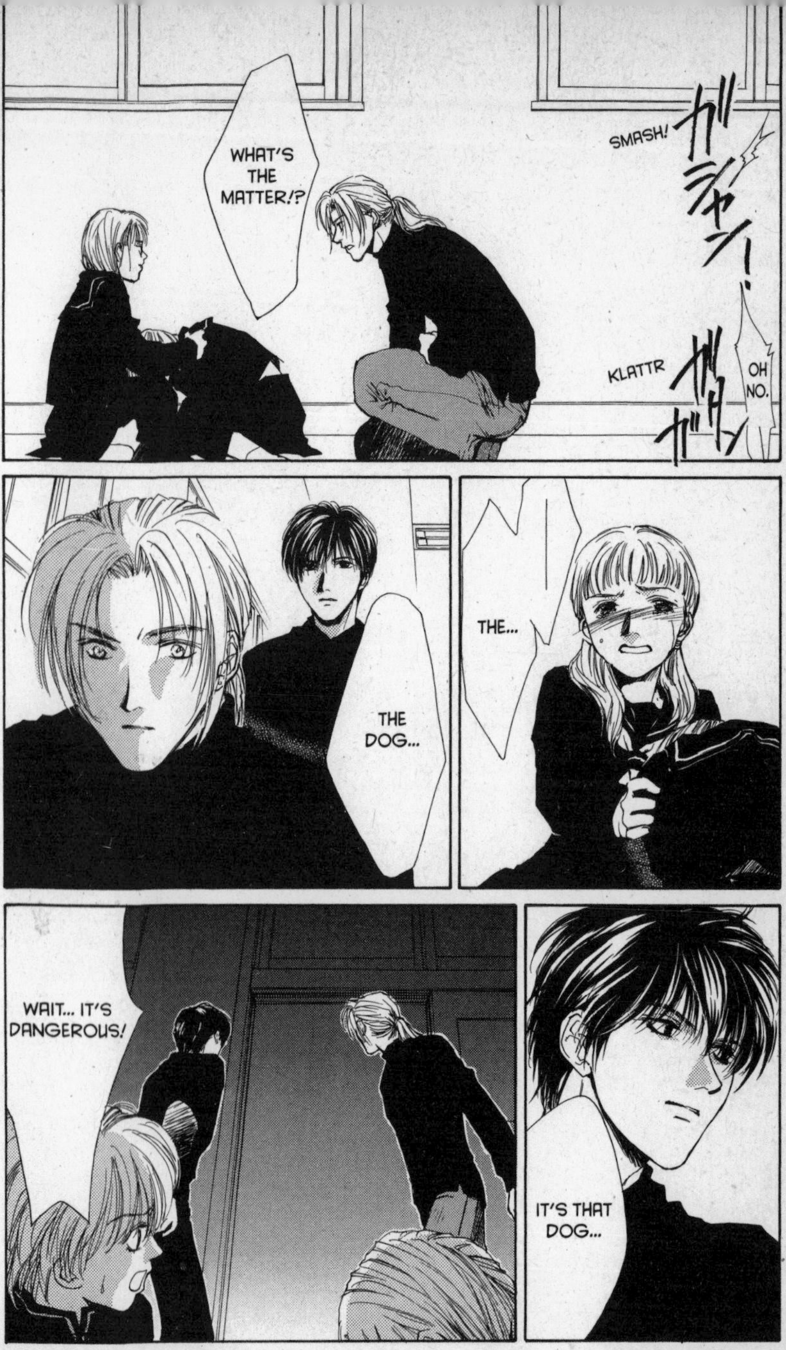
SMASH!
ガシャン!
OH NO.
KLATTR
WHAT'S THE MATTER!?
THE...
THE DOG...
IT'S THAT DOG...
WAIT... IT'S DANGEROUS!

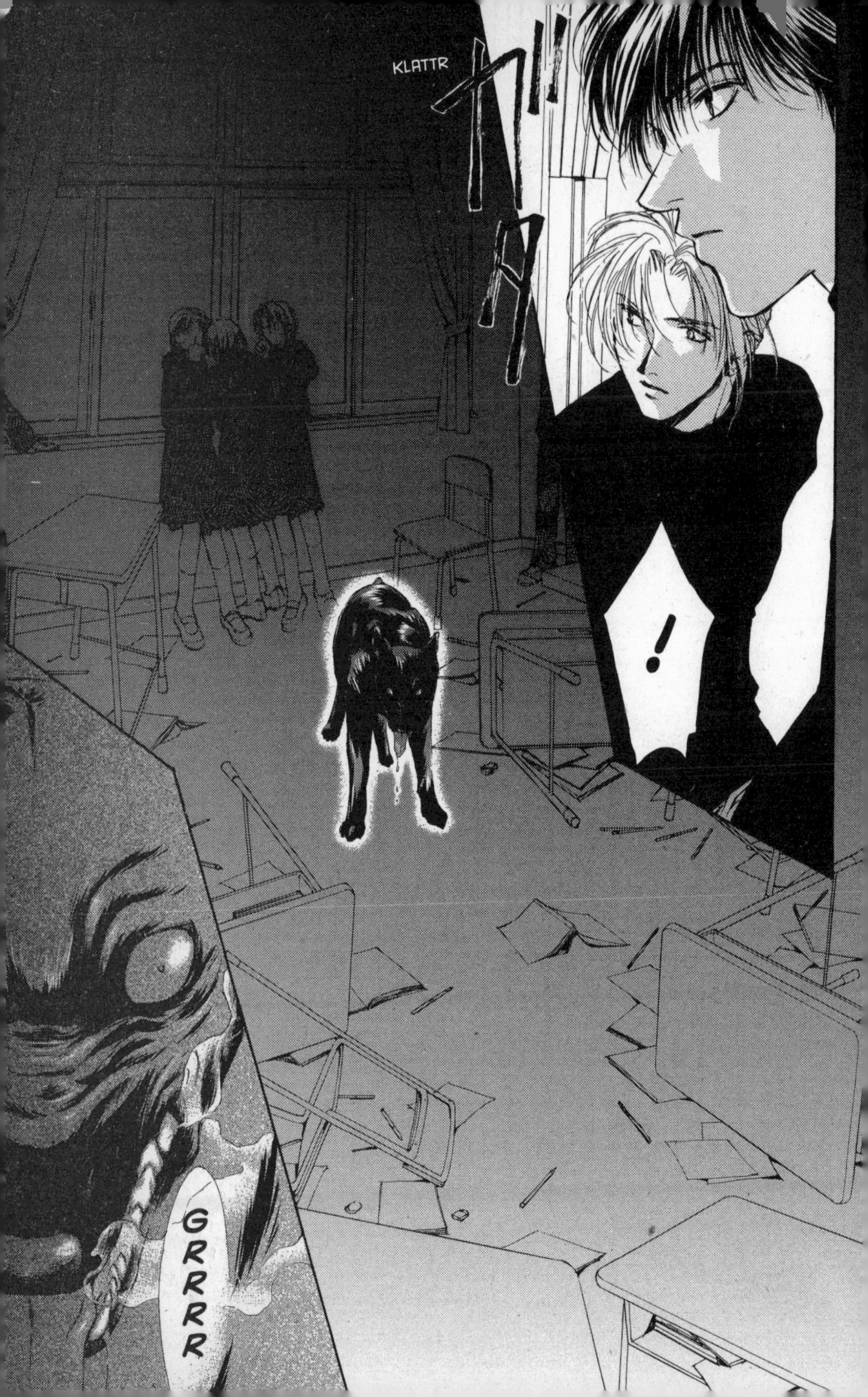
KLATTR
!
GRRRR

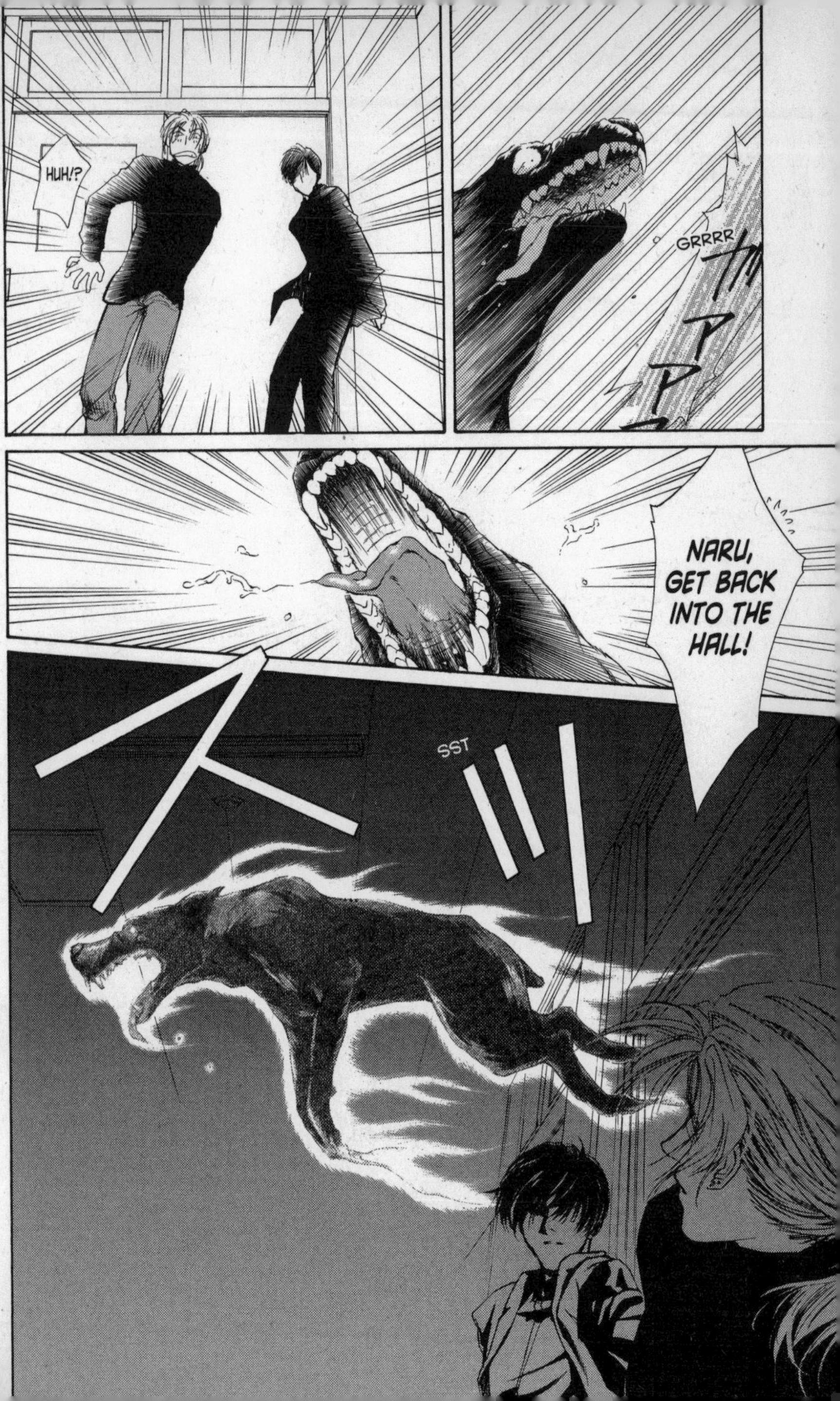
GRRRR
HUH!?
NARU, GET BACK INTO THE HALL!
SST

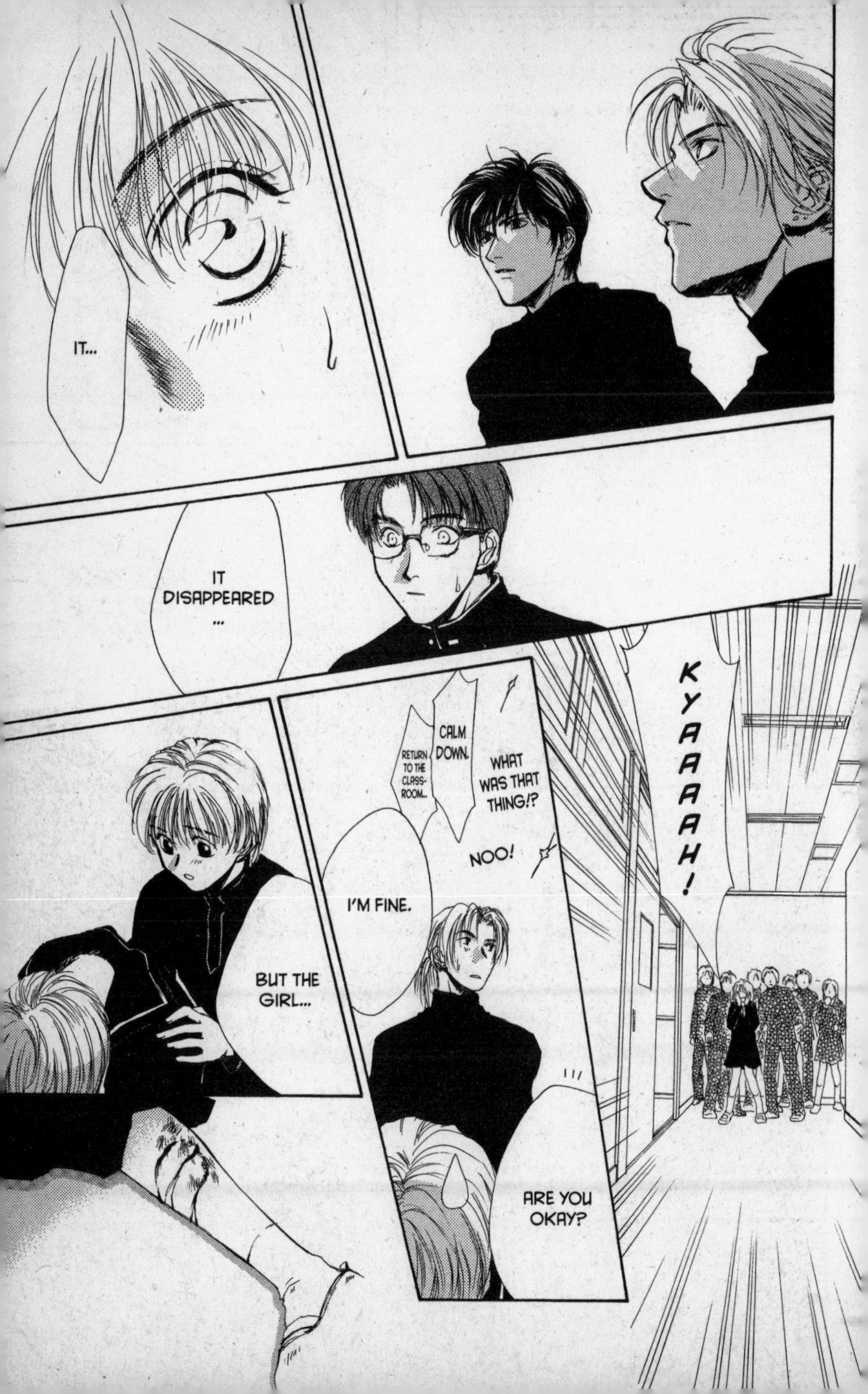
IT...
IT DISAPPEARED ...
KYAAAAAH!
WHAT WAS THAT THING!?
CALM DOWN.
RETURN TO THE CLASS-ROOM...
NOO!
ARE YOU OKAY?
I'M FINE.
BUT THE GIRL...

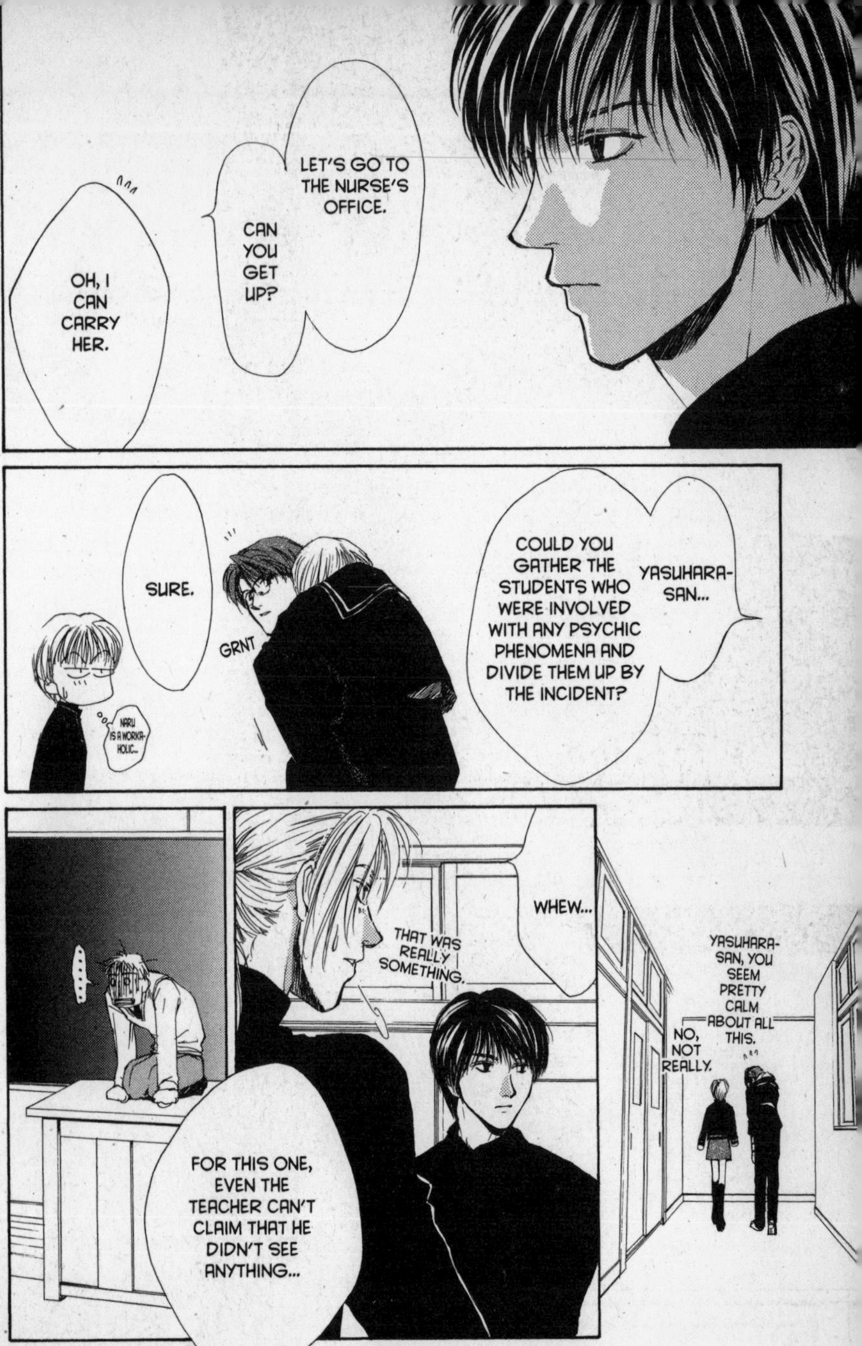
LET'S GO TO THE NURSE'S OFFICE.
CAN YOU GET UP?
OH, I CAN CARRY HER.
YASUHARA-SAN...
COULD YOU GATHER THE STUDENTS WHO WERE INVOLVED WITH ANY PSYCHIC PHENOMENA AND DIVIDE THEM UP BY THE INCIDENT?
GRNT
SURE.
NARU IS A WORKA-HOLIC...
YASUHARA-SAN, YOU SEEM PRETTY CALM ABOUT ALL THIS.
NO, NOT REALLY.
WHEW...
THAT WAS REALLY SOMETHING.
FOR THIS ONE, EVEN THE TEACHER CAN'T CLAIM THAT HE DIDN'T SEE ANYTHING...
...

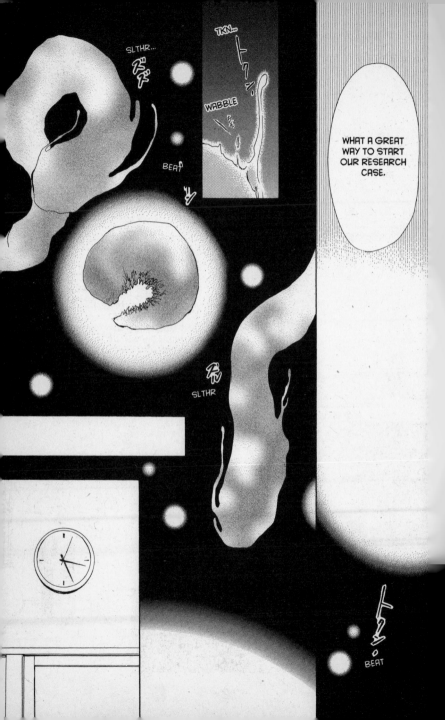

SLTHR...

TKN...

WABBLE

BEAT

WHAT A GREAT
WAY TO START
OUR RESEARCH
CASE.

SLTHR

BEAT

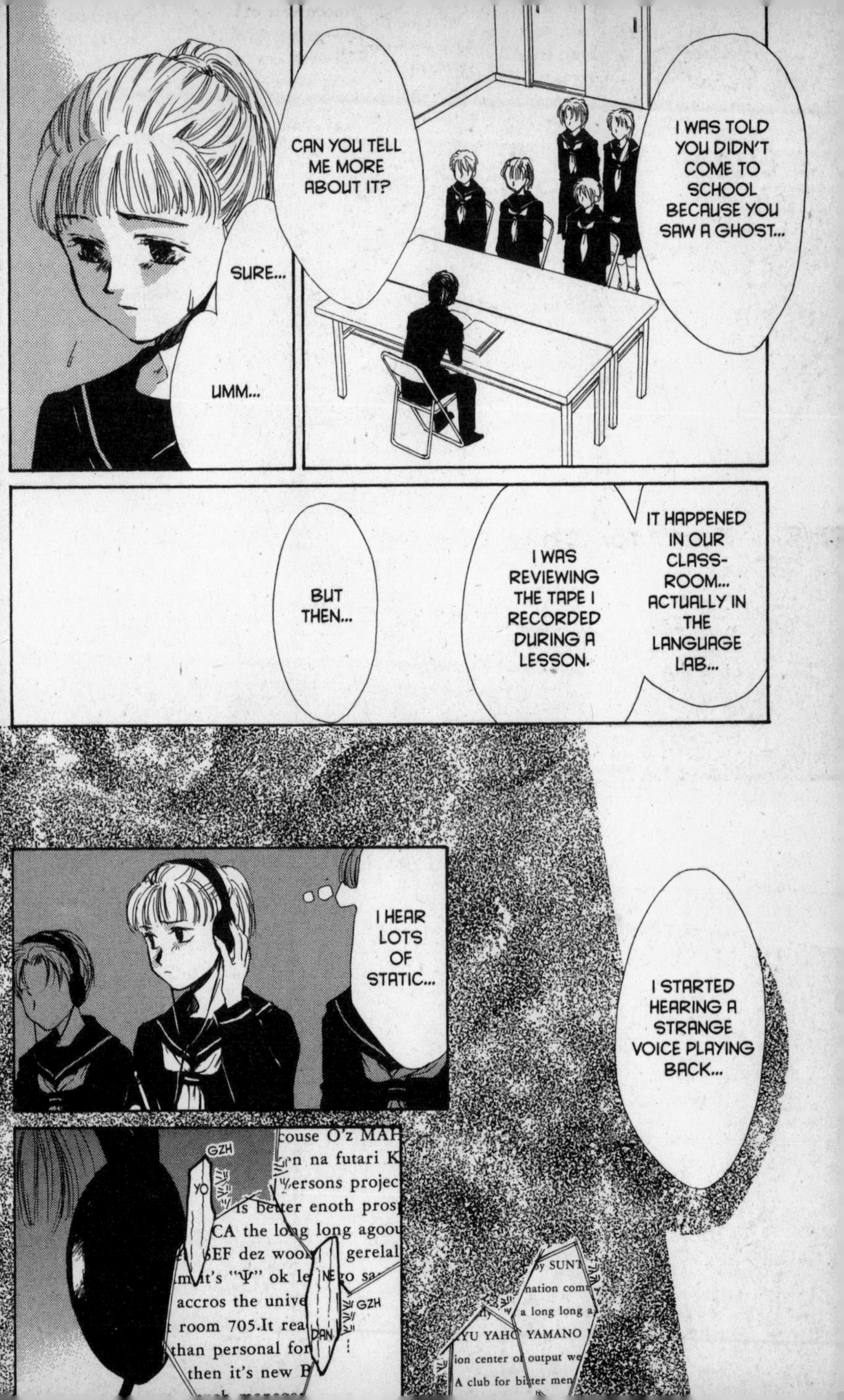
I WAS TOLD YOU DIDN'T COME TO SCHOOL BECAUSE YOU SAW A GHOST...
CAN YOU TELL ME MORE ABOUT IT?
SURE...
UMM...
IT HAPPENED IN OUR CLASS-ROOM... ACTUALLY IN THE LANGUAGE LAB...
I WAS REVIEWING THE TAPE I RECORDED DURING A LESSON.
BUT THEN...
I STARTED HEARING A STRANGE VOICE PLAYING BACK...
I HEAR LOTS OF STATIC...
GZH
YO
NE
GZH
DAN

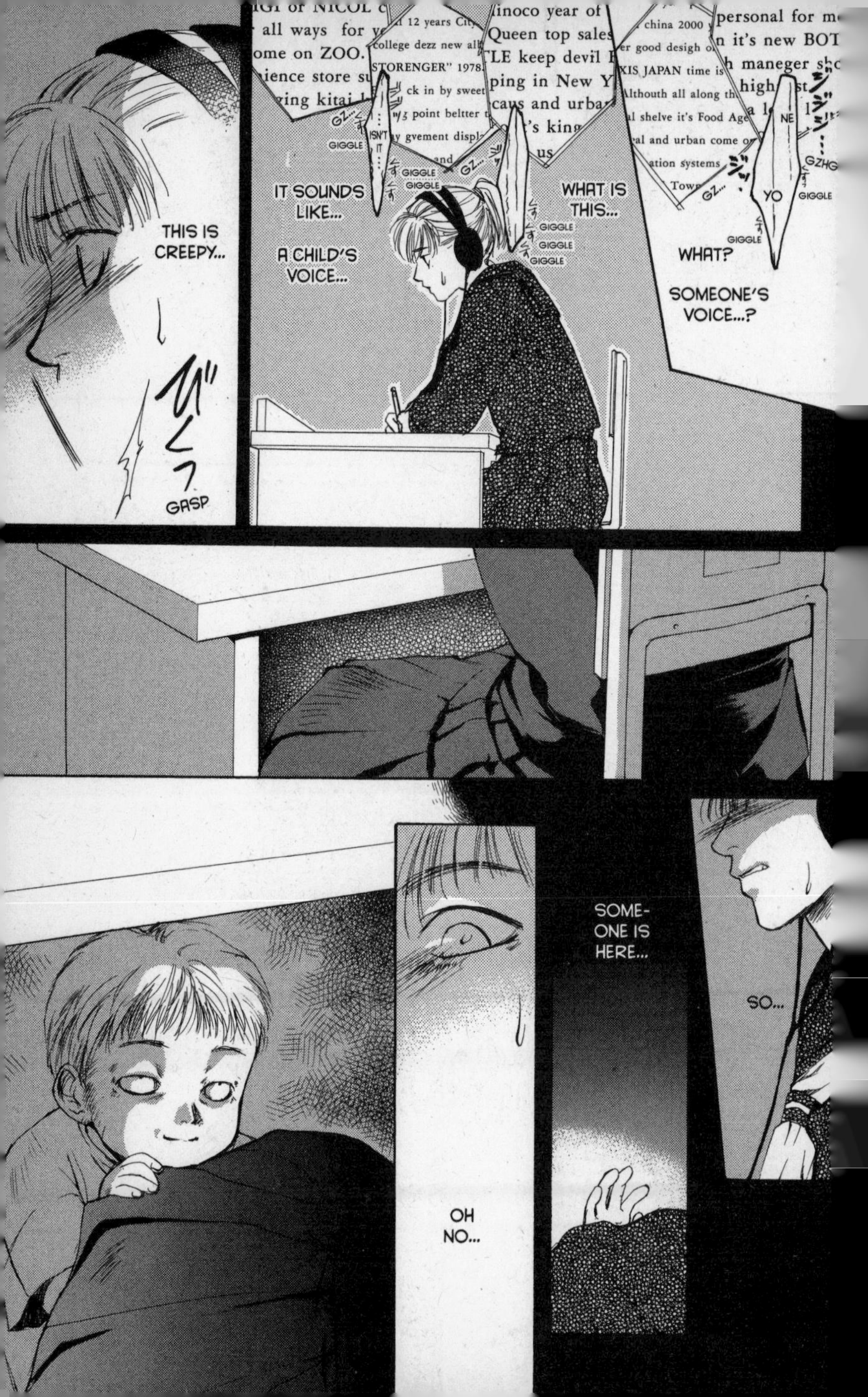
WHAT?
SOMEONE'S VOICE...?
GZHG
NE
YO
GIGGLE
GZ...
GIGGLE
WHAT IS THIS...
GIGGLE
GIGGLE
GIGGLE
GZ...
GIGGLE
GIGGLE
ISN'T IT
GZ...
GIGGLE
IT SOUNDS LIKE...
A CHILD'S VOICE...
THIS IS CREEPY...
GASP
SO...
SOME-ONE IS HERE...
OH NO...

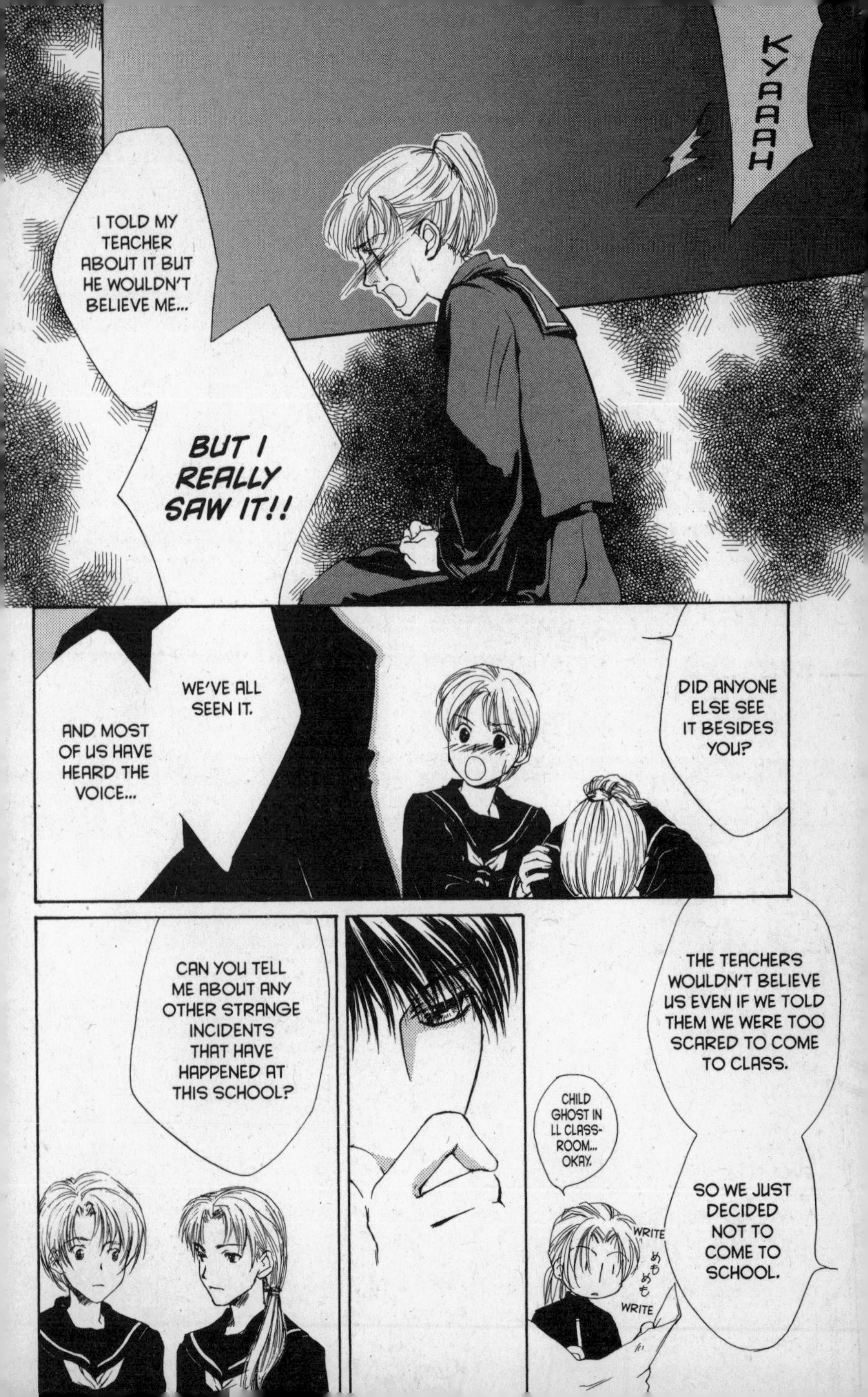
KYAAAAH
I TOLD MY TEACHER ABOUT IT BUT HE WOULDN'T BELIEVE ME...
BUT I REALLY SAW IT!!
DID ANYONE ELSE SEE IT BESIDES YOU?
WE'VE ALL SEEN IT.
AND MOST OF US HAVE HEARD THE VOICE...
THE TEACHERS WOULDN'T BELIEVE US EVEN IF WE TOLD THEM WE WERE TOO SCARED TO COME TO CLASS.
SO WE JUST DECIDED NOT TO COME TO SCHOOL.
CHILD GHOST IN LL CLASS-ROOM... OKAY.
WRITE
めもめも
WRITE
CAN YOU TELL ME ABOUT ANY OTHER STRANGE INCIDENTS THAT HAVE HAPPENED AT THIS SCHOOL?

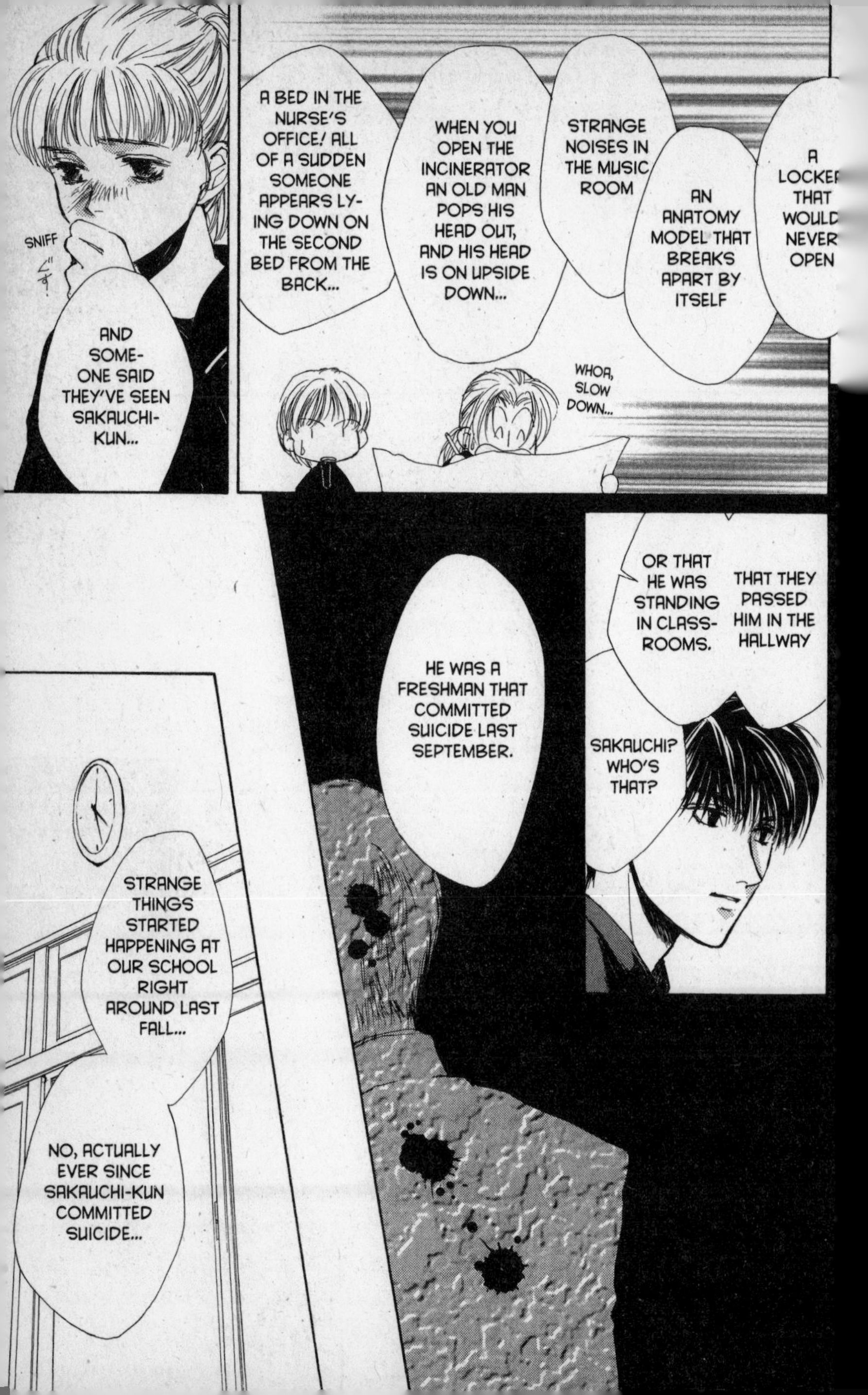
A LOCKER THAT WOULD NEVER OPEN
AN ANATOMY MODEL THAT BREAKS APART BY ITSELF
STRANGE NOISES IN THE MUSIC ROOM
WHEN YOU OPEN THE INCINERATOR AN OLD MAN POPS HIS HEAD OUT, AND HIS HEAD IS ON UPSIDE DOWN...
A BED IN THE NURSE'S OFFICE! ALL OF A SUDDEN SOMEONE APPEARS LY-ING DOWN ON THE SECOND BED FROM THE BACK...
WHOA, SLOW DOWN...
SNIFF
ぐず
AND SOME-ONE SAID THEY'VE SEEN SAKAUCHI-KUN...
THAT THEY PASSED HIM IN THE HALLWAY
OR THAT HE WAS STANDING IN CLASS-ROOMS.
SAKAUCHI? WHO'S THAT?
HE WAS A FRESHMAN THAT COMMITTED SUICIDE LAST SEPTEMBER.
STRANGE THINGS STARTED HAPPENING AT OUR SCHOOL RIGHT AROUND LAST FALL...
NO, ACTUALLY EVER SINCE SAKAUCHI-KUN COMMITTED SUICIDE...

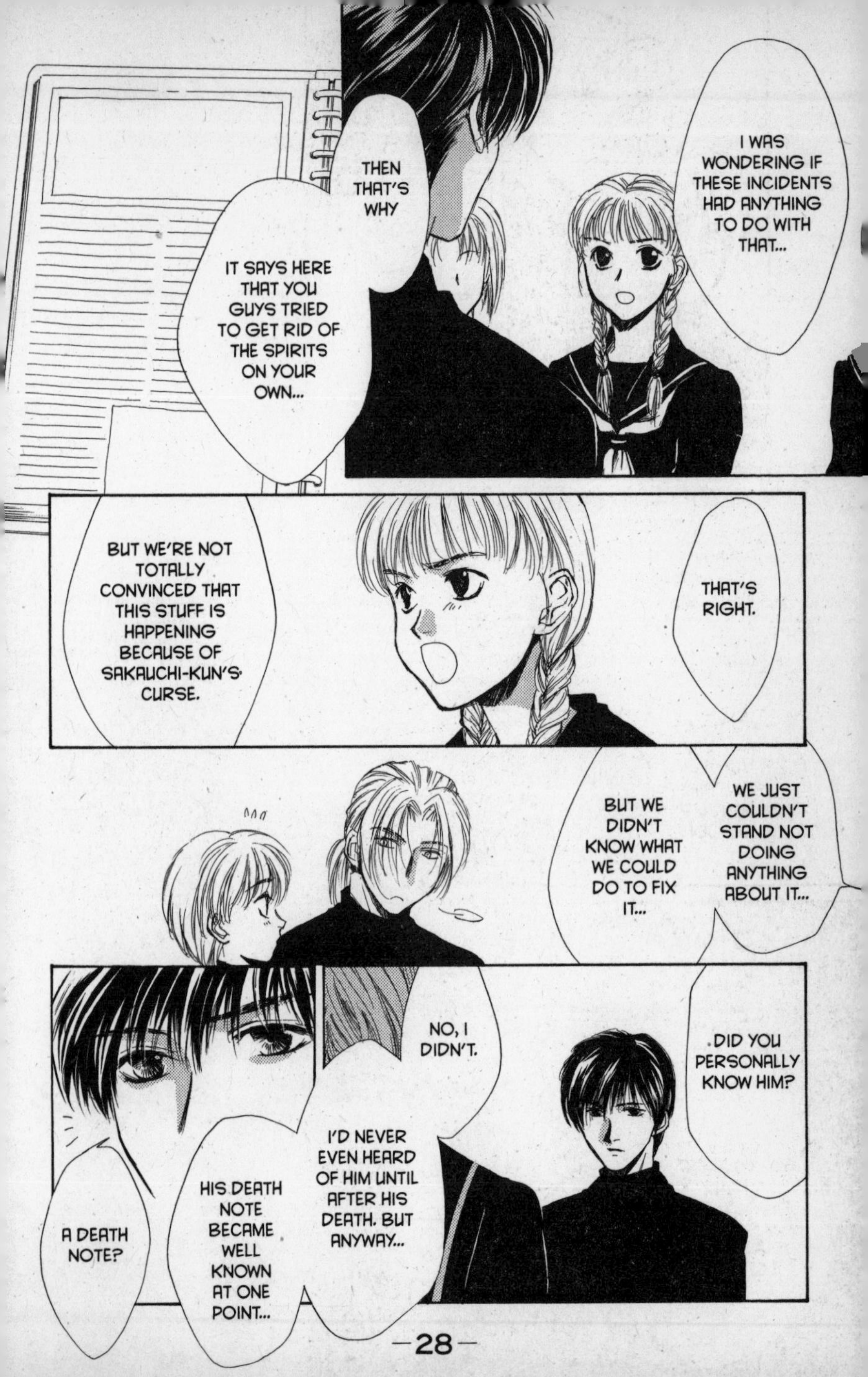
I WAS WONDERING IF THESE INCIDENTS HAD ANYTHING TO DO WITH THAT...
THEN THAT'S WHY
IT SAYS HERE THAT YOU GUYS TRIED TO GET RID OF THE SPIRITS ON YOUR OWN...
THAT'S RIGHT.
BUT WE'RE NOT TOTALLY CONVINCED THAT THIS STUFF IS HAPPENING BECAUSE OF SAKAUCHI-KUN'S CURSE.
WE JUST COULDN'T STAND NOT DOING ANYTHING ABOUT IT...
BUT WE DIDN'T KNOW WHAT WE COULD DO TO FIX IT...
DID YOU PERSONALLY KNOW HIM?
NO, I DIDN'T.
I'D NEVER EVEN HEARD OF HIM UNTIL AFTER HIS DEATH. BUT ANYWAY...
HIS DEATH NOTE BECAME WELL KNOWN AT ONE POINT...
A DEATH NOTE?

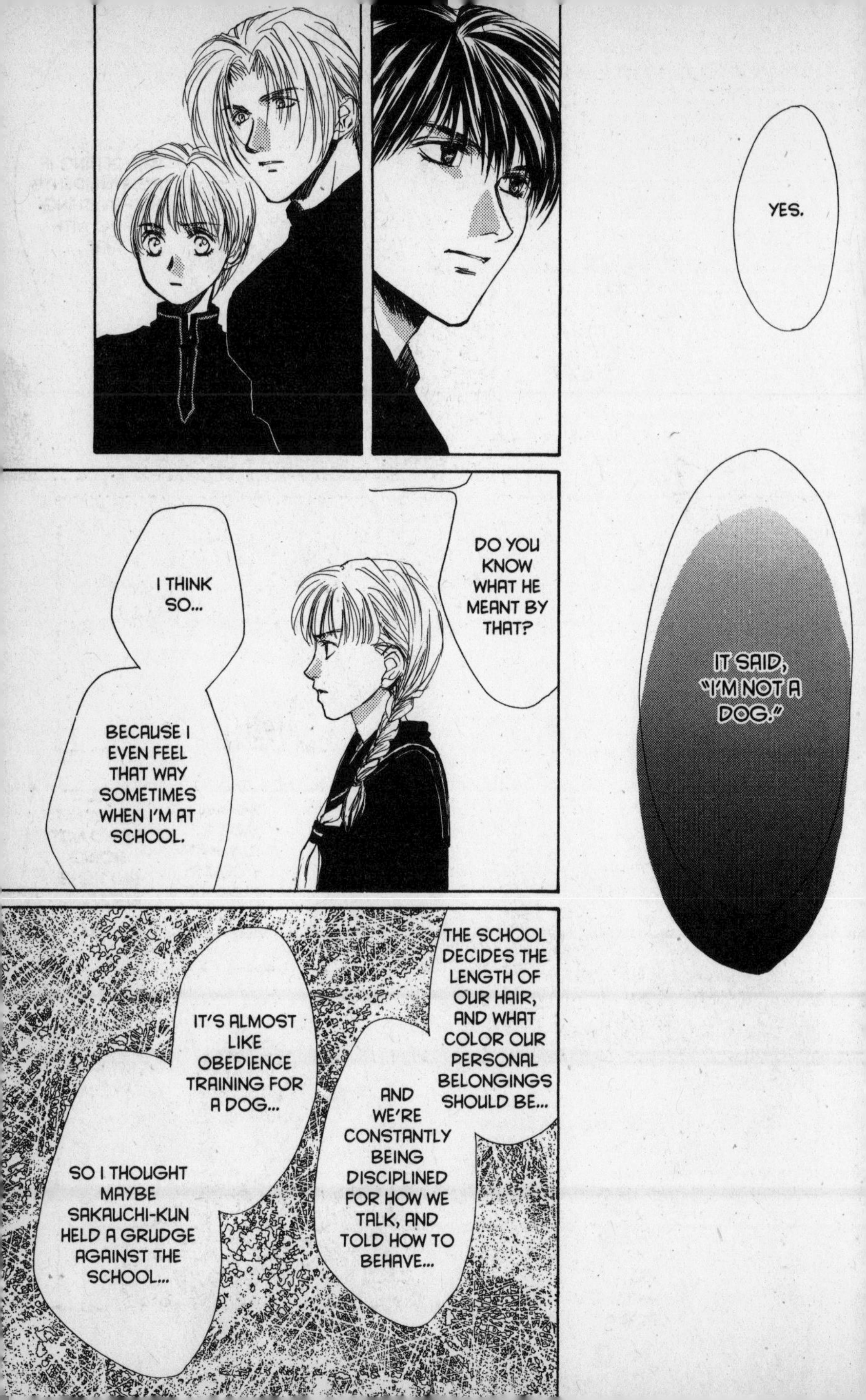
YES.
IT SAID, "I'M NOT A DOG."
DO YOU KNOW WHAT HE MEANT BY THAT?
I THINK SO...
BECAUSE I EVEN FEEL THAT WAY SOMETIMES WHEN I'M AT SCHOOL.
THE SCHOOL DECIDES THE LENGTH OF OUR HAIR, AND WHAT COLOR OUR PERSONAL BELONGINGS SHOULD BE...
AND WE'RE CONSTANTLY BEING DISCIPLINED FOR HOW WE TALK, AND TOLD HOW TO BEHAVE...
IT'S ALMOST LIKE OBEDIENCE TRAINING FOR A DOG...
SO I THOUGHT MAYBE SAKAUCHI-KUN HELD A GRUDGE AGAINST THE SCHOOL...

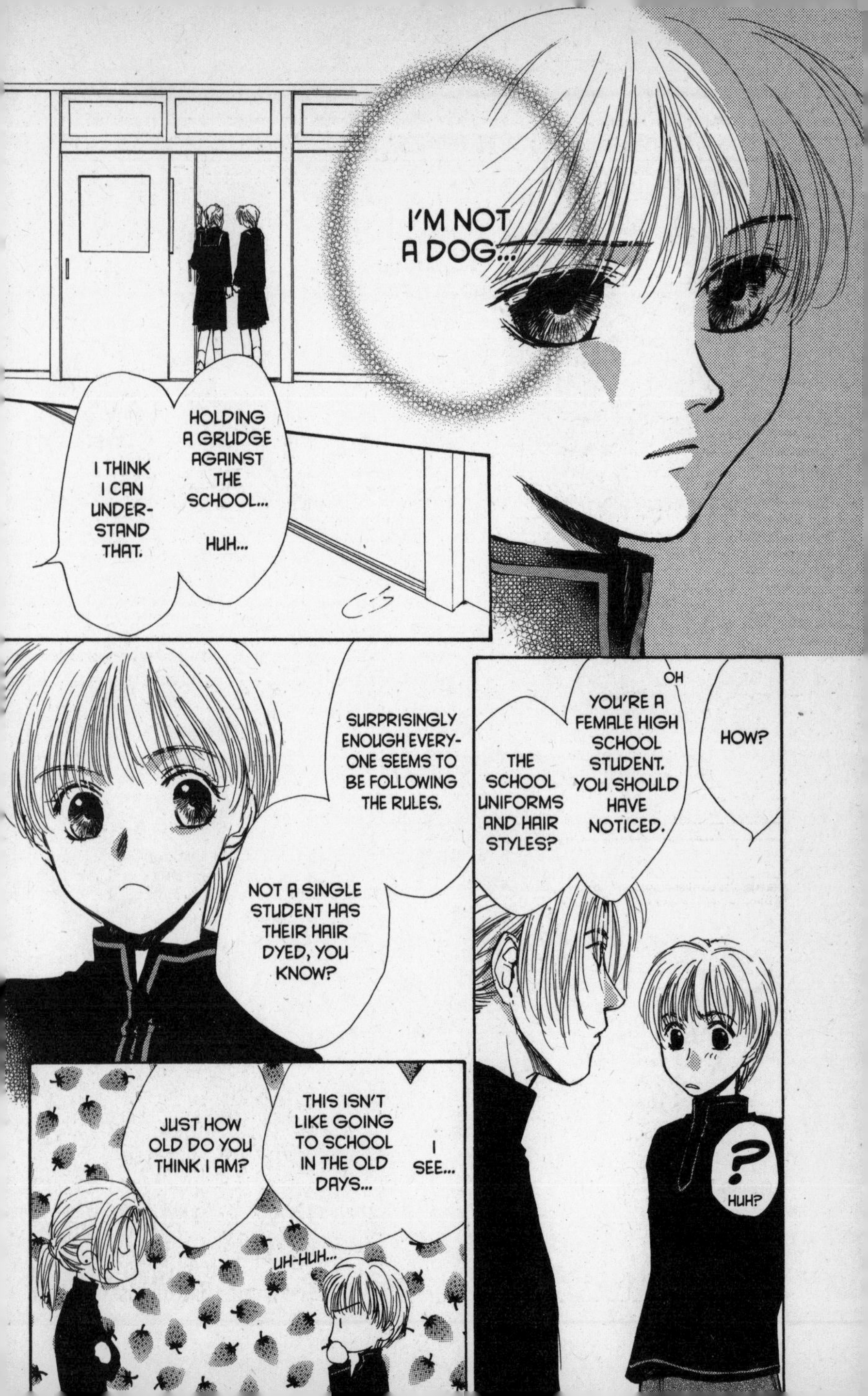
I'M NOT A DOG...
HOLDING A GRUDGE AGAINST THE SCHOOL... HUH...
I THINK I CAN UNDER-STAND THAT.
HOW?
OH YOU'RE A FEMALE HIGH SCHOOL STUDENT. YOU SHOULD HAVE NOTICED.
THE SCHOOL UNIFORMS AND HAIR STYLES?
?
HUH?
SURPRISINGLY ENOUGH EVERY-ONE SEEMS TO BE FOLLOWING THE RULES.
NOT A SINGLE STUDENT HAS THEIR HAIR DYED, YOU KNOW?
I SEE...
THIS ISN'T LIKE GOING TO SCHOOL IN THE OLD DAYS...
JUST HOW OLD DO YOU THINK I AM?
UH-HUH...

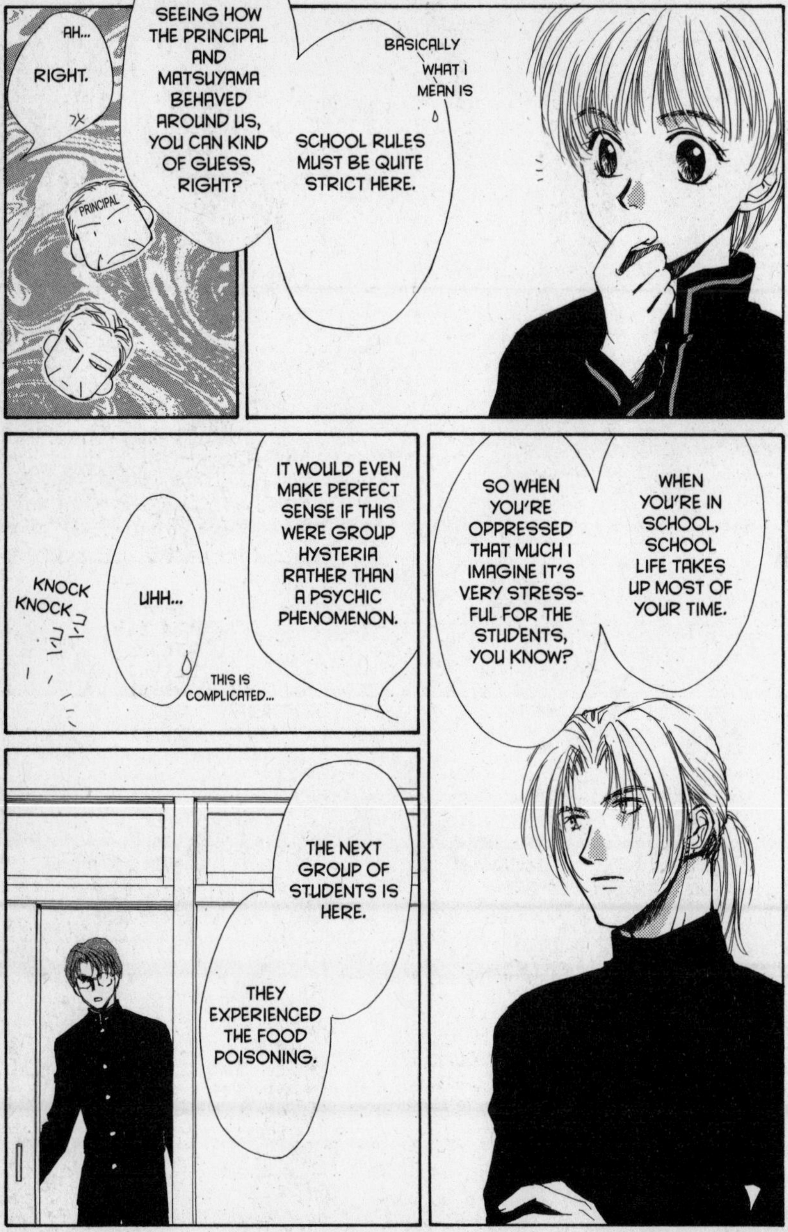
BASICALLY WHAT I MEAN IS
SCHOOL RULES MUST BE QUITE STRICT HERE.
SEEING HOW THE PRINCIPAL AND MATSUYAMA BEHAVED AROUND US, YOU CAN KIND OF GUESS, RIGHT?
AH... RIGHT.
PRINCIPAL
WHEN YOU'RE IN SCHOOL, SCHOOL LIFE TAKES UP MOST OF YOUR TIME.
SO WHEN YOU'RE OPPRESSED THAT MUCH I IMAGINE IT'S VERY STRESS-FUL FOR THE STUDENTS, YOU KNOW?
IT WOULD EVEN MAKE PERFECT SENSE IF THIS WERE GROUP HYSTERIA RATHER THAN A PSYCHIC PHENOMENON.
UHH...
THIS IS COMPLICATED...
KNOCK KNOCK
THE NEXT GROUP OF STUDENTS IS HERE.
THEY EXPERIENCED THE FOOD POISONING.

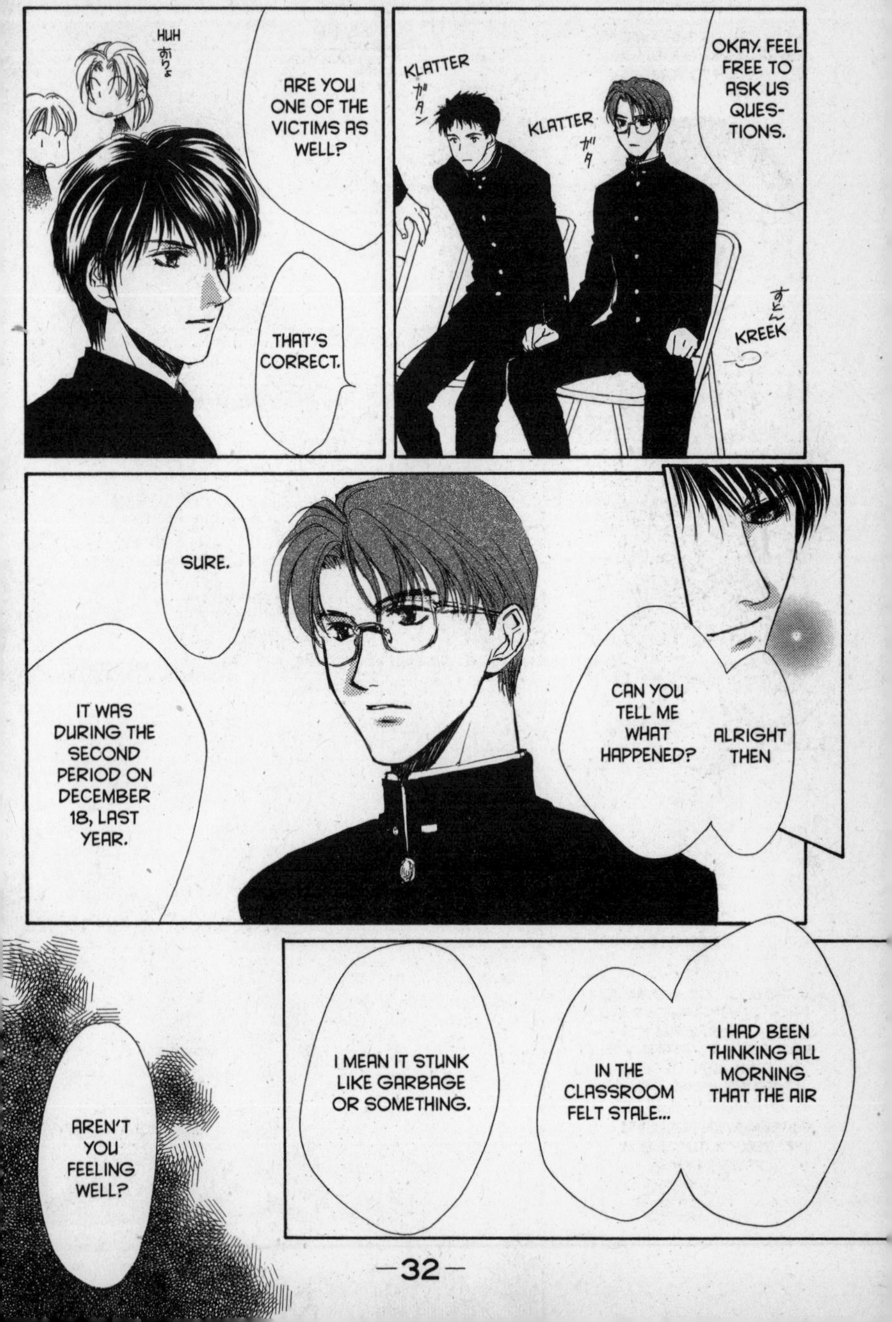
OKAY. FEEL FREE TO ASK US QUES-TIONS.
KLATTER
ガタン
KLATTER
ガタ
KREEK
ARE YOU ONE OF THE VICTIMS AS WELL?
HUH
THAT'S CORRECT.
ALRIGHT THEN
CAN YOU TELL ME WHAT HAPPENED?
SURE.
IT WAS DURING THE SECOND PERIOD ON DECEMBER 18, LAST YEAR.
I HAD BEEN THINKING ALL MORNING THAT THE AIR
IN THE CLASSROOM FELT STALE...
I MEAN IT STUNK LIKE GARBAGE OR SOMETHING.
AREN'T YOU FEELING WELL?

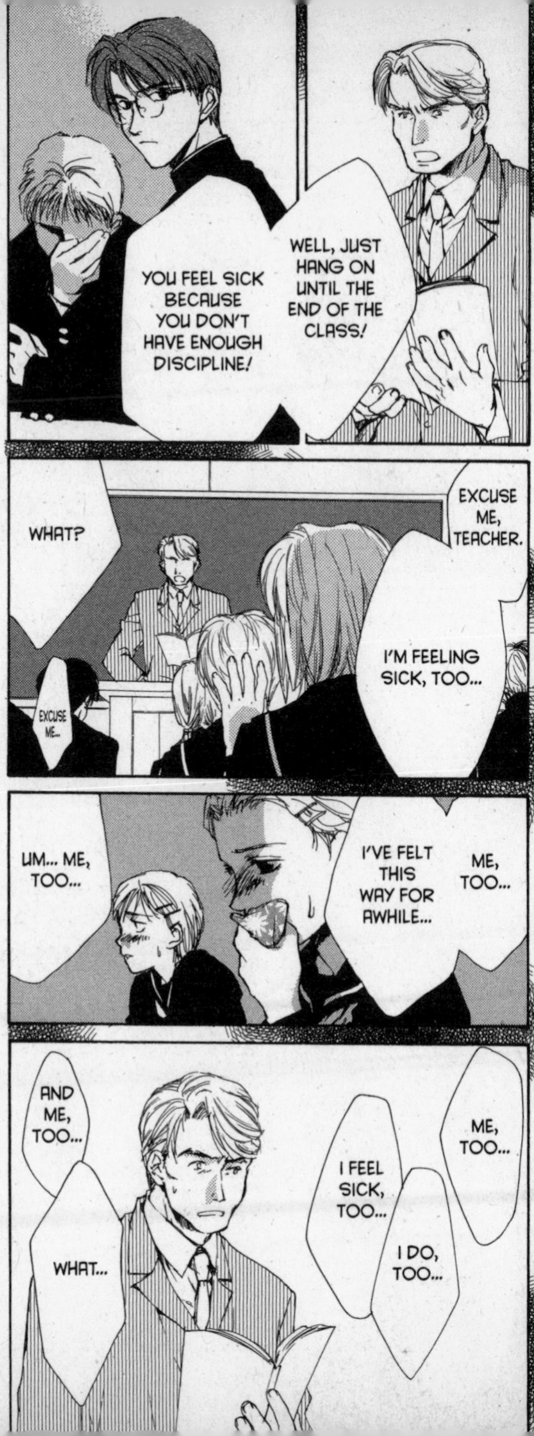
YOU FEEL SICK BECAUSE YOU DON'T HAVE ENOUGH DISCIPLINE!
WELL, JUST HANG ON UNTIL THE END OF THE CLASS!
EXCUSE ME, TEACHER.
I'M FEELING SICK, TOO...
WHAT?
EXCUSE ME...
ME, TOO...
I'VE FELT THIS WAY FOR AWHILE...
UM... ME, TOO...
ME, TOO...
I FEEL SICK, TOO...
I DO, TOO...
AND ME, TOO...
WHAT...

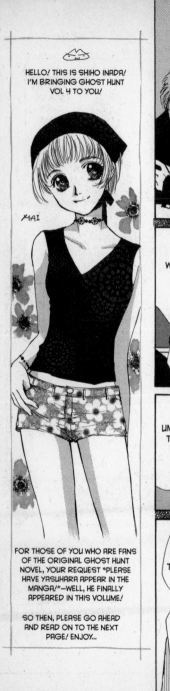

HELLO! THIS IS SHIHO INADA! I'M BRINGING GHOST HUNT VOL 4 TO YOU!

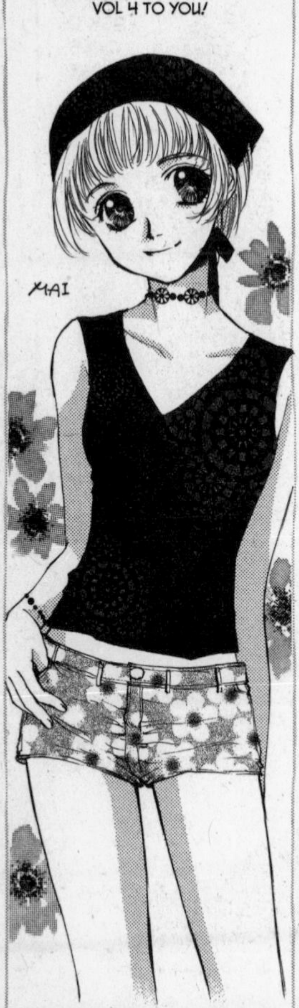
MAI

FOR THOSE OF YOU WHO ARE FANS OF THE ORIGINAL GHOST HUNT NOVEL, YOUR REQUEST "PLEASE HAVE YASUHARA APPEAR IN THE MANGA!"—WELL, HE FINALLY APPEARED IN THIS VOLUME!

SO THEN, PLEASE GO AHEAD AND READ ON TO THE NEXT PAGE! ENJOY...

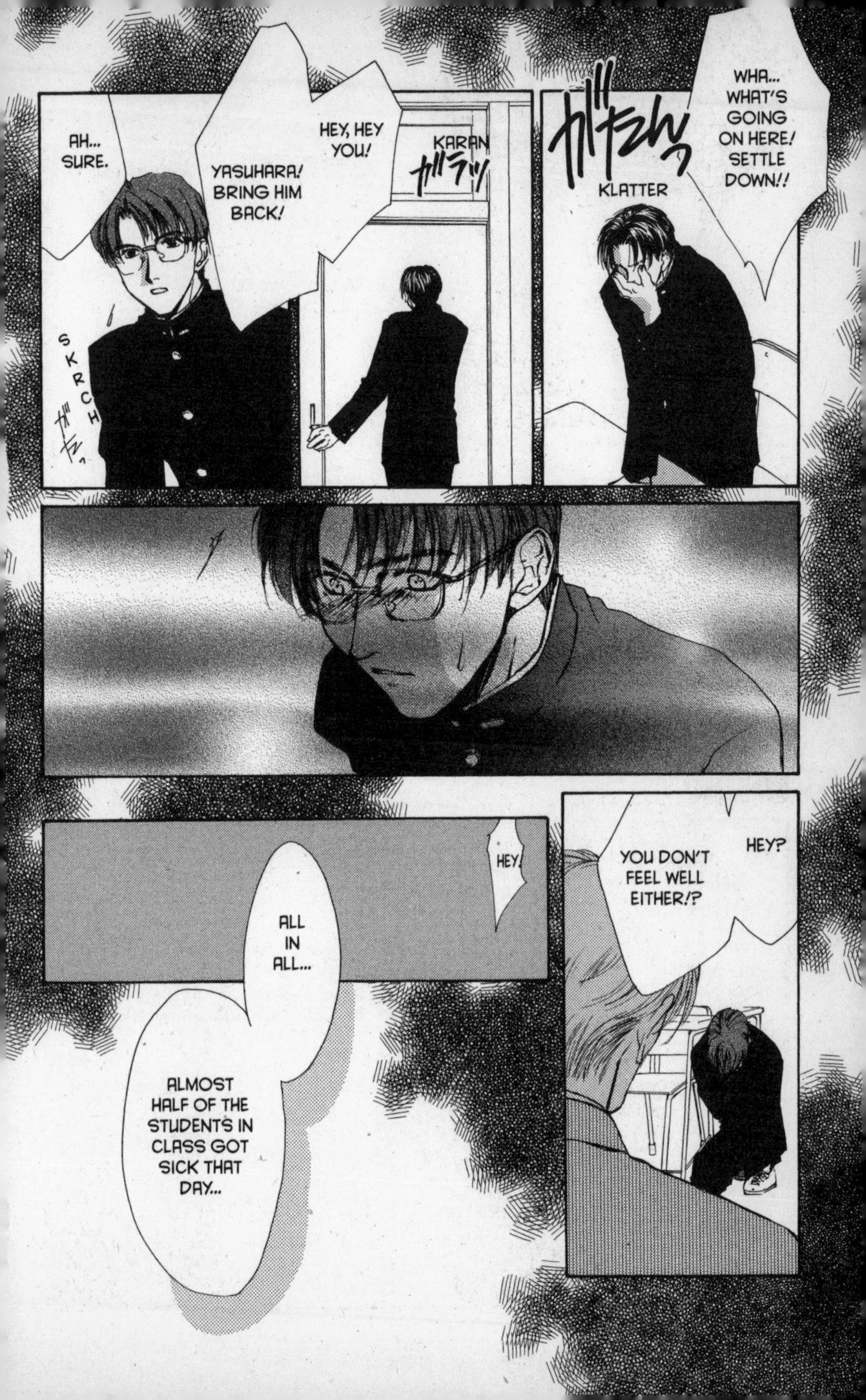
WHA... WHAT'S GOING ON HERE! SETTLE DOWN!!
KLATTER
HEY, HEY YOU!
KARAN
ガラッ
YASUHARA! BRING HIM BACK!
AH... SURE.
SKRCH
HEY?
YOU DON'T FEEL WELL EITHER!?
HEY!
ALL IN ALL...
ALMOST HALF OF THE STUDENTS IN CLASS GOT SICK THAT DAY...

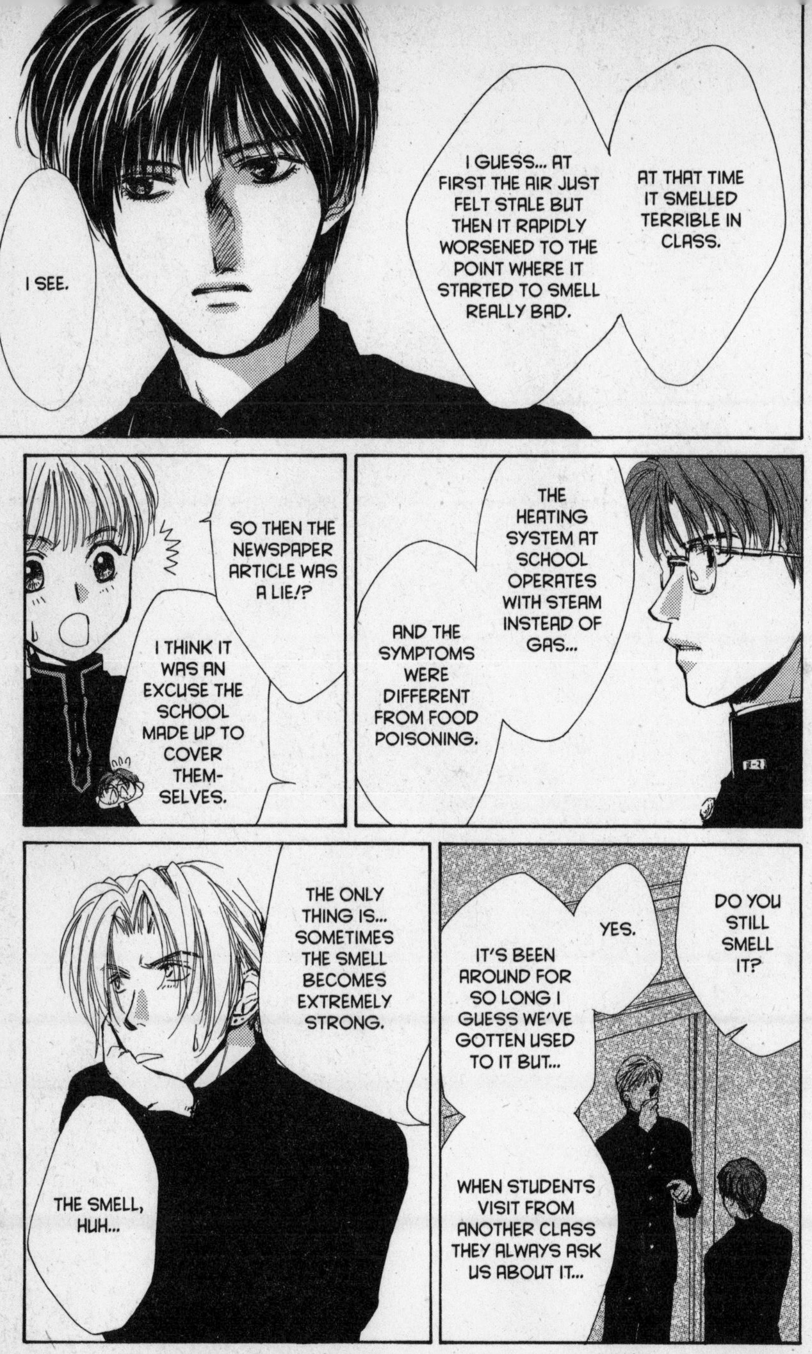
AT THAT TIME IT SMELLED TERRIBLE IN CLASS.
I GUESS... AT FIRST THE AIR JUST FELT STALE BUT THEN IT RAPIDLY WORSENED TO THE POINT WHERE IT STARTED TO SMELL REALLY BAD.
I SEE.
THE HEATING SYSTEM AT SCHOOL OPERATES WITH STEAM INSTEAD OF GAS...
AND THE SYMPTOMS WERE DIFFERENT FROM FOOD POISONING.
SO THEN THE NEWSPAPER ARTICLE WAS A LIE!?
I THINK IT WAS AN EXCUSE THE SCHOOL MADE UP TO COVER THEM-SELVES.
DO YOU STILL SMELL IT?
YES.
IT'S BEEN AROUND FOR SO LONG I GUESS WE'VE GOTTEN USED TO IT BUT...
WHEN STUDENTS VISIT FROM ANOTHER CLASS THEY ALWAYS ASK US ABOUT IT...
THE ONLY THING IS... SOMETIMES THE SMELL BECOMES EXTREMELY STRONG.
THE SMELL, HUH...

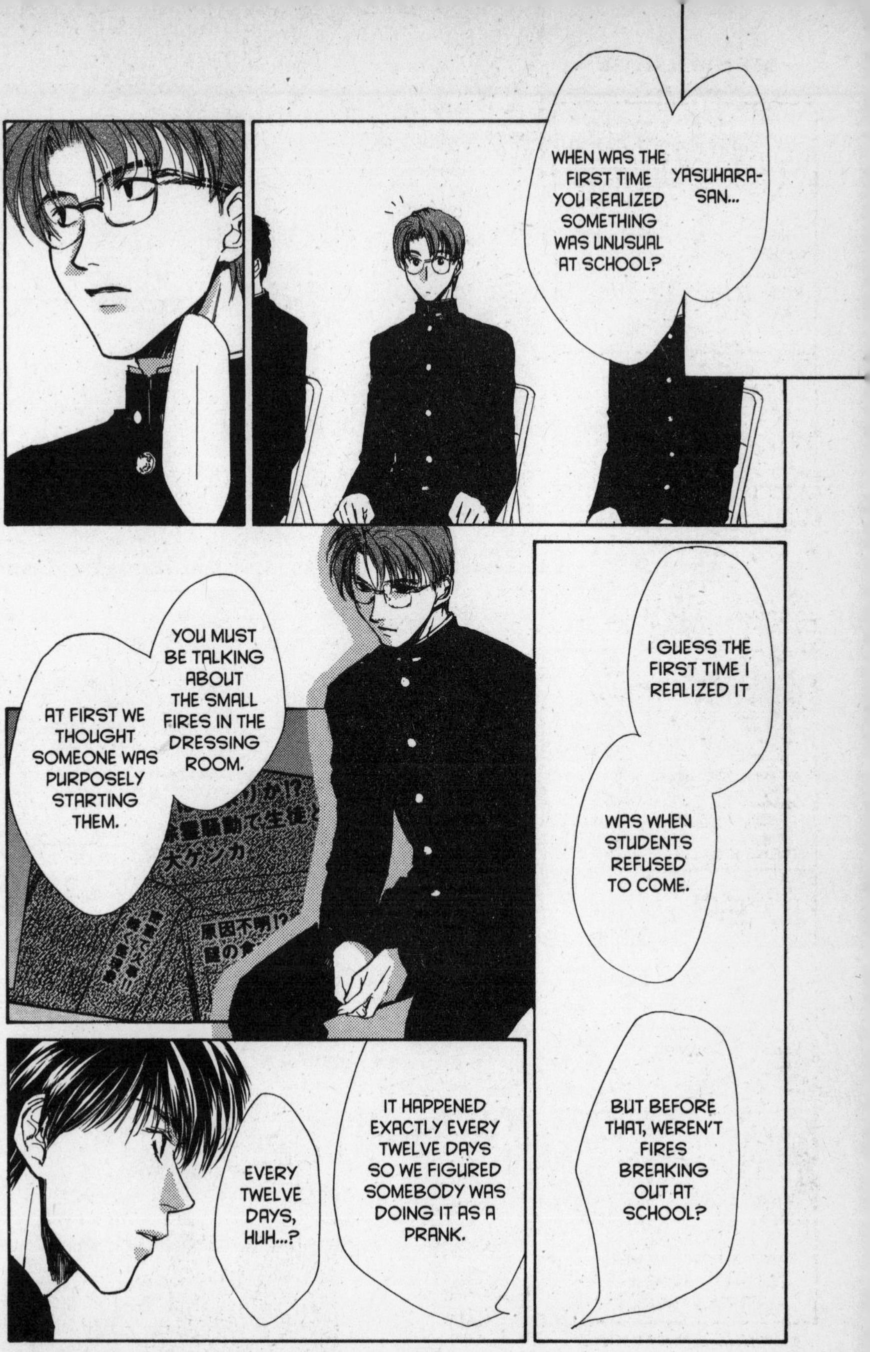
YASUHARA-SAN...
WHEN WAS THE FIRST TIME YOU REALIZED SOMETHING WAS UNUSUAL AT SCHOOL?
I GUESS THE FIRST TIME I REALIZED IT
WAS WHEN STUDENTS REFUSED TO COME.
YOU MUST BE TALKING ABOUT THE SMALL FIRES IN THE DRESSING ROOM.
AT FIRST WE THOUGHT SOMEONE WAS PURPOSELY STARTING THEM.
大ゲンカ
BUT BEFORE THAT, WEREN'T FIRES BREAKING OUT AT SCHOOL?
IT HAPPENED EXACTLY EVERY TWELVE DAYS SO WE FIGURED SOMEBODY WAS DOING IT AS A PRANK.
EVERY TWELVE DAYS, HUH...?

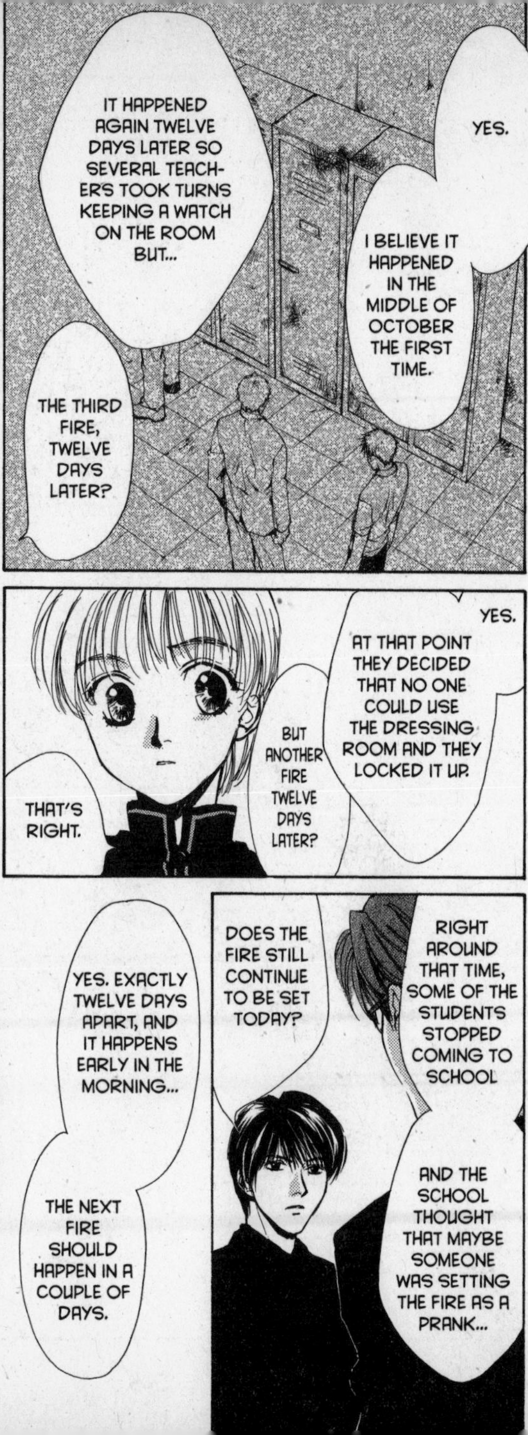
YES.
I BELIEVE IT HAPPENED IN THE MIDDLE OF OCTOBER THE FIRST TIME.
IT HAPPENED AGAIN TWELVE DAYS LATER SO SEVERAL TEACHER'S TOOK TURNS KEEPING A WATCH ON THE ROOM BUT...
THE THIRD FIRE, TWELVE DAYS LATER?
YES.
AT THAT POINT THEY DECIDED THAT NO ONE COULD USE THE DRESSING ROOM AND THEY LOCKED IT UP.
BUT ANOTHER FIRE TWELVE DAYS LATER?
THAT'S RIGHT.
RIGHT AROUND THAT TIME, SOME OF THE STUDENTS STOPPED COMING TO SCHOOL
AND THE SCHOOL THOUGHT THAT MAYBE SOMEONE WAS SETTING THE FIRE AS A PRANK...
DOES THE FIRE STILL CONTINUE TO BE SET TODAY?
YES. EXACTLY TWELVE DAYS APART, AND IT HAPPENS EARLY IN THE MORNING...
THE NEXT FIRE SHOULD HAPPEN IN A COUPLE OF DAYS.

INTERSTITIAL MANGA:
SCARY JOB

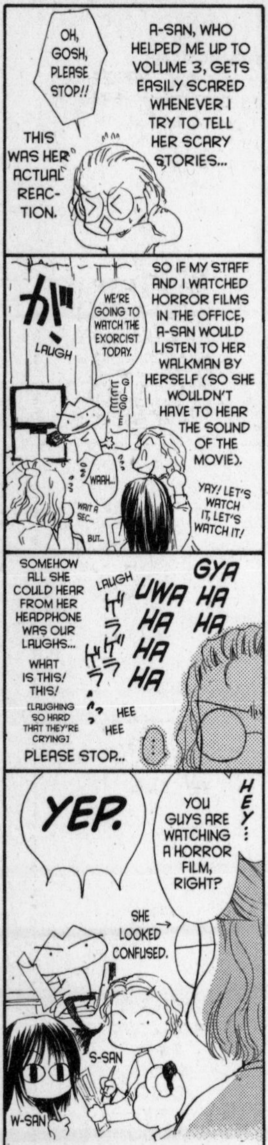
A-SAN, WHO HELPED ME UP TO VOLUME 3, GETS EASILY SCARED WHENEVER I TRY TO TELL HER SCARY STORIES...
OH, GOSH, PLEASE STOP!!
THIS WAS HER ACTUAL REACTION.
SO IF MY STAFF AND I WATCHED HORROR FILMS IN THE OFFICE, A-SAN WOULD LISTEN TO HER WALKMAN BY HERSELF (SO SHE WOULDN'T HAVE TO HEAR THE SOUND OF THE MOVIE).
WE'RE GOING TO WATCH THE EXORCIST TODAY.
が、
LAUGH
GIGGLE
WAAH...
YAY! LET'S WATCH IT, LET'S WATCH IT!
WAIT A SEC...
BUT...
SOMEHOW ALL SHE COULD HEAR FROM HER HEADPHONE WAS OUR LAUGHS...
GYA HA HA
UWA HA HA HA HA
LAUGH
ゲラゲラゲラ
WHAT IS THIS! THIS!
[LAUGHING SO HARD THAT THEY'RE CRYING]
HEE HEE
PLEASE STOP...
YEP.
HEY...
YOU GUYS ARE WATCHING A HORROR FILM, RIGHT?
SHE LOOKED CONFUSED.
S-SAN
W-SAN
AT THAT TIME WE WERE CERTAINLY WATCHING A HORROR MOVIE...

WE WATCHED EXORCIST 1 AND 3 REPEATEDLY...

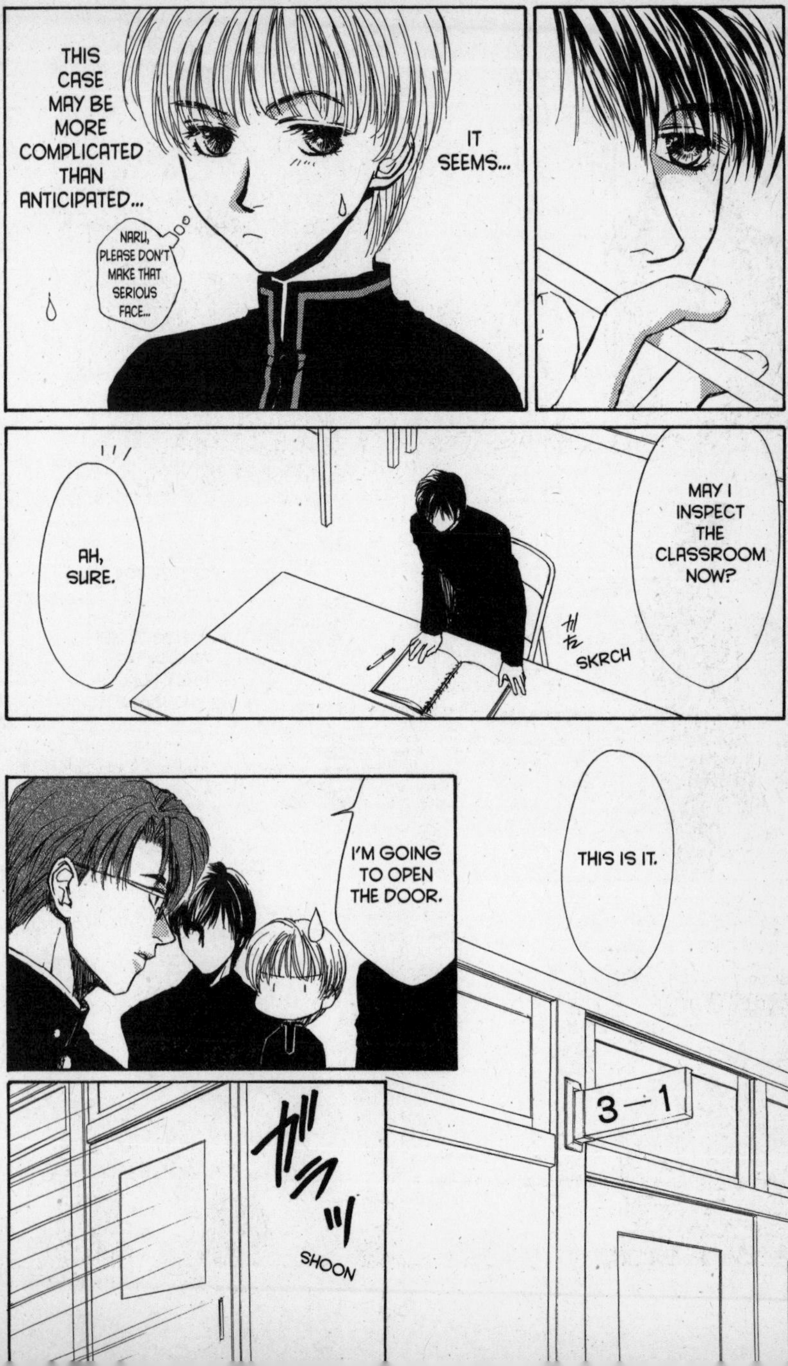
IT SEEMS...
THIS CASE MAY BE MORE COMPLICATED THAN ANTICIPATED...
NARU, PLEASE DON'T MAKE THAT SERIOUS FACE...
MAY I INSPECT THE CLASSROOM NOW?
カタ
SKRCH
AH, SURE.
THIS IS IT.
3-1
I'M GOING TO OPEN THE DOOR.
ガラッ
SHOON

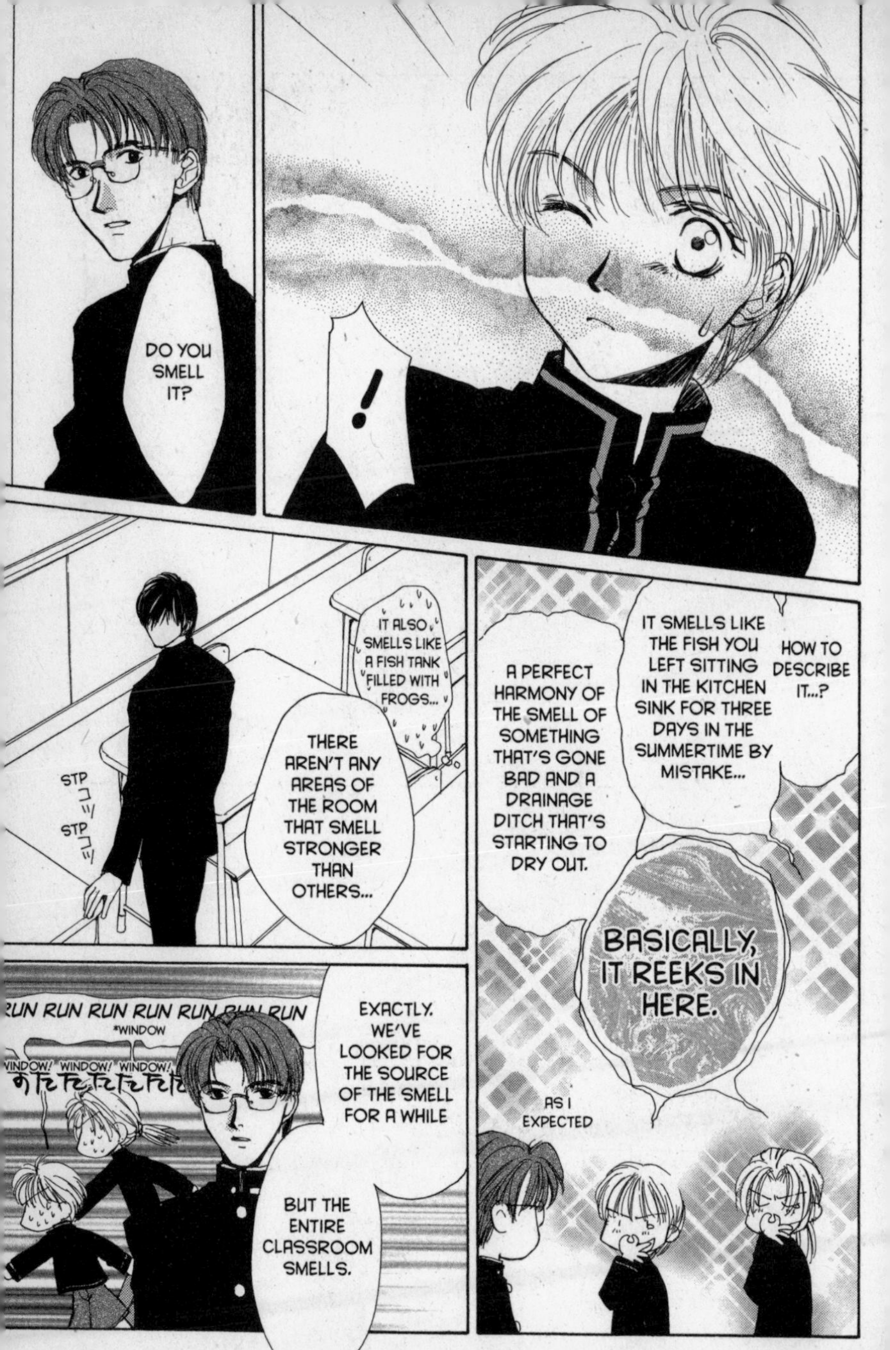
!
DO YOU SMELL IT?
HOW TO DESCRIBE IT...?
IT SMELLS LIKE THE FISH YOU LEFT SITTING IN THE KITCHEN SINK FOR THREE DAYS IN THE SUMMERTIME BY MISTAKE...
A PERFECT HARMONY OF THE SMELL OF SOMETHING THAT'S GONE BAD AND A DRAINAGE DITCH THAT'S STARTING TO DRY OUT.
BASICALLY, IT REEKS IN HERE.
AS I EXPECTED
IT ALSO SMELLS LIKE A FISH TANK FILLED WITH FROGS...
THERE AREN'T ANY AREAS OF THE ROOM THAT SMELL STRONGER THAN OTHERS...
STP コツ
STP コツ
EXACTLY. WE'VE LOOKED FOR THE SOURCE OF THE SMELL FOR A WHILE
BUT THE ENTIRE CLASSROOM SMELLS.
RUN RUN RUN RUN RUN RUN RUN
*WINDOW
WINDOW! WINDOW! WINDOW!

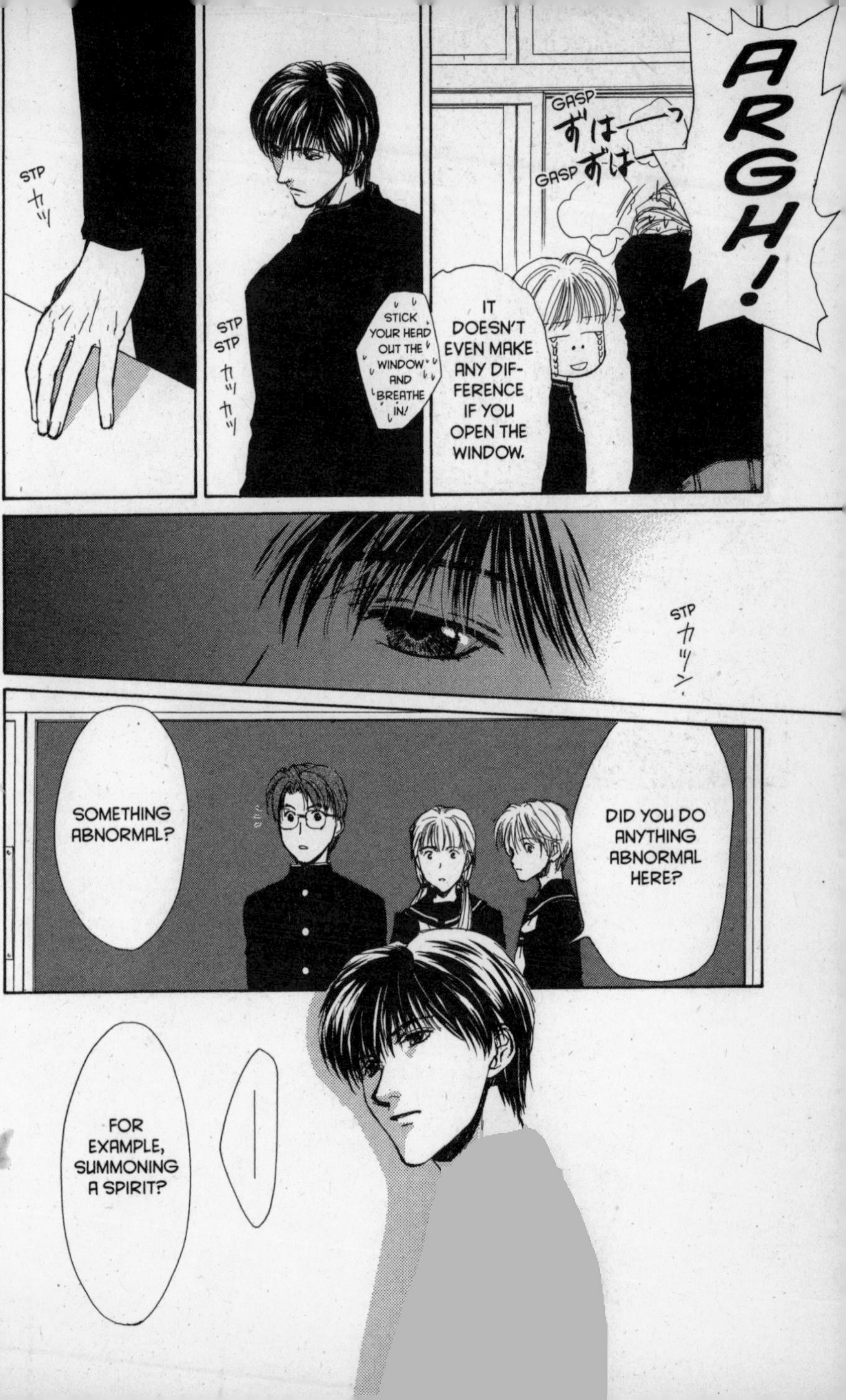
ARGH!
GASP
ずはーっ
GASP
ずは
IT DOESN'T EVEN MAKE ANY DIF-FERENCE IF YOU OPEN THE WINDOW.
STICK YOUR HEAD OUT THE WINDOW AND BREATHE IN!
STP STP
カッカッ
STP
カッ
STP
カツン
DID YOU DO ANYTHING ABNORMAL HERE?
SOMETHING ABNORMAL?
—
FOR EXAMPLE, SUMMONING A SPIRIT?

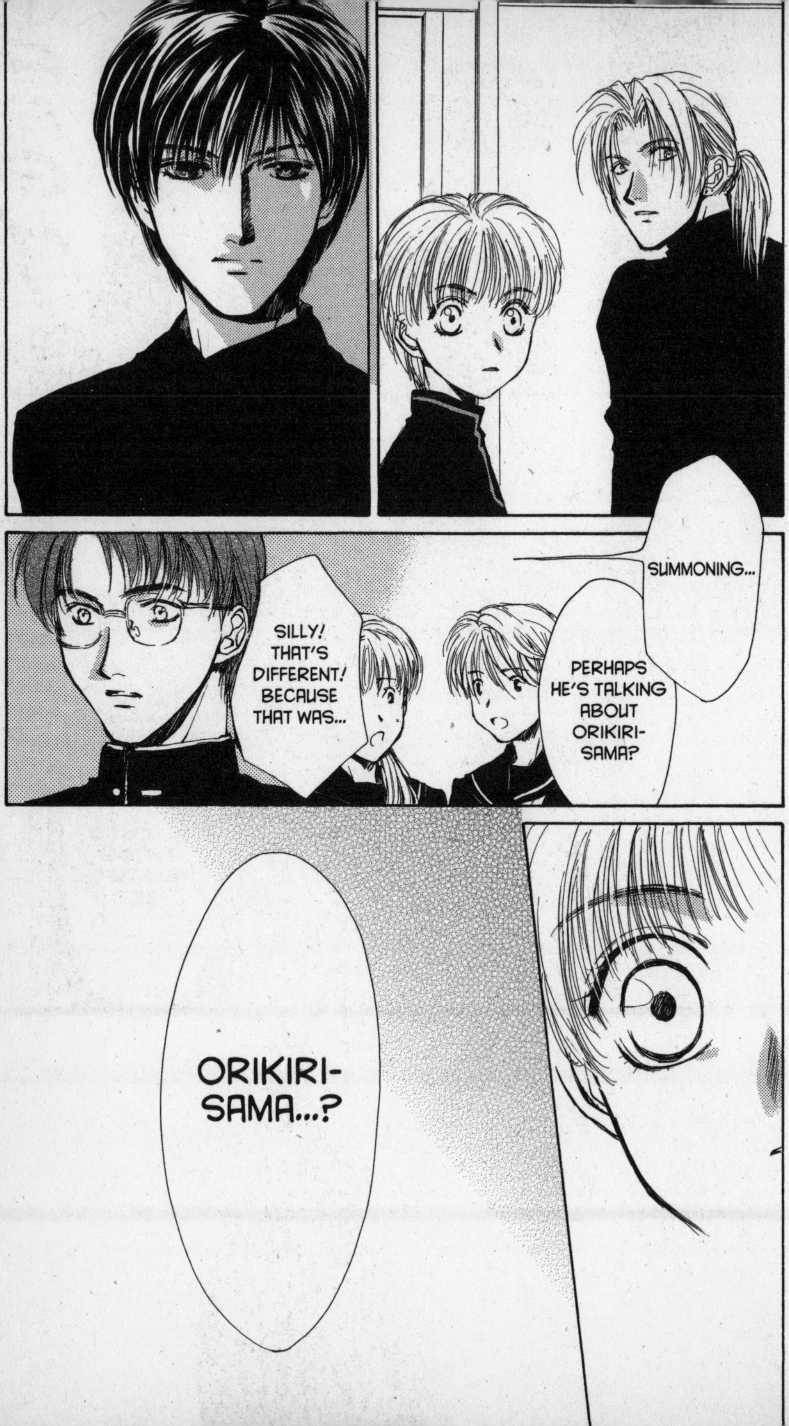
SUMMONING...
PERHAPS HE'S TALKING ABOUT ORIKIRI-SAMA?
SILLY! THAT'S DIFFERENT! BECAUSE THAT WAS...
ORIKIRI-SAMA...?

FILE 2

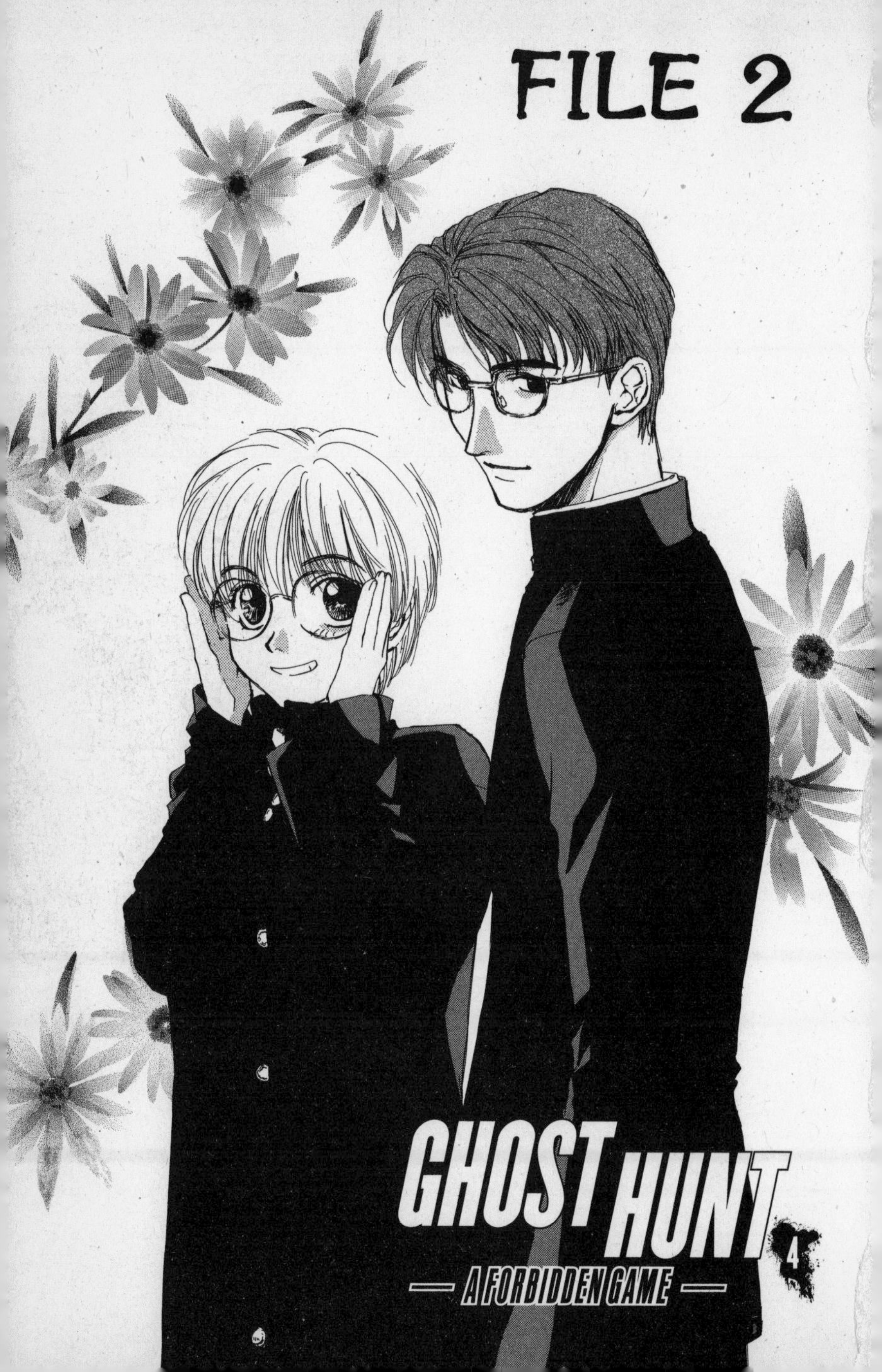
GHOST HUNT
4
A FORBIDDEN GAME

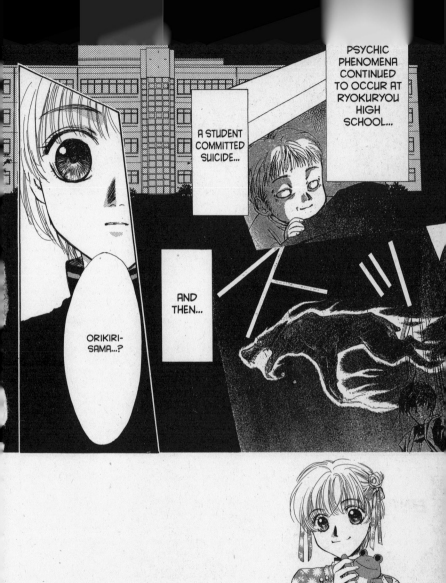

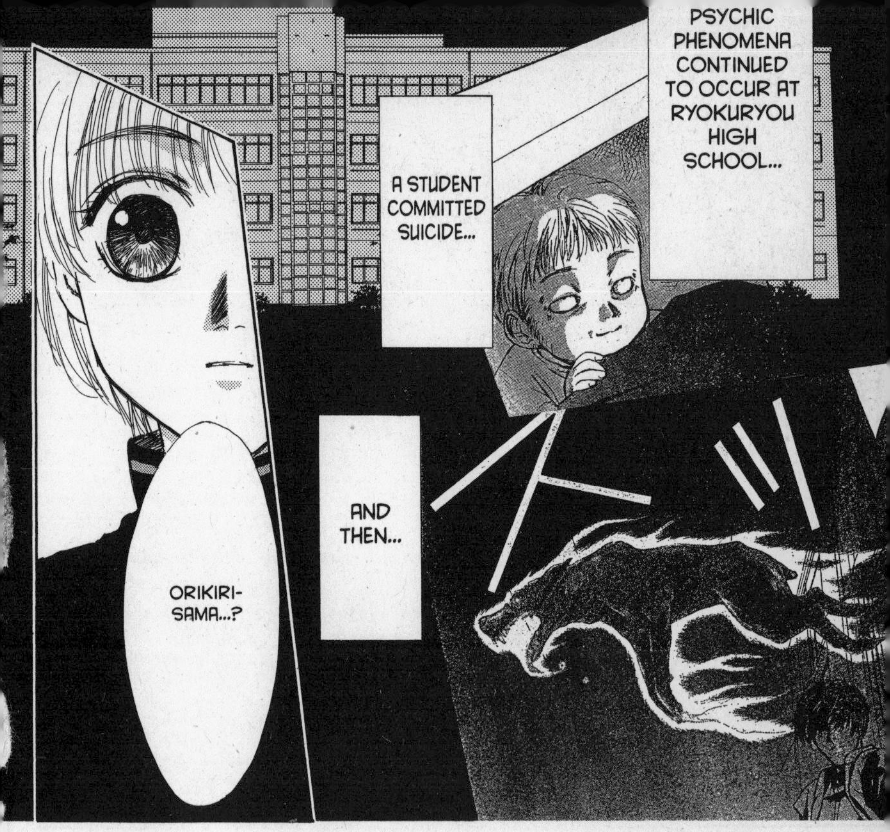
PSYCHIC PHENOMENA CONTINUED TO OCCUR AT RYOKURYOU HIGH SCHOOL...
A STUDENT COMMITTED SUICIDE...
AND THEN...
ORIKIRI-SAMA...?

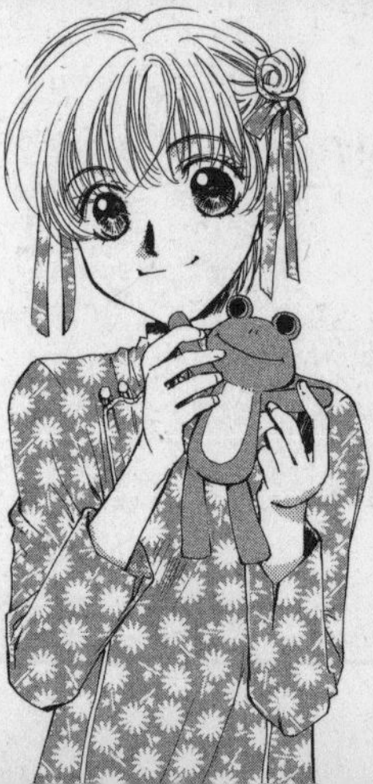

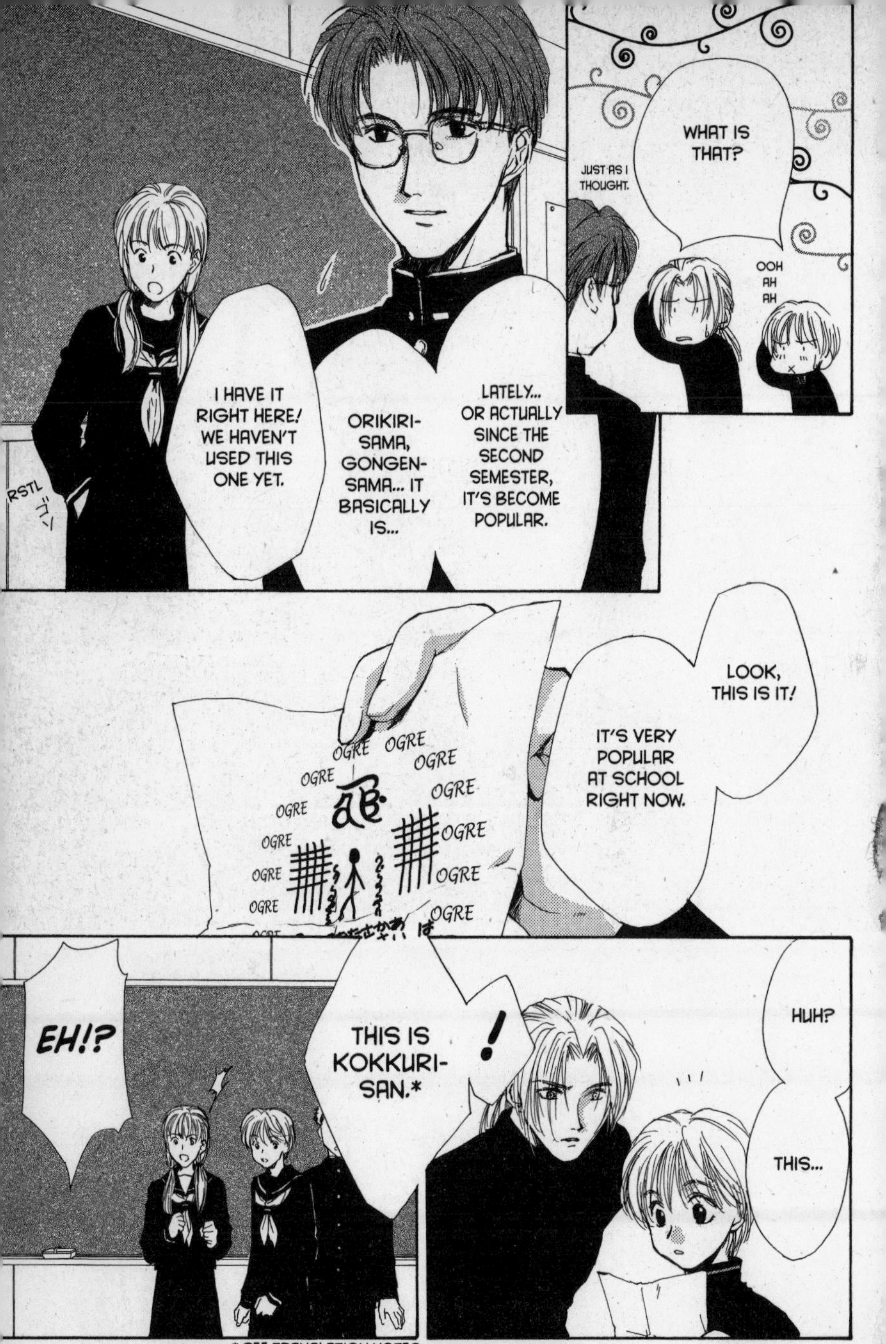
WHAT IS THAT?
JUST AS I THOUGHT.
OOH AH AH
LATELY... OR ACTUALLY SINCE THE SECOND SEMESTER, IT'S BECOME POPULAR.
ORIKIRI-SAMA, GONGEN-SAMA... IT BASICALLY IS...
I HAVE IT RIGHT HERE! WE HAVEN'T USED THIS ONE YET.
RSTL
LOOK, THIS IS IT!
IT'S VERY POPULAR AT SCHOOL RIGHT NOW.
OGRE OGRE OGRE OGRE OGRE OGRE OGRE OGRE OGRE OGRE OGRE OGRE OGRE
HUH?
THIS...
!
THIS IS KOKKURI-SAN.*
EH!?

* SEE TRANSLATION NOTES

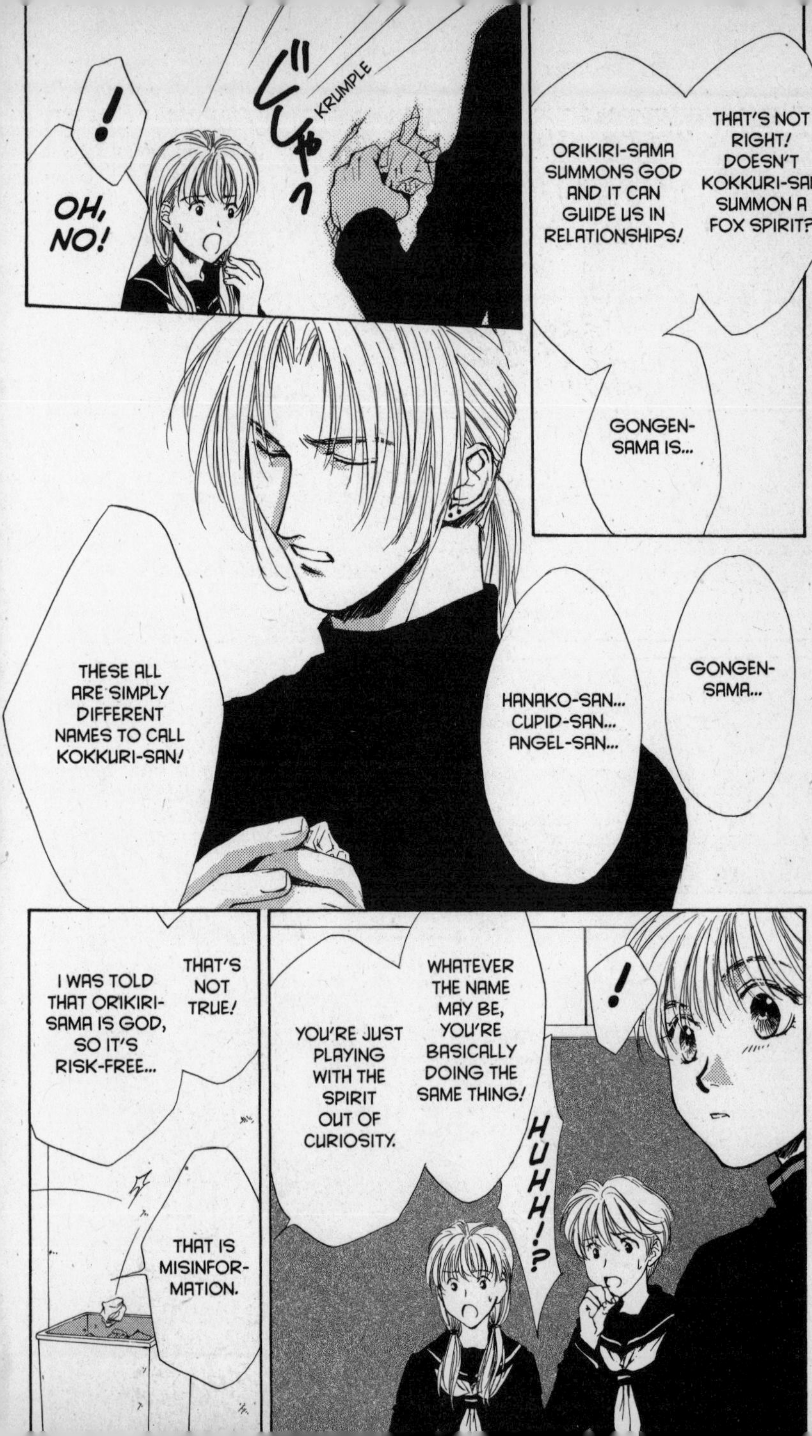
THAT'S NOT RIGHT! DOESN'T KOKKURI-SAN SUMMON A FOX SPIRIT?
ORIKIRI-SAMA SUMMONS GOD AND IT CAN GUIDE US IN RELATIONSHIPS!
GONGEN-SAMA IS...
KRUMPLE
!
OH, NO!
GONGEN-SAMA...
HANAKO-SAN... CUPID-SAN... ANGEL-SAN...
THESE ALL ARE SIMPLY DIFFERENT NAMES TO CALL KOKKURI-SAN!
!
WHATEVER THE NAME MAY BE, YOU'RE BASICALLY DOING THE SAME THING!
YOU'RE JUST PLAYING WITH THE SPIRIT OUT OF CURIOSITY.
HUHH!?
THAT'S NOT TRUE!
I WAS TOLD THAT ORIKIRI-SAMA IS GOD, SO IT'S RISK-FREE...
THAT IS MISINFORMATION.

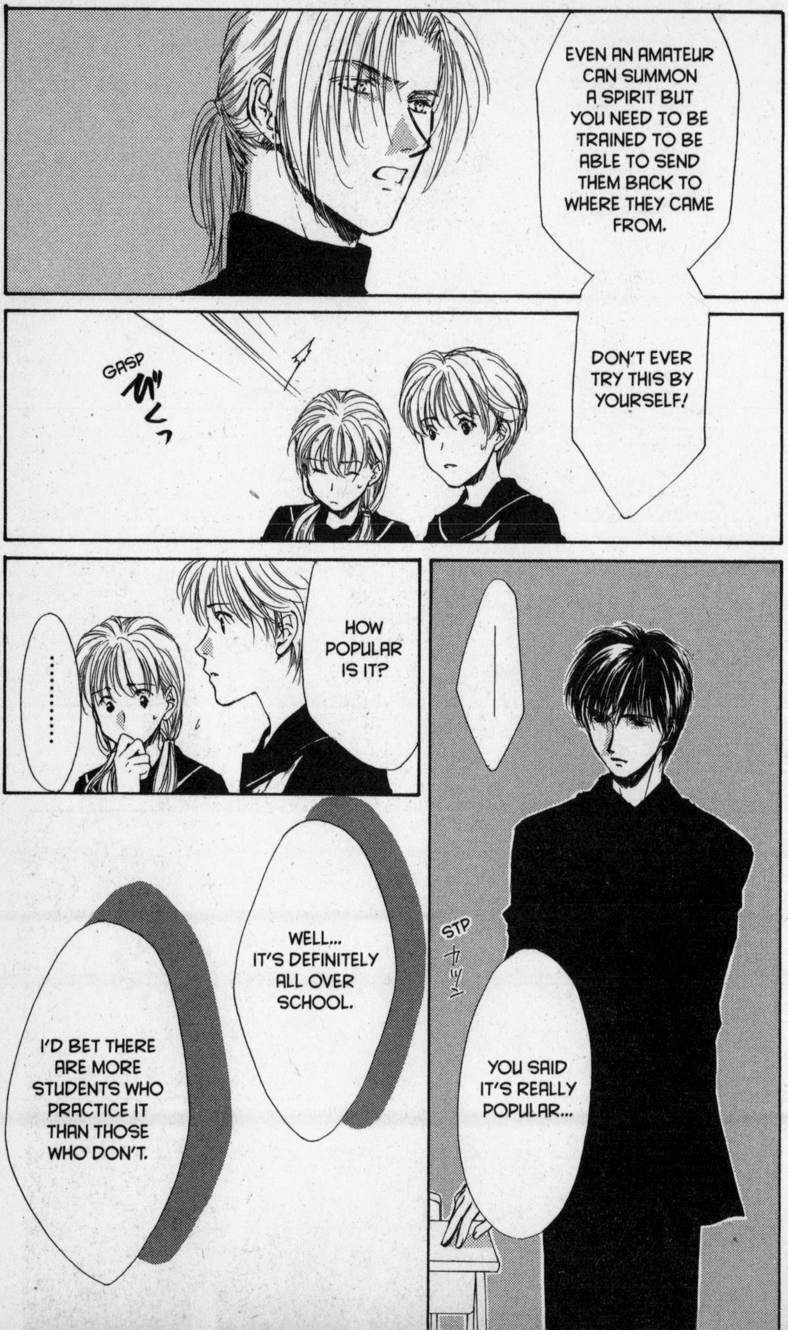
EVEN AN AMATEUR CAN SUMMON A SPIRIT BUT YOU NEED TO BE TRAINED TO BE ABLE TO SEND THEM BACK TO WHERE THEY CAME FROM.
DON'T EVER TRY THIS BY YOURSELF!
GASP
—
STP
YOU SAID IT'S REALLY POPULAR...
HOW POPULAR IS IT?
....
WELL... IT'S DEFINITELY ALL OVER SCHOOL.
I'D BET THERE ARE MORE STUDENTS WHO PRACTICE IT THAN THOSE WHO DON'T.

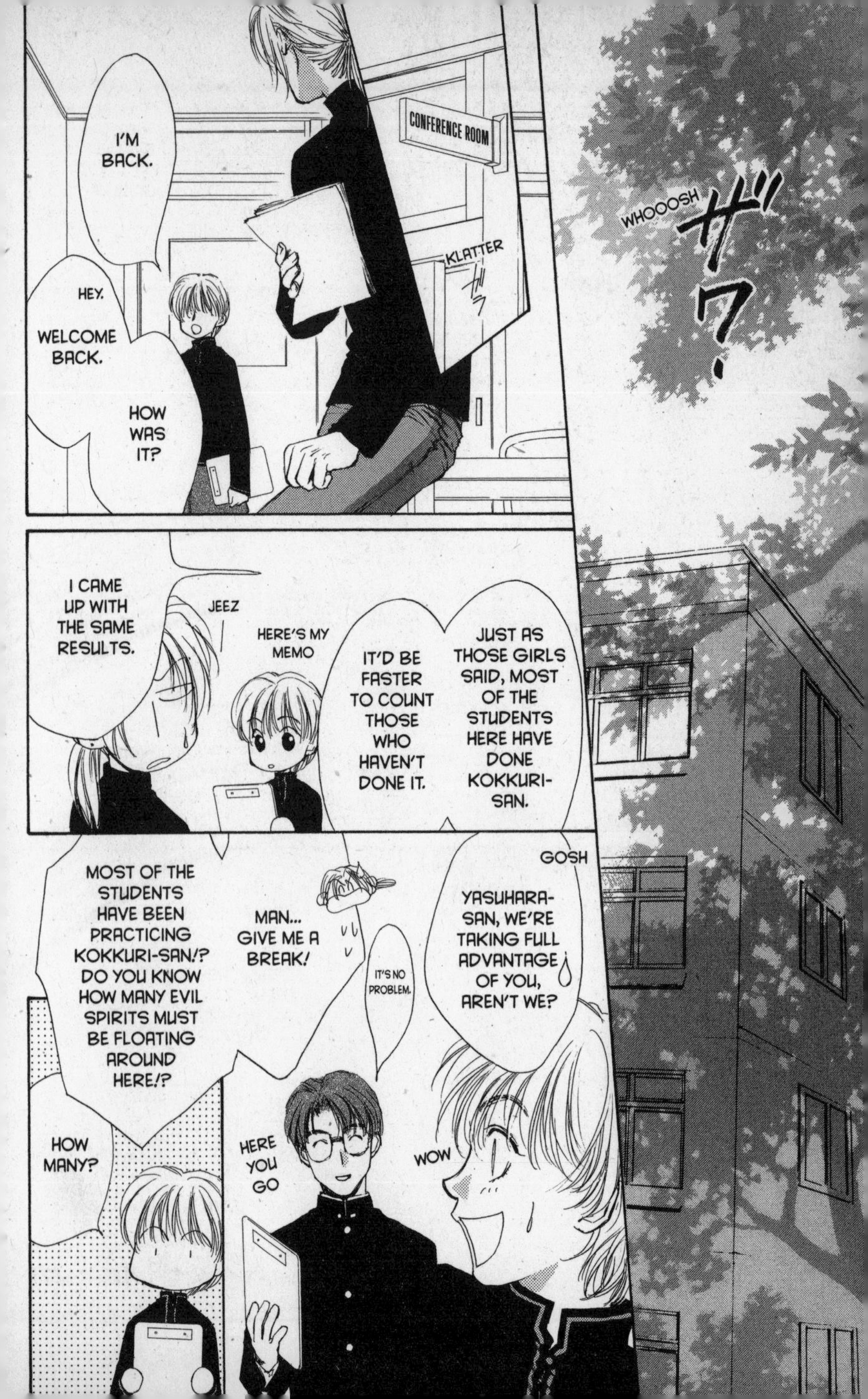
WHOOOSH
ザワ
CONFERENCE ROOM
KLATTER
I'M BACK.
HEY.
WELCOME BACK.
HOW WAS IT?
JUST AS THOSE GIRLS SAID, MOST OF THE STUDENTS HERE HAVE DONE KOKKURI-SAN.
IT'D BE FASTER TO COUNT THOSE WHO HAVEN'T DONE IT.
HERE'S MY MEMO
JEEZ
I CAME UP WITH THE SAME RESULTS.
GOSH
YASUHARA-SAN, WE'RE TAKING FULL ADVANTAGE OF YOU, AREN'T WE?
IT'S NO PROBLEM.
MAN... GIVE ME A BREAK!
MOST OF THE STUDENTS HAVE BEEN PRACTICING KOKKURI-SAN!? DO YOU KNOW HOW MANY EVIL SPIRITS MUST BE FLOATING AROUND HERE!?
WOW
HERE YOU GO
HOW MANY?

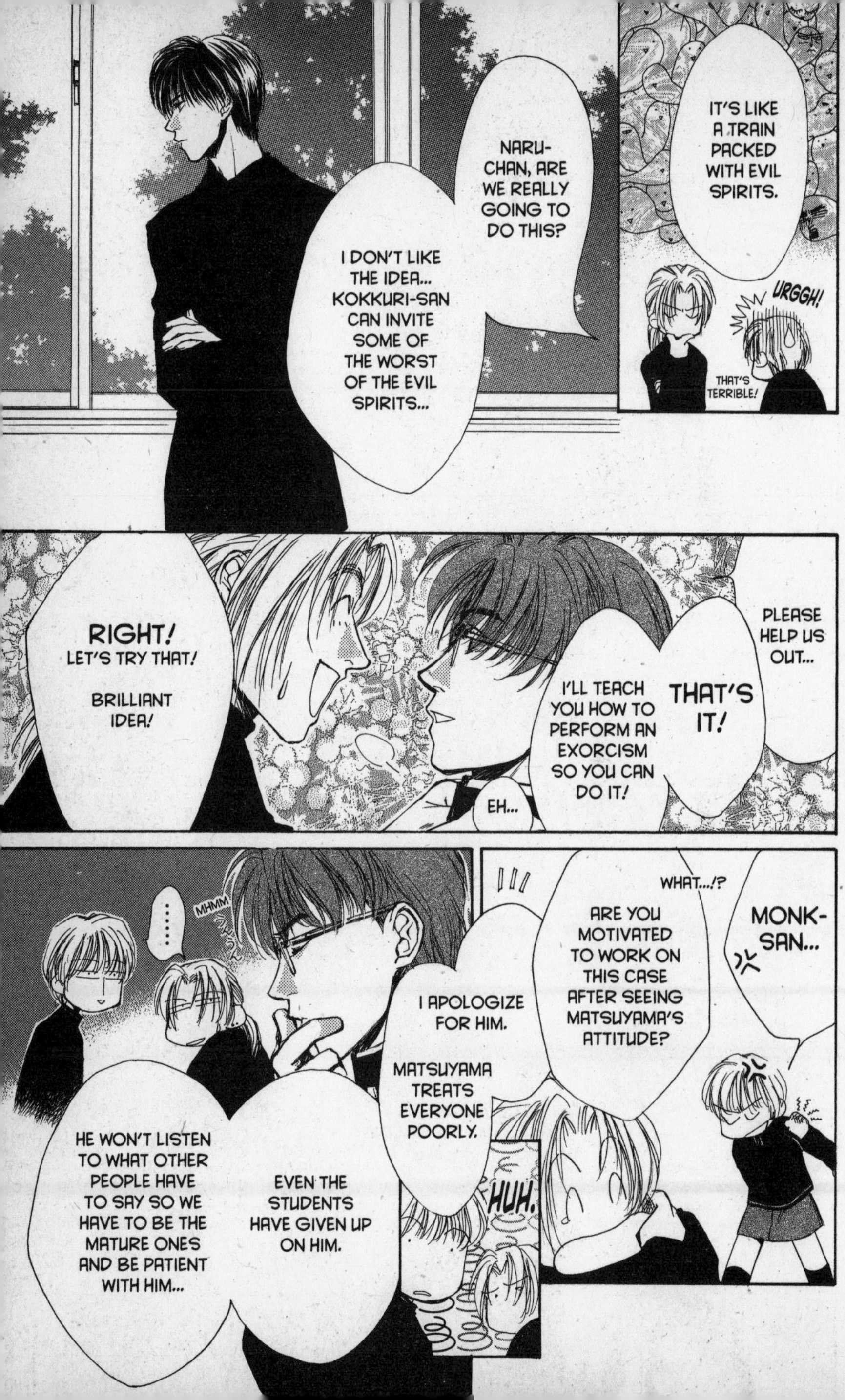
IT'S LIKE A TRAIN PACKED WITH EVIL SPIRITS.
URGGH!
THAT'S TERRIBLE!
NARU-CHAN, ARE WE REALLY GOING TO DO THIS?
I DON'T LIKE THE IDEA... KOKKURI-SAN CAN INVITE SOME OF THE WORST OF THE EVIL SPIRITS...
PLEASE HELP US OUT...
THAT'S IT!
I'LL TEACH YOU HOW TO PERFORM AN EXORCISM SO YOU CAN DO IT!
EH...
RIGHT! LET'S TRY THAT!
BRILLIANT IDEA!
MONK-SAN...
WHAT...!?
ARE YOU MOTIVATED TO WORK ON THIS CASE AFTER SEEING MATSUYAMA'S ATTITUDE?
I APOLOGIZE FOR HIM.
MATSUYAMA TREATS EVERYONE POORLY.
HUH.
......
MHMM
EVEN THE STUDENTS HAVE GIVEN UP ON HIM.
HE WON'T LISTEN TO WHAT OTHER PEOPLE HAVE TO SAY SO WE HAVE TO BE THE MATURE ONES AND BE PATIENT WITH HIM...

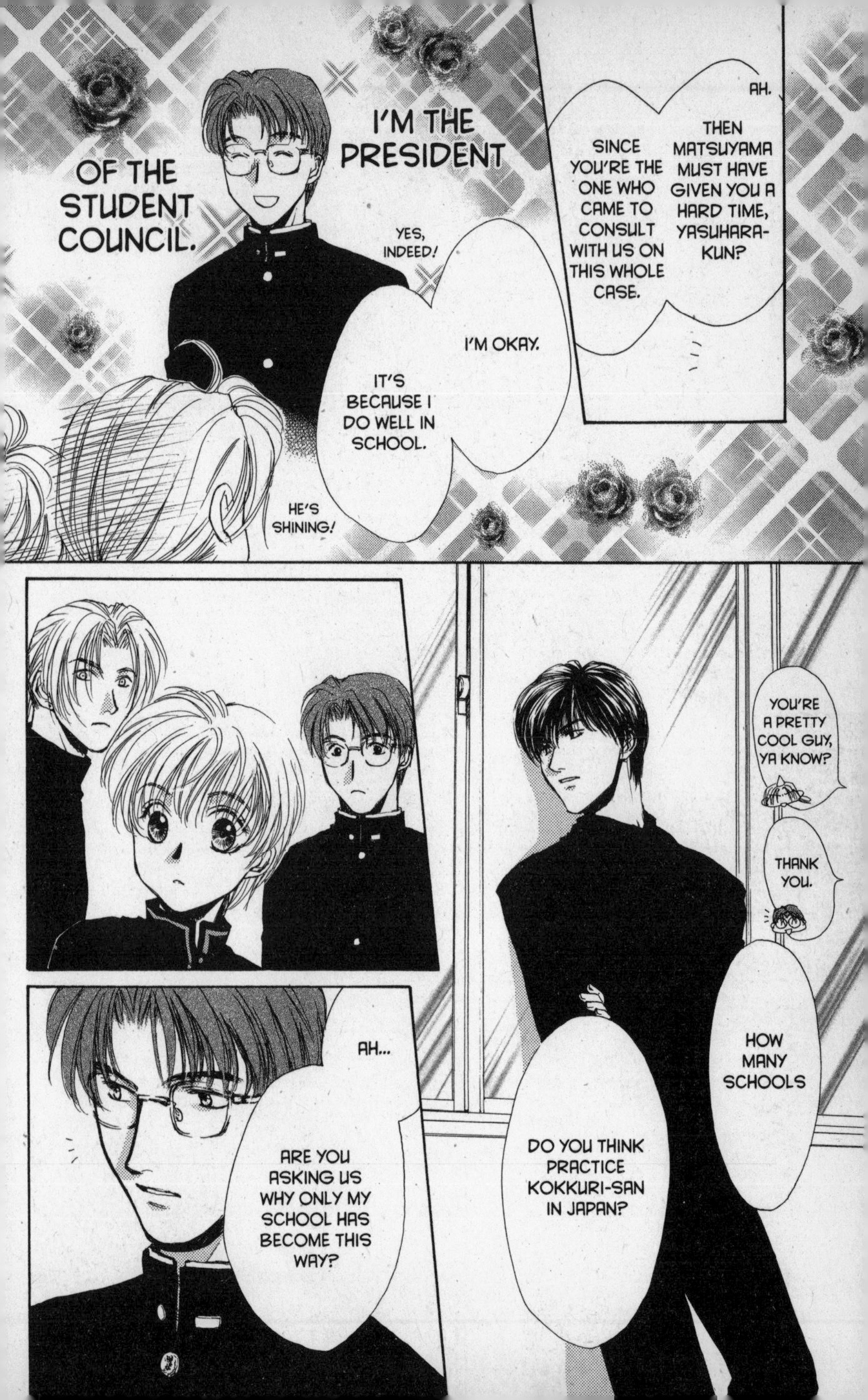
AH.
THEN MATSUYAMA MUST HAVE GIVEN YOU A HARD TIME, YASUHARA-KUN?
SINCE YOU'RE THE ONE WHO CAME TO CONSULT WITH US ON THIS WHOLE CASE.
I'M OKAY.
IT'S BECAUSE I DO WELL IN SCHOOL.
YES, INDEED!
I'M THE PRESIDENT
OF THE STUDENT COUNCIL.
HE'S SHINING!
YOU'RE A PRETTY COOL GUY, YA KNOW?
THANK YOU.
HOW MANY SCHOOLS
DO YOU THINK PRACTICE KOKKURI-SAN IN JAPAN?
AH...
ARE YOU ASKING US WHY ONLY MY SCHOOL HAS BECOME THIS WAY?

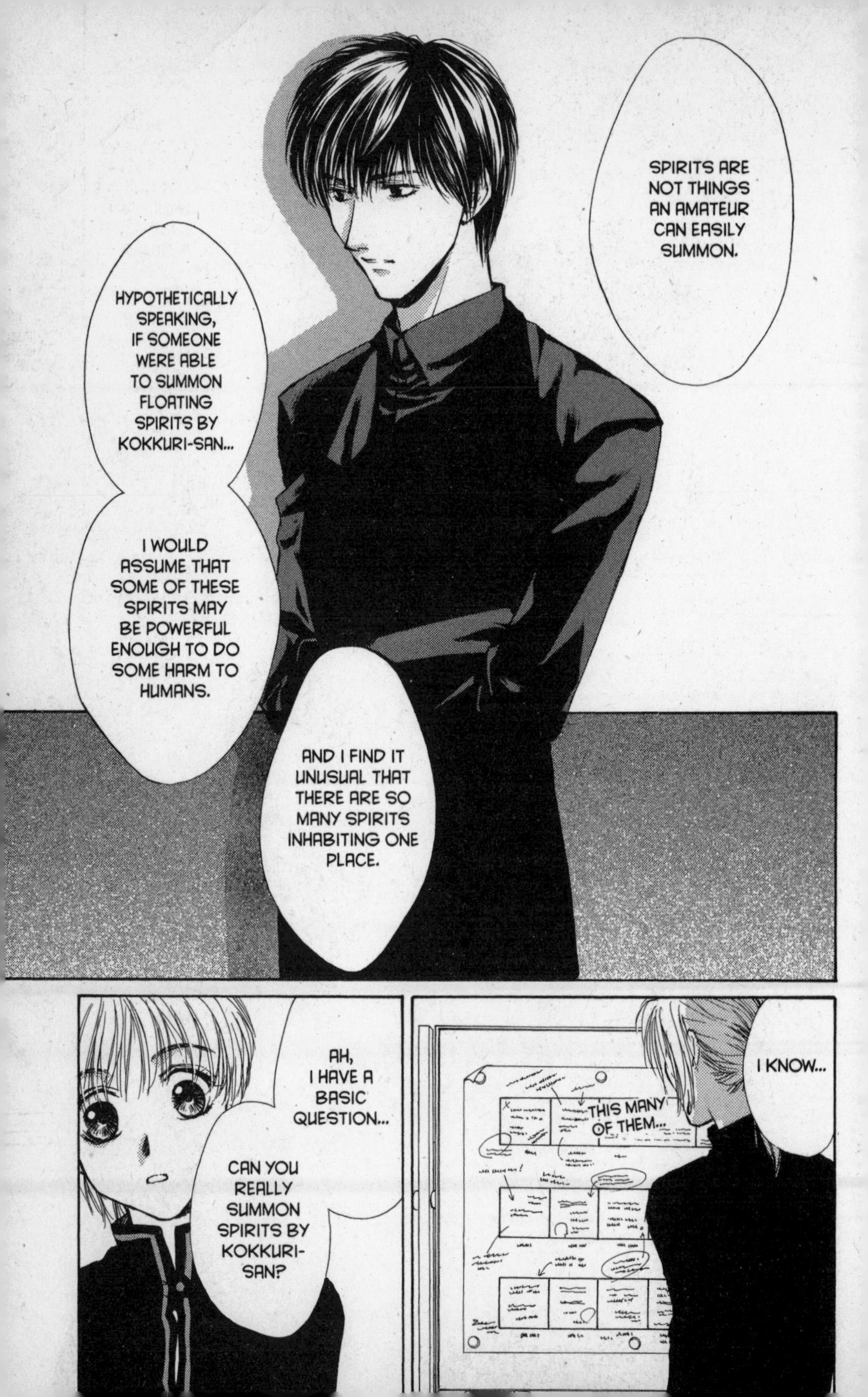
SPIRITS ARE NOT THINGS AN AMATEUR CAN EASILY SUMMON.
HYPOTHETICALLY SPEAKING, IF SOMEONE WERE ABLE TO SUMMON FLOATING SPIRITS BY KOKKURI-SAN...
I WOULD ASSUME THAT SOME OF THESE SPIRITS MAY BE POWERFUL ENOUGH TO DO SOME HARM TO HUMANS.
AND I FIND IT UNUSUAL THAT THERE ARE SO MANY SPIRITS INHABITING ONE PLACE.
I KNOW...
THIS MANY OF THEM...
AH, I HAVE A BASIC QUESTION...
CAN YOU REALLY SUMMON SPIRITS BY KOKKURI-SAN?

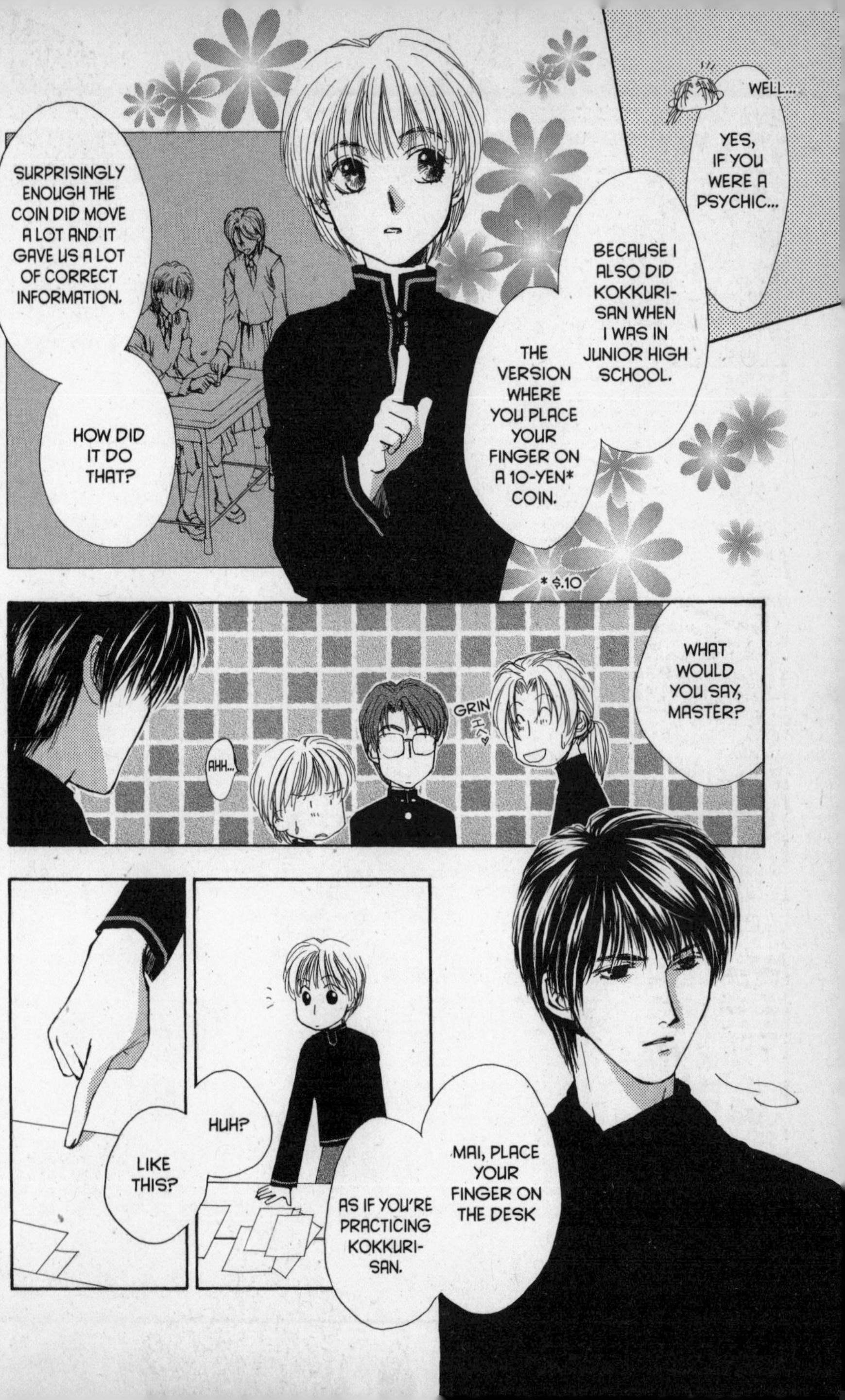
WELL...
YES, IF YOU WERE A PSYCHIC...
BECAUSE I ALSO DID KOKKURI-SAN WHEN I WAS IN JUNIOR HIGH SCHOOL.
THE VERSION WHERE YOU PLACE YOUR FINGER ON A 10-YEN* COIN.
* $.10
SURPRISINGLY ENOUGH THE COIN DID MOVE A LOT AND IT GAVE US A LOT OF CORRECT INFORMATION.
HOW DID IT DO THAT?
WHAT WOULD YOU SAY, MASTER?
GRIN
AHH...
MAI, PLACE YOUR FINGER ON THE DESK
AS IF YOU'RE PRACTICING KOKKURI-SAN.
HUH?
LIKE THIS?

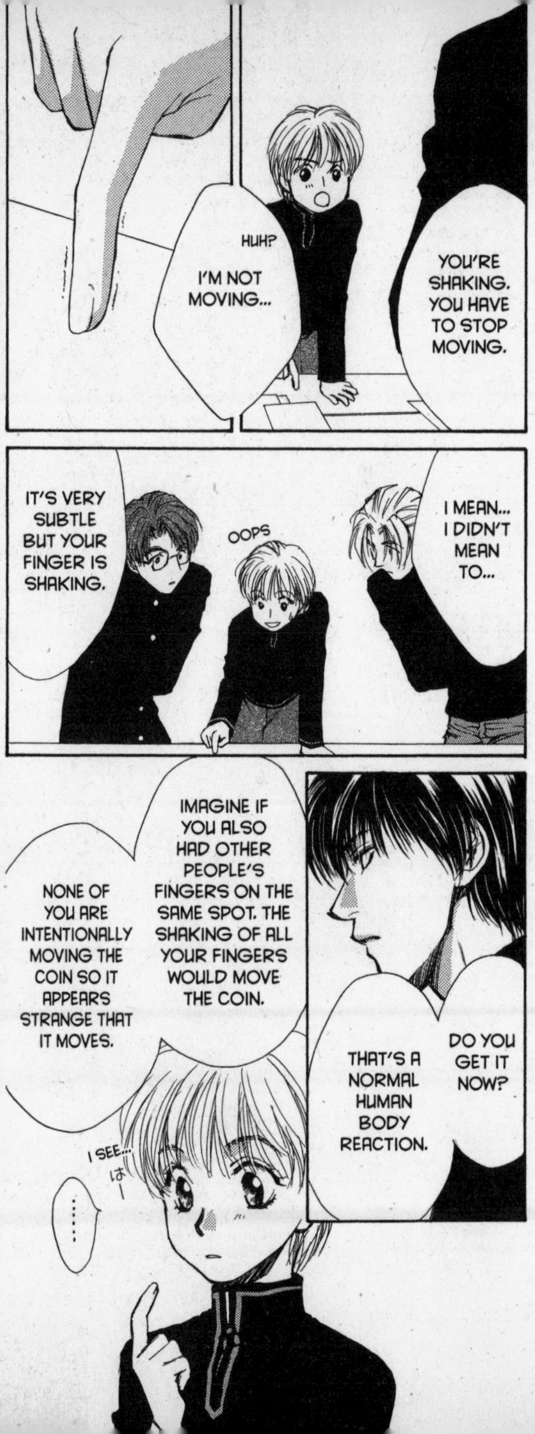
YOU'RE SHAKING. YOU HAVE TO STOP MOVING.
HUH?
I'M NOT MOVING...
I MEAN... I DIDN'T MEAN TO...
OOPS
IT'S VERY SUBTLE BUT YOUR FINGER IS SHAKING.
DO YOU GET IT NOW?
THAT'S A NORMAL HUMAN BODY REACTION.
IMAGINE IF YOU ALSO HAD OTHER PEOPLE'S FINGERS ON THE SAME SPOT. THE SHAKING OF ALL YOUR FINGERS WOULD MOVE THE COIN.
NONE OF YOU ARE INTENTIONALLY MOVING THE COIN SO IT APPEARS STRANGE THAT IT MOVES.
I SEE...
は
......

SCARY JOB PART 2

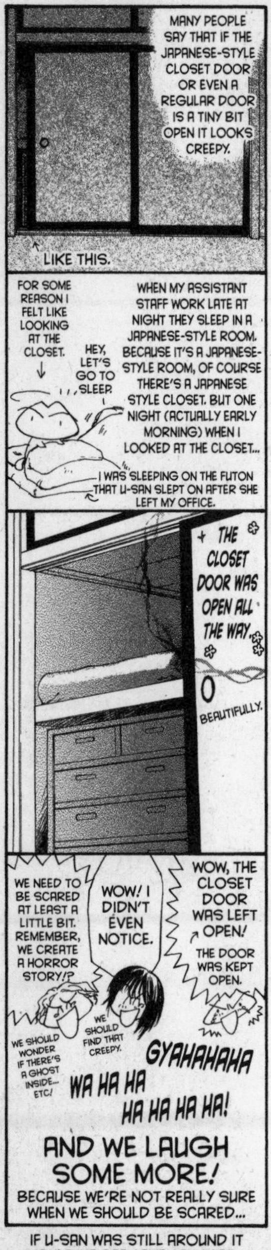
MANY PEOPLE SAY THAT IF THE JAPANESE-STYLE CLOSET DOOR OR EVEN A REGULAR DOOR IS A TINY BIT OPEN IT LOOKS CREEPY.
LIKE THIS.
WHEN MY ASSISTANT STAFF WORK LATE AT NIGHT THEY SLEEP IN A JAPANESE-STYLE ROOM. BECAUSE IT'S A JAPANESE-STYLE ROOM, OF COURSE THERE'S A JAPANESE STYLE CLOSET. BUT ONE NIGHT (ACTUALLY EARLY MORNING) WHEN I LOOKED AT THE CLOSET...
FOR SOME REASON I FELT LIKE LOOKING AT THE CLOSET.
HEY, LET'S GO TO SLEEP.
I WAS SLEEPING ON THE FUTON THAT U-SAN SLEPT ON AFTER SHE LEFT MY OFFICE.
THE CLOSET DOOR WAS OPEN ALL THE WAY.
BEAUTIFULLY.
WOW, THE CLOSET DOOR WAS LEFT OPEN!
THE DOOR WAS KEPT OPEN.
WOW! I DIDN'T EVEN NOTICE.
WE NEED TO BE SCARED AT LEAST A LITTLE BIT. REMEMBER, WE CREATE A HORROR STORY!?
WE SHOULD FIND THAT CREEPY.
WE SHOULD WONDER IF THERE'S A GHOST INSIDE... ETC!
GYAHAHAHA
WA HA HA HA HA HA HA!
AND WE LAUGH SOME MORE!
BECAUSE WE'RE NOT REALLY SURE WHEN WE SHOULD BE SCARED...

IF U-SAN WAS STILL AROUND IT WOULD'VE BEEN EVEN FUNNIER...

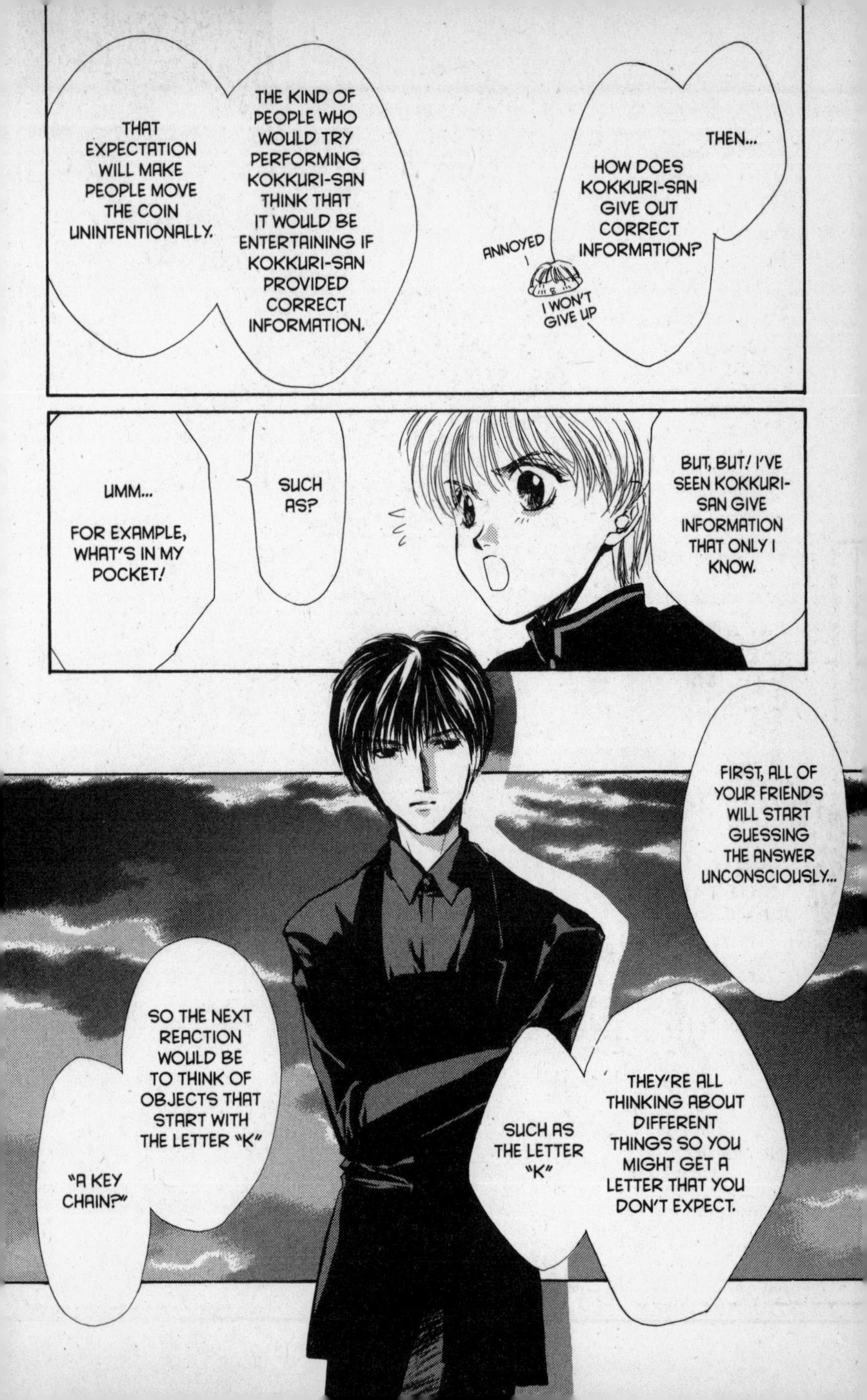
THEN...
HOW DOES KOKKURI-SAN GIVE OUT CORRECT INFORMATION?
ANNOYED
I WON'T GIVE UP
THE KIND OF PEOPLE WHO WOULD TRY PERFORMING KOKKURI-SAN THINK THAT IT WOULD BE ENTERTAINING IF KOKKURI-SAN PROVIDED CORRECT INFORMATION.
THAT EXPECTATION WILL MAKE PEOPLE MOVE THE COIN UNINTENTIONALLY.
BUT, BUT! I'VE SEEN KOKKURI-SAN GIVE INFORMATION THAT ONLY I KNOW.
SUCH AS?
UMM...
FOR EXAMPLE, WHAT'S IN MY POCKET!
FIRST, ALL OF YOUR FRIENDS WILL START GUESSING THE ANSWER UNCONSCIOUSLY...
THEY'RE ALL THINKING ABOUT DIFFERENT THINGS SO YOU MIGHT GET A LETTER THAT YOU DON'T EXPECT.
SUCH AS THE LETTER "K"
SO THE NEXT REACTION WOULD BE TO THINK OF OBJECTS THAT START WITH THE LETTER "K"
"A KEY CHAIN?"

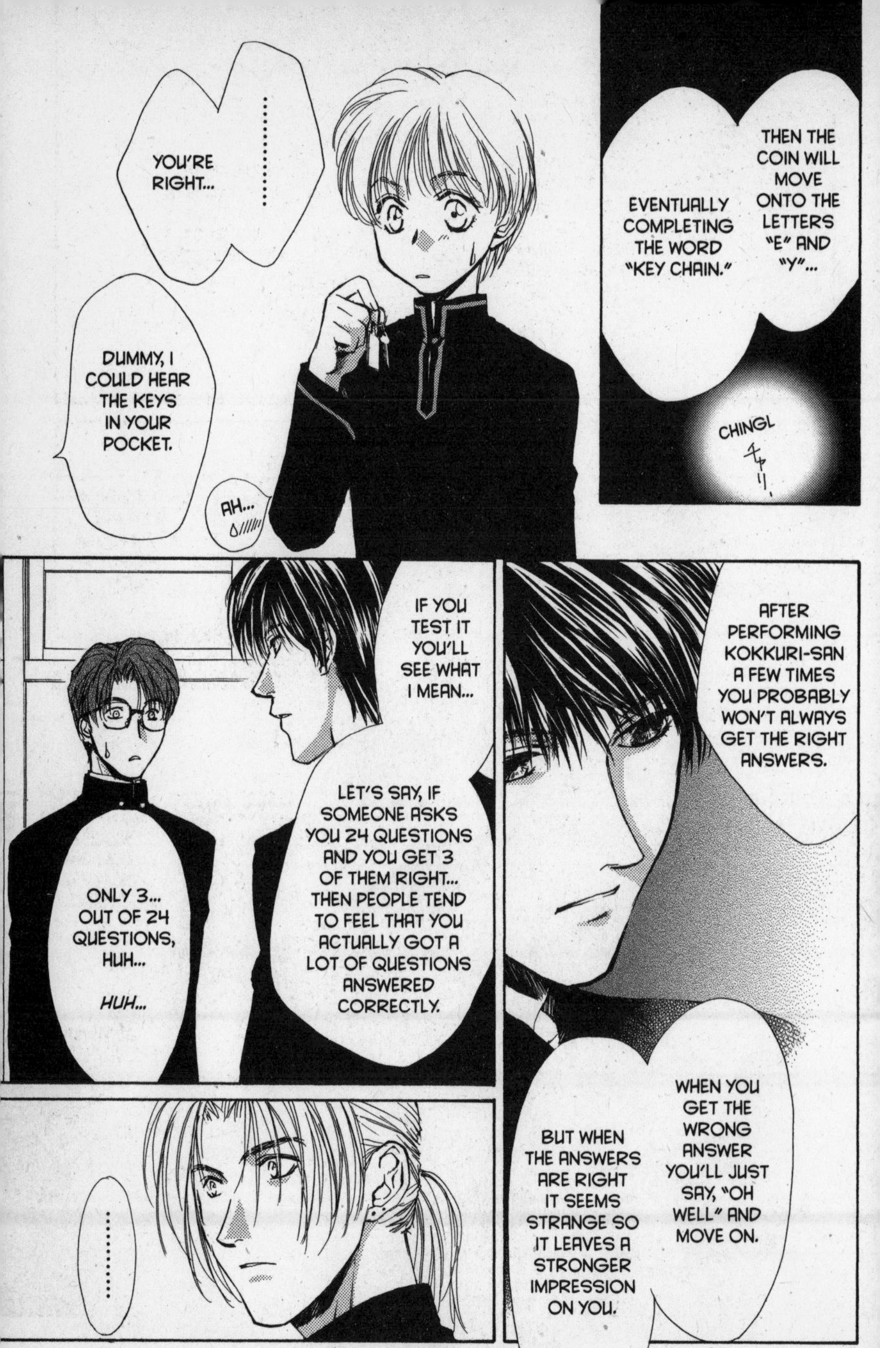
THEN THE COIN WILL MOVE ONTO THE LETTERS "E" AND "Y"...
EVENTUALLY COMPLETING THE WORD "KEY CHAIN."
CHINGL
......
YOU'RE RIGHT...
DUMMY, I COULD HEAR THE KEYS IN YOUR POCKET.
AH...
AFTER PERFORMING KOKKURI-SAN A FEW TIMES YOU PROBABLY WON'T ALWAYS GET THE RIGHT ANSWERS.
WHEN YOU GET THE WRONG ANSWER YOU'LL JUST SAY, "OH WELL" AND MOVE ON.
BUT WHEN THE ANSWERS ARE RIGHT IT SEEMS STRANGE SO IT LEAVES A STRONGER IMPRESSION ON YOU.
IF YOU TEST IT YOU'LL SEE WHAT I MEAN...
LET'S SAY, IF SOMEONE ASKS YOU 24 QUESTIONS AND YOU GET 3 OF THEM RIGHT... THEN PEOPLE TEND TO FEEL THAT YOU ACTUALLY GOT A LOT OF QUESTIONS ANSWERED CORRECTLY.
ONLY 3... OUT OF 24 QUESTIONS, HUH...
HUH...
......

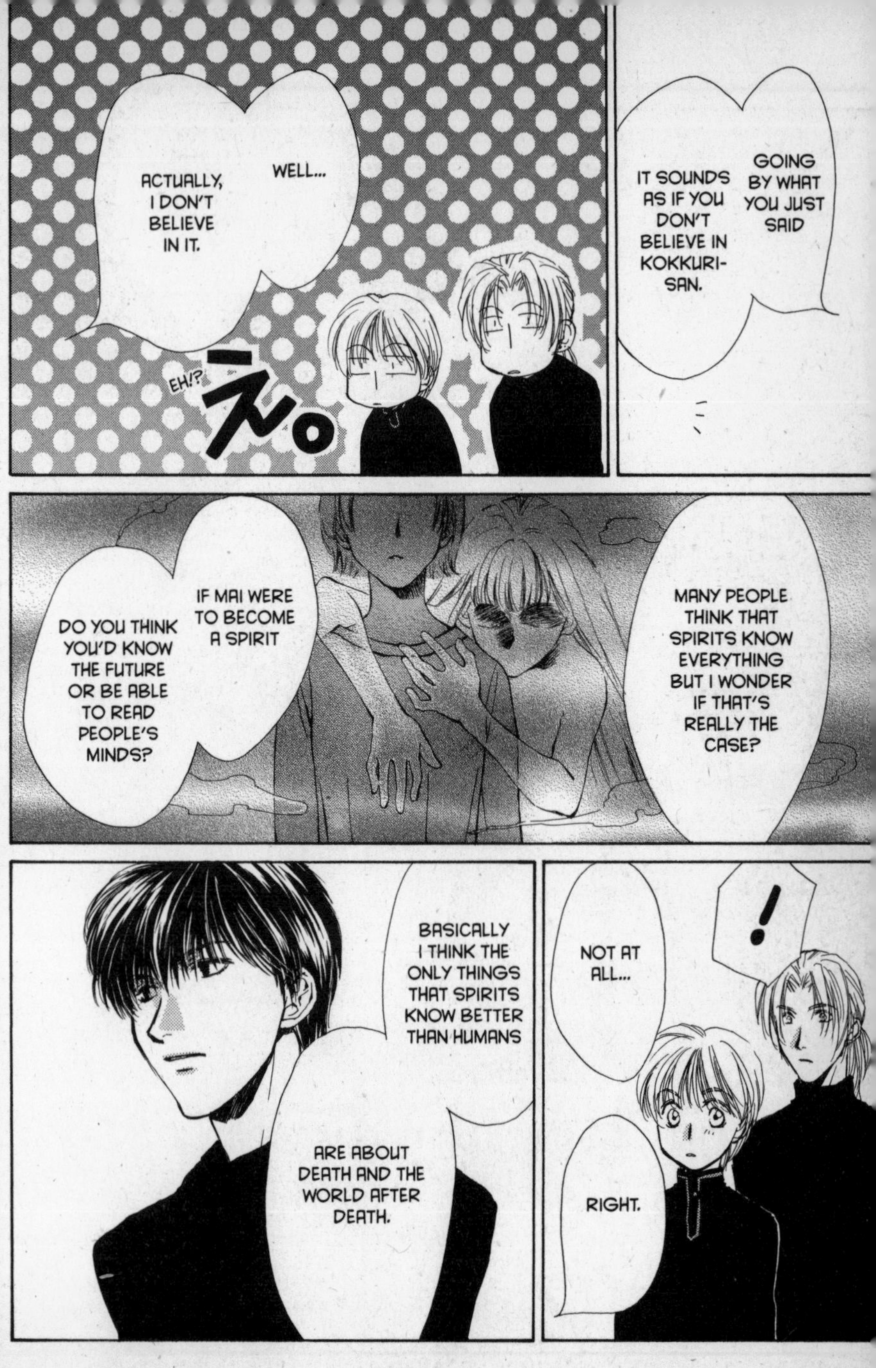
GOING BY WHAT YOU JUST SAID
IT SOUNDS AS IF YOU DON'T BELIEVE IN KOKKURI-SAN.
WELL...
ACTUALLY, I DON'T BELIEVE IN IT.
EH!?
MANY PEOPLE THINK THAT SPIRITS KNOW EVERYTHING BUT I WONDER IF THAT'S REALLY THE CASE?
IF MAI WERE TO BECOME A SPIRIT
DO YOU THINK YOU'D KNOW THE FUTURE OR BE ABLE TO READ PEOPLE'S MINDS?
!
NOT AT ALL...
RIGHT.
BASICALLY I THINK THE ONLY THINGS THAT SPIRITS KNOW BETTER THAN HUMANS
ARE ABOUT DEATH AND THE WORLD AFTER DEATH.

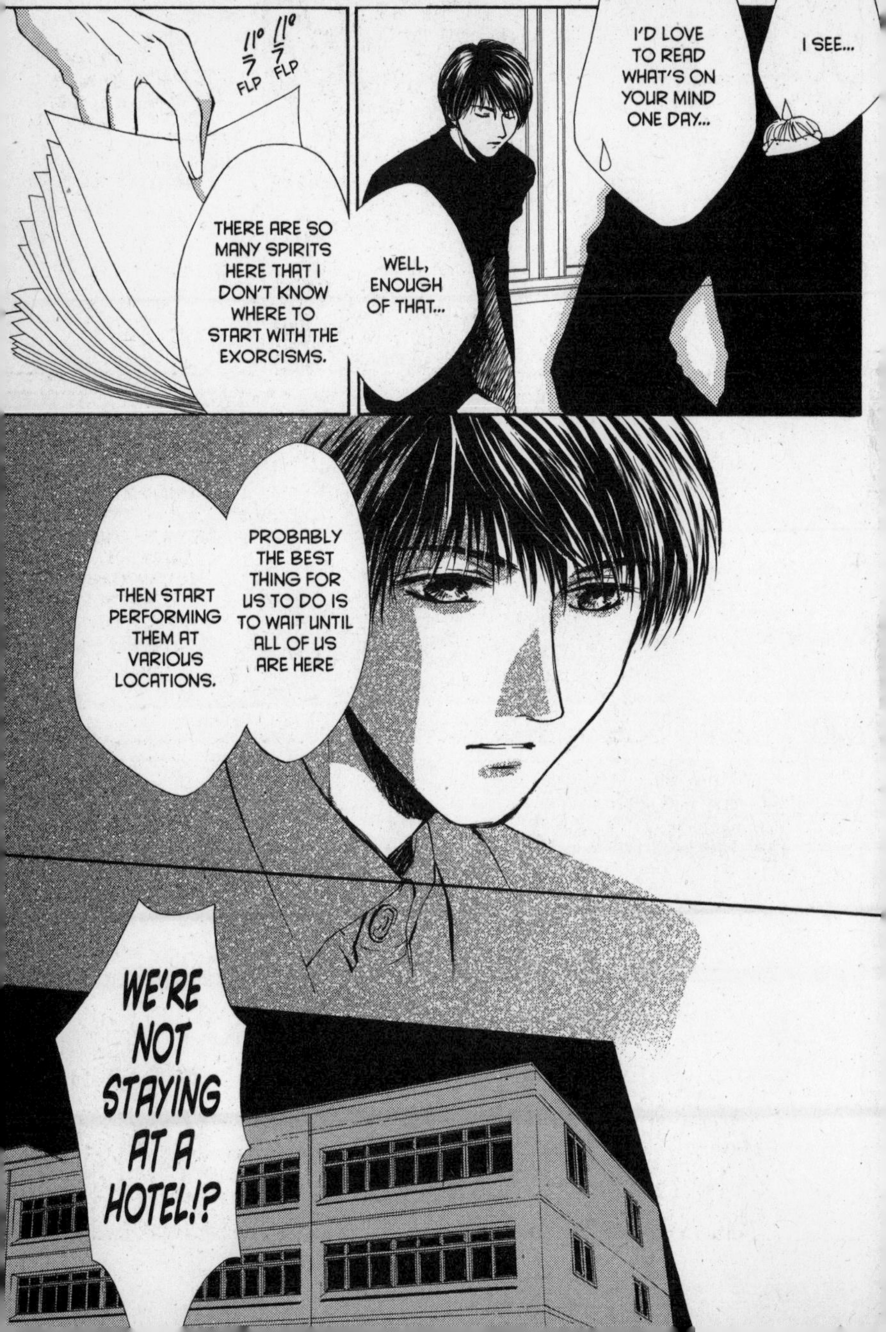
I SEE...
I'D LOVE TO READ WHAT'S ON YOUR MIND ONE DAY...
WELL, ENOUGH OF THAT...
FLP FLP
THERE ARE SO MANY SPIRITS HERE THAT I DON'T KNOW WHERE TO START WITH THE EXORCISMS.
PROBABLY THE BEST THING FOR US TO DO IS TO WAIT UNTIL ALL OF US ARE HERE
THEN START PERFORMING THEM AT VARIOUS LOCATIONS.
WE'RE NOT STAYING AT A HOTEL!?

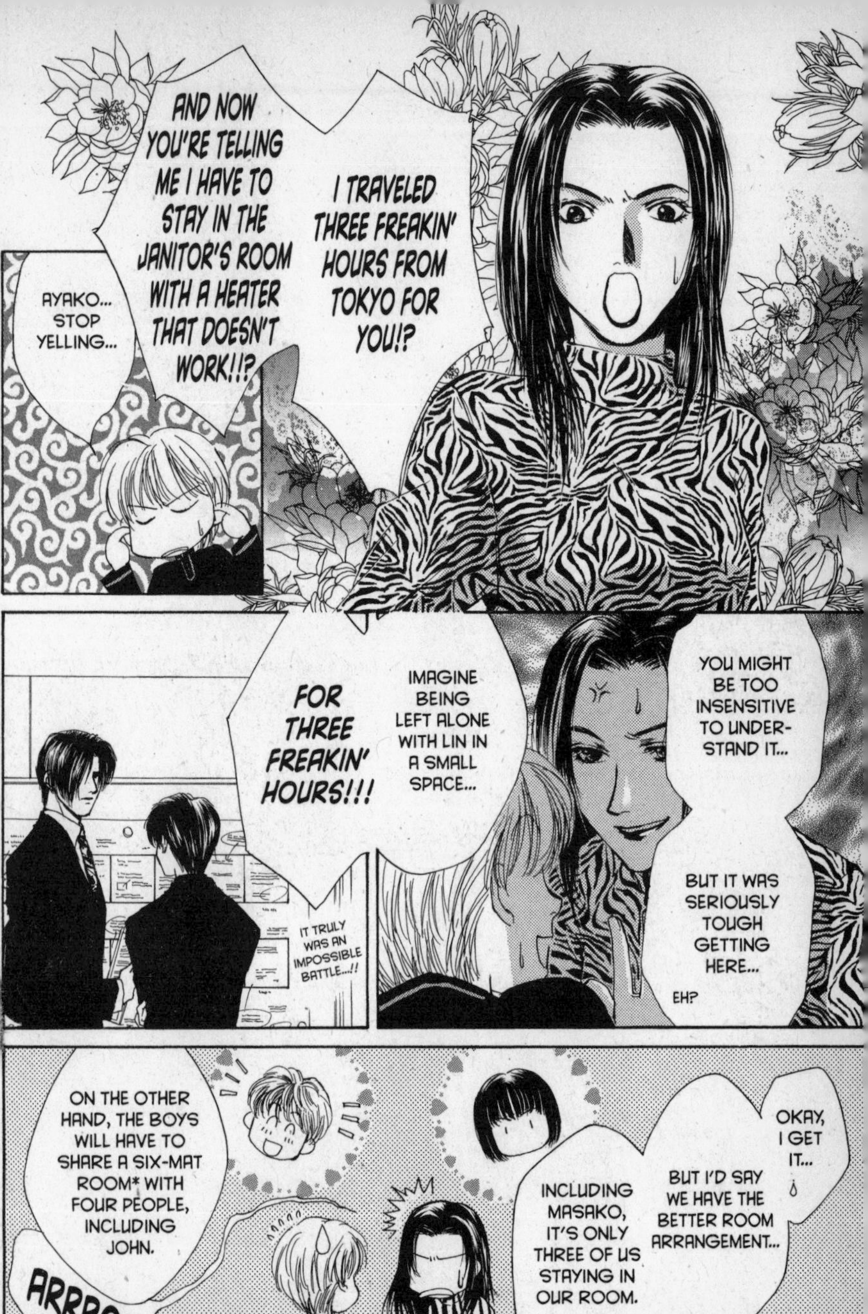
I TRAVELED THREE FREAKIN' HOURS FROM TOKYO FOR YOU!?
AND NOW YOU'RE TELLING ME I HAVE TO STAY IN THE JANITOR'S ROOM WITH A HEATER THAT DOESN'T WORK!!?
AYAKO... STOP YELLING...
YOU MIGHT BE TOO INSENSITIVE TO UNDER-STAND IT...
BUT IT WAS SERIOUSLY TOUGH GETTING HERE...
EH?
IMAGINE BEING LEFT ALONE WITH LIN IN A SMALL SPACE...
FOR THREE FREAKIN' HOURS!!!
IT TRULY WAS AN IMPOSSIBLE BATTLE...!!
OKAY, I GET IT...
BUT I'D SAY WE HAVE THE BETTER ROOM ARRANGEMENT...
INCLUDING MASAKO, IT'S ONLY THREE OF US STAYING IN OUR ROOM.
ON THE OTHER HAND, THE BOYS WILL HAVE TO SHARE A SIX-MAT ROOM* WITH FOUR PEOPLE, INCLUDING JOHN.
ARRRGH...

*SEE TRANSLATION NOTES

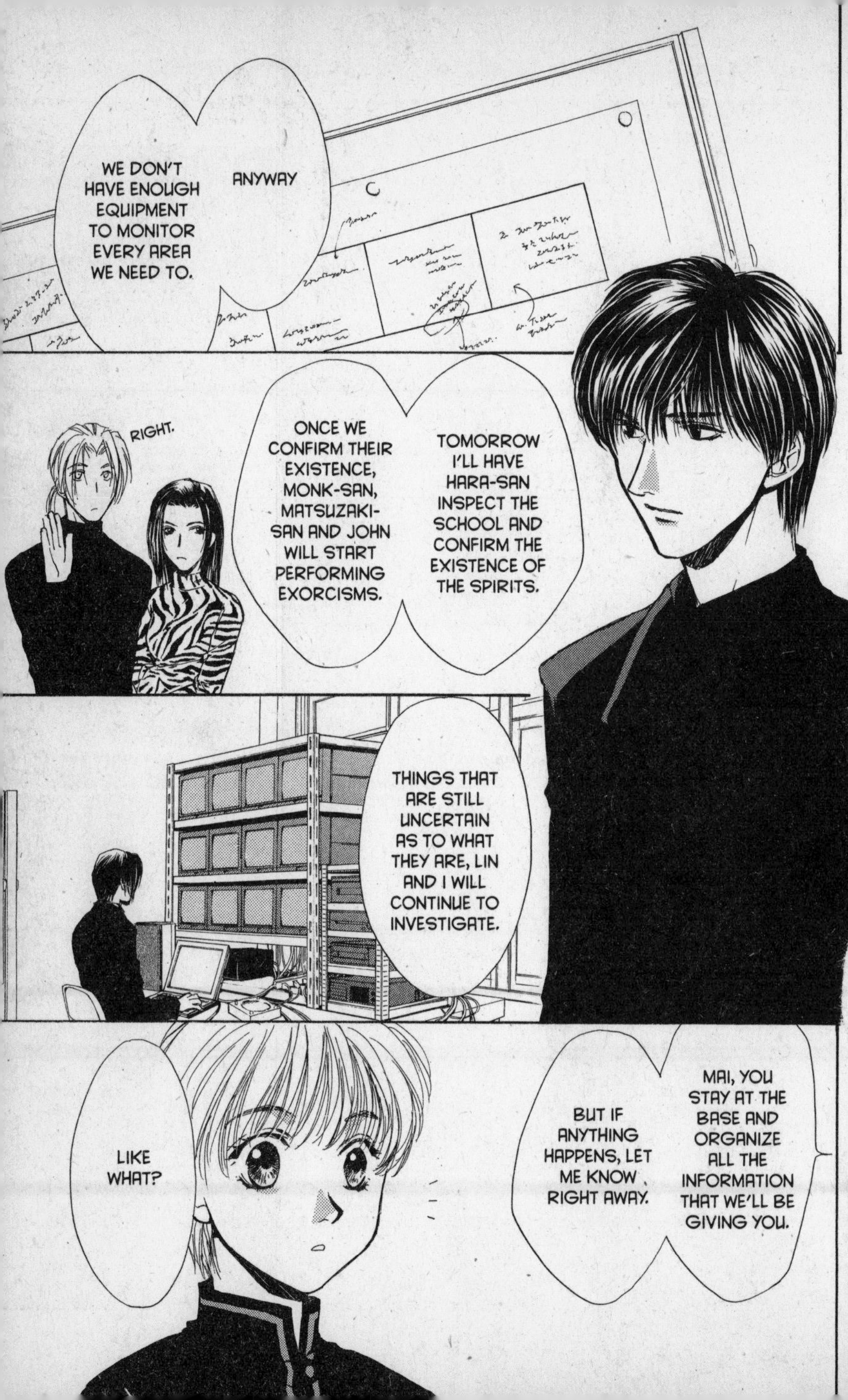
ANYWAY
WE DON'T HAVE ENOUGH EQUIPMENT TO MONITOR EVERY AREA WE NEED TO.
TOMORROW I'LL HAVE HARA-SAN INSPECT THE SCHOOL AND CONFIRM THE EXISTENCE OF THE SPIRITS.
ONCE WE CONFIRM THEIR EXISTENCE, MONK-SAN, MATSUZAKI-SAN AND JOHN WILL START PERFORMING EXORCISMS.
RIGHT.
THINGS THAT ARE STILL UNCERTAIN AS TO WHAT THEY ARE, LIN AND I WILL CONTINUE TO INVESTIGATE.
MAI, YOU STAY AT THE BASE AND ORGANIZE ALL THE INFORMATION THAT WE'LL BE GIVING YOU.
BUT IF ANYTHING HAPPENS, LET ME KNOW RIGHT AWAY.
LIKE WHAT?

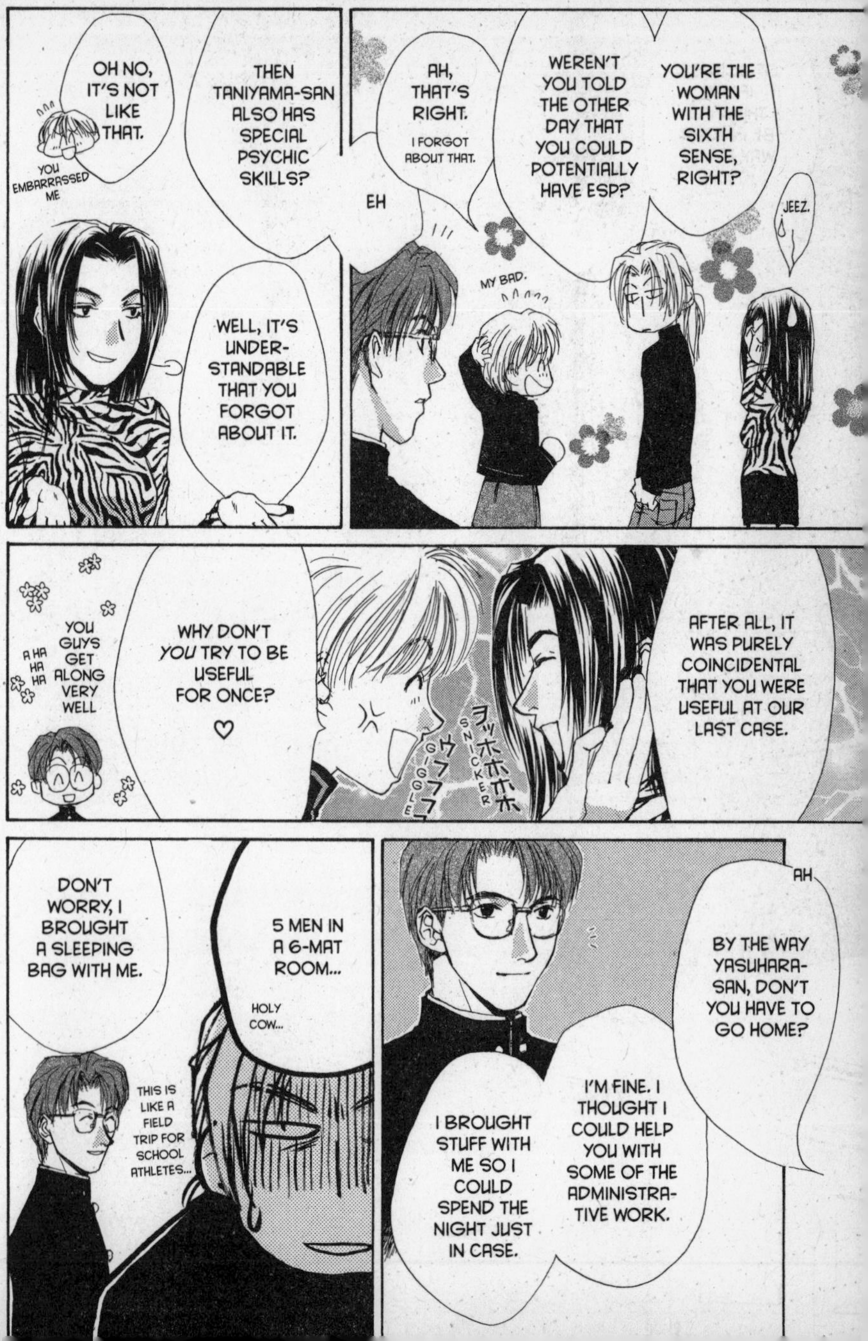
YOU'RE THE WOMAN WITH THE SIXTH SENSE, RIGHT?
JEEZ.
WEREN'T YOU TOLD THE OTHER DAY THAT YOU COULD POTENTIALLY HAVE ESP?
AH, THAT'S RIGHT.
I FORGOT ABOUT THAT.
EH
MY BAD.
THEN TANIYAMA-SAN ALSO HAS SPECIAL PSYCHIC SKILLS?
OH NO, IT'S NOT LIKE THAT.
YOU EMBARRASSED ME
WELL, IT'S UNDER-STANDABLE THAT YOU FORGOT ABOUT IT.
AFTER ALL, IT WAS PURELY COINCIDENTAL THAT YOU WERE USEFUL AT OUR LAST CASE.
ヨッホホホホ SNICKER
ウフフフ GIGGLE
WHY DON'T *YOU* TRY TO BE USEFUL FOR ONCE? ♡
YOU GUYS GET ALONG VERY WELL
A HA HA HA
AH
BY THE WAY YASUHARA-SAN, DON'T YOU HAVE TO GO HOME?
I'M FINE. I THOUGHT I COULD HELP YOU WITH SOME OF THE ADMINISTRA-TIVE WORK.
I BROUGHT STUFF WITH ME SO I COULD SPEND THE NIGHT JUST IN CASE.
5 MEN IN A 6-MAT ROOM...
HOLY COW...
DON'T WORRY, I BROUGHT A SLEEPING BAG WITH ME.
THIS IS LIKE A FIELD TRIP FOR SCHOOL ATHLETES...

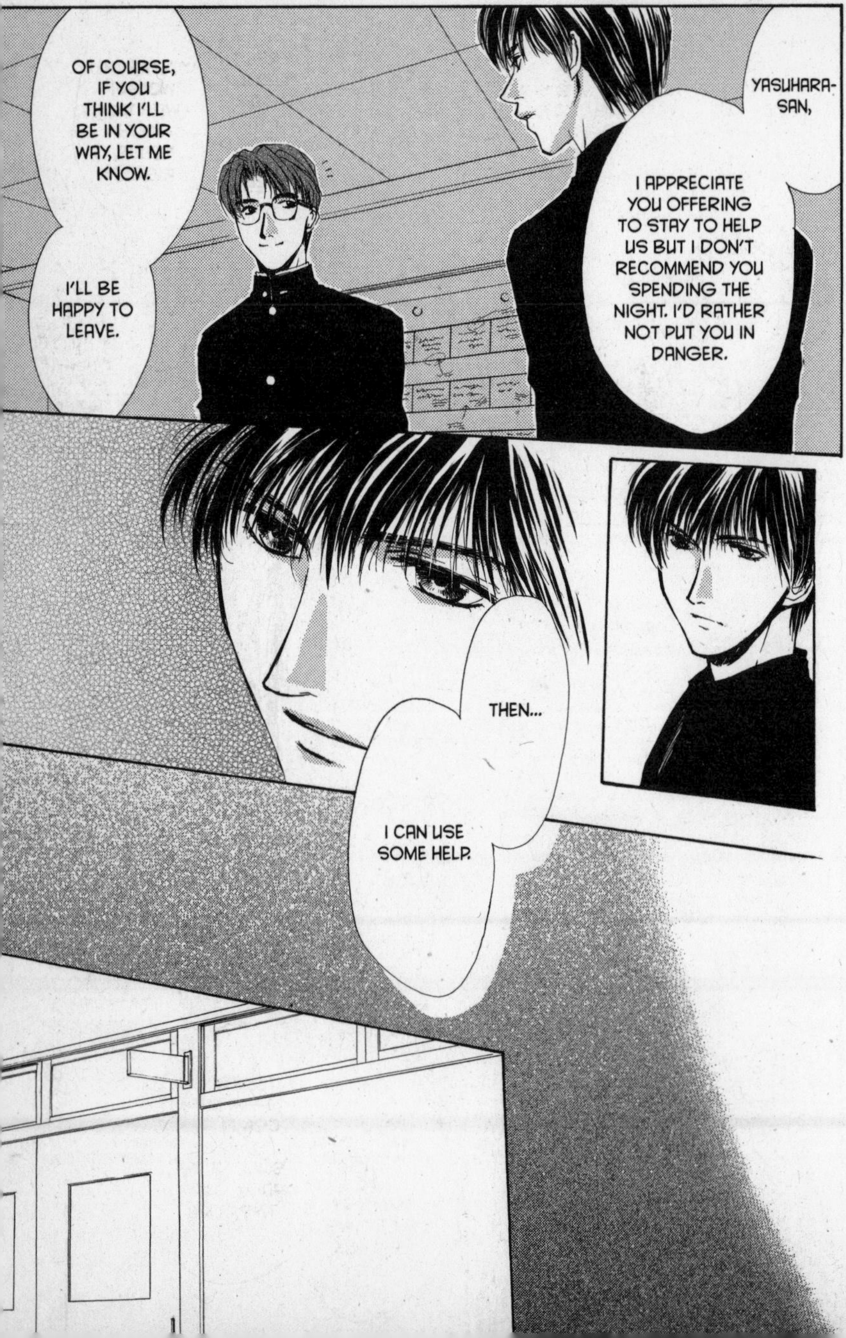
YASUHARA-SAN,
I APPRECIATE YOU OFFERING TO STAY TO HELP US BUT I DON'T RECOMMEND YOU SPENDING THE NIGHT. I'D RATHER NOT PUT YOU IN DANGER.
OF COURSE, IF YOU THINK I'LL BE IN YOUR WAY, LET ME KNOW.
I'LL BE HAPPY TO LEAVE.
THEN...
I CAN USE SOME HELP.

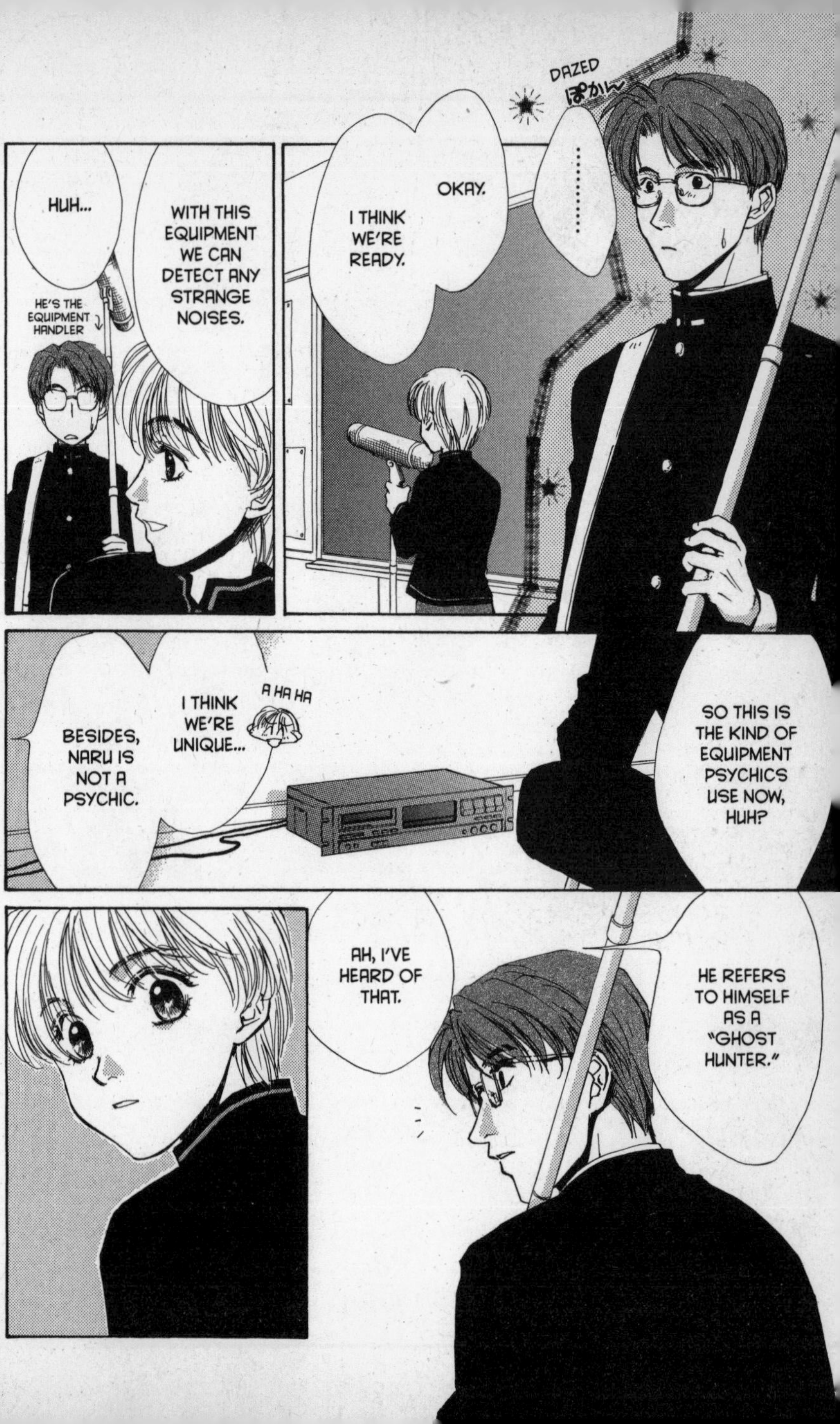
DAZED
ぽかん
......
OKAY.
I THINK WE'RE READY.
WITH THIS EQUIPMENT WE CAN DETECT ANY STRANGE NOISES.
HUH...
HE'S THE EQUIPMENT HANDLER
SO THIS IS THE KIND OF EQUIPMENT PSYCHICS USE NOW, HUH?
I THINK WE'RE UNIQUE...
A HA HA
BESIDES, NARU IS NOT A PSYCHIC.
HE REFERS TO HIMSELF AS A "GHOST HUNTER."
AH, I'VE HEARD OF THAT.

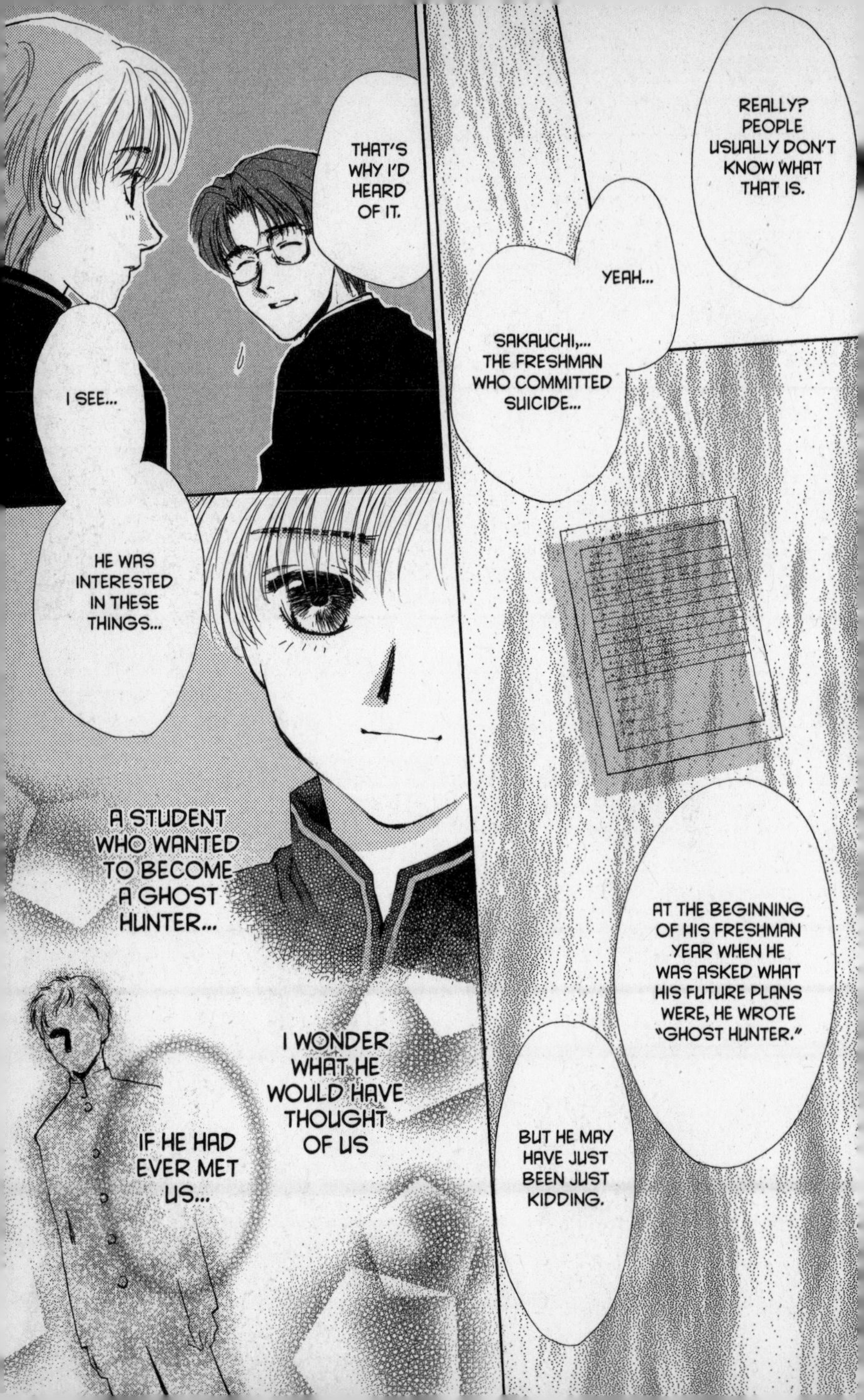
REALLY? PEOPLE USUALLY DON'T KNOW WHAT THAT IS.
YEAH...
SAKAUCHI,... THE FRESHMAN WHO COMMITTED SUICIDE...
AT THE BEGINNING OF HIS FRESHMAN YEAR WHEN HE WAS ASKED WHAT HIS FUTURE PLANS WERE, HE WROTE "GHOST HUNTER."
BUT HE MAY HAVE JUST BEEN JUST KIDDING.
THAT'S WHY I'D HEARD OF IT.
I SEE...
HE WAS INTERESTED IN THESE THINGS...
A STUDENT WHO WANTED TO BECOME A GHOST HUNTER...
I WONDER WHAT HE WOULD HAVE THOUGHT OF US
IF HE HAD EVER MET US...

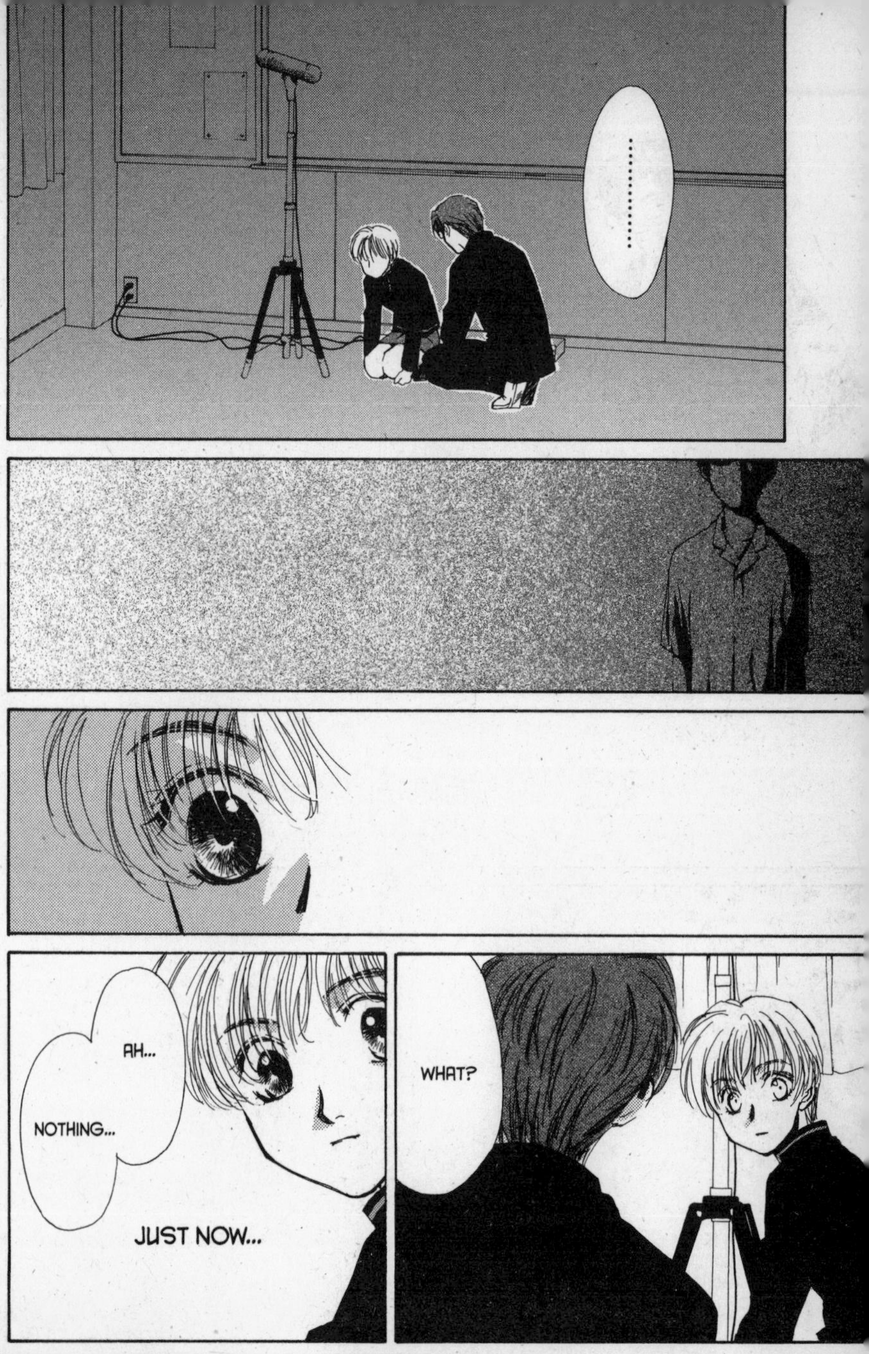
......
WHAT?
AH...
NOTHING...
JUST NOW...

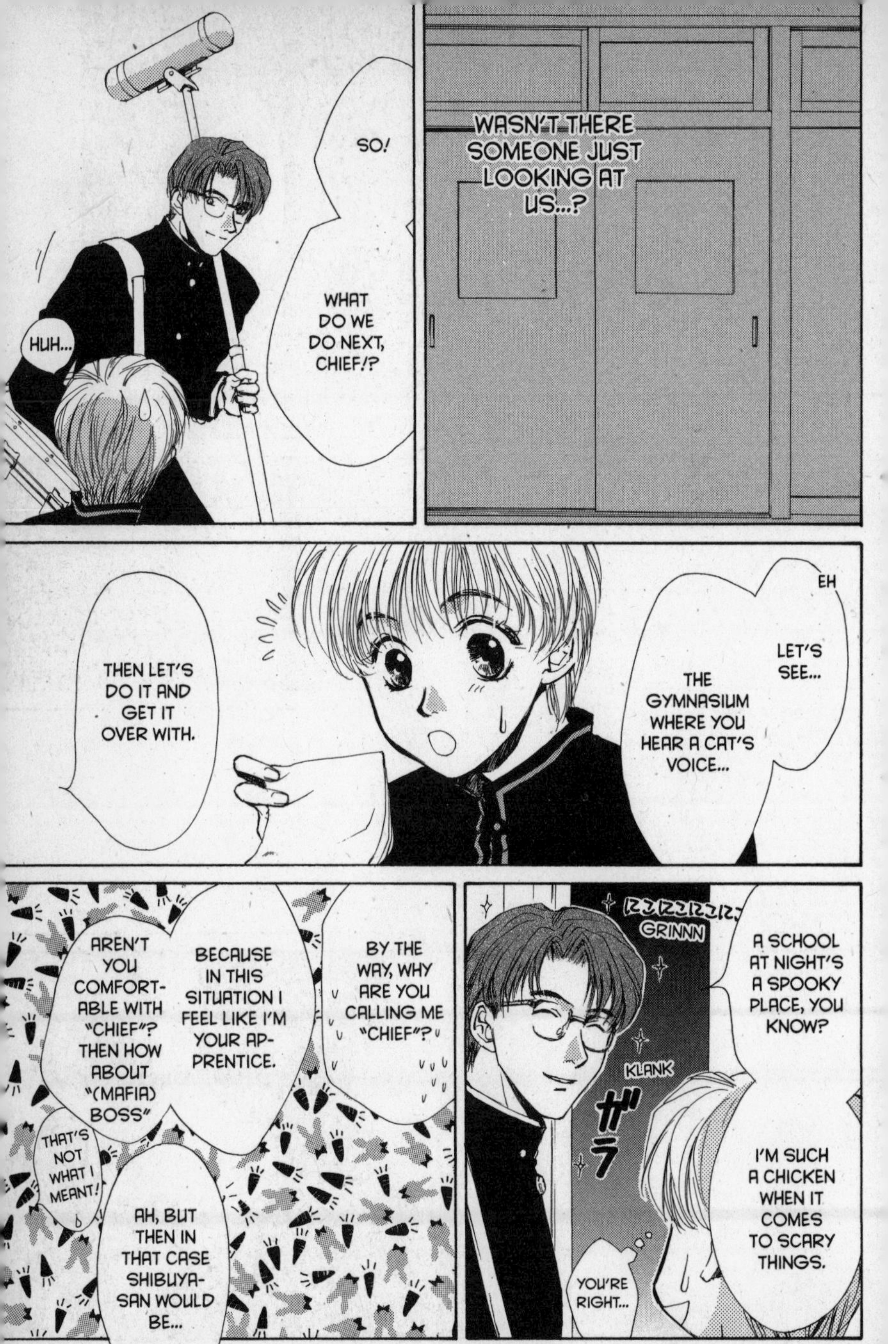
WASN'T THERE SOMEONE JUST LOOKING AT US...?
SO!
WHAT DO WE DO NEXT, CHIEF!?
HUH...
EH
LET'S SEE...
THE GYMNASIUM WHERE YOU HEAR A CAT'S VOICE...
THEN LET'S DO IT AND GET IT OVER WITH.
A SCHOOL AT NIGHT'S A SPOOKY PLACE, YOU KNOW?
GRINNN
KLANK
ガラ
I'M SUCH A CHICKEN WHEN IT COMES TO SCARY THINGS.
YOU'RE RIGHT...
BY THE WAY, WHY ARE YOU CALLING ME "CHIEF"?
BECAUSE IN THIS SITUATION I FEEL LIKE I'M YOUR APPRENTICE.
AREN'T YOU COMFORTABLE WITH "CHIEF"? THEN HOW ABOUT "(MAFIA) BOSS"
THAT'S NOT WHAT I MEANT!
AH, BUT THEN IN THAT CASE SHIBUYA-SAN WOULD BE...

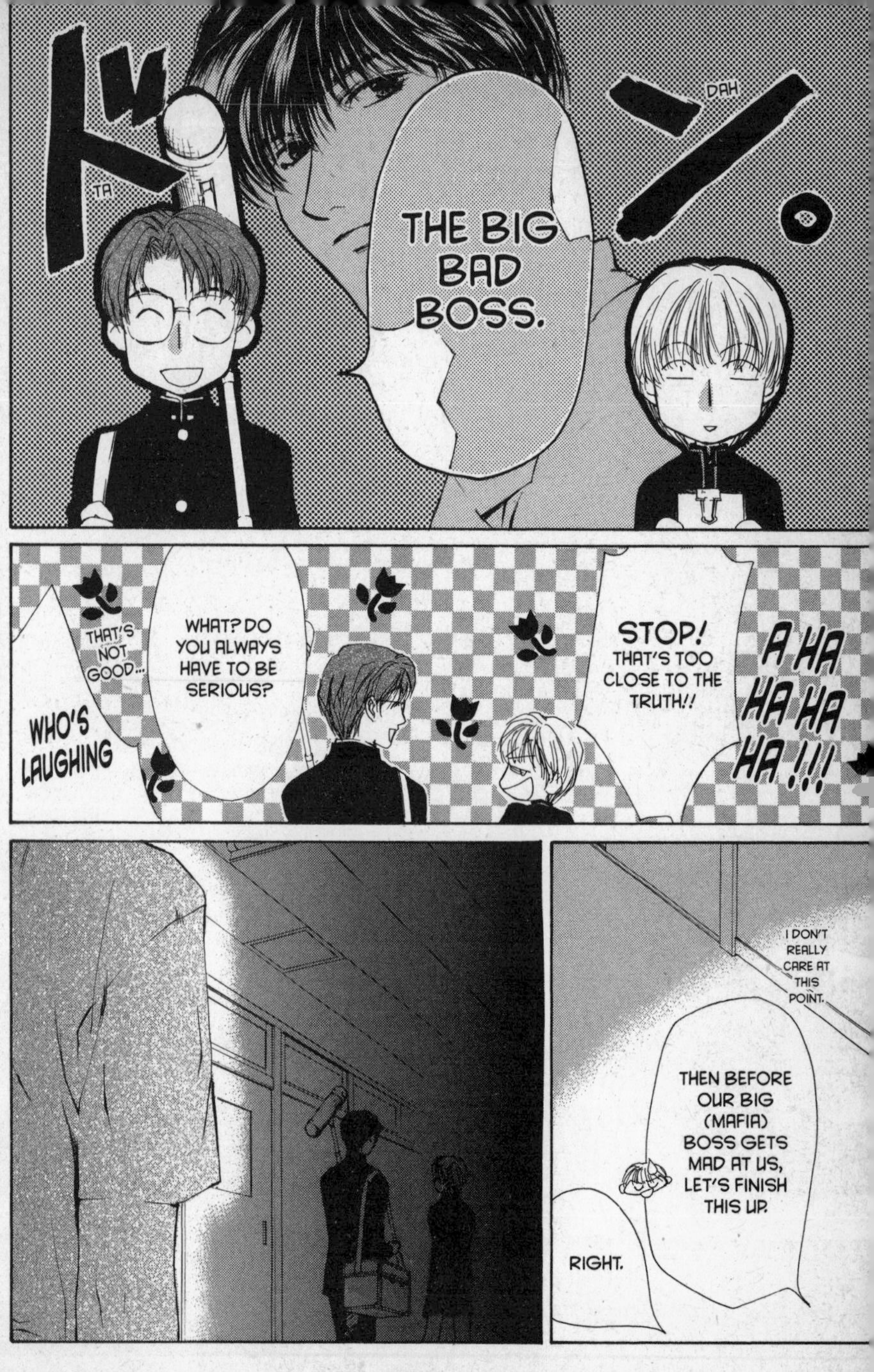
DAH
THE BIG BAD BOSS.
TA
A HA HA HA HA !!!
STOP! THAT'S TOO CLOSE TO THE TRUTH!!
WHAT? DO YOU ALWAYS HAVE TO BE SERIOUS?
THAT'S NOT GOOD...
WHO'S LAUGHING
I DON'T REALLY CARE AT THIS POINT.
THEN BEFORE OUR BIG (MAFIA) BOSS GETS MAD AT US, LET'S FINISH THIS UP.
RIGHT.

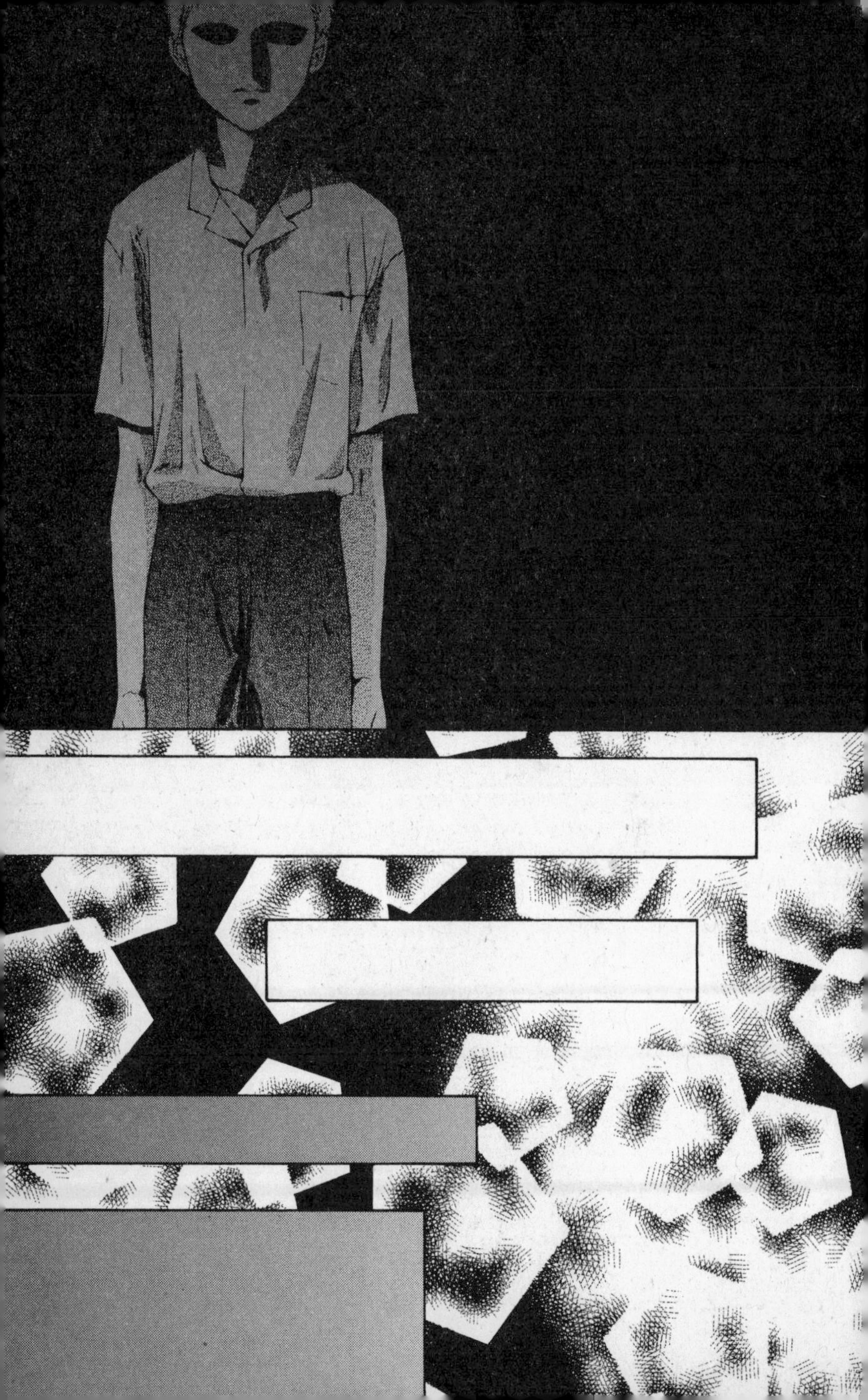

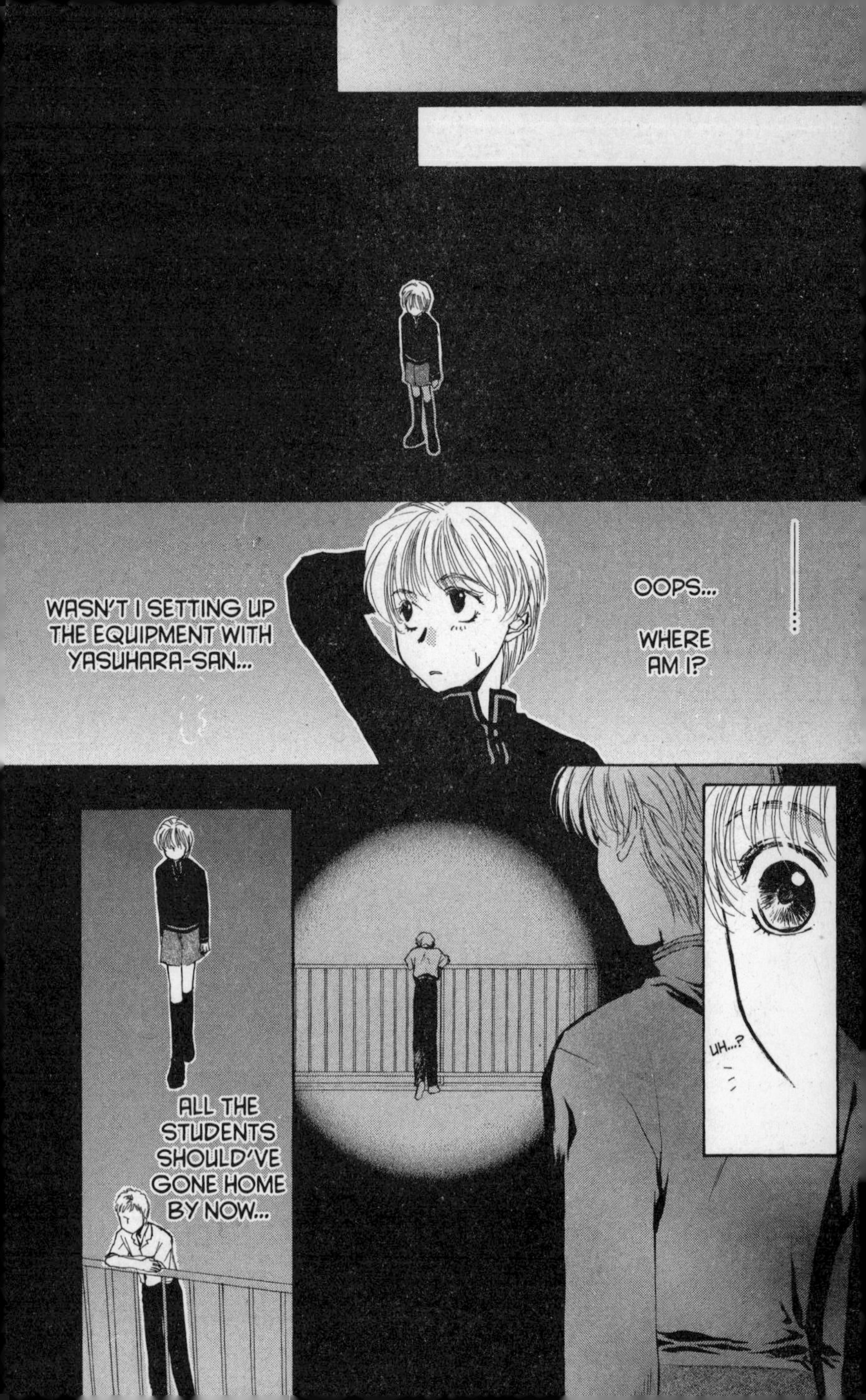

OOPS...
WHERE AM I?
WASN'T I SETTING UP THE EQUIPMENT WITH YASUHARA-SAN...
UH...?
ALL THE STUDENTS SHOULD'VE GONE HOME BY NOW...

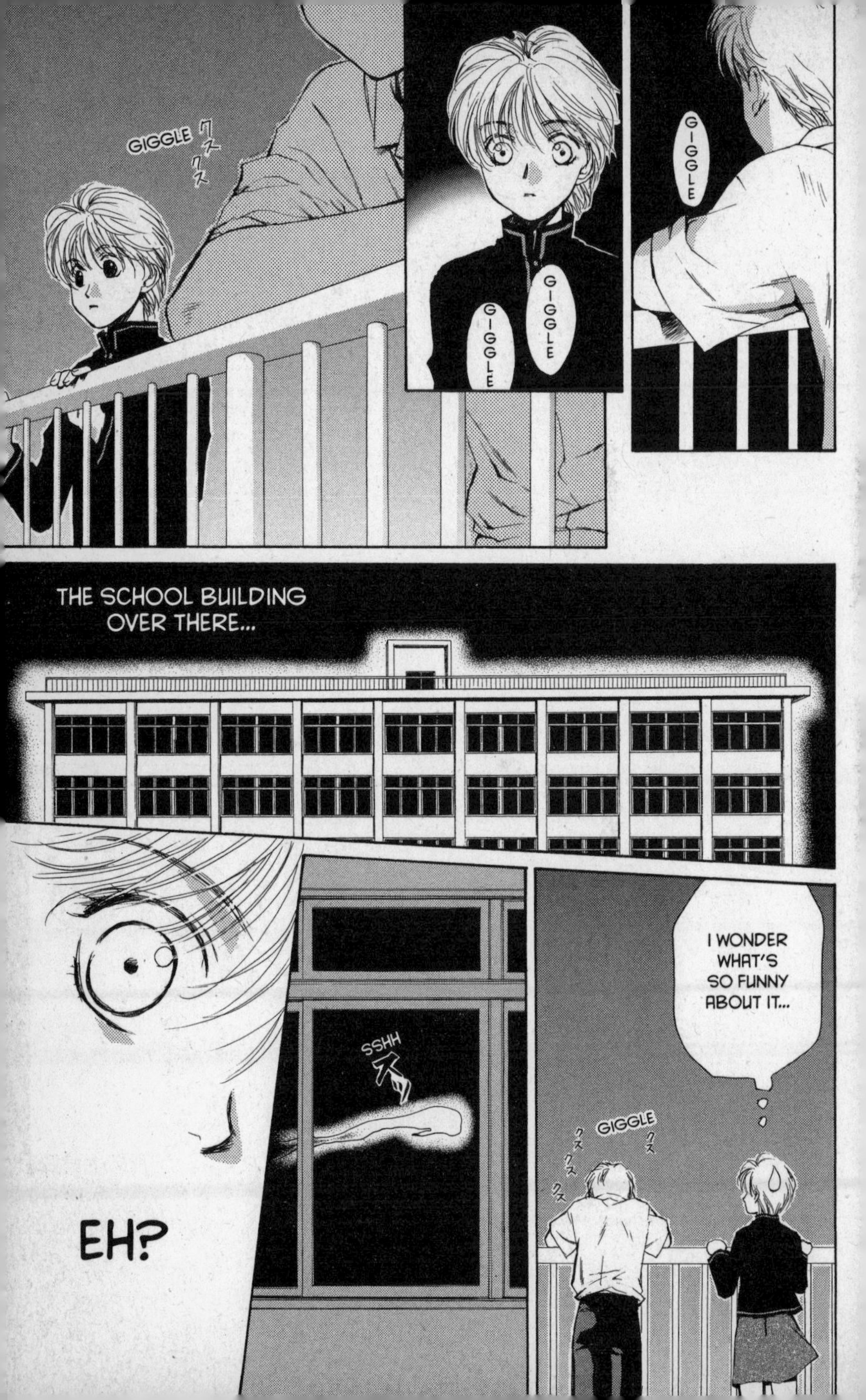
GIGGLE
GIGGLE
GIGGLE
GIGGLE クスクス
THE SCHOOL BUILDING OVER THERE...
I WONDER WHAT'S SO FUNNY ABOUT IT...
GIGGLE クスクス
SSHH ス
EH?

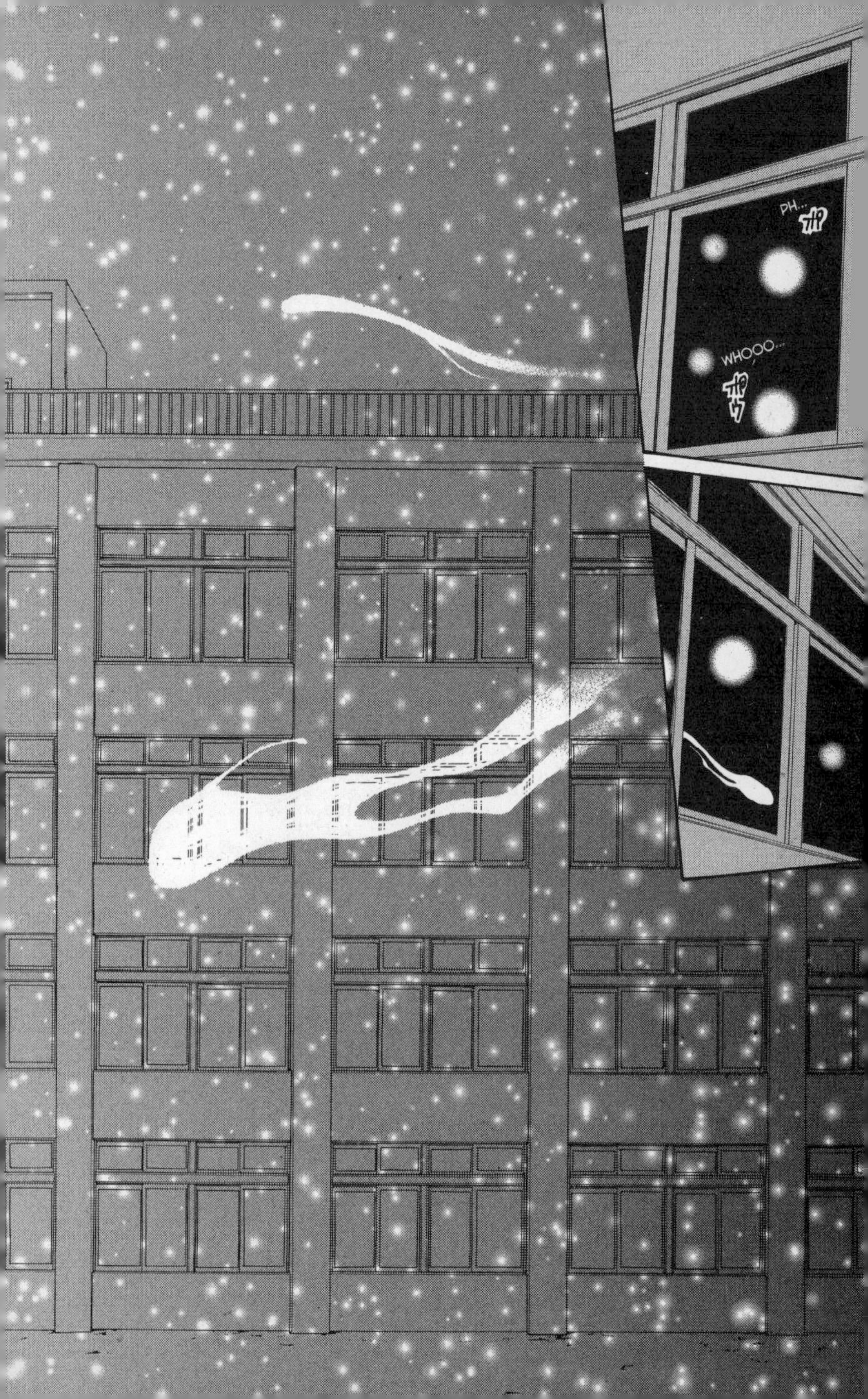
PH...
WHOOO...

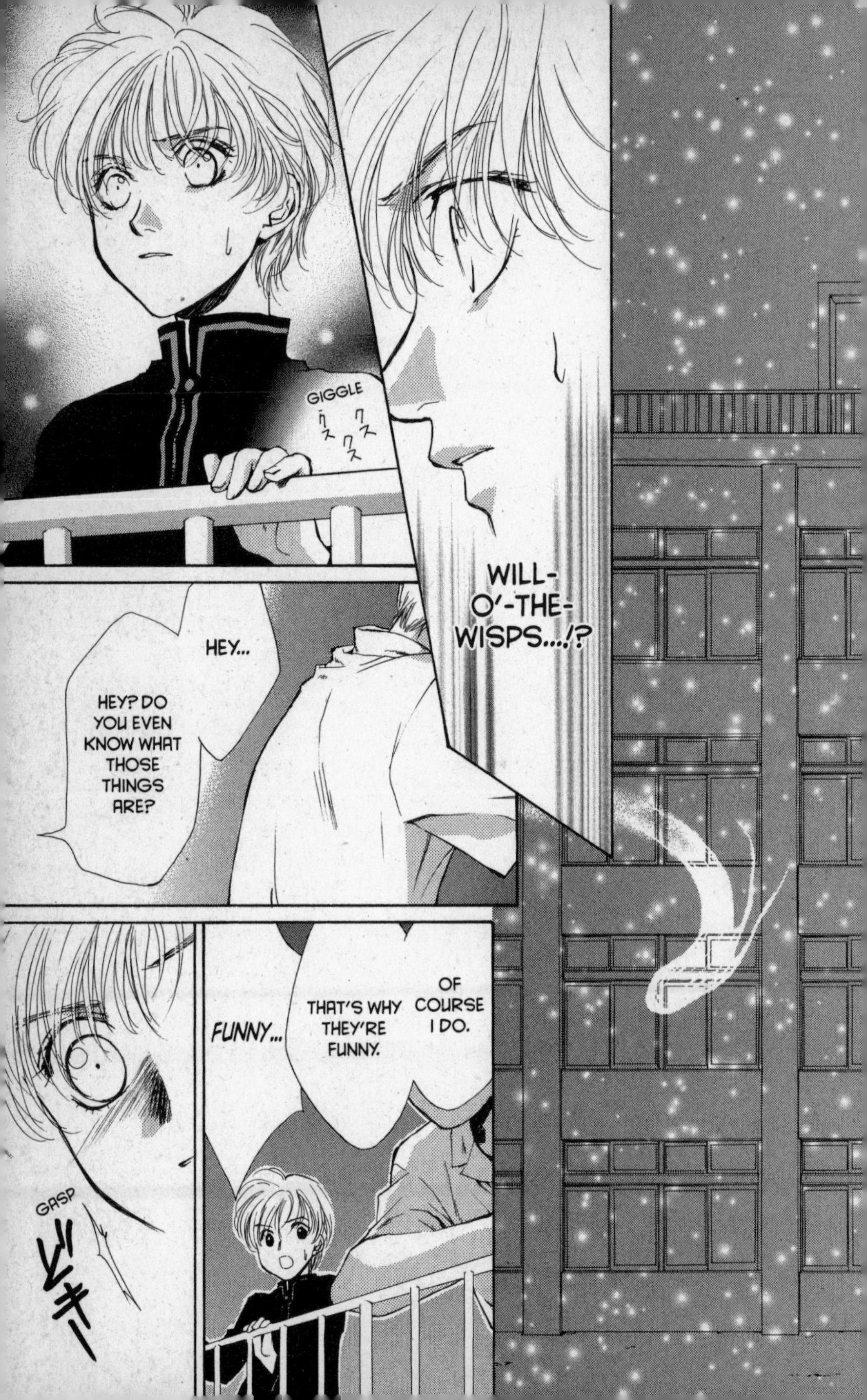
WILL-O'-THE-WISPS...!?
GIGGLE
クスクスクス
HEY...
HEY? DO YOU EVEN KNOW WHAT THOSE THINGS ARE?
OF COURSE I DO.
THAT'S WHY THEY'RE FUNNY.
FUNNY...
GASP
ドキー

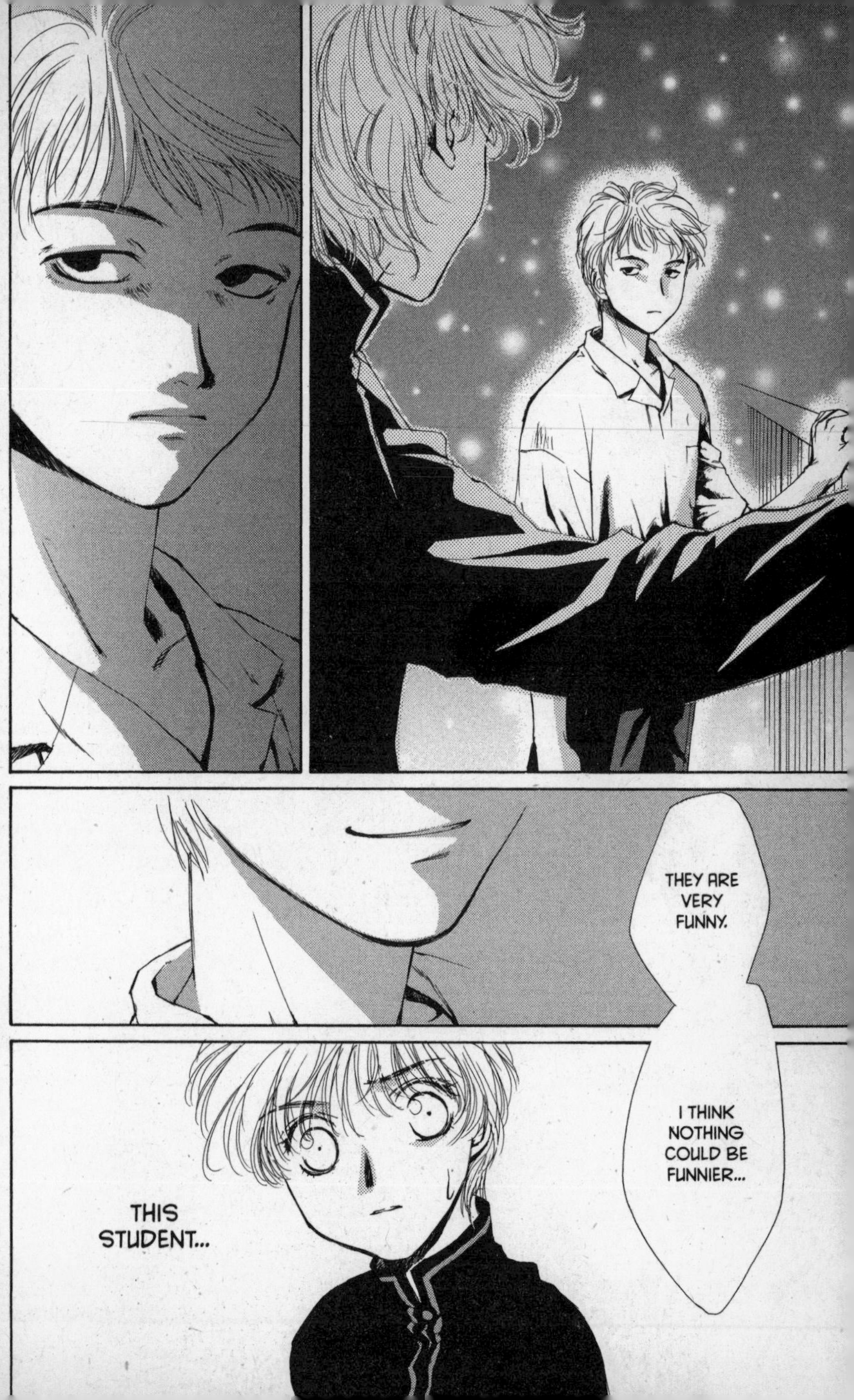
THEY ARE VERY FUNNY.
I THINK NOTHING COULD BE FUNNIER...
THIS STUDENT...

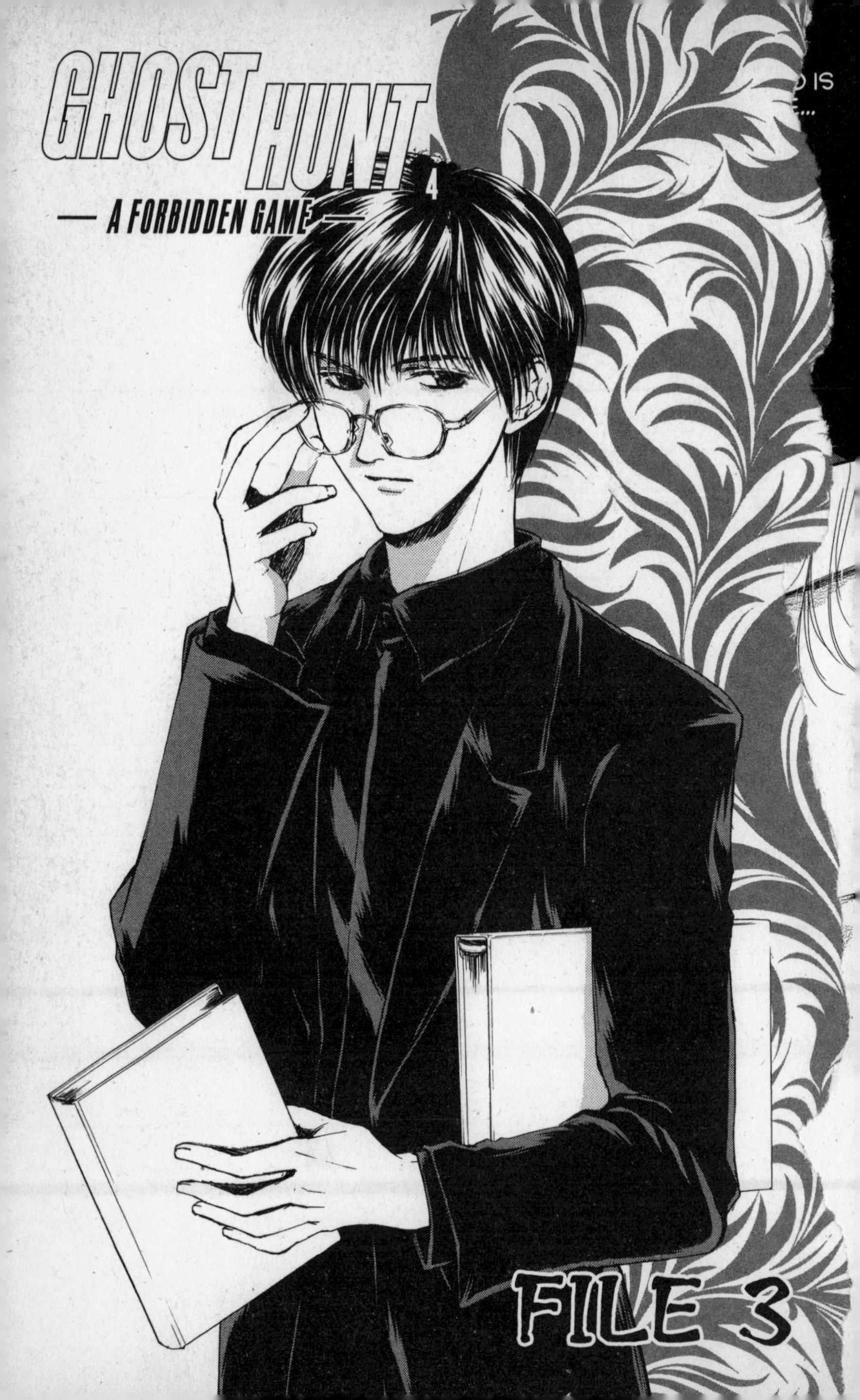
GHOST HUNT 4
— A FORBIDDEN GAME —
FILE 3

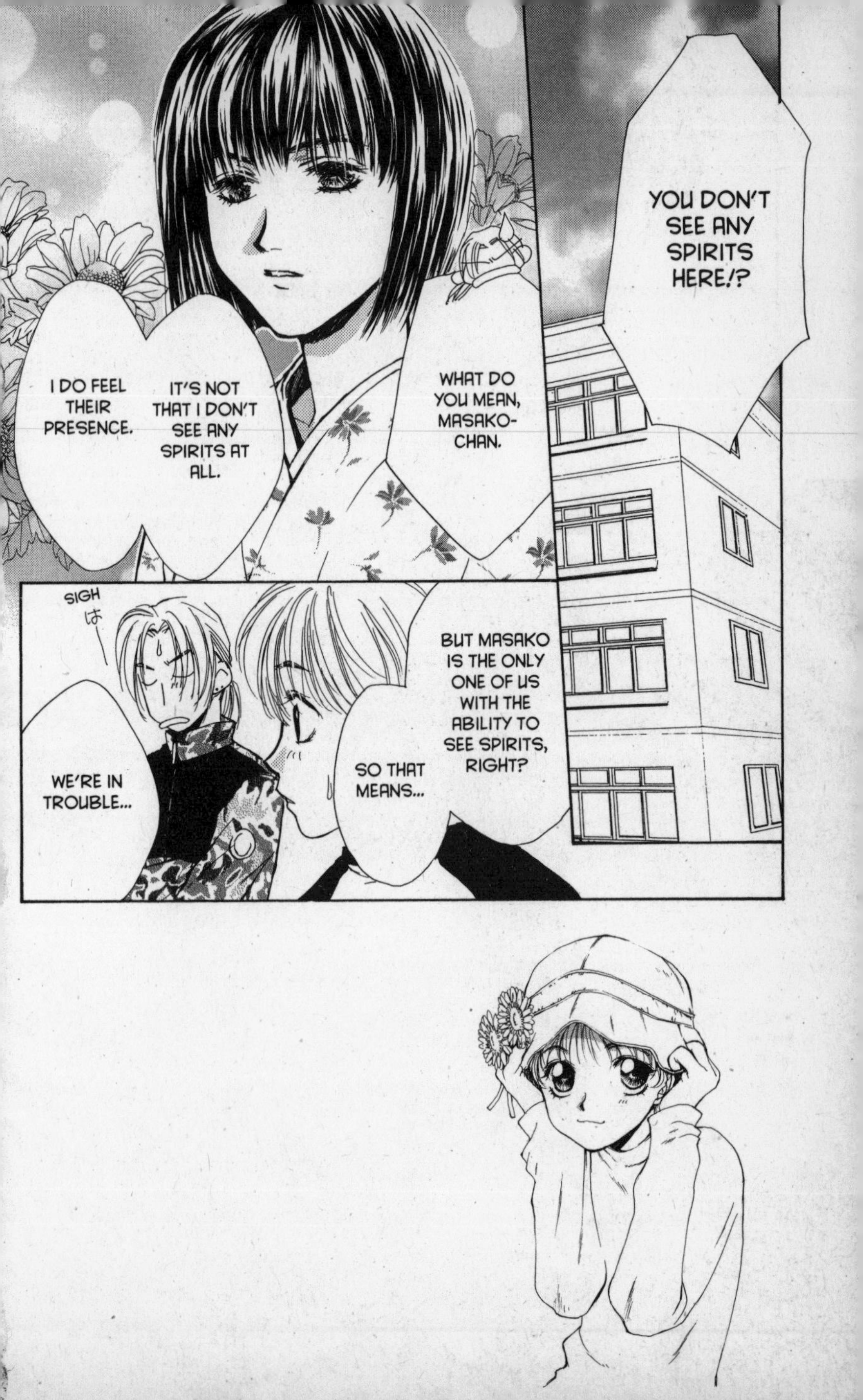
YOU DON'T SEE ANY SPIRITS HERE!?
WHAT DO YOU MEAN, MASAKO-CHAN.
IT'S NOT THAT I DON'T SEE ANY SPIRITS AT ALL.
I DO FEEL THEIR PRESENCE.
BUT MASAKO IS THE ONLY ONE OF US WITH THE ABILITY TO SEE SPIRITS, RIGHT?
SO THAT MEANS...
SIGH
は―
WE'RE IN TROUBLE...

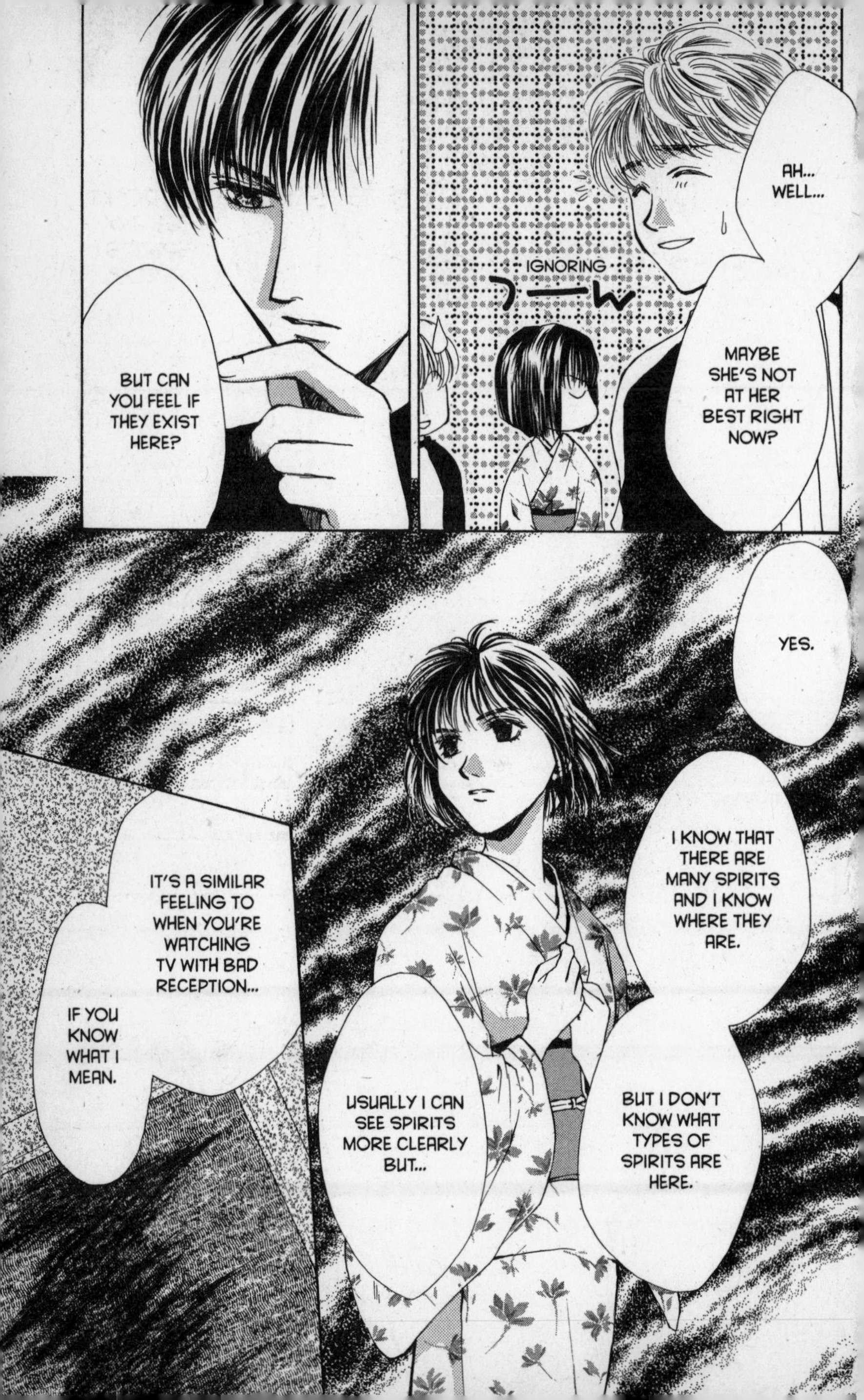
AH... WELL...
IGNORING
MAYBE SHE'S NOT AT HER BEST RIGHT NOW?
BUT CAN YOU FEEL IF THEY EXIST HERE?
YES.
I KNOW THAT THERE ARE MANY SPIRITS AND I KNOW WHERE THEY ARE.
BUT I DON'T KNOW WHAT TYPES OF SPIRITS ARE HERE.
USUALLY I CAN SEE SPIRITS MORE CLEARLY BUT...
IT'S A SIMILAR FEELING TO WHEN YOU'RE WATCHING TV WITH BAD RECEPTION...
IF YOU KNOW WHAT I MEAN.

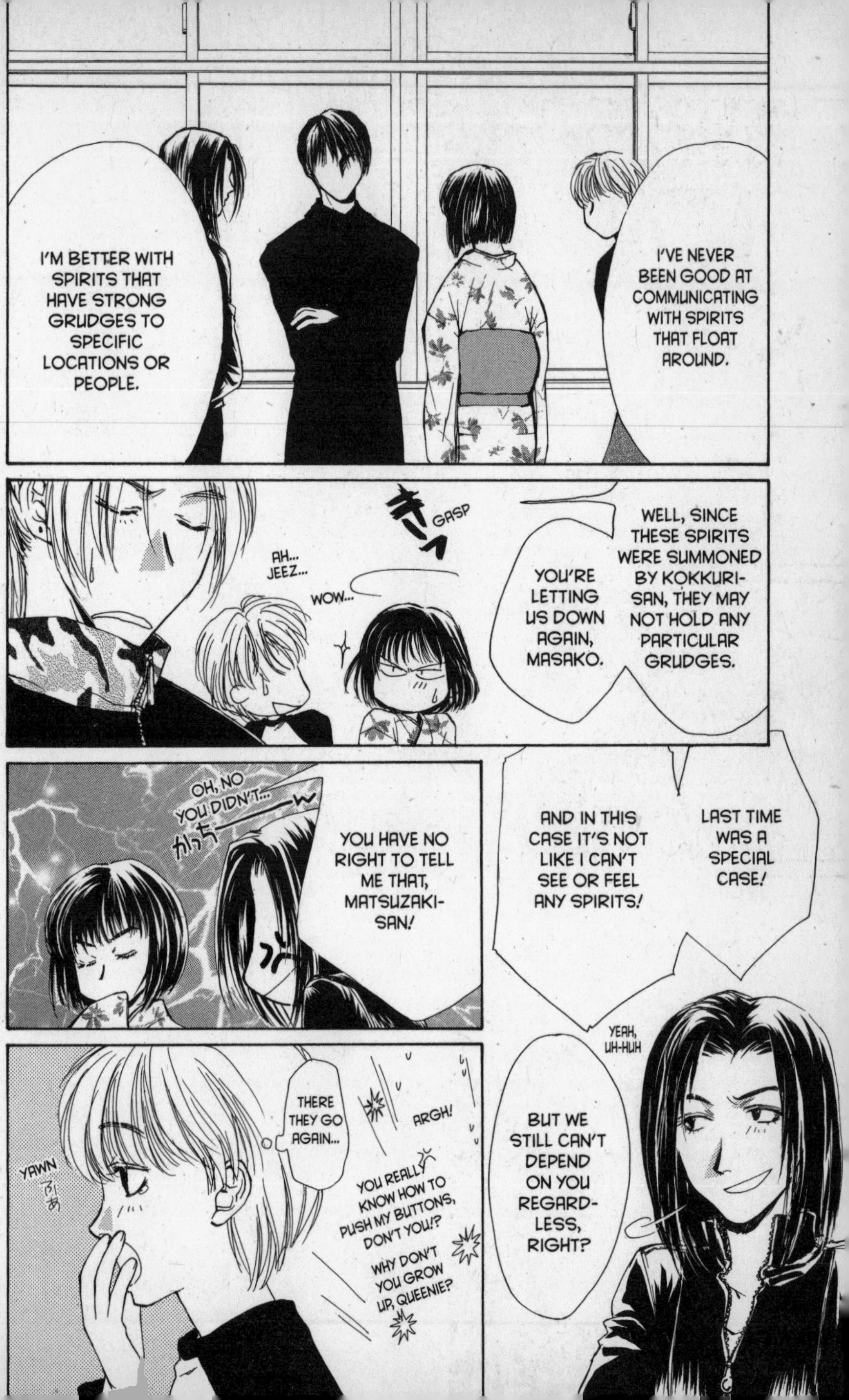
I'VE NEVER BEEN GOOD AT COMMUNICATING WITH SPIRITS THAT FLOAT AROUND.
I'M BETTER WITH SPIRITS THAT HAVE STRONG GRUDGES TO SPECIFIC LOCATIONS OR PEOPLE.
WELL, SINCE THESE SPIRITS WERE SUMMONED BY KOKKURI-SAN, THEY MAY NOT HOLD ANY PARTICULAR GRUDGES.
YOU'RE LETTING US DOWN AGAIN, MASAKO.
き GASP
WOW...
AH... JEEZ...
LAST TIME WAS A SPECIAL CASE!
AND IN THIS CASE IT'S NOT LIKE I CAN'T SEE OR FEEL ANY SPIRITS!
YOU HAVE NO RIGHT TO TELL ME THAT, MATSUZAKI-SAN!
OH, NO YOU DIDN'T...
かっち
YEAH, UH-HUH
BUT WE STILL CAN'T DEPEND ON YOU REGARDLESS, RIGHT?
THERE THEY GO AGAIN...
ARGH!
YOU REALLY KNOW HOW TO PUSH MY BUTTONS, DON'T YOU!?
WHY DON'T YOU GROW UP, QUEENIE?
YAWN
ふあ

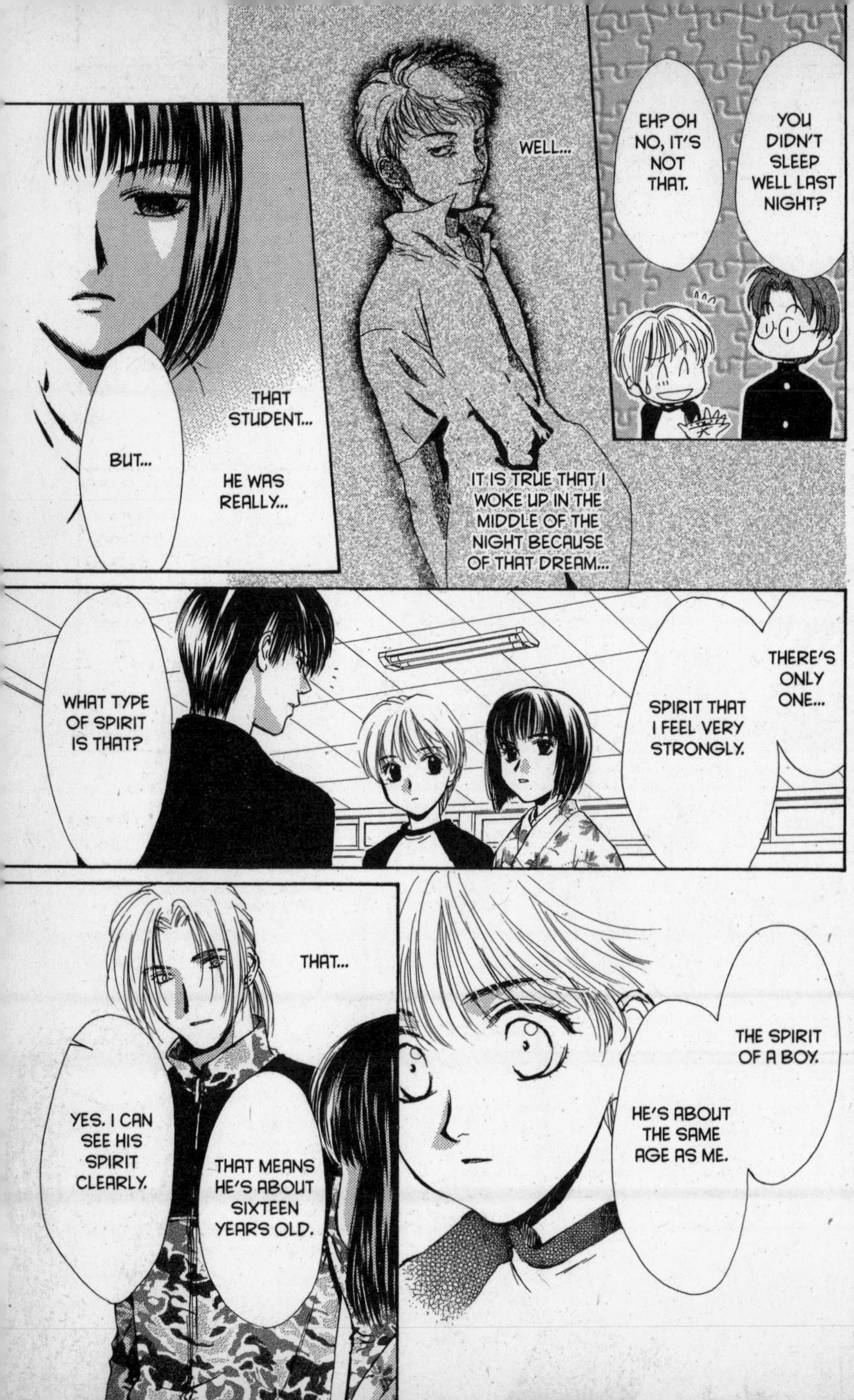
YOU DIDN'T SLEEP WELL LAST NIGHT?
EH? OH NO, IT'S NOT THAT.
WELL...
IT IS TRUE THAT I WOKE UP IN THE MIDDLE OF THE NIGHT BECAUSE OF THAT DREAM...
THAT STUDENT...
HE WAS REALLY...
BUT...
THERE'S ONLY ONE...
SPIRIT THAT I FEEL VERY STRONGLY.
WHAT TYPE OF SPIRIT IS THAT?
THE SPIRIT OF A BOY.
HE'S ABOUT THE SAME AGE AS ME.
THAT...
THAT MEANS HE'S ABOUT SIXTEEN YEARS OLD.
YES. I CAN SEE HIS SPIRIT CLEARLY.

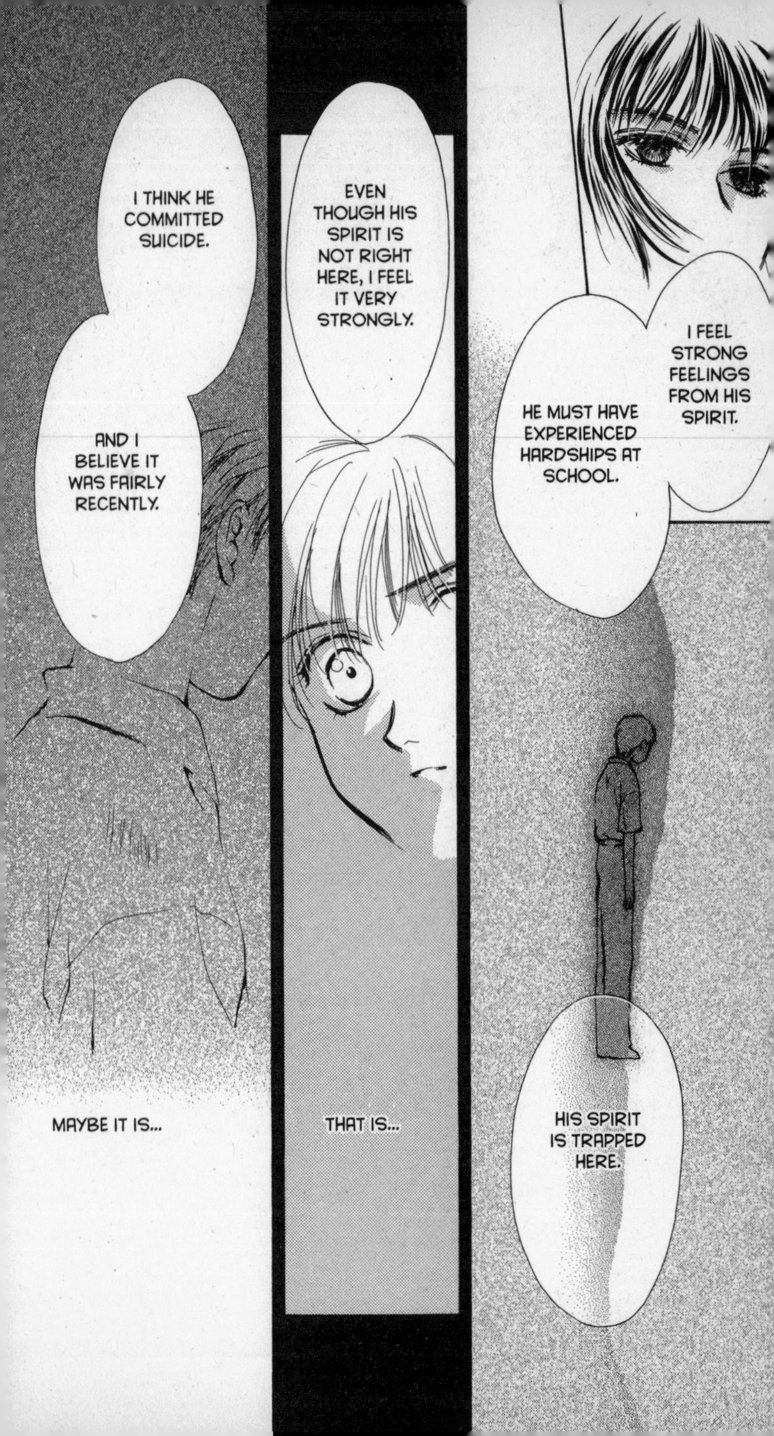
I FEEL STRONG FEELINGS FROM HIS SPIRIT.
HE MUST HAVE EXPERIENCED HARDSHIPS AT SCHOOL.
HIS SPIRIT IS TRAPPED HERE.
EVEN THOUGH HIS SPIRIT IS NOT RIGHT HERE, I FEEL IT VERY STRONGLY.
THAT IS...
I THINK HE COMMITTED SUICIDE.
AND I BELIEVE IT WAS FAIRLY RECENTLY.
MAYBE IT IS...

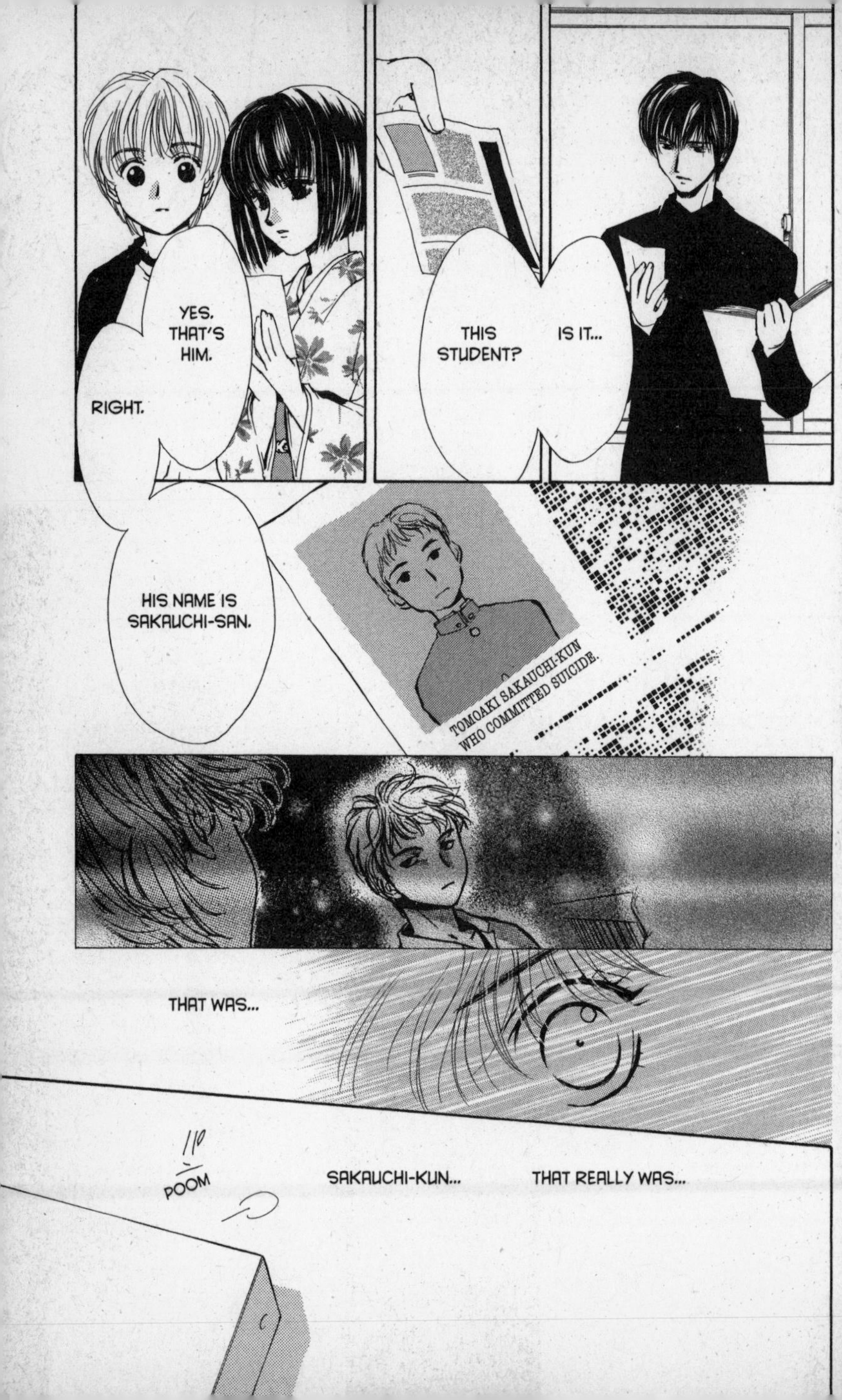
IS IT...
THIS STUDENT?
YES. THAT'S HIM.
RIGHT.
HIS NAME IS SAKAUCHI-SAN.
TOMOAKI SAKAUCHI-KUN WHO COMMITTED SUICIDE.
THAT WAS...
THAT REALLY WAS...
SAKAUCHI-KUN...
POOM

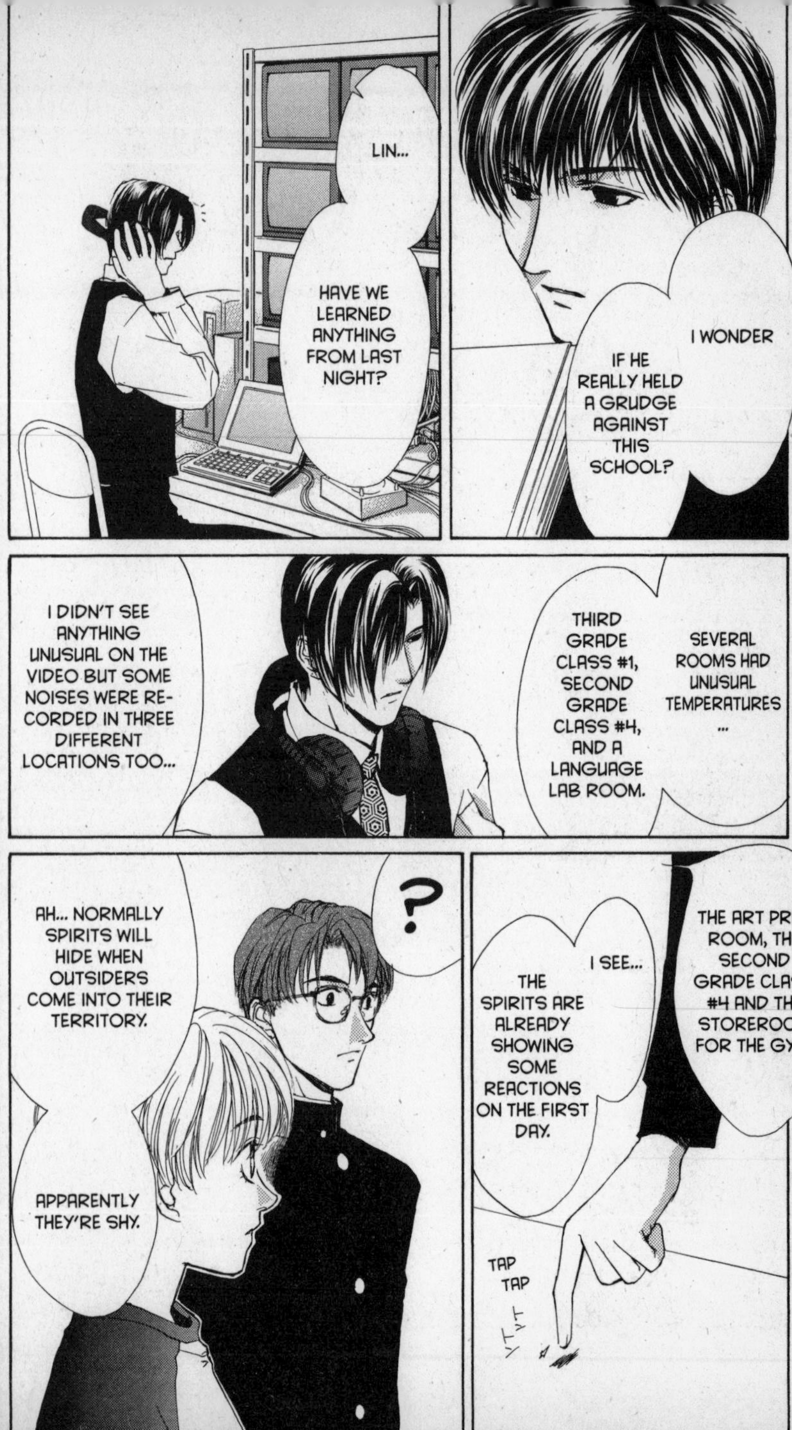
I WONDER IF HE REALLY HELD A GRUDGE AGAINST THIS SCHOOL?
LIN...
HAVE WE LEARNED ANYTHING FROM LAST NIGHT?
SEVERAL ROOMS HAD UNUSUAL TEMPERATURES ...
THIRD GRADE CLASS #1, SECOND GRADE CLASS #4, AND A LANGUAGE LAB ROOM.
I DIDN'T SEE ANYTHING UNUSUAL ON THE VIDEO BUT SOME NOISES WERE RE-CORDED IN THREE DIFFERENT LOCATIONS TOO...
THE ART PREP ROOM, THE SECOND GRADE CLASS #4 AND THE STOREROOM FOR THE GYM.
I SEE... THE SPIRITS ARE ALREADY SHOWING SOME REACTIONS ON THE FIRST DAY.
TAP TAP
?
AH... NORMALLY SPIRITS WILL HIDE WHEN OUTSIDERS COME INTO THEIR TERRITORY.
APPARENTLY THEY'RE SHY.

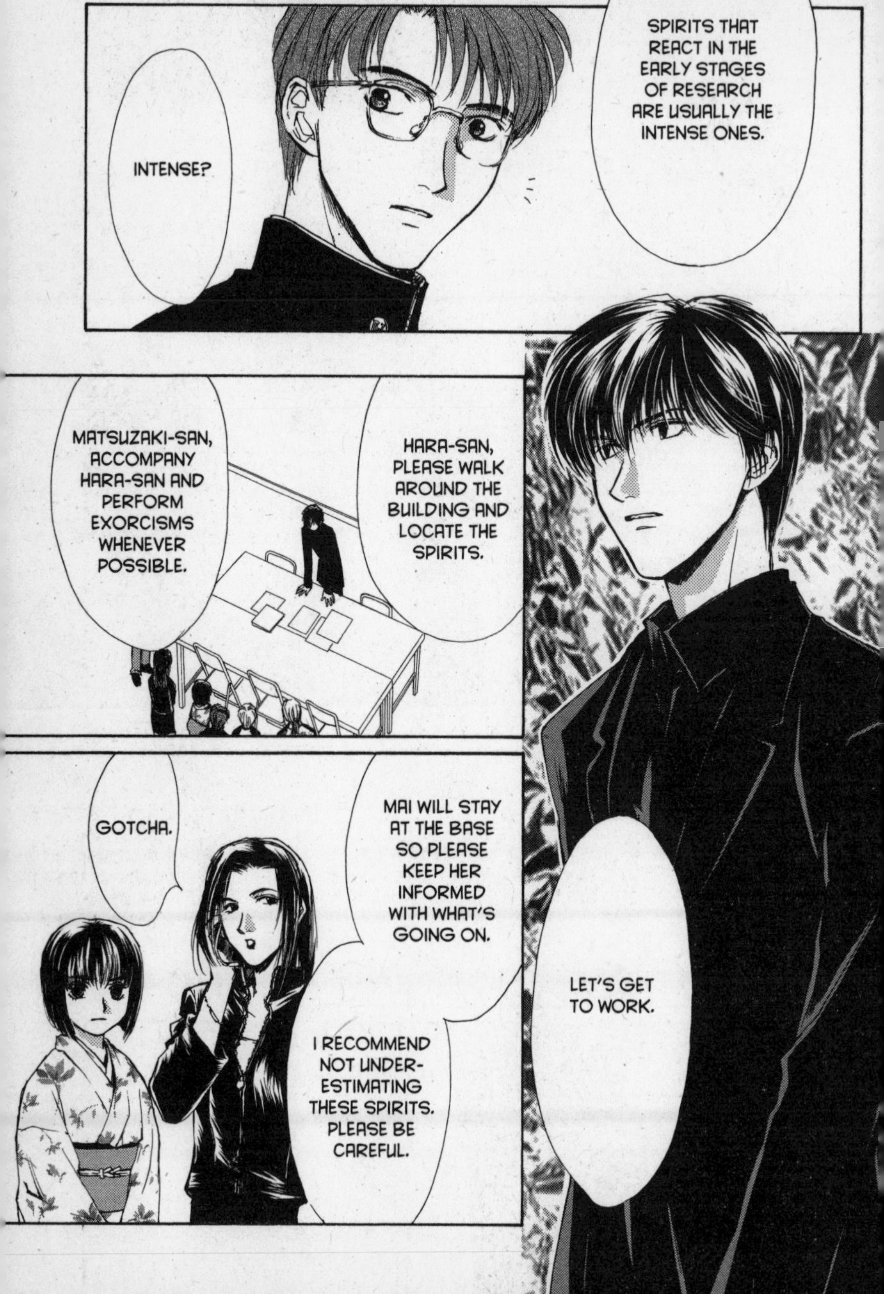
SPIRITS THAT REACT IN THE EARLY STAGES OF RESEARCH ARE USUALLY THE INTENSE ONES.
INTENSE?
LET'S GET TO WORK.
HARA-SAN, PLEASE WALK AROUND THE BUILDING AND LOCATE THE SPIRITS.
MATSUZAKI-SAN, ACCOMPANY HARA-SAN AND PERFORM EXORCISMS WHENEVER POSSIBLE.
MAI WILL STAY AT THE BASE SO PLEASE KEEP HER INFORMED WITH WHAT'S GOING ON.
I RECOMMEND NOT UNDER-ESTIMATING THESE SPIRITS. PLEASE BE CAREFUL.
GOTCHA.

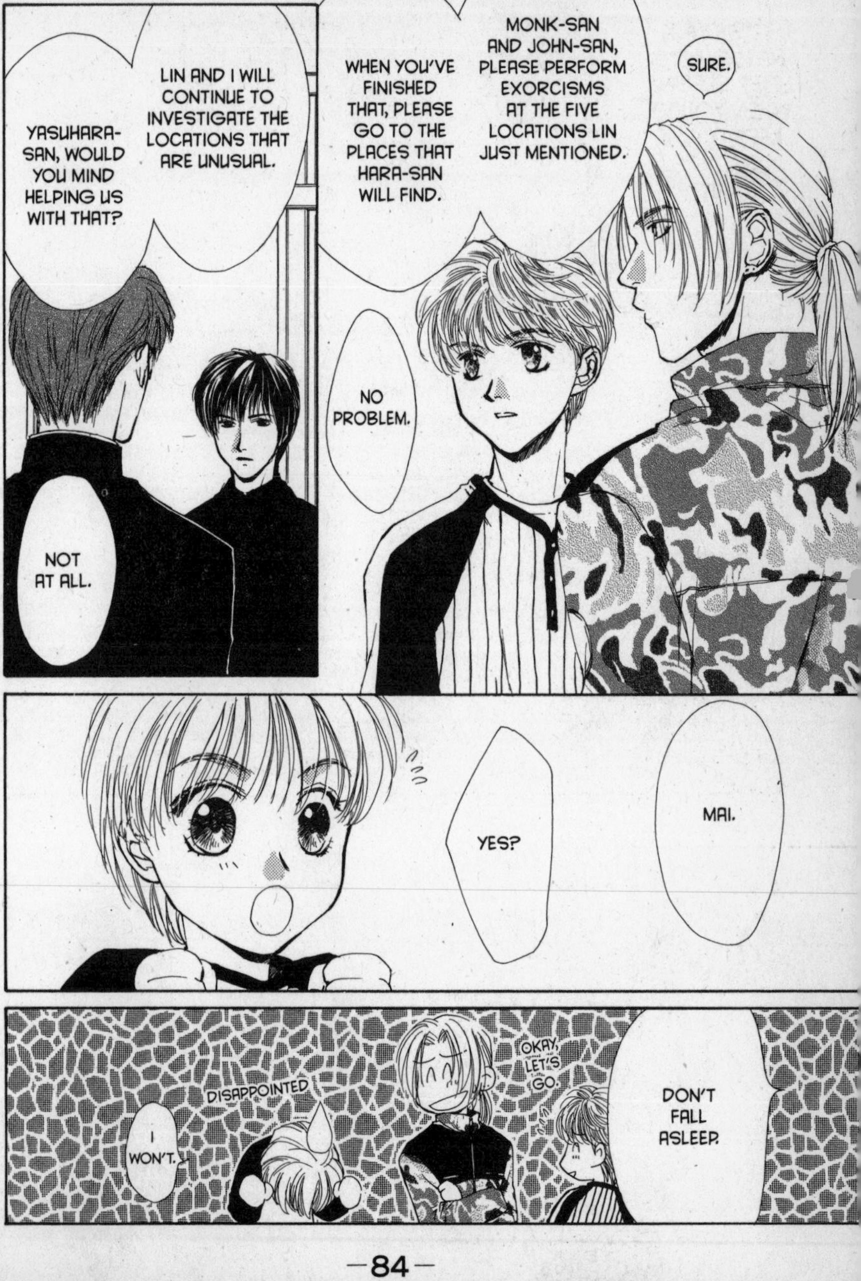
MONK-SAN AND JOHN-SAN, PLEASE PERFORM EXORCISMS AT THE FIVE LOCATIONS LIN JUST MENTIONED.
WHEN YOU'VE FINISHED THAT, PLEASE GO TO THE PLACES THAT HARA-SAN WILL FIND.
SURE.
NO PROBLEM.
LIN AND I WILL CONTINUE TO INVESTIGATE THE LOCATIONS THAT ARE UNUSUAL.
YASUHARA-SAN, WOULD YOU MIND HELPING US WITH THAT?
NOT AT ALL.
MAI.
YES?
DON'T FALL ASLEEP.
OKAY, LET'S GO.
DISAPPOINTED
I WON'T.

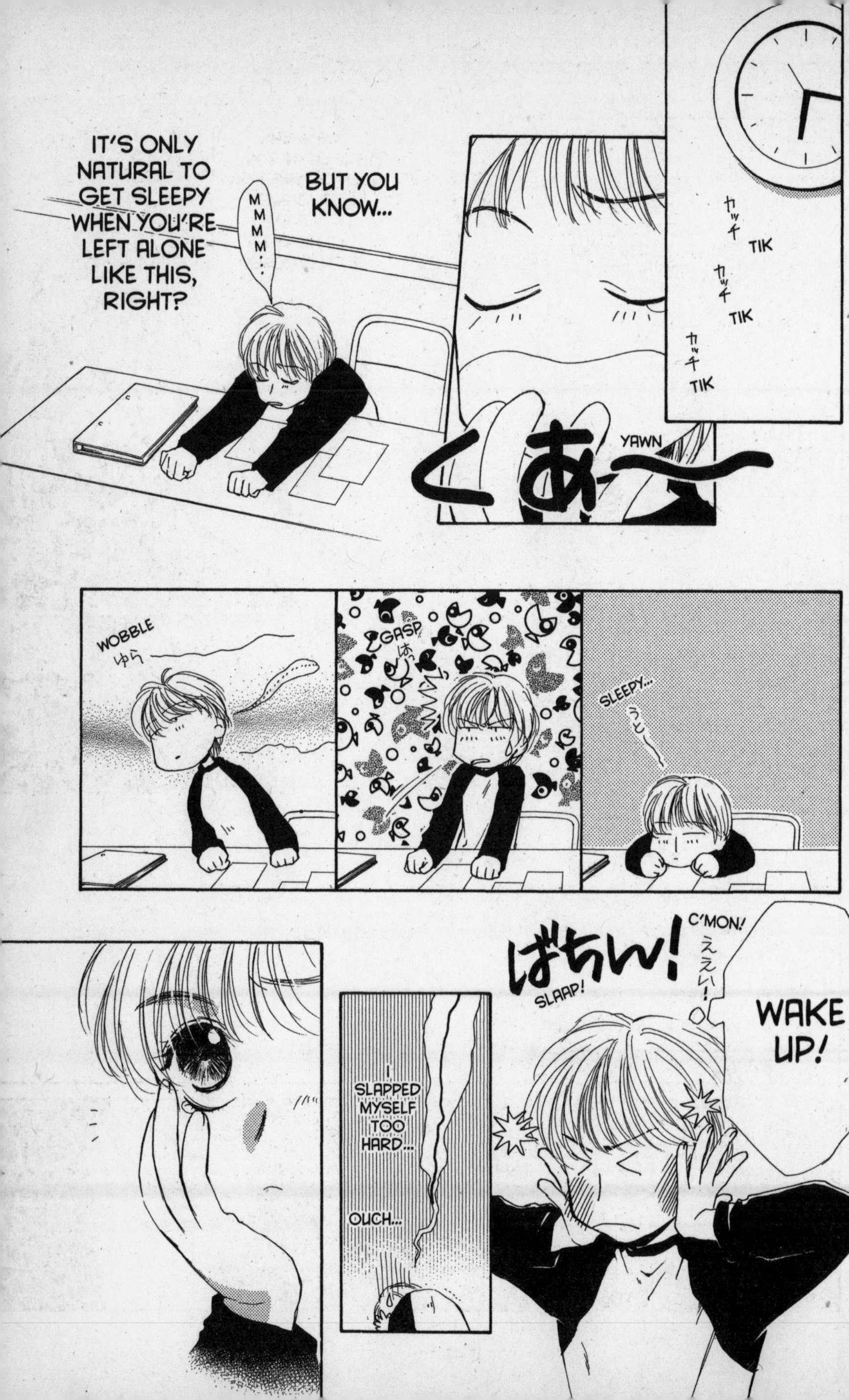

カッチ
TIK
カッチ
TIK
カッチ
TIK
くあ～～
YAWN
BUT YOU KNOW...
MMMM...
IT'S ONLY NATURAL TO GET SLEEPY WHEN YOU'RE LEFT ALONE LIKE THIS, RIGHT?
SLEEPY...
うと～～
GASP
はっ
WOBBLE
ゆら
C'MON!
ええい!
WAKE UP!
ばちん!
SLAAP!
I SLAPPED MYSELF TOO HARD...
OUCH...

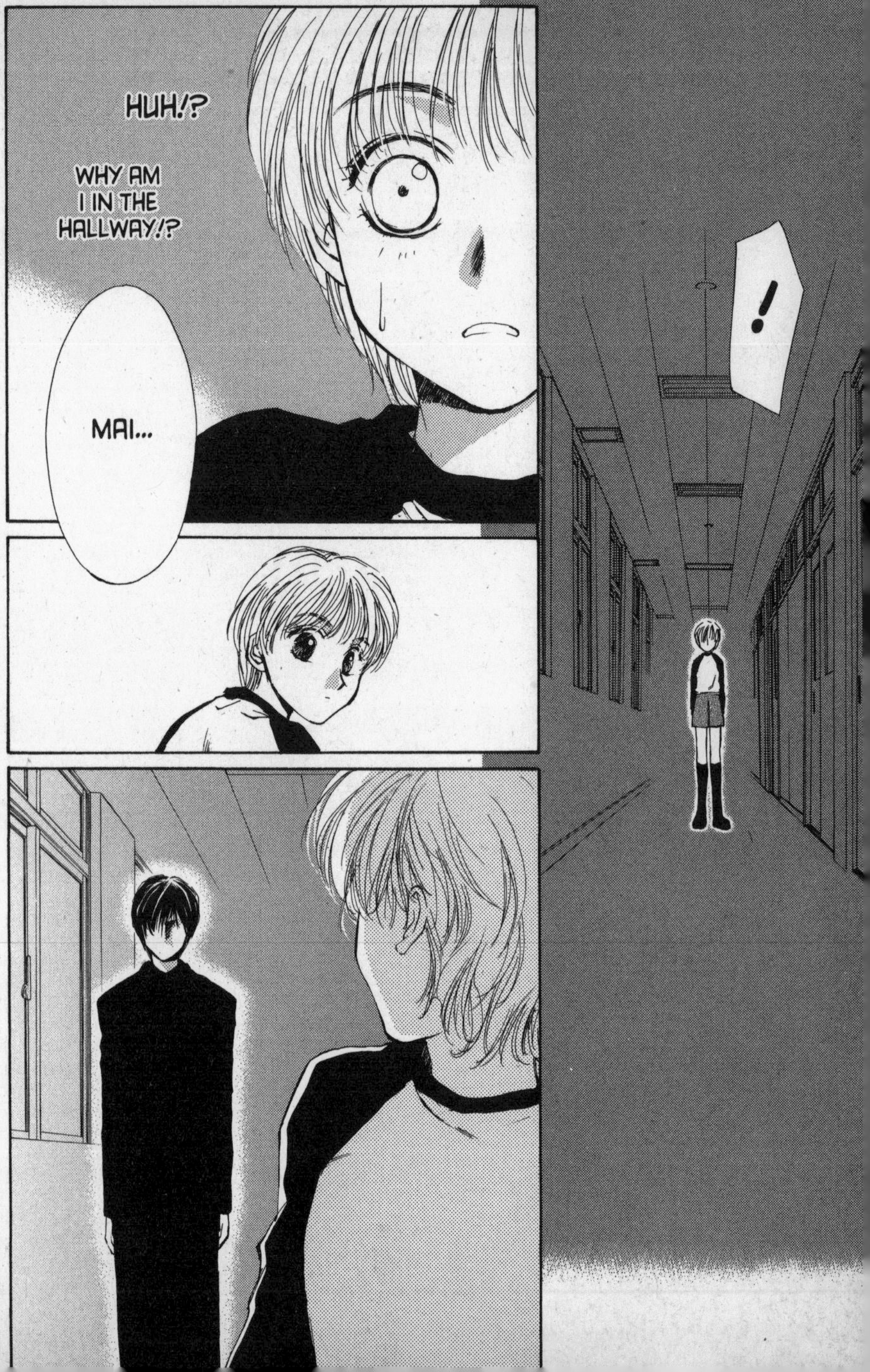
!
HUH!?
WHY AM I IN THE HALLWAY!?
MAI...

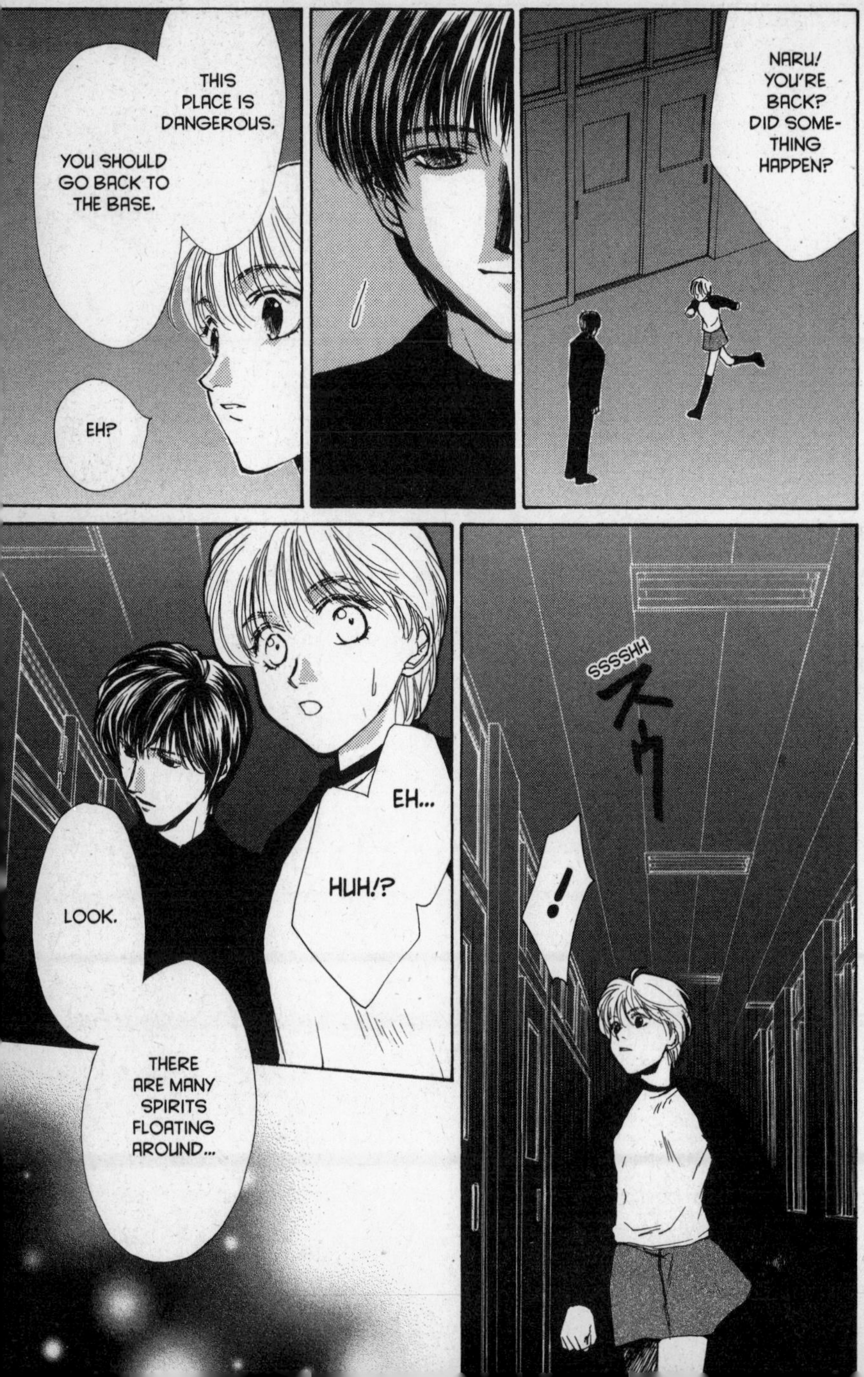
NARU! YOU'RE BACK? DID SOME-THING HAPPEN?
THIS PLACE IS DANGEROUS.
YOU SHOULD GO BACK TO THE BASE.
EH?
SSSSHH
!
EH... HUH!?
LOOK.
THERE ARE MANY SPIRITS FLOATING AROUND...

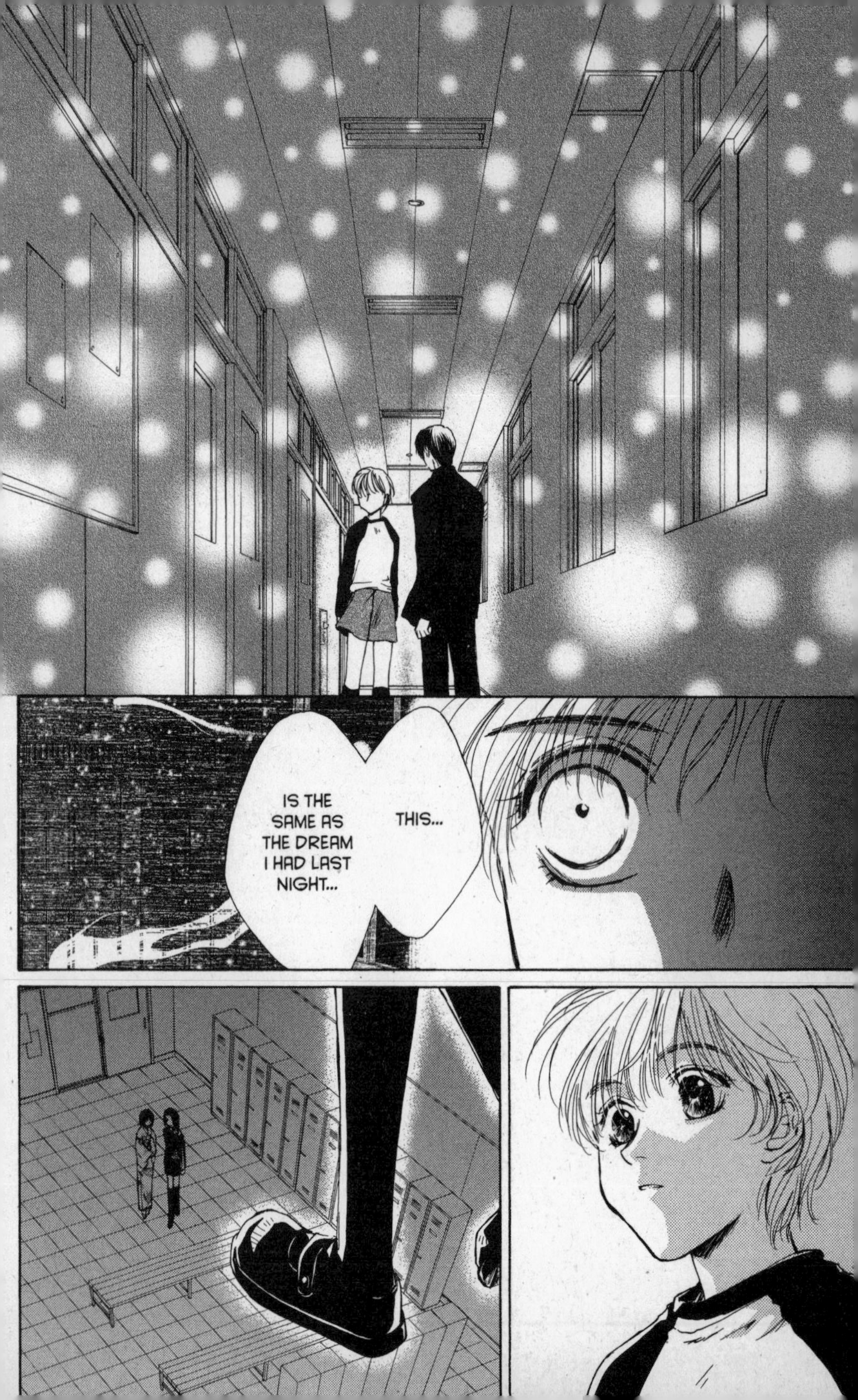
THIS...
IS THE SAME AS THE DREAM I HAD LAST NIGHT...

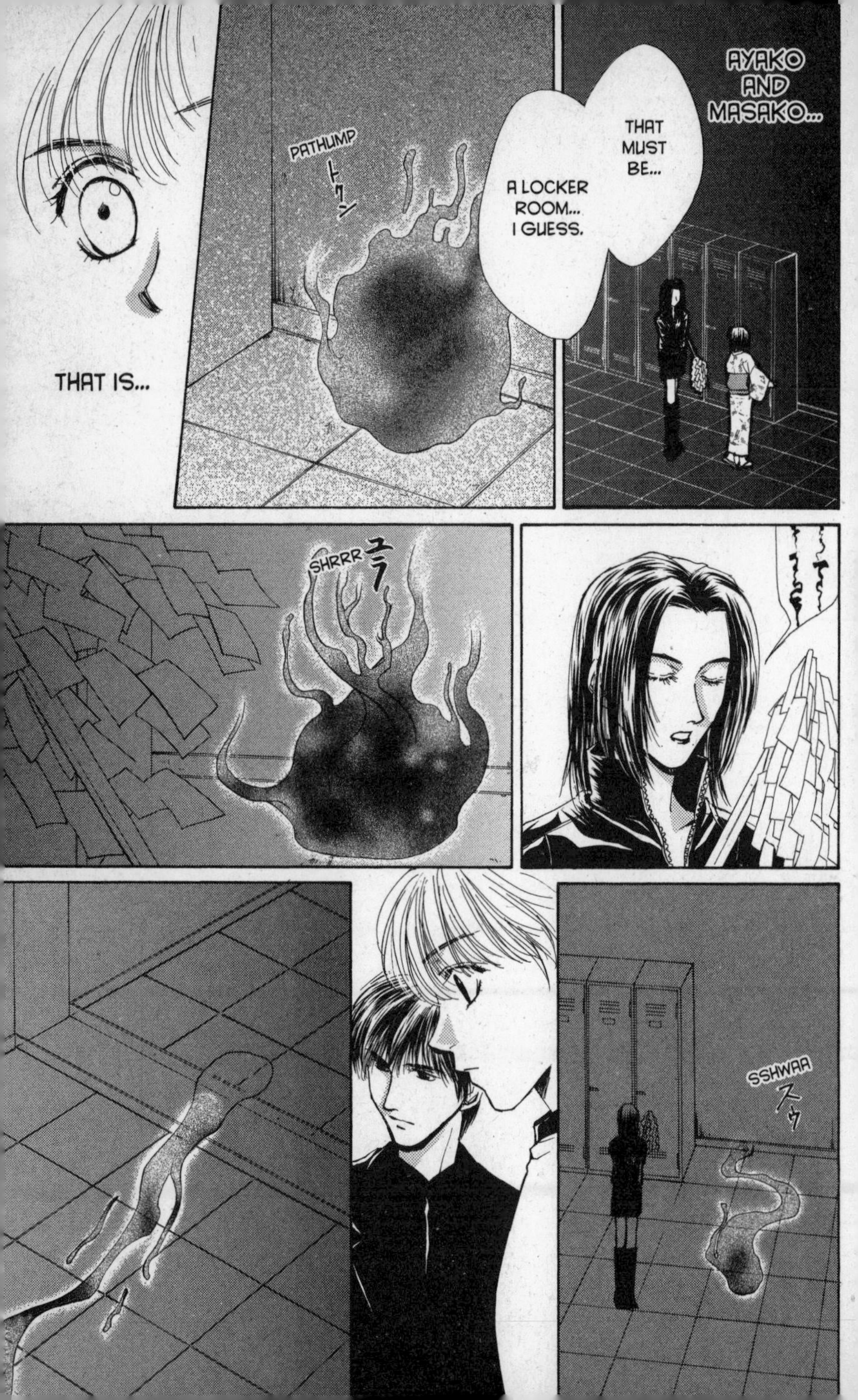
AYAKO AND MASAKO...
THAT MUST BE...
A LOCKER ROOM... I GUESS.
PATHUMP
トクン
THAT IS...
SHRRR
ユラ
SSHWAA
スゥ

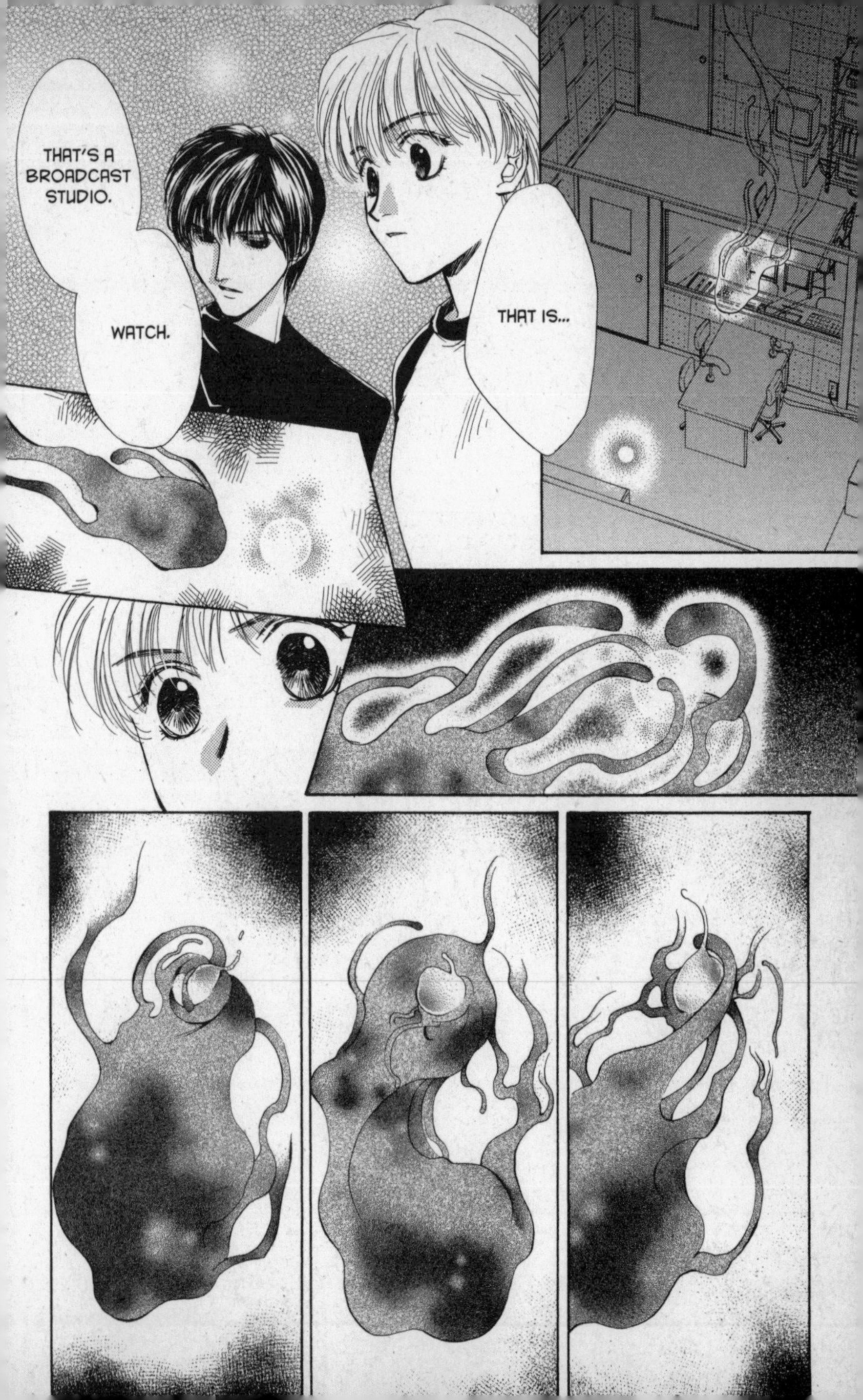
THAT IS...
THAT'S A BROADCAST STUDIO.
WATCH.

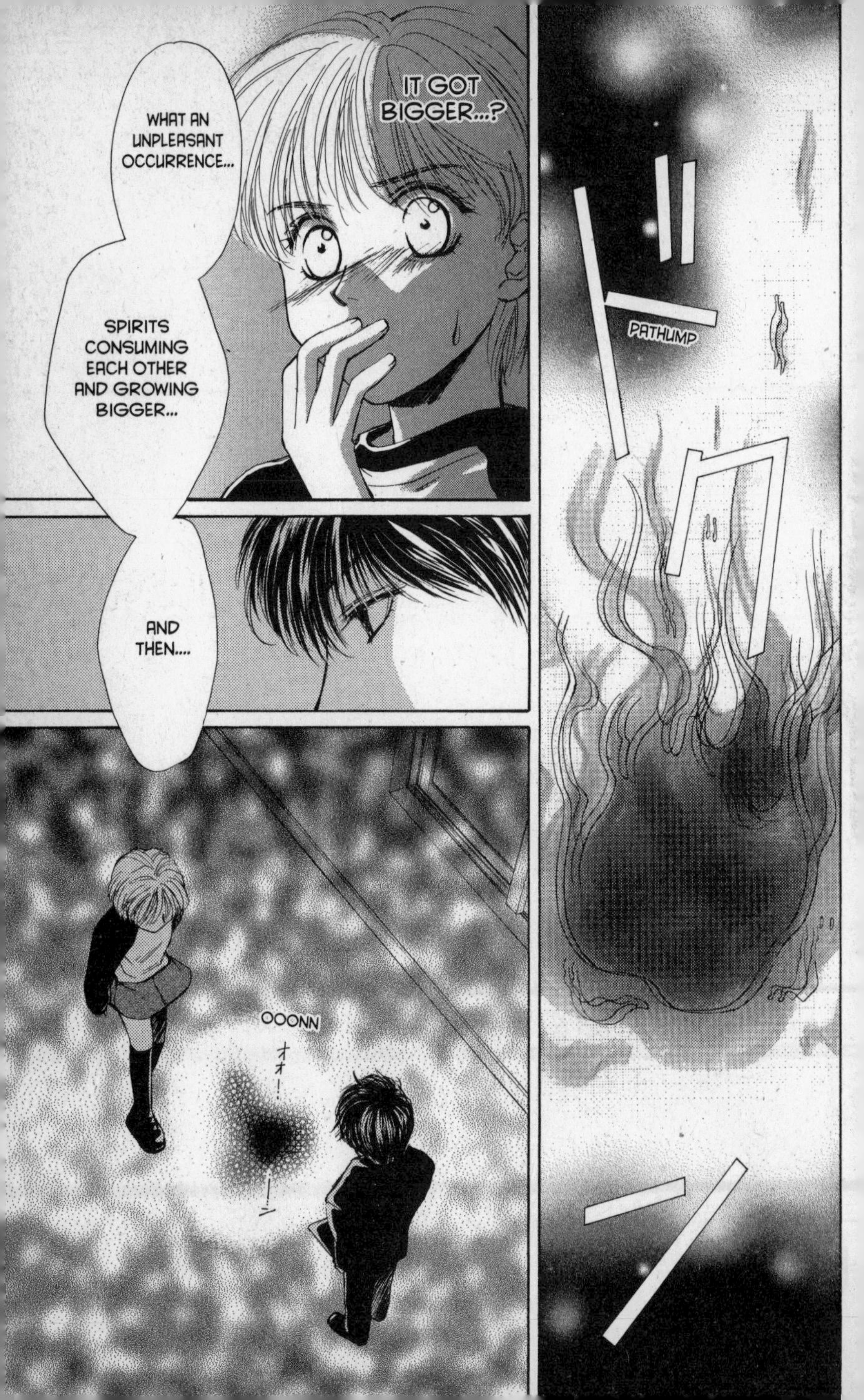
PATHUMP
IT GOT BIGGER...?
WHAT AN UNPLEASANT OCCURRENCE...
SPIRITS CONSUMING EACH OTHER AND GROWING BIGGER...
AND THEN....
OOONN

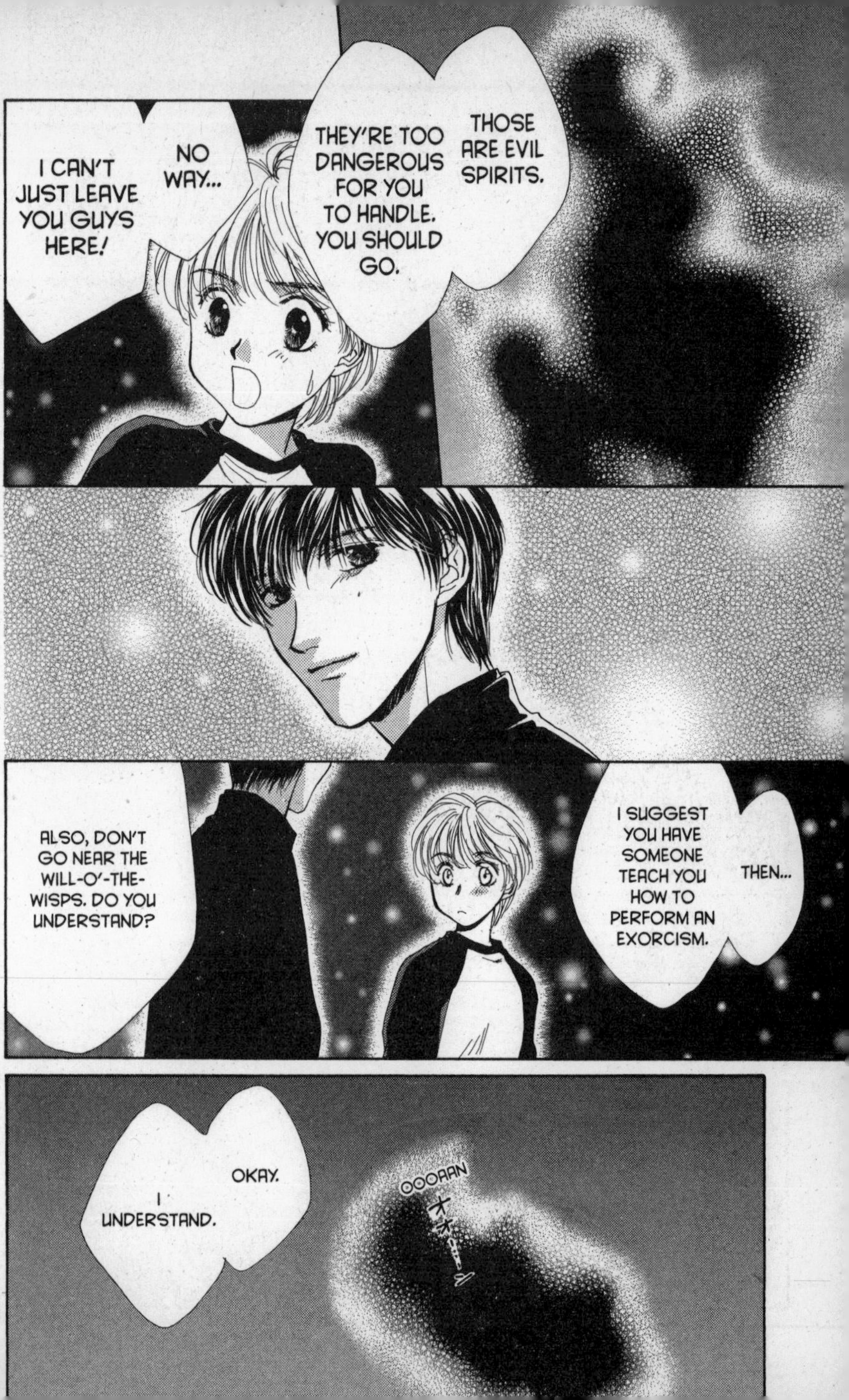
THOSE ARE EVIL SPIRITS.
THEY'RE TOO DANGEROUS FOR YOU TO HANDLE. YOU SHOULD GO.
NO WAY...
I CAN'T JUST LEAVE YOU GUYS HERE!
THEN...
I SUGGEST YOU HAVE SOMEONE TEACH YOU HOW TO PERFORM AN EXORCISM.
ALSO, DON'T GO NEAR THE WILL-O'-THE-WISPS. DO YOU UNDERSTAND?
OOOAAN
OKAY.
I UNDERSTAND.

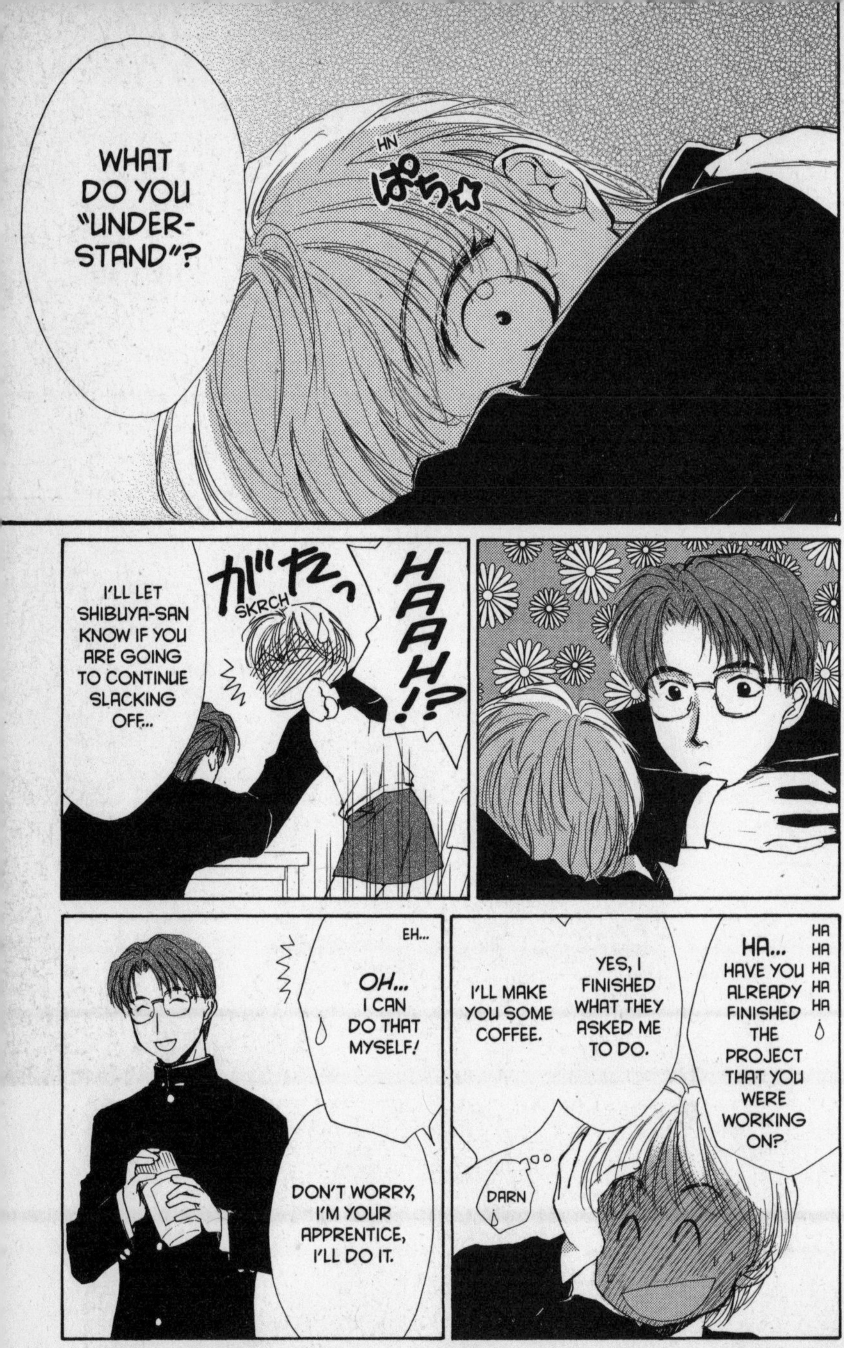
HN
ぱち☆
WHAT DO YOU "UNDER-STAND"?
HAAH!?
がたっ
SKRCH
I'LL LET SHIBUYA-SAN KNOW IF YOU ARE GOING TO CONTINUE SLACKING OFF...
HA HA HA HA HA HA
HA... HAVE YOU ALREADY FINISHED THE PROJECT THAT YOU WERE WORKING ON?
YES, I FINISHED WHAT THEY ASKED ME TO DO.
I'LL MAKE YOU SOME COFFEE.
DARN
EH...
OH... I CAN DO THAT MYSELF!
DON'T WORRY, I'M YOUR APPRENTICE, I'LL DO IT.

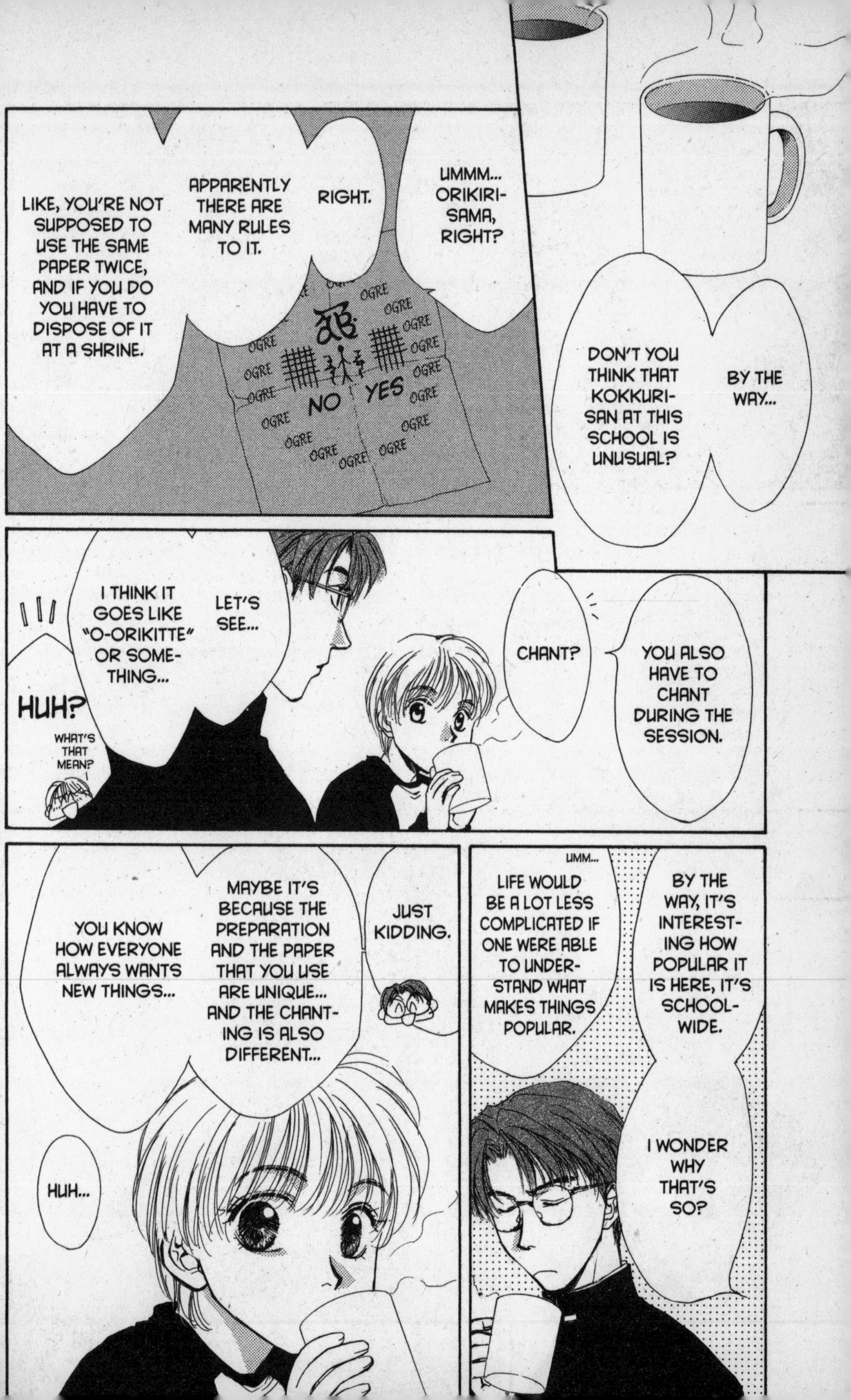
BY THE WAY...
DON'T YOU THINK THAT KOKKURI-SAN AT THIS SCHOOL IS UNUSUAL?
UMMM... ORIKIRI-SAMA, RIGHT?
RIGHT.
APPARENTLY THERE ARE MANY RULES TO IT.
LIKE, YOU'RE NOT SUPPOSED TO USE THE SAME PAPER TWICE, AND IF YOU DO YOU HAVE TO DISPOSE OF IT AT A SHRINE.
OGRE
NO
YES
YOU ALSO HAVE TO CHANT DURING THE SESSION.
CHANT?
LET'S SEE...
I THINK IT GOES LIKE "O-ORIKITTE" OR SOME-THING...
HUH?
WHAT'S THAT MEAN?
BY THE WAY, IT'S INTEREST-ING HOW POPULAR IT IS HERE, IT'S SCHOOL-WIDE.
I WONDER WHY THAT'S SO?
UMM...
LIFE WOULD BE A LOT LESS COMPLICATED IF ONE WERE ABLE TO UNDER-STAND WHAT MAKES THINGS POPULAR.
JUST KIDDING.
MAYBE IT'S BECAUSE THE PREPARATION AND THE PAPER THAT YOU USE ARE UNIQUE... AND THE CHANT-ING IS ALSO DIFFERENT...
YOU KNOW HOW EVERYONE ALWAYS WANTS NEW THINGS...
HUH...

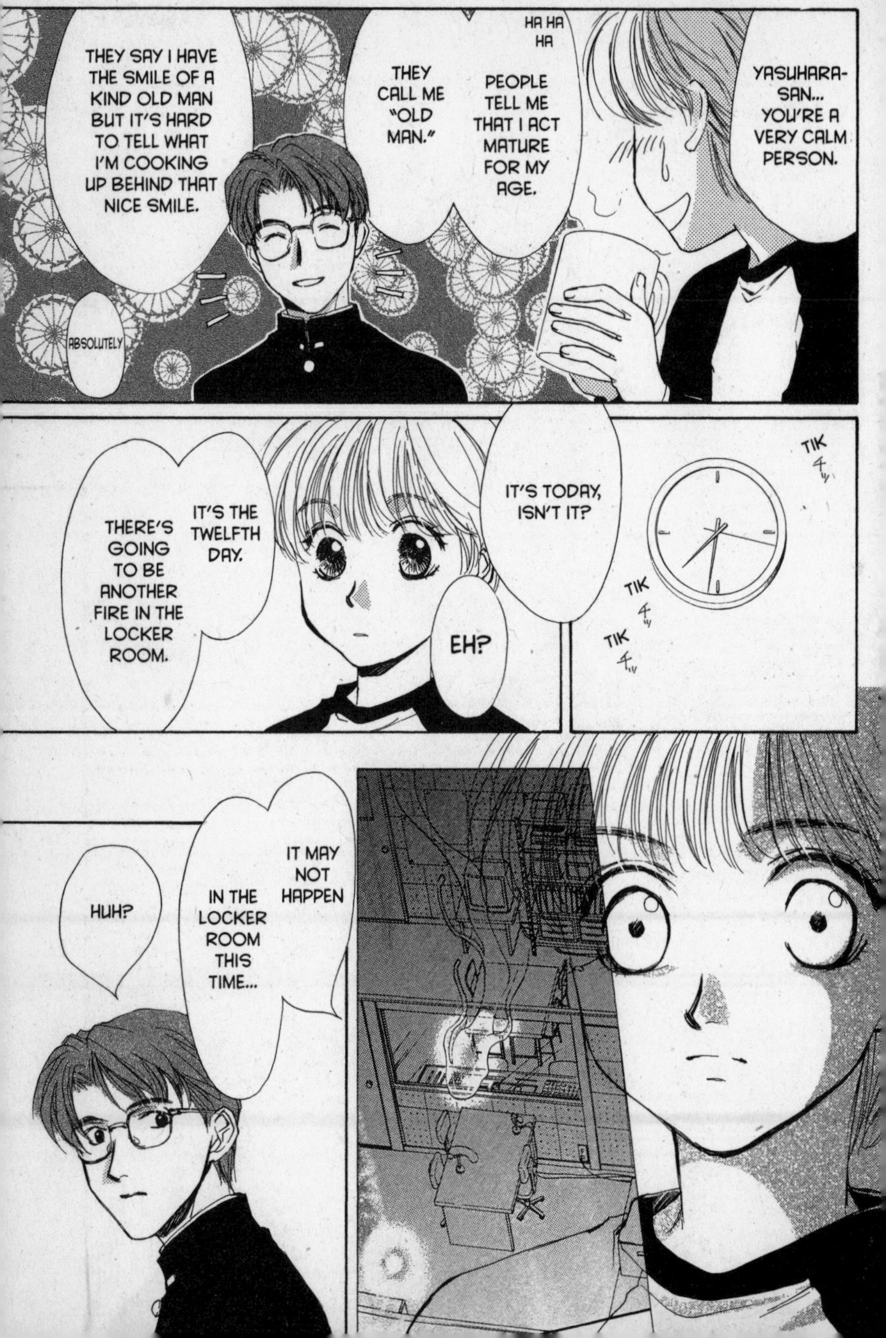
YASUHARA-SAN... YOU'RE A VERY CALM PERSON.
HA HA HA
PEOPLE TELL ME THAT I ACT MATURE FOR MY AGE.
THEY CALL ME "OLD MAN."
THEY SAY I HAVE THE SMILE OF A KIND OLD MAN BUT IT'S HARD TO TELL WHAT I'M COOKING UP BEHIND THAT NICE SMILE.
ABSOLUTELY
TIK
TIK
TIK
IT'S TODAY, ISN'T IT?
EH?
IT'S THE TWELFTH DAY.
THERE'S GOING TO BE ANOTHER FIRE IN THE LOCKER ROOM.
IT MAY NOT HAPPEN
IN THE LOCKER ROOM THIS TIME...
HUH?

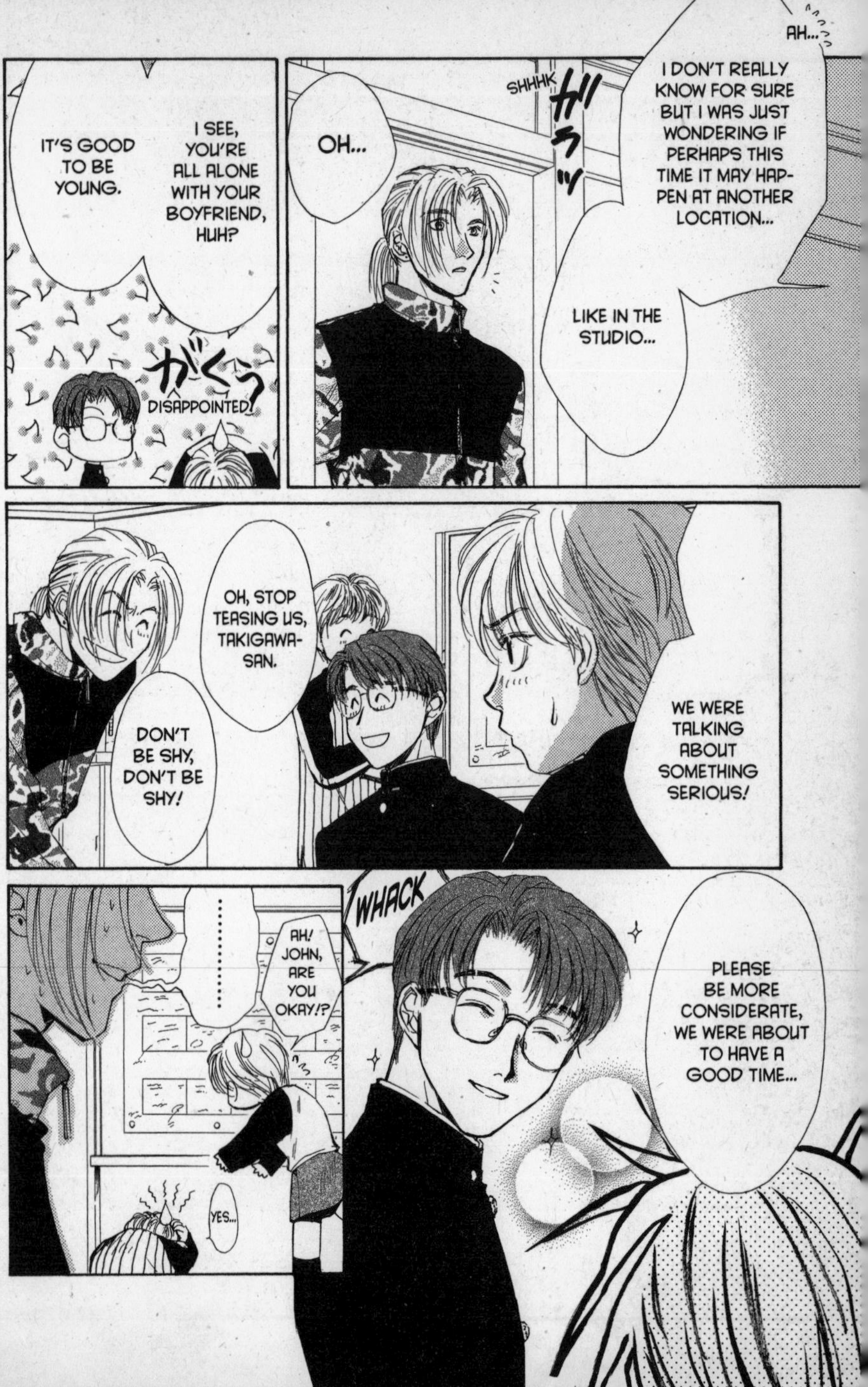
AH...
I DON'T REALLY KNOW FOR SURE BUT I WAS JUST WONDERING IF PERHAPS THIS TIME IT MAY HAP-PEN AT ANOTHER LOCATION...
LIKE IN THE STUDIO...
SHHHK
ガラッ
OH...
I SEE, YOU'RE ALL ALONE WITH YOUR BOYFRIEND, HUH?
IT'S GOOD TO BE YOUNG.
がくぅ
DISAPPOINTED
WE WERE TALKING ABOUT SOMETHING SERIOUS!
OH, STOP TEASING US, TAKIGAWA-SAN.
DON'T BE SHY, DON'T BE SHY!
WHACK
PLEASE BE MORE CONSIDERATE, WE WERE ABOUT TO HAVE A GOOD TIME...
AH! JOHN, ARE YOU OKAY!?
......
YES...

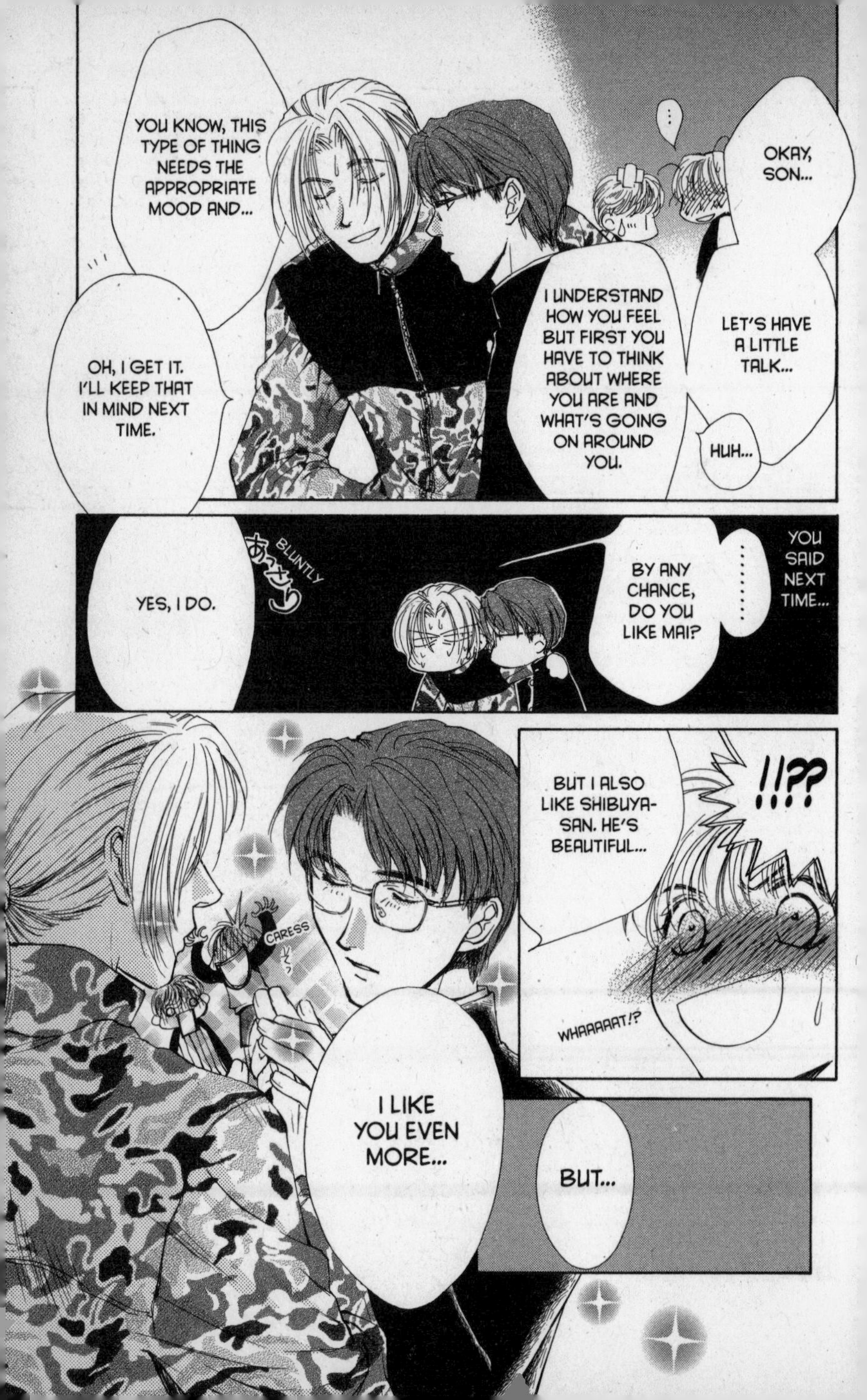
...
OKAY, SON...
LET'S HAVE A LITTLE TALK...
HUH...
YOU KNOW, THIS TYPE OF THING NEEDS THE APPROPRIATE MOOD AND...
I UNDERSTAND HOW YOU FEEL BUT FIRST YOU HAVE TO THINK ABOUT WHERE YOU ARE AND WHAT'S GOING ON AROUND YOU.
OH, I GET IT. I'LL KEEP THAT IN MIND NEXT TIME.
YOU SAID NEXT TIME...
....
BY ANY CHANCE, DO YOU LIKE MAI?
BLUNTLY
YES, I DO.
!!??
BUT I ALSO LIKE SHIBUYA-SAN. HE'S BEAUTIFUL...
WHAAAAAT!?
BUT...
I LIKE YOU EVEN MORE...
CARESS

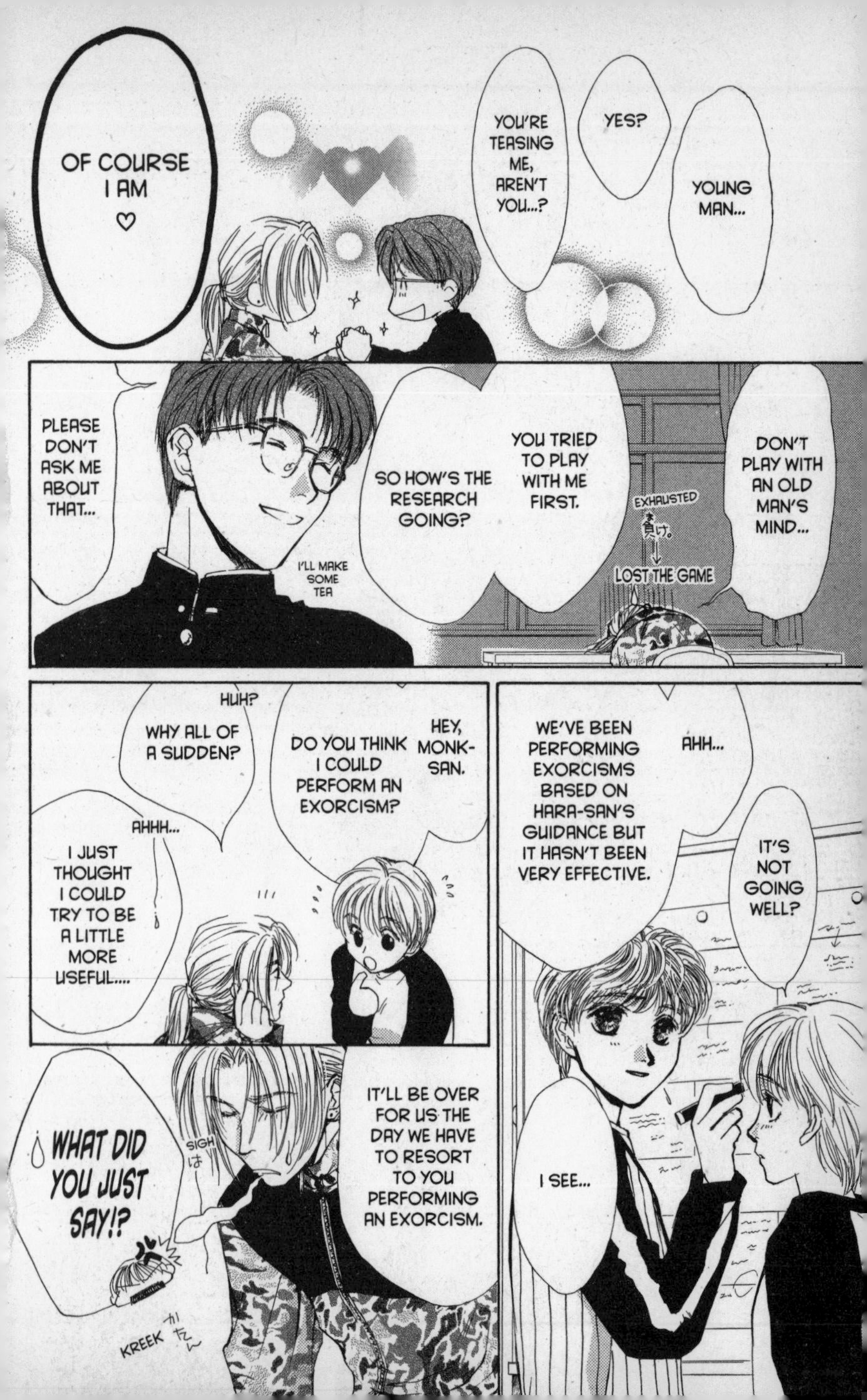
YOUNG MAN...
YES?
YOU'RE TEASING ME, AREN'T YOU...?
OF COURSE I AM ♡
DON'T PLAY WITH AN OLD MAN'S MIND...
EXHAUSTED
負け。
LOST THE GAME
YOU TRIED TO PLAY WITH ME FIRST.
SO HOW'S THE RESEARCH GOING?
I'LL MAKE SOME TEA
PLEASE DON'T ASK ME ABOUT THAT...
AHH...
WE'VE BEEN PERFORMING EXORCISMS BASED ON HARA-SAN'S GUIDANCE BUT IT HASN'T BEEN VERY EFFECTIVE.
IT'S NOT GOING WELL?
I SEE...
HEY, MONK-SAN.
DO YOU THINK I COULD PERFORM AN EXORCISM?
HUH?
WHY ALL OF A SUDDEN?
AHHH...
I JUST THOUGHT I COULD TRY TO BE A LITTLE MORE USEFUL....
IT'LL BE OVER FOR US THE DAY WE HAVE TO RESORT TO YOU PERFORMING AN EXORCISM.
SIGH
は
WHAT DID YOU JUST SAY!?
KREEK
かたん

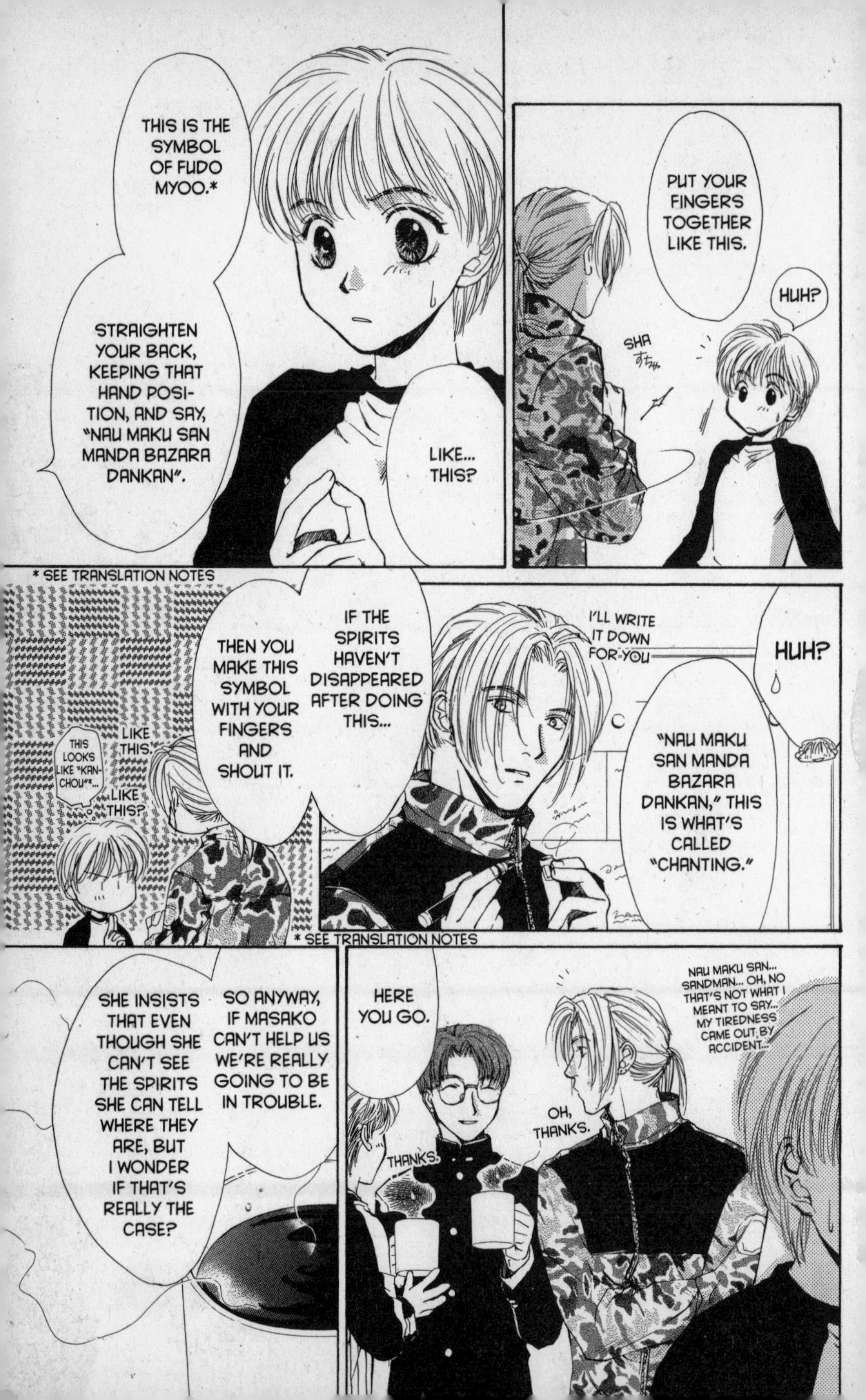
PUT YOUR FINGERS TOGETHER LIKE THIS.
HUH?
SHA
すちゃ
THIS IS THE SYMBOL OF FUDO MYOO.*
STRAIGHTEN YOUR BACK, KEEPING THAT HAND POSI-TION, AND SAY, "NAU MAKU SAN MANDA BAZARA DANKAN".
LIKE... THIS?
* SEE TRANSLATION NOTES
HUH?
I'LL WRITE IT DOWN FOR YOU
"NAU MAKU SAN MANDA BAZARA DANKAN," THIS IS WHAT'S CALLED "CHANTING."
IF THE SPIRITS HAVEN'T DISAPPEARED AFTER DOING THIS...
THEN YOU MAKE THIS SYMBOL WITH YOUR FINGERS AND SHOUT IT.
LIKE THIS.
THIS LOOKS LIKE "KAN-CHOU"*...
LIKE THIS?
* SEE TRANSLATION NOTES
NAU MAKU SAN... SANDMAN... OH, NO THAT'S NOT WHAT I MEANT TO SAY... MY TIREDNESS CAME OUT BY ACCIDENT...
HERE YOU GO.
OH, THANKS.
THANKS.
SO ANYWAY, IF MASAKO CAN'T HELP US WE'RE REALLY GOING TO BE IN TROUBLE.
SHE INSISTS THAT EVEN THOUGH SHE CAN'T SEE THE SPIRITS SHE CAN TELL WHERE THEY ARE, BUT I WONDER IF THAT'S REALLY THE CASE?

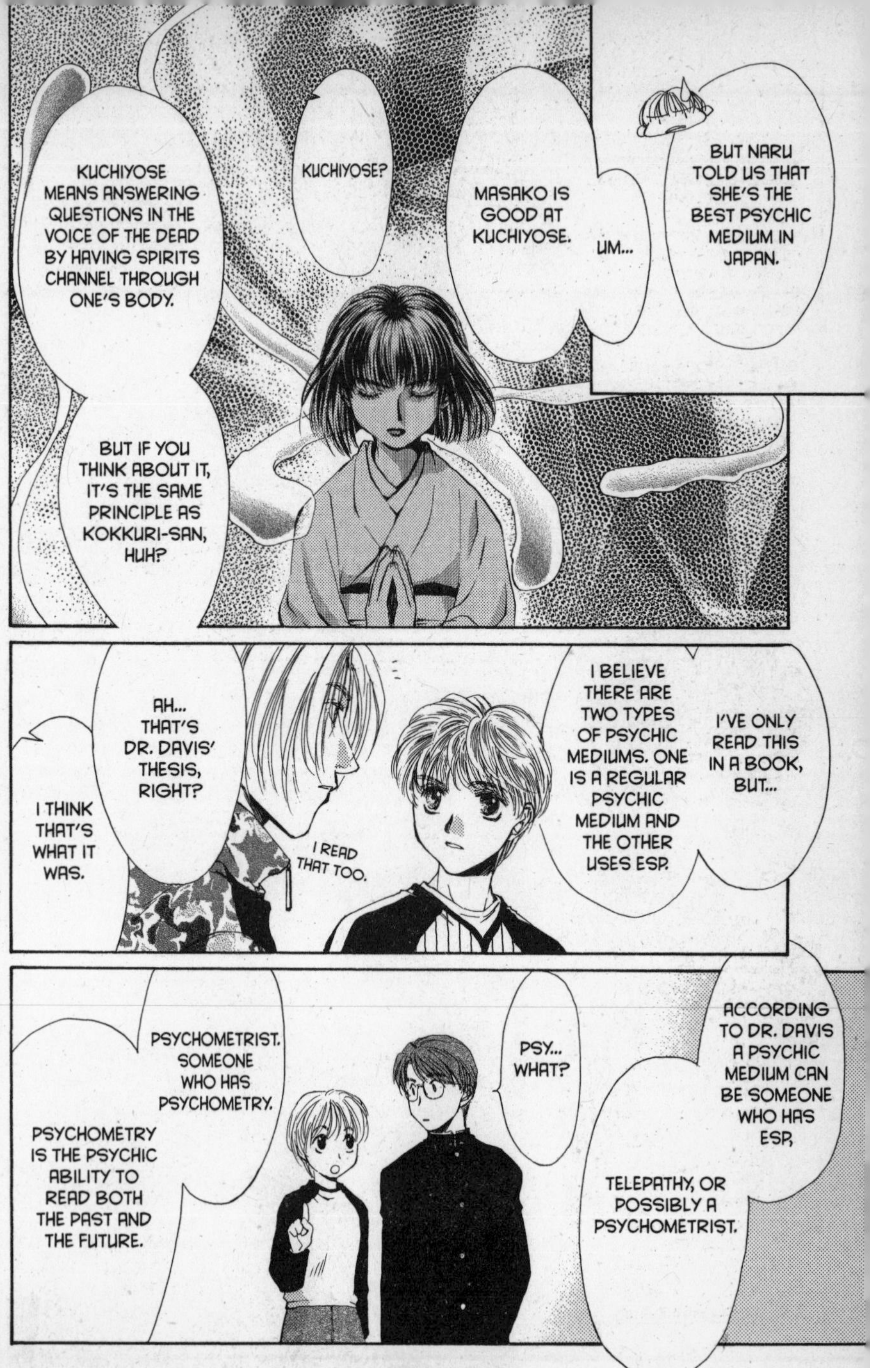
BUT NARU TOLD US THAT SHE'S THE BEST PSYCHIC MEDIUM IN JAPAN.
UM...
MASAKO IS GOOD AT KUCHIYOSE.
KUCHIYOSE?
KUCHIYOSE MEANS ANSWERING QUESTIONS IN THE VOICE OF THE DEAD BY HAVING SPIRITS CHANNEL THROUGH ONE'S BODY.
BUT IF YOU THINK ABOUT IT, IT'S THE SAME PRINCIPLE AS KOKKURI-SAN, HUH?
I'VE ONLY READ THIS IN A BOOK, BUT...
I BELIEVE THERE ARE TWO TYPES OF PSYCHIC MEDIUMS. ONE IS A REGULAR PSYCHIC MEDIUM AND THE OTHER USES ESP.
I READ THAT TOO.
AH... THAT'S DR. DAVIS' THESIS, RIGHT?
I THINK THAT'S WHAT IT WAS.
ACCORDING TO DR. DAVIS A PSYCHIC MEDIUM CAN BE SOMEONE WHO HAS ESP,
TELEPATHY, OR POSSIBLY A PSYCHOMETRIST.
PSY... WHAT?
PSYCHOMETRIST. SOMEONE WHO HAS PSYCHOMETRY.
PSYCHOMETRY IS THE PSYCHIC ABILITY TO READ BOTH THE PAST AND THE FUTURE.

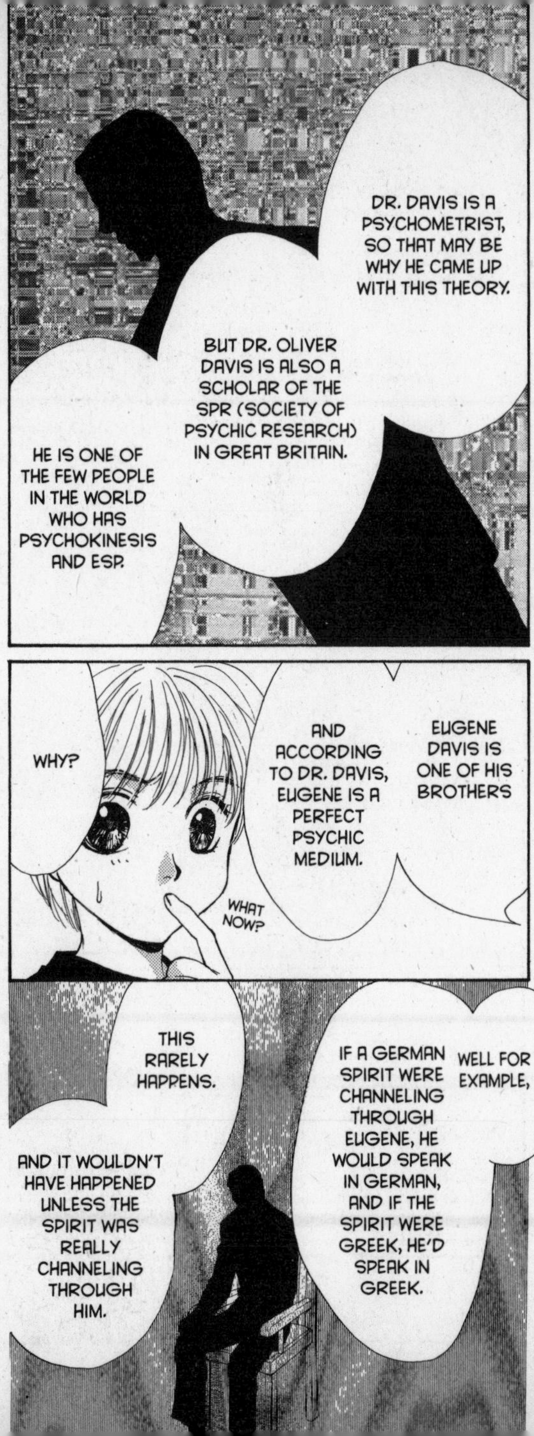
DR. DAVIS IS A PSYCHOMETRIST, SO THAT MAY BE WHY HE CAME UP WITH THIS THEORY.
BUT DR. OLIVER DAVIS IS ALSO A SCHOLAR OF THE SPR (SOCIETY OF PSYCHIC RESEARCH) IN GREAT BRITAIN.
HE IS ONE OF THE FEW PEOPLE IN THE WORLD WHO HAS PSYCHOKINESIS AND ESP.
EUGENE DAVIS IS ONE OF HIS BROTHERS
AND ACCORDING TO DR. DAVIS, EUGENE IS A PERFECT PSYCHIC MEDIUM.
WHY?
WHAT NOW?
WELL FOR EXAMPLE,
IF A GERMAN SPIRIT WERE CHANNELING THROUGH EUGENE, HE WOULD SPEAK IN GERMAN, AND IF THE SPIRIT WERE GREEK, HE'D SPEAK IN GREEK.
THIS RARELY HAPPENS.
AND IT WOULDN'T HAVE HAPPENED UNLESS THE SPIRIT WAS REALLY CHANNELING THROUGH HIM.

BY THE WAY, THIS STORY WILL BE CONTINUED INTO THE NEXT VOLUME!

SO WE ADDED A SIDE STORY FOR YOU AFTER PART 1 OF THE MAIN STORY (FORBIDDEN GAME). ONO-SENSEI SPECIALLY CAME UP WITH THIS SIDE STORY. THANK YOU, SENSEI.

OUR GOAL WAS TO MAKE SIDE CHARACTERS THAT NORMALLY DON'T GET TO STAND OUT VERY MUCH, STAND OUT. SO WE SELECTED "THAT CHARACTER" BUT MONK-SAN ENDED UP STEALING HIS SPOTLIGHT. OH HOW PITIFUL! (SOB)

WELL THEN, I'LL SEE YOU AGAIN IN VOLUME 5!

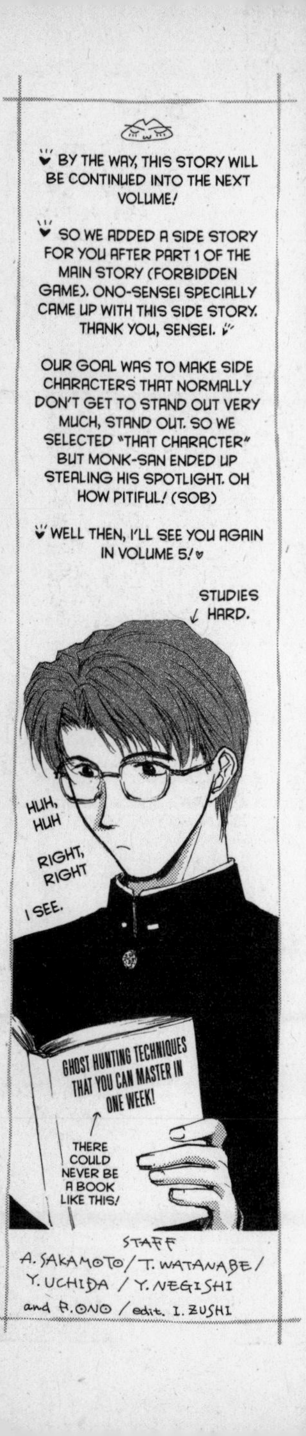
STUDIES HARD.
HUH, HUH
RIGHT, RIGHT
I SEE.
GHOST HUNTING TECHNIQUES THAT YOU CAN MASTER IN ONE WEEK!
THERE COULD NEVER BE A BOOK LIKE THIS!

STAFF
A. SAKAMOTO / T. WATANABE / Y. UCHIDA / Y. NEGISHI and A. ONO / edit. I. ZUSHI

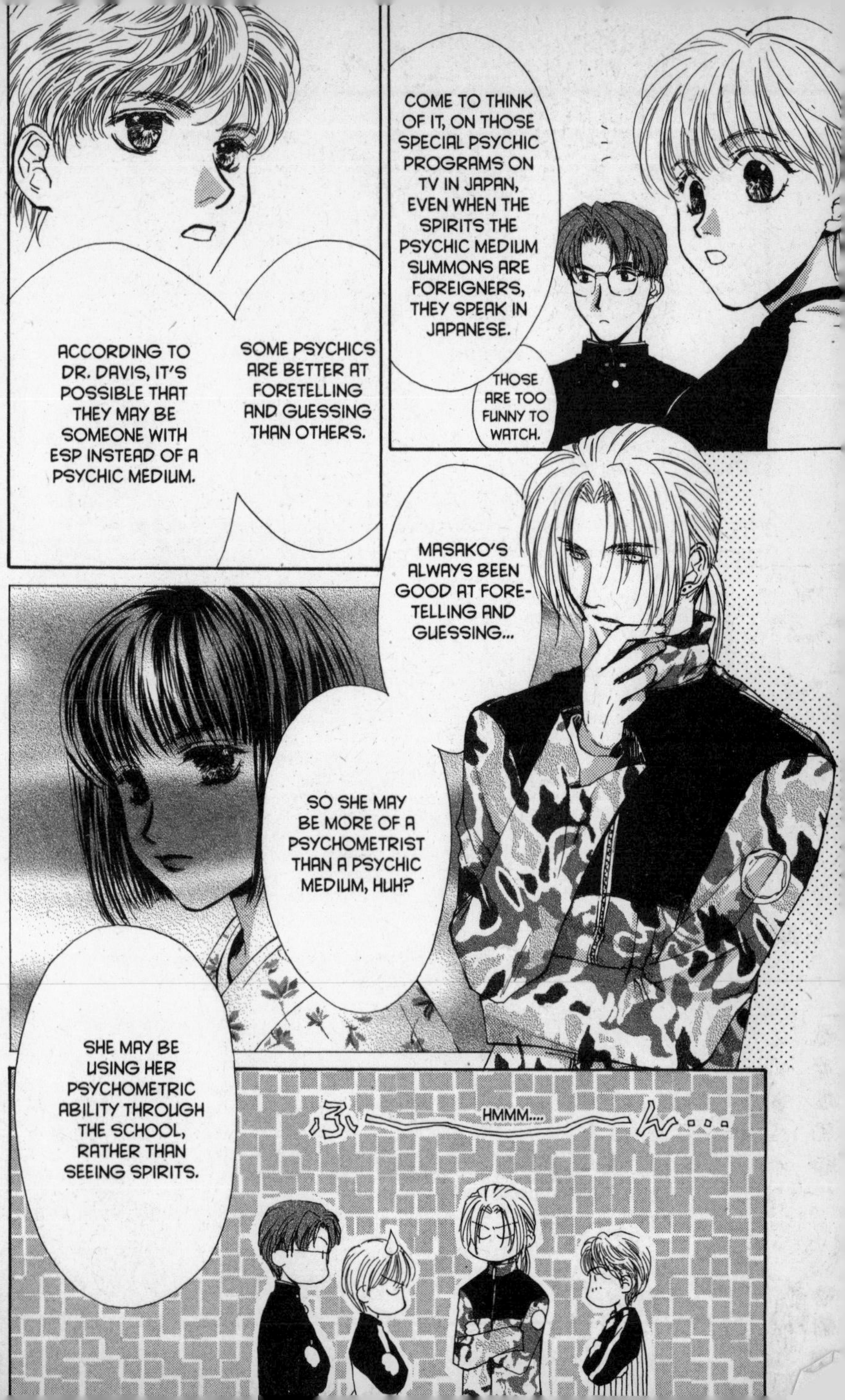
COME TO THINK OF IT, ON THOSE SPECIAL PSYCHIC PROGRAMS ON TV IN JAPAN, EVEN WHEN THE SPIRITS THE PSYCHIC MEDIUM SUMMONS ARE FOREIGNERS, THEY SPEAK IN JAPANESE.
THOSE ARE TOO FUNNY TO WATCH.
SOME PSYCHICS ARE BETTER AT FORETELLING AND GUESSING THAN OTHERS.
ACCORDING TO DR. DAVIS, IT'S POSSIBLE THAT THEY MAY BE SOMEONE WITH ESP INSTEAD OF A PSYCHIC MEDIUM.
MASAKO'S ALWAYS BEEN GOOD AT FORE-TELLING AND GUESSING...
SO SHE MAY BE MORE OF A PSYCHOMETRIST THAN A PSYCHIC MEDIUM, HUH?
SHE MAY BE USING HER PSYCHOMETRIC ABILITY THROUGH THE SCHOOL, RATHER THAN SEEING SPIRITS.
ふーーーん...
HMMM....

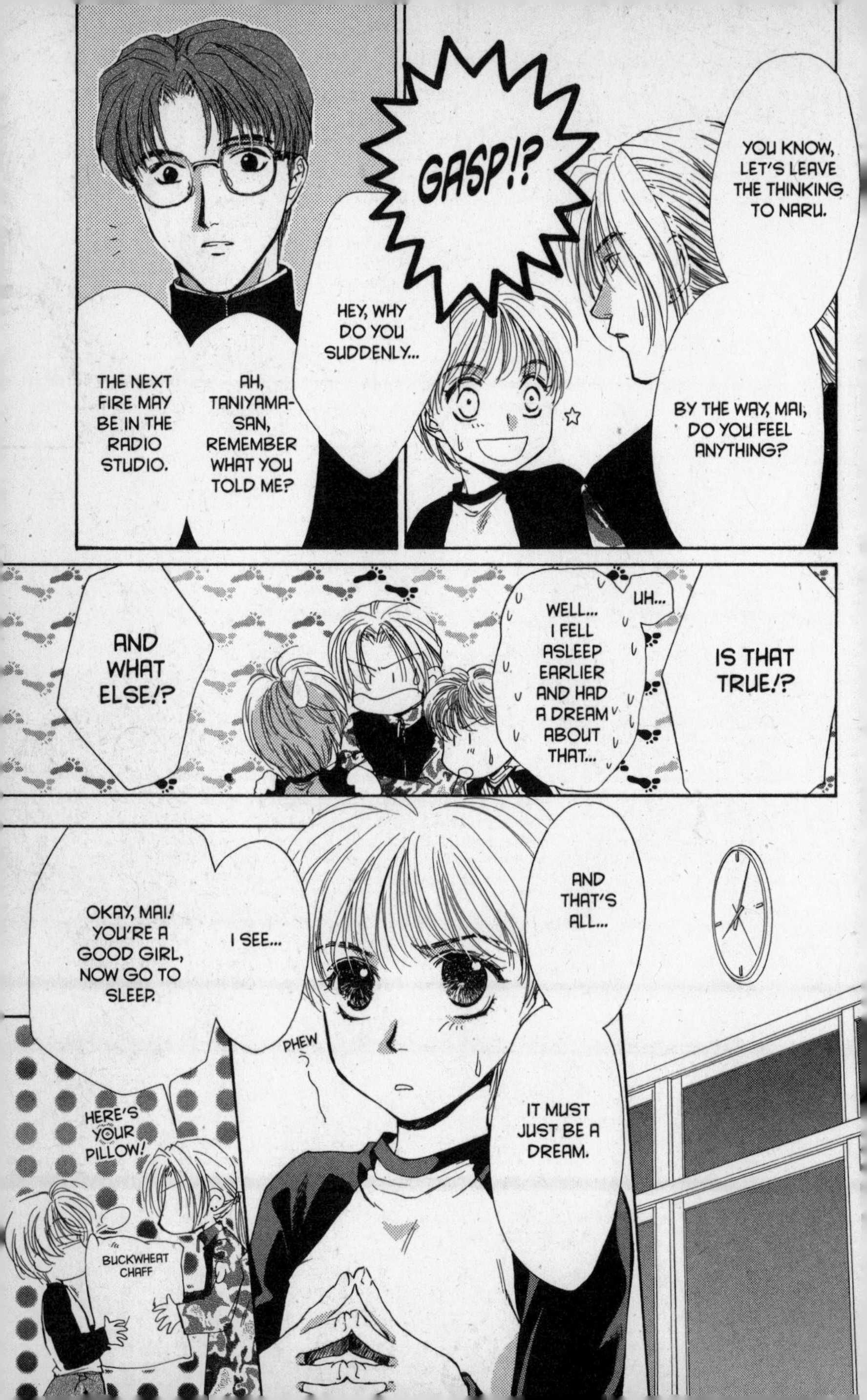
YOU KNOW, LET'S LEAVE THE THINKING TO NARU.
BY THE WAY, MAI, DO YOU FEEL ANYTHING?
GASP!?
HEY, WHY DO YOU SUDDENLY...
AH, TANIYAMA-SAN, REMEMBER WHAT YOU TOLD ME?
THE NEXT FIRE MAY BE IN THE RADIO STUDIO.
IS THAT TRUE!?
UH...
WELL... I FELL ASLEEP EARLIER AND HAD A DREAM ABOUT THAT...
AND WHAT ELSE!?
AND THAT'S ALL...
IT MUST JUST BE A DREAM.
I SEE...
OKAY, MAI! YOU'RE A GOOD GIRL, NOW GO TO SLEEP.
PHEW
HERE'S YOUR PILLOW!
BUCKWHEAT CHAFF

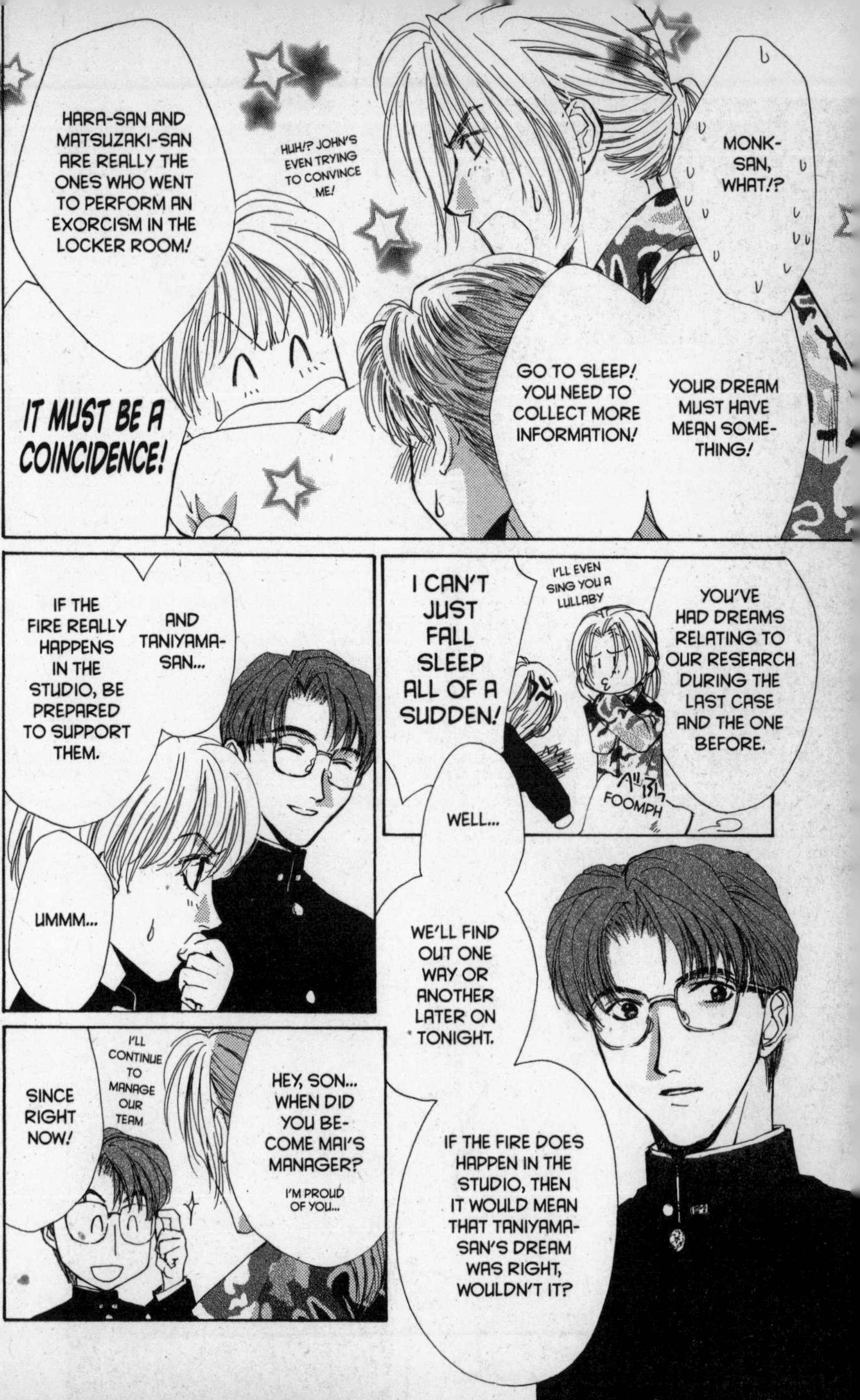
MONK-SAN, WHAT!?
YOUR DREAM MUST HAVE MEAN SOME-THING!
GO TO SLEEP! YOU NEED TO COLLECT MORE INFORMATION!
HUH!? JOHN'S EVEN TRYING TO CONVINCE ME!
HARA-SAN AND MATSUZAKI-SAN ARE REALLY THE ONES WHO WENT TO PERFORM AN EXORCISM IN THE LOCKER ROOM!
IT MUST BE A COINCIDENCE!
YOU'VE HAD DREAMS RELATING TO OUR RESEARCH DURING THE LAST CASE AND THE ONE BEFORE.
I'LL EVEN SING YOU A LULLABY
FOOMPH
I CAN'T JUST FALL SLEEP ALL OF A SUDDEN!
WELL...
WE'LL FIND OUT ONE WAY OR ANOTHER LATER ON TONIGHT.
IF THE FIRE DOES HAPPEN IN THE STUDIO, THEN IT WOULD MEAN THAT TANIYAMA-SAN'S DREAM WAS RIGHT, WOULDN'T IT?
AND TANIYAMA-SAN...
IF THE FIRE REALLY HAPPENS IN THE STUDIO, BE PREPARED TO SUPPORT THEM.
UMMM...
HEY, SON... WHEN DID YOU BE-COME MAI'S MANAGER?
I'M PROUD OF YOU...
I'LL CONTINUE TO MANAGE OUR TEAM
SINCE RIGHT NOW!

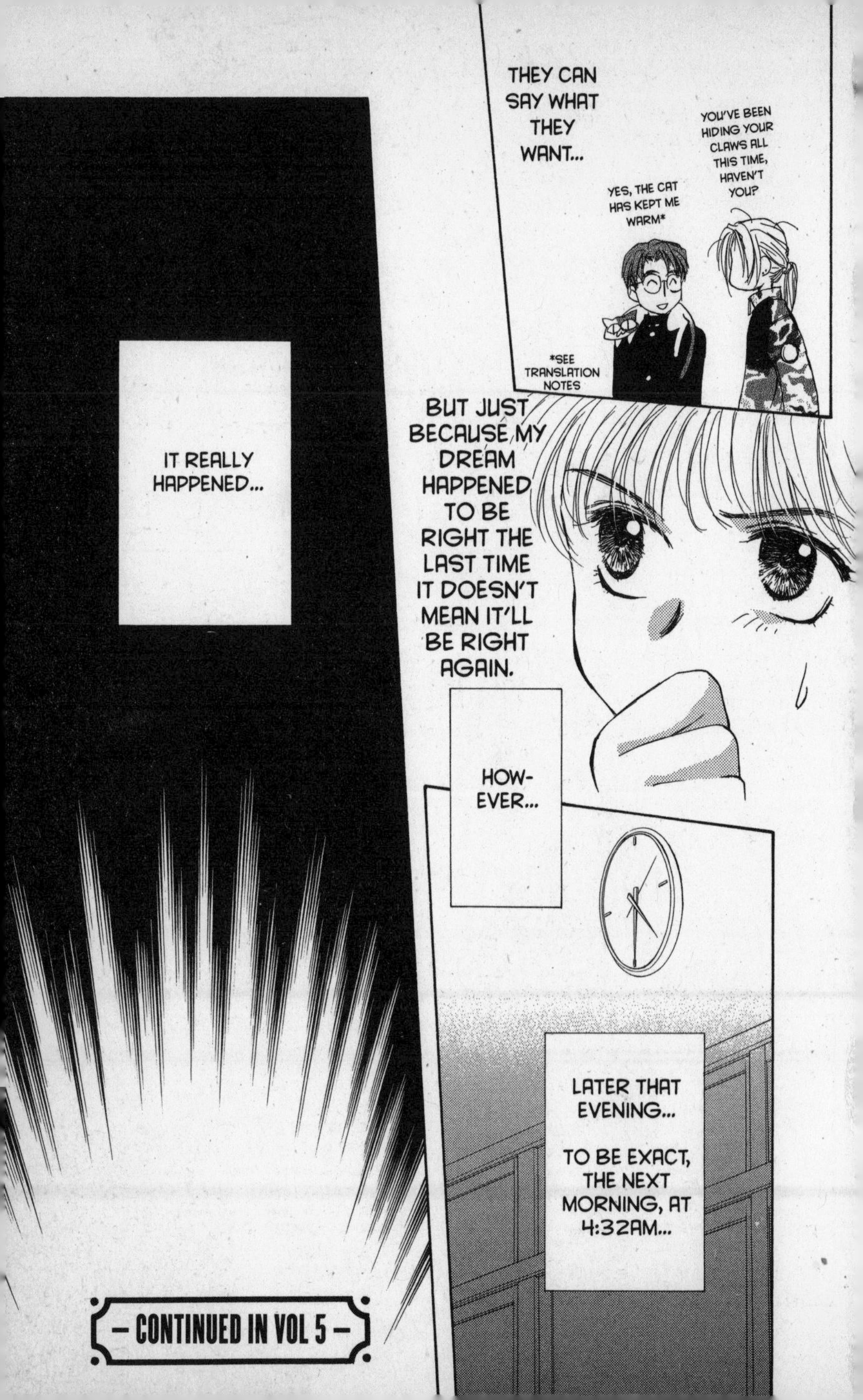
THEY CAN SAY WHAT THEY WANT...
YOU'VE BEEN HIDING YOUR CLAWS ALL THIS TIME, HAVEN'T YOU?
YES, THE CAT HAS KEPT ME WARM*
*SEE TRANSLATION NOTES
BUT JUST BECAUSE MY DREAM HAPPENED TO BE RIGHT THE LAST TIME IT DOESN'T MEAN IT'LL BE RIGHT AGAIN.
HOW-EVER...
LATER THAT EVENING...
TO BE EXACT, THE NEXT MORNING, AT 4:32AM...
IT REALLY HAPPENED...
– CONTINUED IN VOL 5 –

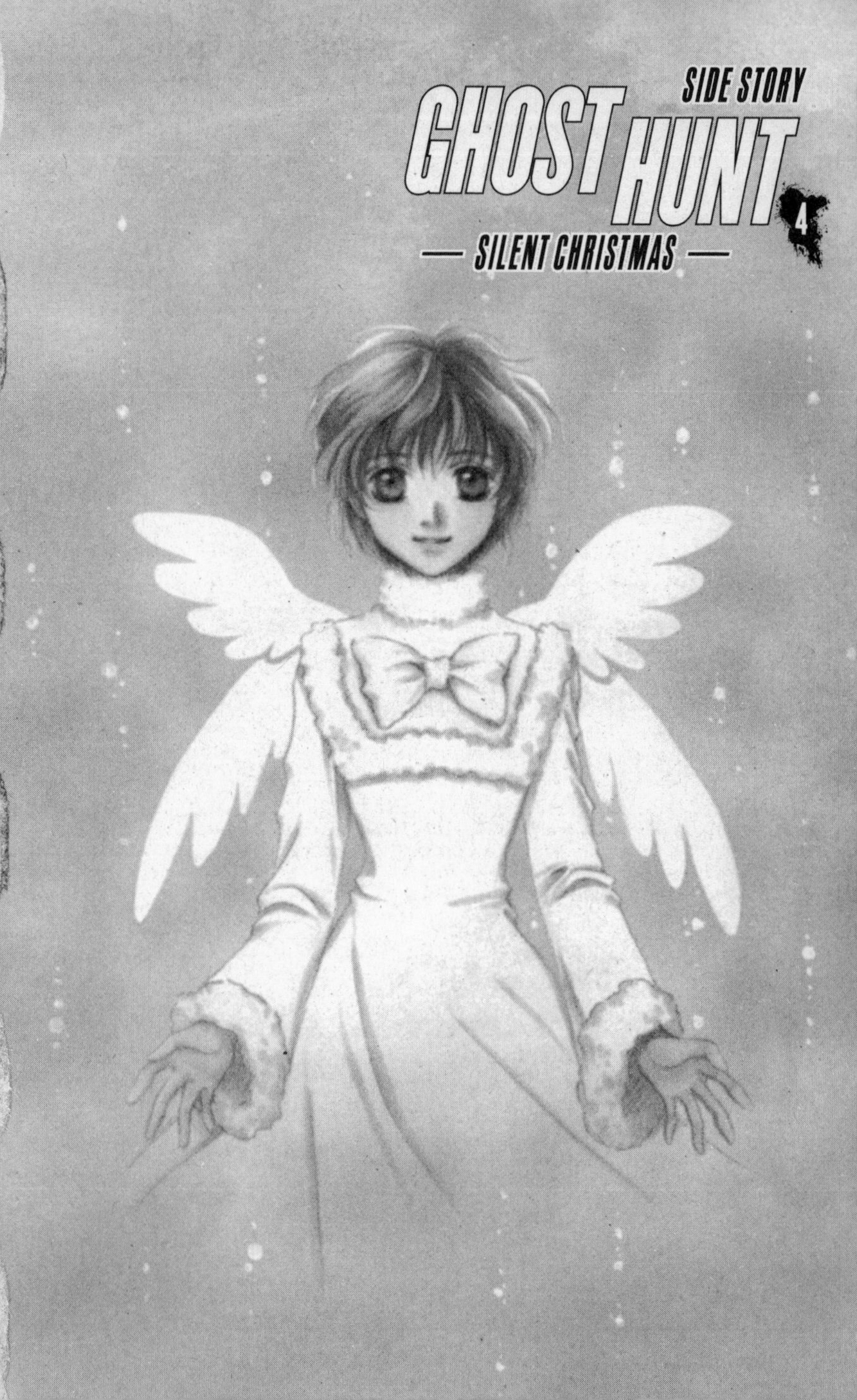
SIDE STORY
GHOST HUNT
4
— SILENT CHRISTMAS —

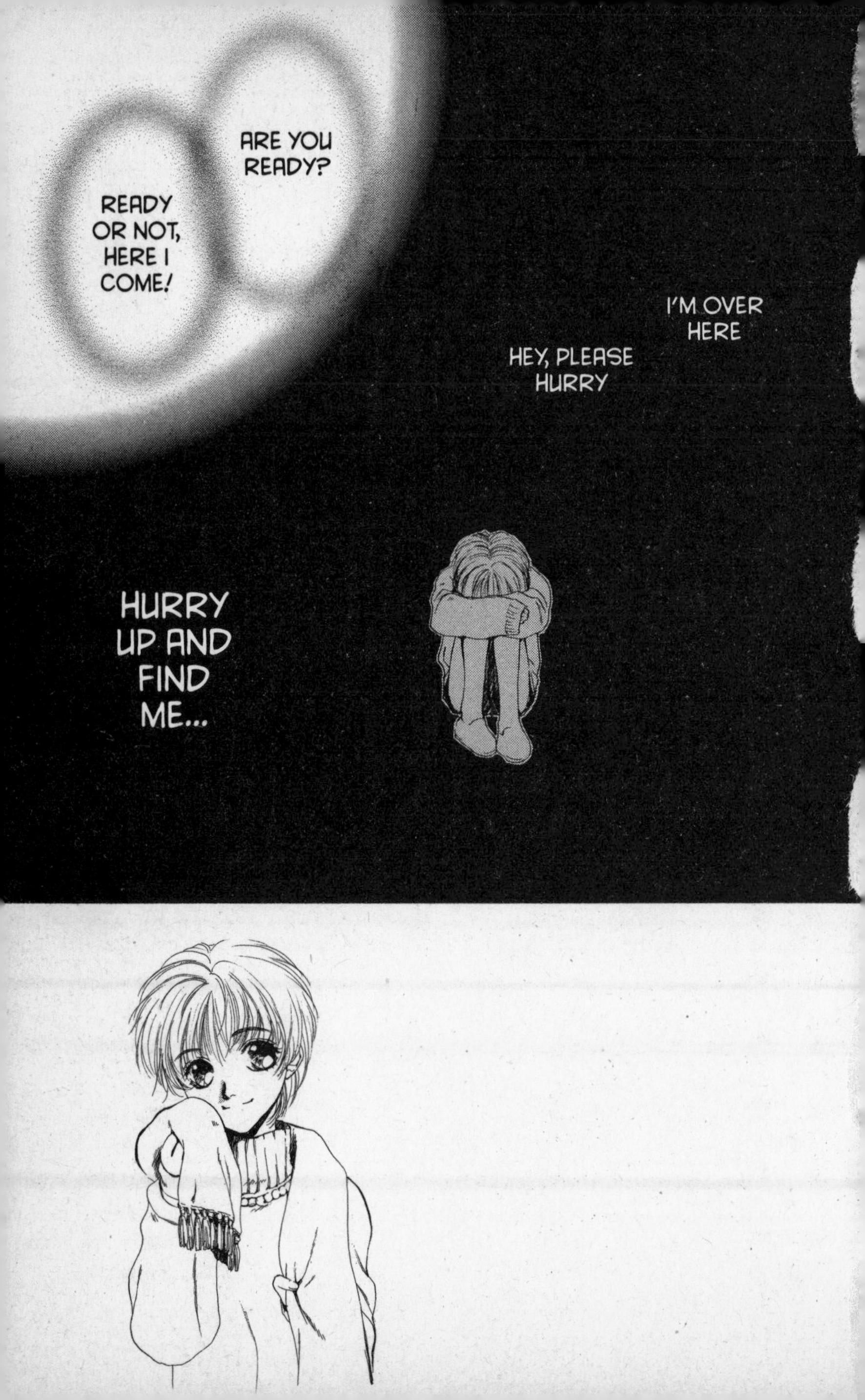
ARE YOU READY?
READY OR NOT, HERE I COME!
I'M OVER HERE
HEY, PLEASE HURRY
HURRY UP AND FIND ME...

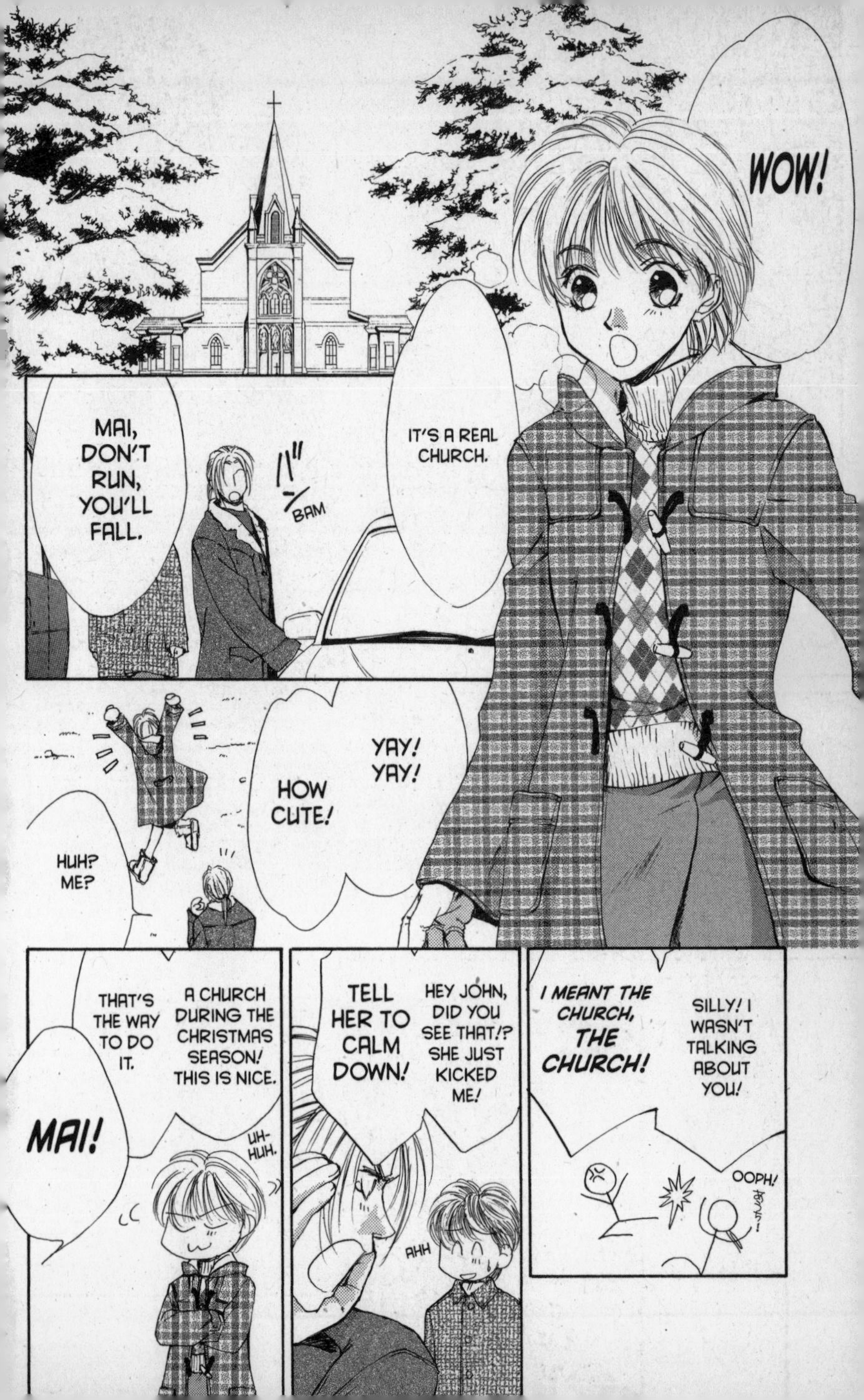
WOW!
IT'S A REAL CHURCH.
MAI, DON'T RUN, YOU'LL FALL.
BAM
YAY! YAY!
HOW CUTE!
HUH? ME?
SILLY! I WASN'T TALKING ABOUT YOU!
I MEANT THE CHURCH, THE CHURCH!
OOPH!
HEY JOHN, DID YOU SEE THAT!? SHE JUST KICKED ME!
TELL HER TO CALM DOWN!
AHH
A CHURCH DURING THE CHRISTMAS SEASON! THIS IS NICE.
THAT'S THE WAY TO DO IT.
UH-HUH.
MAI!

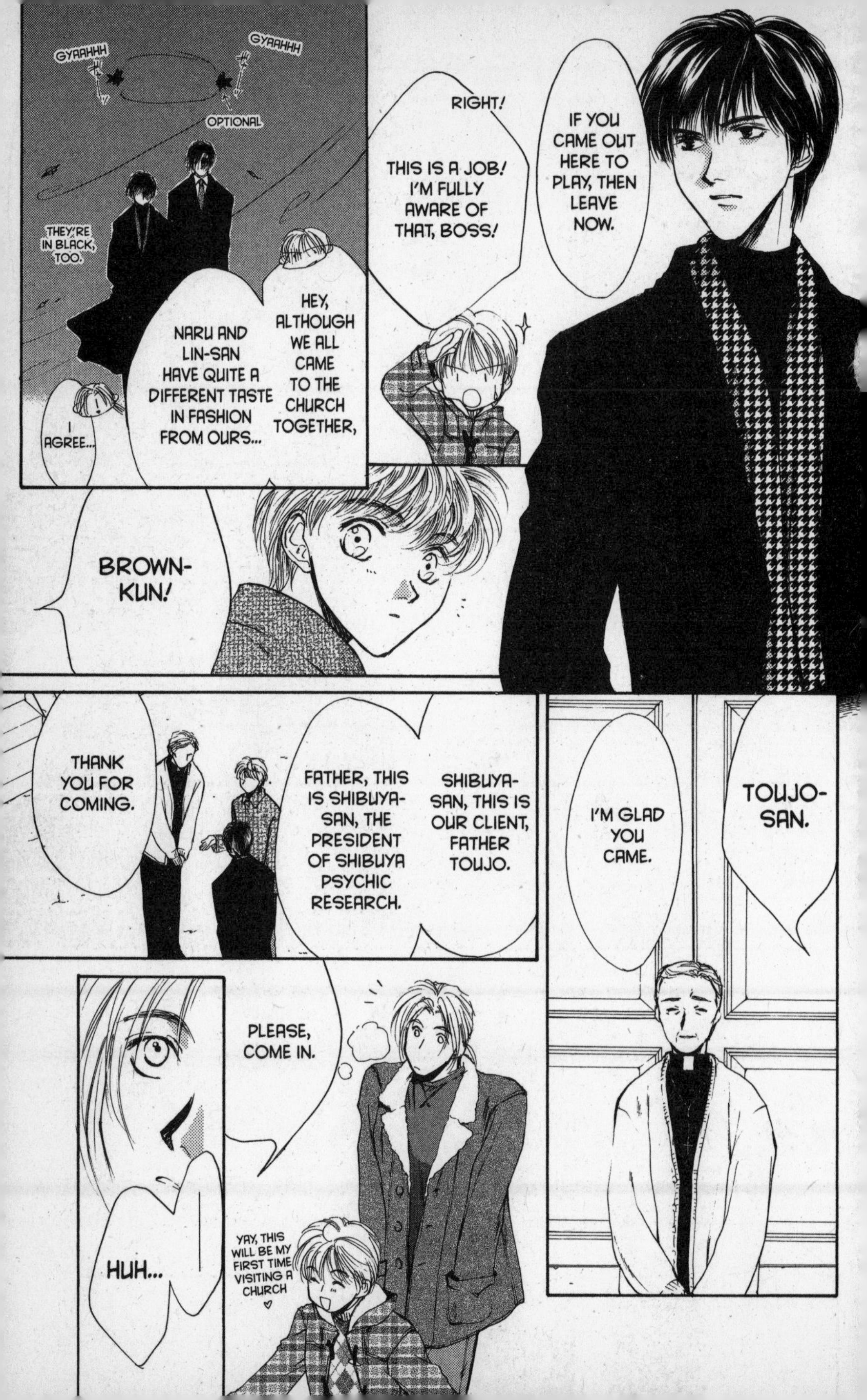
IF YOU CAME OUT HERE TO PLAY, THEN LEAVE NOW.
RIGHT!
THIS IS A JOB! I'M FULLY AWARE OF THAT, BOSS!
GYAAHHH
GYAAHHH
OPTIONAL
THEY'RE IN BLACK, TOO.
HEY, ALTHOUGH WE ALL CAME TO THE CHURCH TOGETHER,
NARU AND LIN-SAN HAVE QUITE A DIFFERENT TASTE IN FASHION FROM OURS...
I AGREE...
BROWN-KUN!
TOUJO-SAN.
I'M GLAD YOU CAME.
SHIBUYA-SAN, THIS IS OUR CLIENT, FATHER TOUJO.
FATHER, THIS IS SHIBUYA-SAN, THE PRESIDENT OF SHIBUYA PSYCHIC RESEARCH.
THANK YOU FOR COMING.
PLEASE, COME IN.
YAY, THIS WILL BE MY FIRST TIME VISITING A CHURCH ♡
HUH...

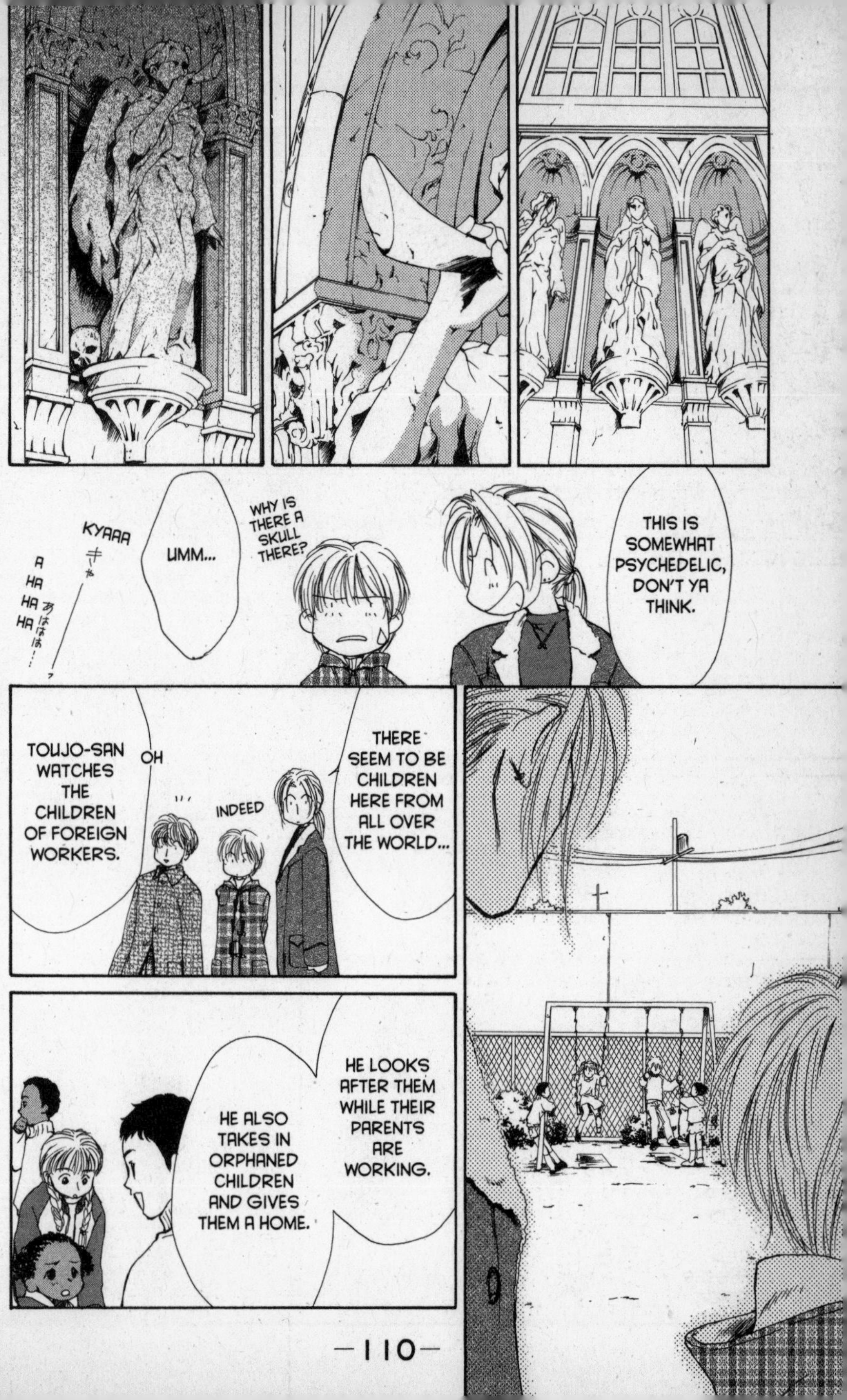
THIS IS SOMEWHAT PSYCHEDELIC, DON'T YA THINK.
WHY IS THERE A SKULL THERE?
UMM...
KYAAA キャ
A HA HA HA あははは…
THERE SEEM TO BE CHILDREN HERE FROM ALL OVER THE WORLD...
INDEED
OH
TOUJO-SAN WATCHES THE CHILDREN OF FOREIGN WORKERS.
HE LOOKS AFTER THEM WHILE THEIR PARENTS ARE WORKING.
HE ALSO TAKES IN ORPHANED CHILDREN AND GIVES THEM A HOME.

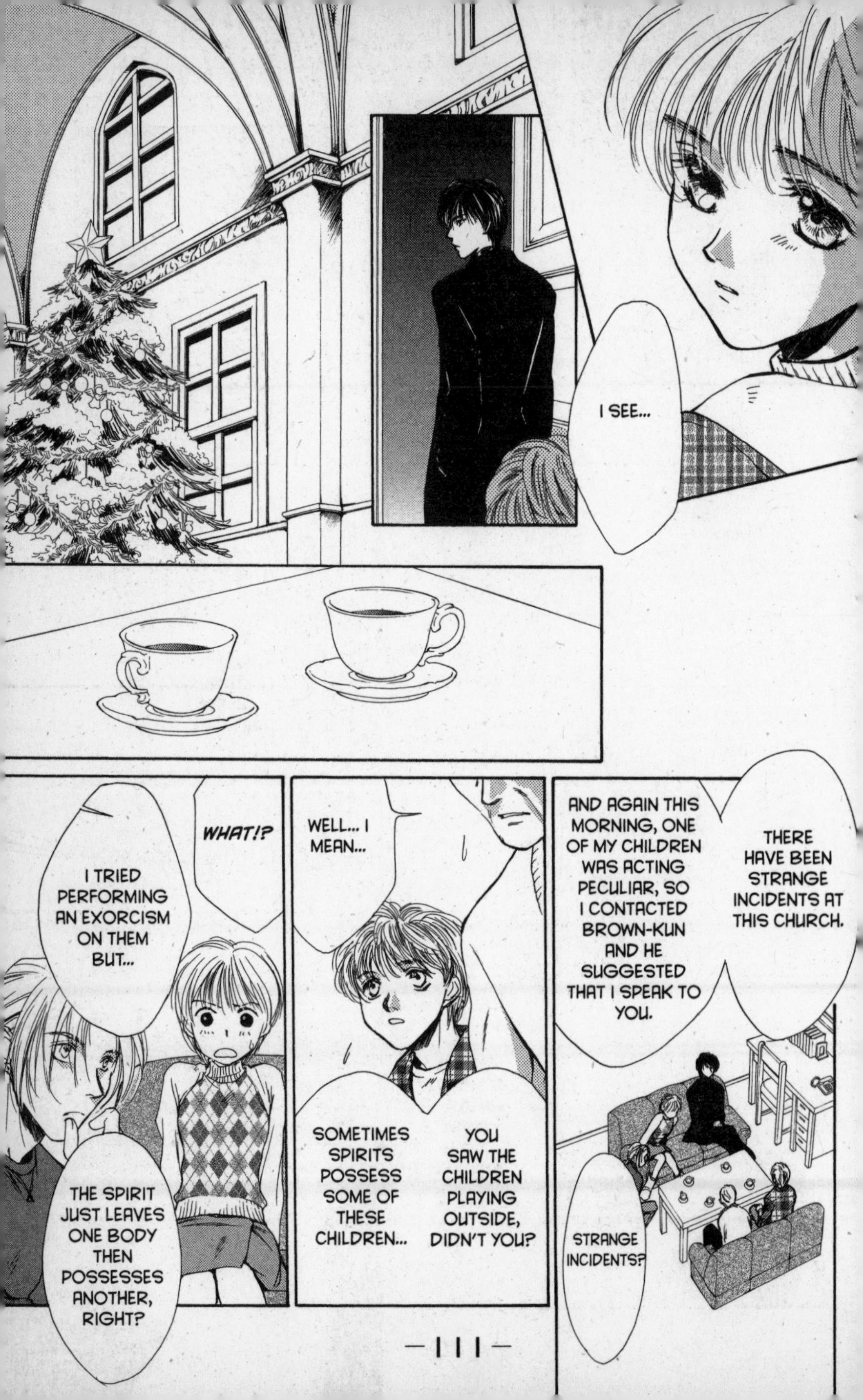
I SEE...
THERE HAVE BEEN STRANGE INCIDENTS AT THIS CHURCH.
AND AGAIN THIS MORNING, ONE OF MY CHILDREN WAS ACTING PECULIAR, SO I CONTACTED BROWN-KUN AND HE SUGGESTED THAT I SPEAK TO YOU.
STRANGE INCIDENTS?
WELL... I MEAN...
YOU SAW THE CHILDREN PLAYING OUTSIDE, DIDN'T YOU?
SOMETIMES SPIRITS POSSESS SOME OF THESE CHILDREN...
WHAT!?
I TRIED PERFORMING AN EXORCISM ON THEM BUT...
THE SPIRIT JUST LEAVES ONE BODY THEN POSSESSES ANOTHER, RIGHT?

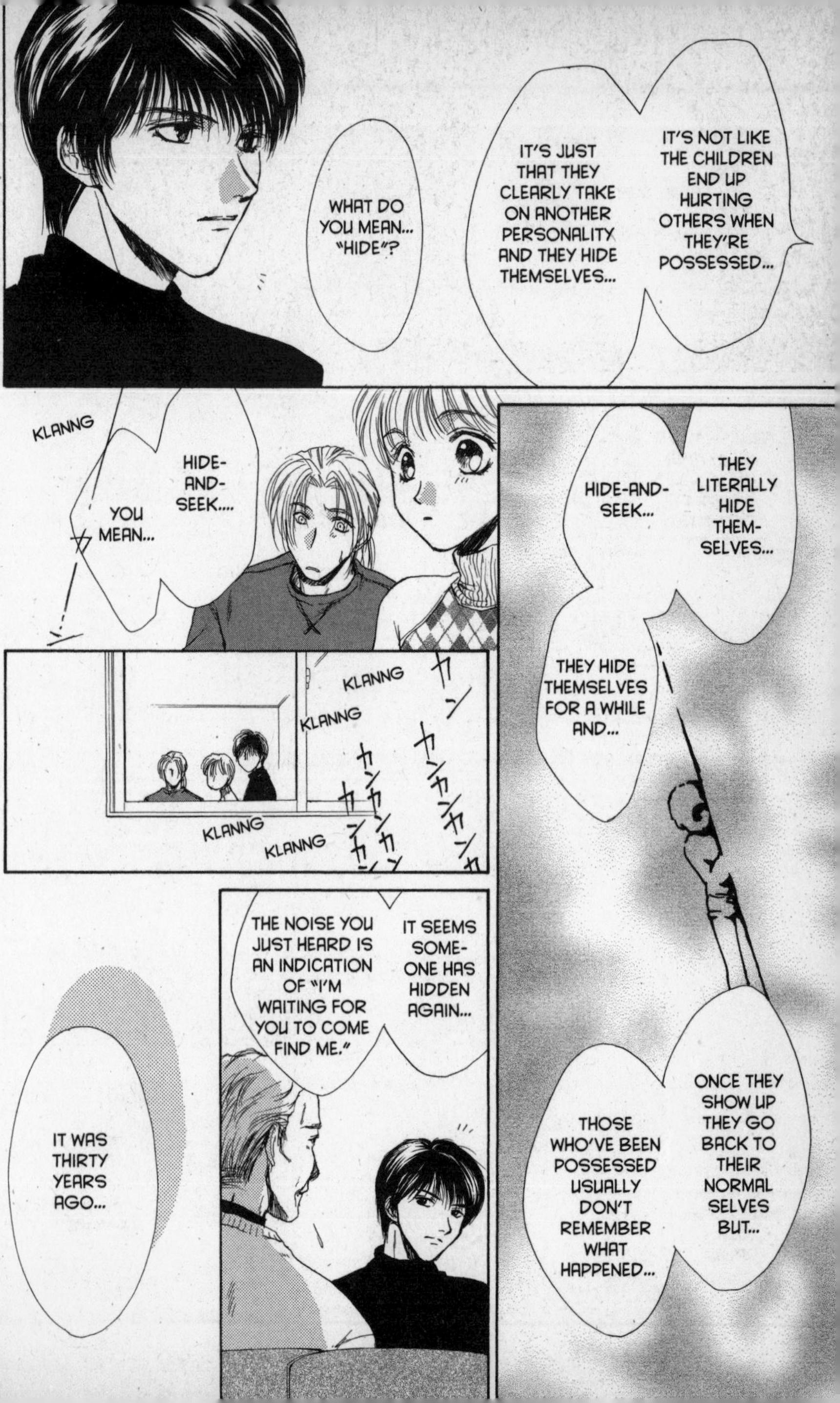
IT'S NOT LIKE THE CHILDREN END UP HURTING OTHERS WHEN THEY'RE POSSESSED...
IT'S JUST THAT THEY CLEARLY TAKE ON ANOTHER PERSONALITY AND THEY HIDE THEMSELVES...
WHAT DO YOU MEAN... "HIDE"?
THEY LITERALLY HIDE THEM-SELVES...
HIDE-AND-SEEK...
THEY HIDE THEMSELVES FOR A WHILE AND...
ONCE THEY SHOW UP THEY GO BACK TO THEIR NORMAL SELVES BUT...
THOSE WHO'VE BEEN POSSESSED USUALLY DON'T REMEMBER WHAT HAPPENED...
HIDE-AND-SEEK....
YOU MEAN...
KLANNG
KLANNG
KLANNG
KLANNG
KLANNG
IT SEEMS SOME-ONE HAS HIDDEN AGAIN...
THE NOISE YOU JUST HEARD IS AN INDICATION OF "I'M WAITING FOR YOU TO COME FIND ME."
IT WAS THIRTY YEARS AGO...

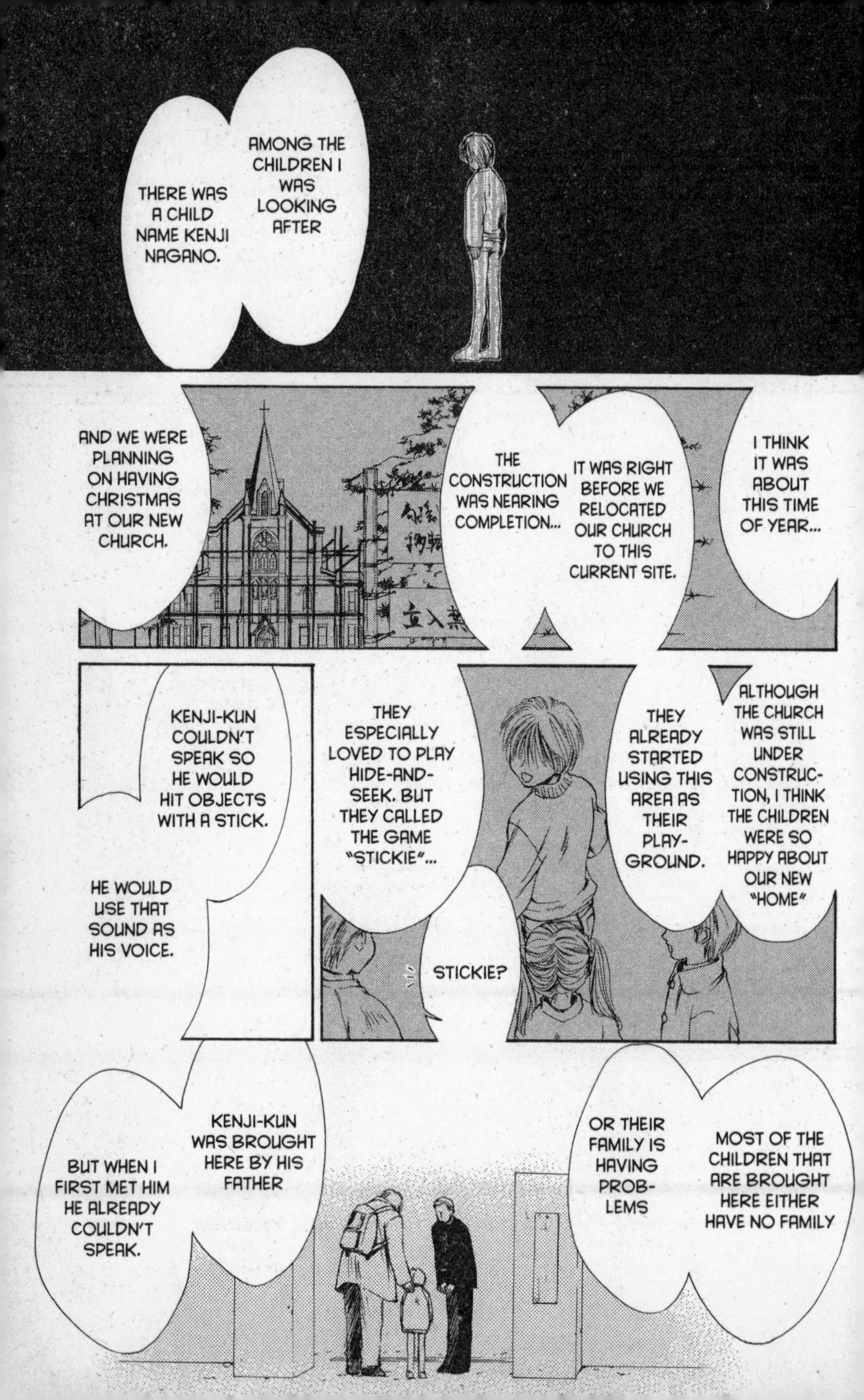
AMONG THE CHILDREN I WAS LOOKING AFTER
THERE WAS A CHILD NAME KENJI NAGANO.
I THINK IT WAS ABOUT THIS TIME OF YEAR...
IT WAS RIGHT BEFORE WE RELOCATED OUR CHURCH TO THIS CURRENT SITE.
THE CONSTRUCTION WAS NEARING COMPLETION...
AND WE WERE PLANNING ON HAVING CHRISTMAS AT OUR NEW CHURCH.
ALTHOUGH THE CHURCH WAS STILL UNDER CONSTRUC-TION, I THINK THE CHILDREN WERE SO HAPPY ABOUT OUR NEW "HOME"
THEY ALREADY STARTED USING THIS AREA AS THEIR PLAY-GROUND.
THEY ESPECIALLY LOVED TO PLAY HIDE-AND-SEEK. BUT THEY CALLED THE GAME "STICKIE"...
STICKIE?
KENJI-KUN COULDN'T SPEAK SO HE WOULD HIT OBJECTS WITH A STICK.
HE WOULD USE THAT SOUND AS HIS VOICE.
MOST OF THE CHILDREN THAT ARE BROUGHT HERE EITHER HAVE NO FAMILY
OR THEIR FAMILY IS HAVING PROB-LEMS
KENJI-KUN WAS BROUGHT HERE BY HIS FATHER
BUT WHEN I FIRST MET HIM HE ALREADY COULDN'T SPEAK.

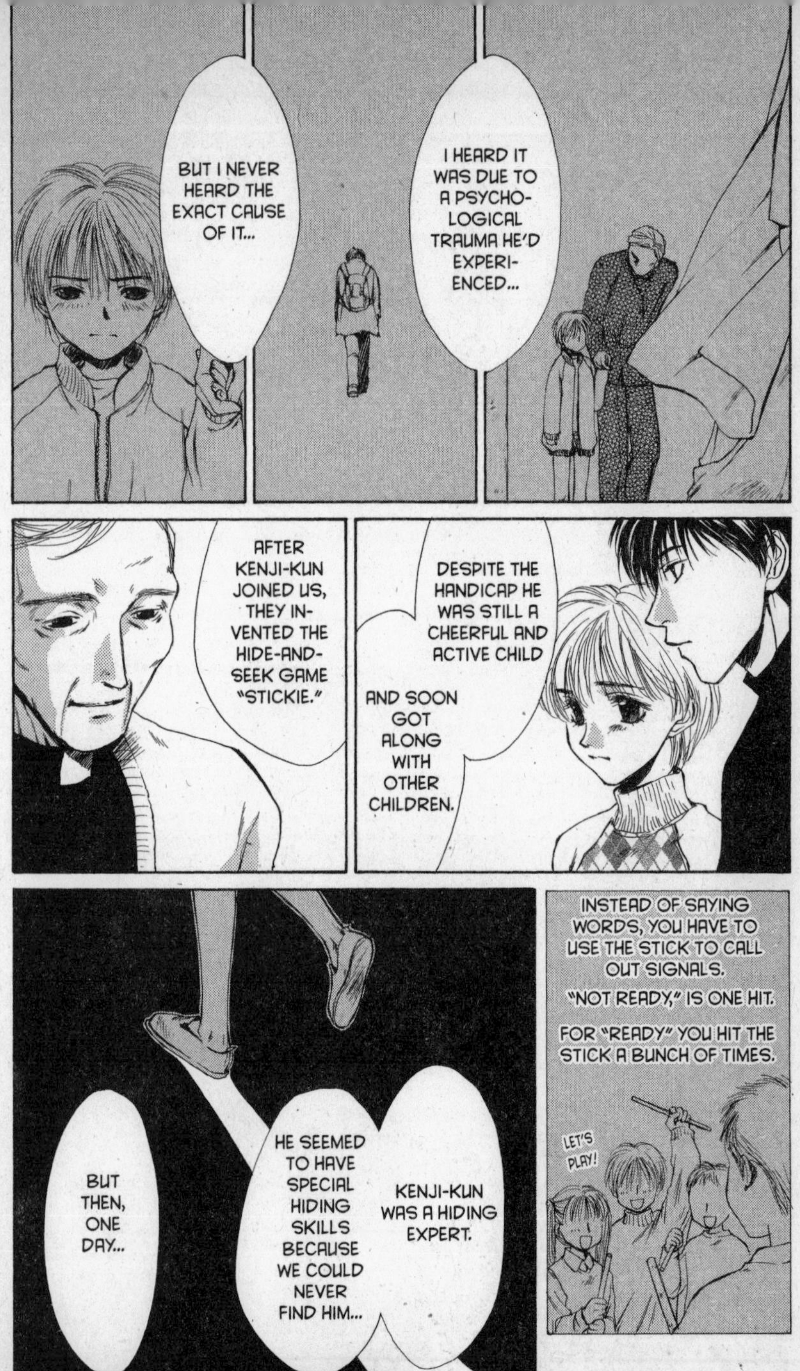
I HEARD IT WAS DUE TO A PSYCHO-LOGICAL TRAUMA HE'D EXPERI-ENCED...
BUT I NEVER HEARD THE EXACT CAUSE OF IT...
DESPITE THE HANDICAP HE WAS STILL A CHEERFUL AND ACTIVE CHILD
AND SOON GOT ALONG WITH OTHER CHILDREN.
AFTER KENJI-KUN JOINED US, THEY IN-VENTED THE HIDE-AND-SEEK GAME "STICKIE."
INSTEAD OF SAYING WORDS, YOU HAVE TO USE THE STICK TO CALL OUT SIGNALS.
"NOT READY," IS ONE HIT.
FOR "READY" YOU HIT THE STICK A BUNCH OF TIMES.
LET'S PLAY!
KENJI-KUN WAS A HIDING EXPERT.
HE SEEMED TO HAVE SPECIAL HIDING SKILLS BECAUSE WE COULD NEVER FIND HIM...
BUT THEN, ONE DAY...

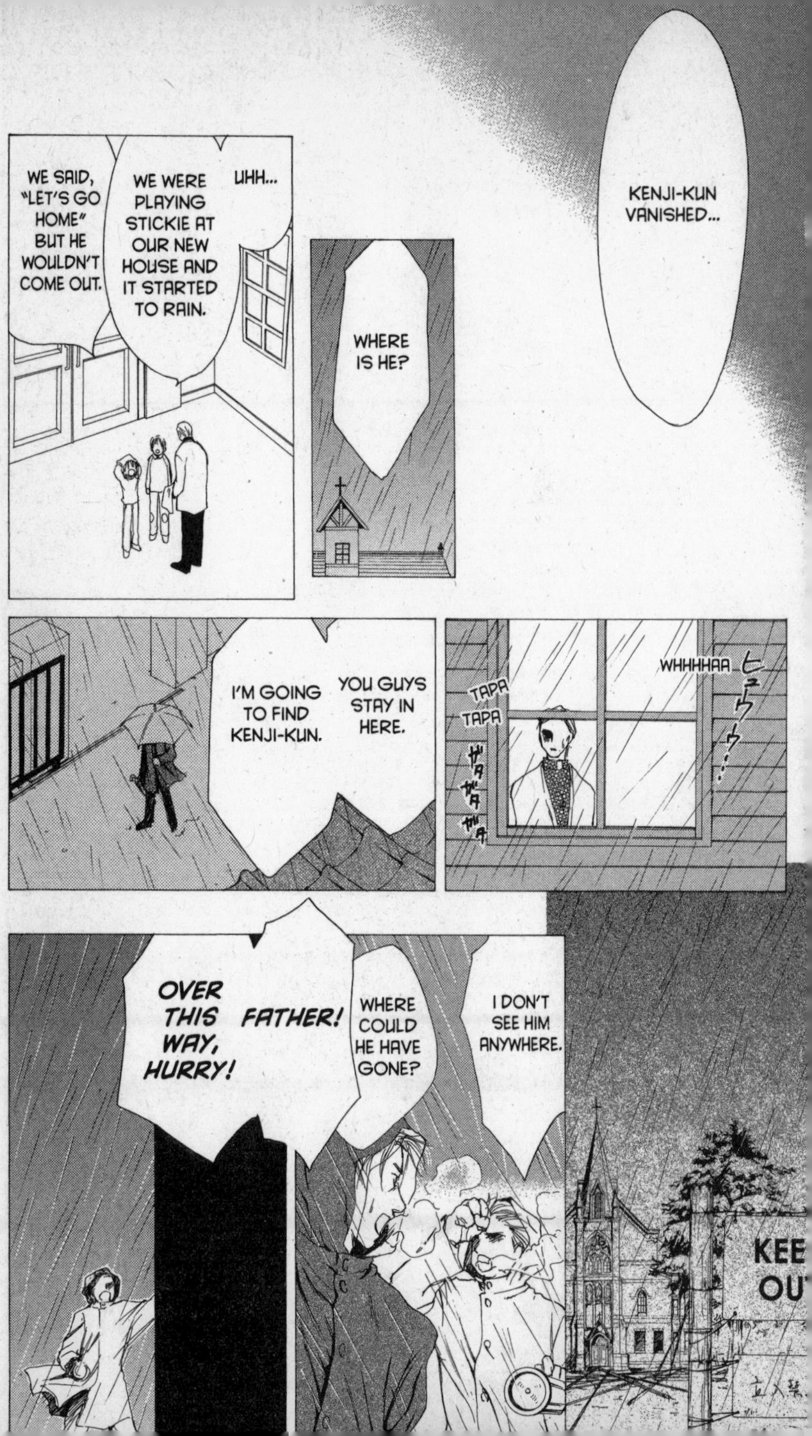
KENJI-KUN VANISHED...
WHERE IS HE?
UHH...
WE WERE PLAYING STICKIE AT OUR NEW HOUSE AND IT STARTED TO RAIN.
WE SAID, "LET'S GO HOME" BUT HE WOULDN'T COME OUT.
WHHHHAA ヒュウゥ...
TAPA TAPA
ガタガタガタ
YOU GUYS STAY IN HERE.
I'M GOING TO FIND KENJI-KUN.
KEE
OU
I DON'T SEE HIM ANYWHERE.
WHERE COULD HE HAVE GONE?
FATHER!
OVER THIS WAY, HURRY!

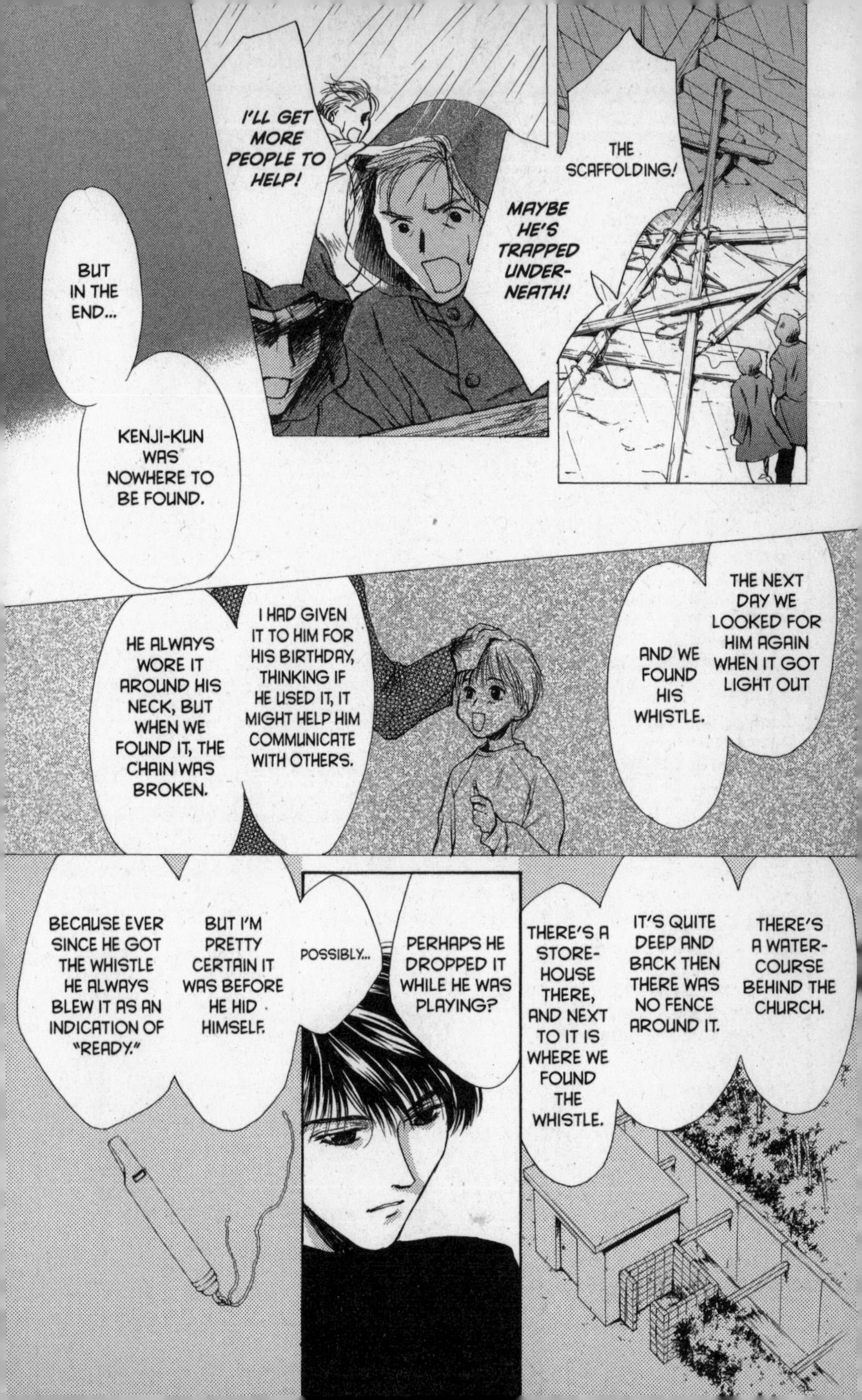
THE SCAFFOLDING!
MAYBE HE'S TRAPPED UNDER-NEATH!
I'LL GET MORE PEOPLE TO HELP!
BUT IN THE END...
KENJI-KUN WAS NOWHERE TO BE FOUND.
THE NEXT DAY WE LOOKED FOR HIM AGAIN WHEN IT GOT LIGHT OUT
AND WE FOUND HIS WHISTLE.
I HAD GIVEN IT TO HIM FOR HIS BIRTHDAY, THINKING IF HE USED IT, IT MIGHT HELP HIM COMMUNICATE WITH OTHERS.
HE ALWAYS WORE IT AROUND HIS NECK, BUT WHEN WE FOUND IT, THE CHAIN WAS BROKEN.
THERE'S A WATER-COURSE BEHIND THE CHURCH.
IT'S QUITE DEEP AND BACK THEN THERE WAS NO FENCE AROUND IT.
THERE'S A STORE-HOUSE THERE, AND NEXT TO IT IS WHERE WE FOUND THE WHISTLE.
PERHAPS HE DROPPED IT WHILE HE WAS PLAYING?
POSSIBLY...
BUT I'M PRETTY CERTAIN IT WAS BEFORE HE HID HIMSELF.
BECAUSE EVER SINCE HE GOT THE WHISTLE HE ALWAYS BLEW IT AS AN INDICATION OF "READY."

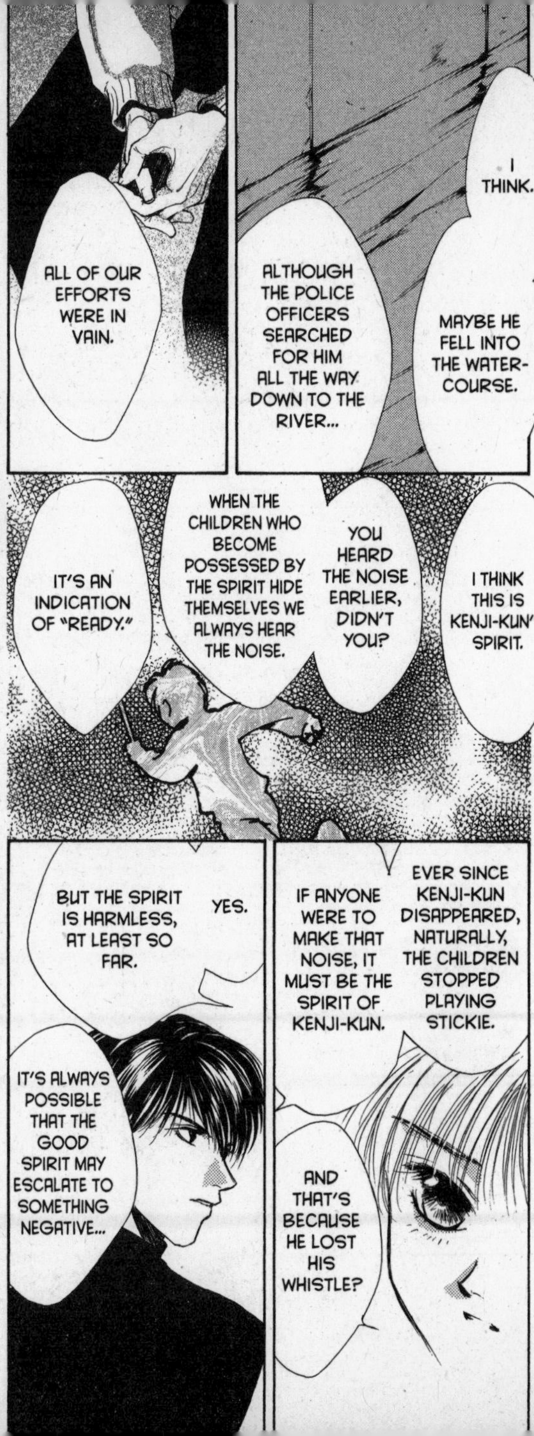
I THINK...
MAYBE HE FELL INTO THE WATER-COURSE.
ALTHOUGH THE POLICE OFFICERS SEARCHED FOR HIM ALL THE WAY DOWN TO THE RIVER...
ALL OF OUR EFFORTS WERE IN VAIN.
I THINK THIS IS KENJI-KUN'S SPIRIT.
YOU HEARD THE NOISE EARLIER, DIDN'T YOU?
WHEN THE CHILDREN WHO BECOME POSSESSED BY THE SPIRIT HIDE THEMSELVES WE ALWAYS HEAR THE NOISE.
IT'S AN INDICATION OF "READY."
EVER SINCE KENJI-KUN DISAPPEARED, NATURALLY, THE CHILDREN STOPPED PLAYING STICKIE.
IF ANYONE WERE TO MAKE THAT NOISE, IT MUST BE THE SPIRIT OF KENJI-KUN.
AND THAT'S BECAUSE HE LOST HIS WHISTLE?
YES.
BUT THE SPIRIT IS HARMLESS, AT LEAST SO FAR.
IT'S ALWAYS POSSIBLE THAT THE GOOD SPIRIT MAY ESCALATE TO SOMETHING NEGATIVE...

BONUS STORY... FIVE MEN TO SHARE A SIX MAT ROOM.

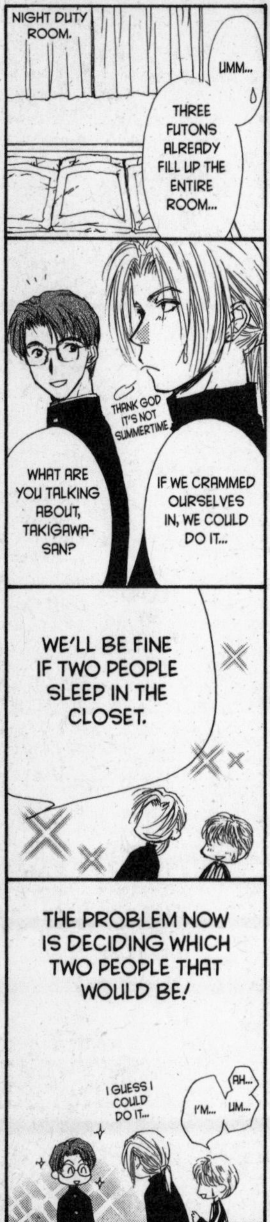
NIGHT DUTY ROOM.
UMM...
THREE FUTONS ALREADY FILL UP THE ENTIRE ROOM...
IF WE CRAMMED OURSELVES IN, WE COULD DO IT...
THANK GOD IT'S NOT SUMMERTIME
WHAT ARE YOU TALKING ABOUT, TAKIGAWA-SAN?
WE'LL BE FINE IF TWO PEOPLE SLEEP IN THE CLOSET.
THE PROBLEM NOW IS DECIDING WHICH TWO PEOPLE THAT WOULD BE!
AH...
I'M... UM...
I GUESS I COULD DO IT...

I MEAN, YOU CAN'T POSSIBLY ALL SLEEP AT ONCE THOUGH...

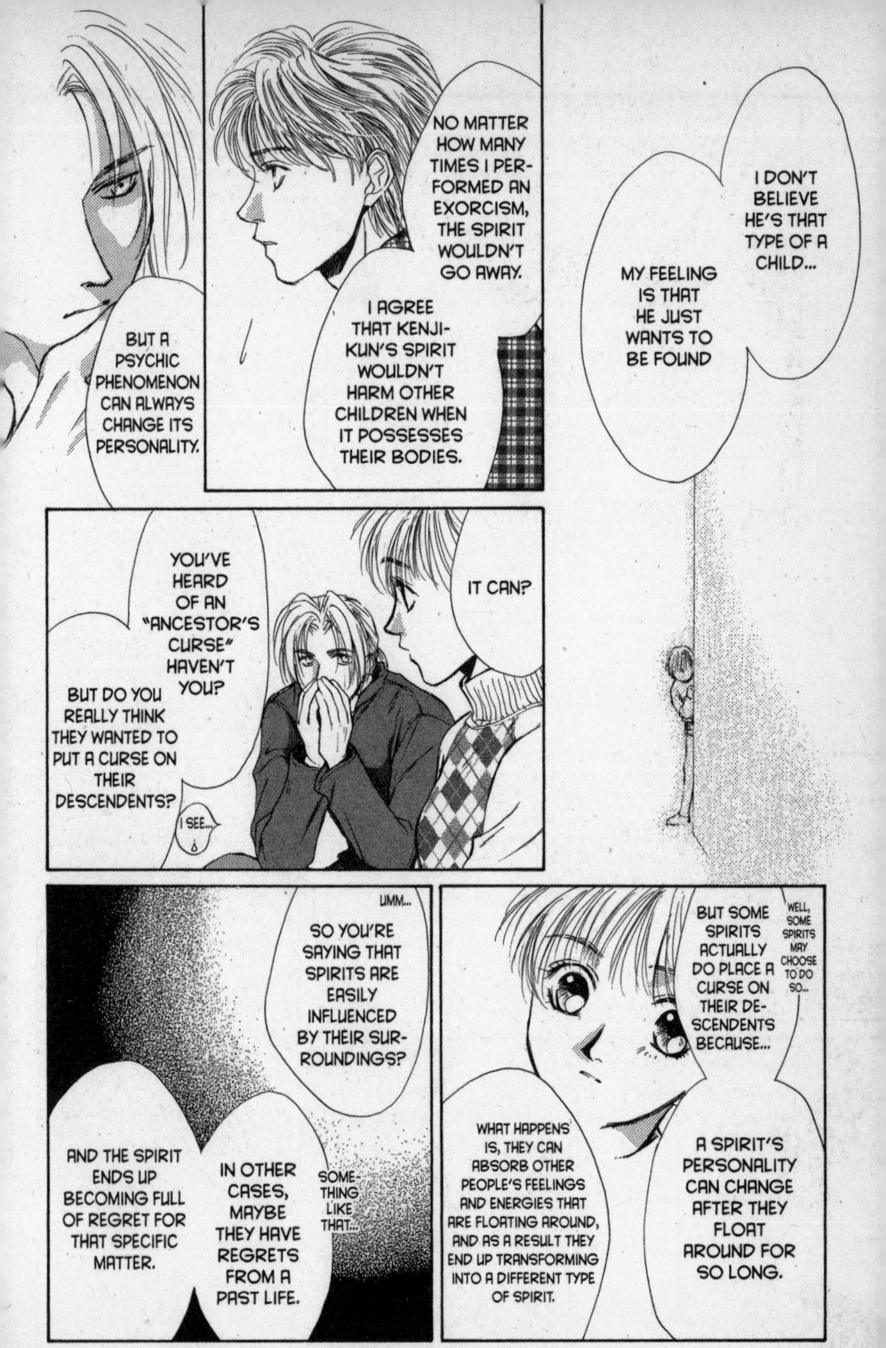
I DON'T BELIEVE HE'S THAT TYPE OF A CHILD...
MY FEELING IS THAT HE JUST WANTS TO BE FOUND
NO MATTER HOW MANY TIMES I PERFORMED AN EXORCISM, THE SPIRIT WOULDN'T GO AWAY.
I AGREE THAT KENJI-KUN'S SPIRIT WOULDN'T HARM OTHER CHILDREN WHEN IT POSSESSES THEIR BODIES.
BUT A PSYCHIC PHENOMENON CAN ALWAYS CHANGE ITS PERSONALITY.
IT CAN?
YOU'VE HEARD OF AN "ANCESTOR'S CURSE" HAVEN'T YOU?
BUT DO YOU REALLY THINK THEY WANTED TO PUT A CURSE ON THEIR DESCENDENTS?
I SEE...
WELL, SOME SPIRITS MAY CHOOSE TO DO SO...
BUT SOME SPIRITS ACTUALLY DO PLACE A CURSE ON THEIR DESCENDENTS BECAUSE...
A SPIRIT'S PERSONALITY CAN CHANGE AFTER THEY FLOAT AROUND FOR SO LONG.
WHAT HAPPENS IS, THEY CAN ABSORB OTHER PEOPLE'S FEELINGS AND ENERGIES THAT ARE FLOATING AROUND, AND AS A RESULT THEY END UP TRANSFORMING INTO A DIFFERENT TYPE OF SPIRIT.
UMM...
SO YOU'RE SAYING THAT SPIRITS ARE EASILY INFLUENCED BY THEIR SURROUNDINGS?
SOMETHING LIKE THAT...
IN OTHER CASES, MAYBE THEY HAVE REGRETS FROM A PAST LIFE.
AND THE SPIRIT ENDS UP BECOMING FULL OF REGRET FOR THAT SPECIFIC MATTER.

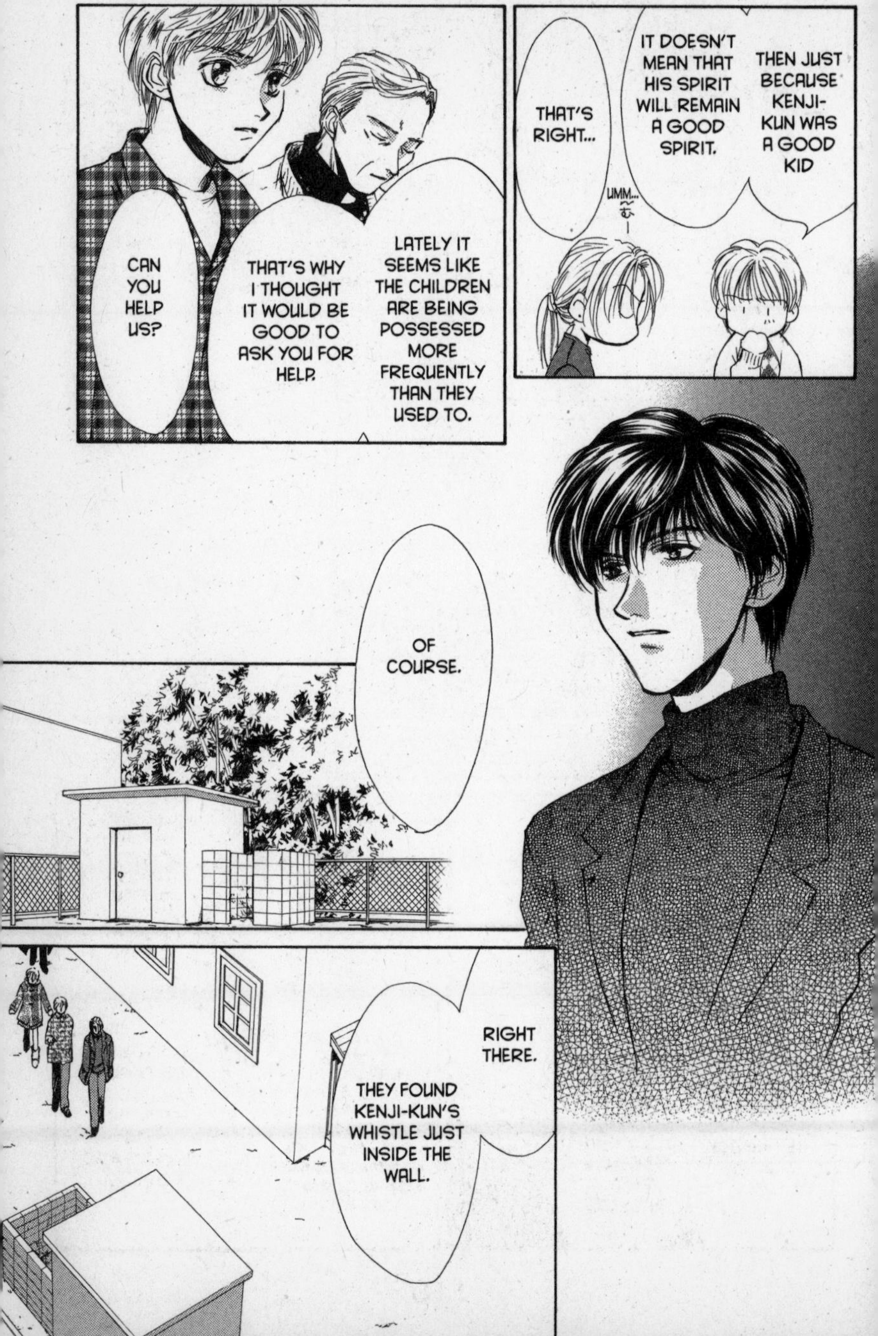
THEN JUST BECAUSE KENJI-KUN WAS A GOOD KID
IT DOESN'T MEAN THAT HIS SPIRIT WILL REMAIN A GOOD SPIRIT.
THAT'S RIGHT...
UMM...
LATELY IT SEEMS LIKE THE CHILDREN ARE BEING POSSESSED MORE FREQUENTLY THAN THEY USED TO.
THAT'S WHY I THOUGHT IT WOULD BE GOOD TO ASK YOU FOR HELP.
CAN YOU HELP US?
OF COURSE.
RIGHT THERE.
THEY FOUND KENJI-KUN'S WHISTLE JUST INSIDE THE WALL.

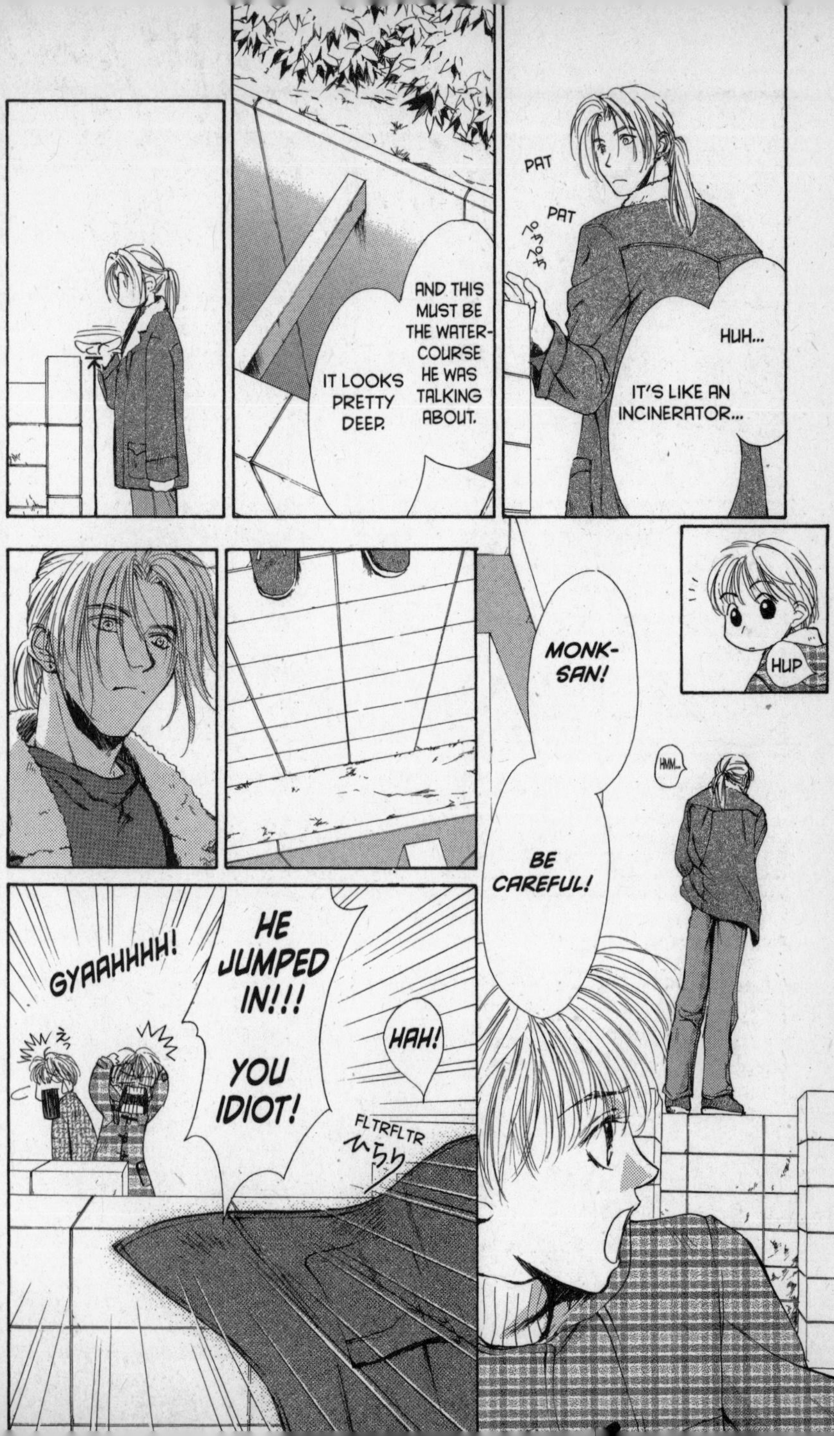
PAT
PAT
HUH...
IT'S LIKE AN INCINERATOR...
AND THIS MUST BE THE WATER-COURSE HE WAS TALKING ABOUT.
IT LOOKS PRETTY DEEP.
HUP
HMM...
MONK-SAN!
BE CAREFUL!
HE JUMPED IN!!!
YOU IDIOT!
HAH!
FLTRFLTR
ひらり
GYAAHHHH!
えっ

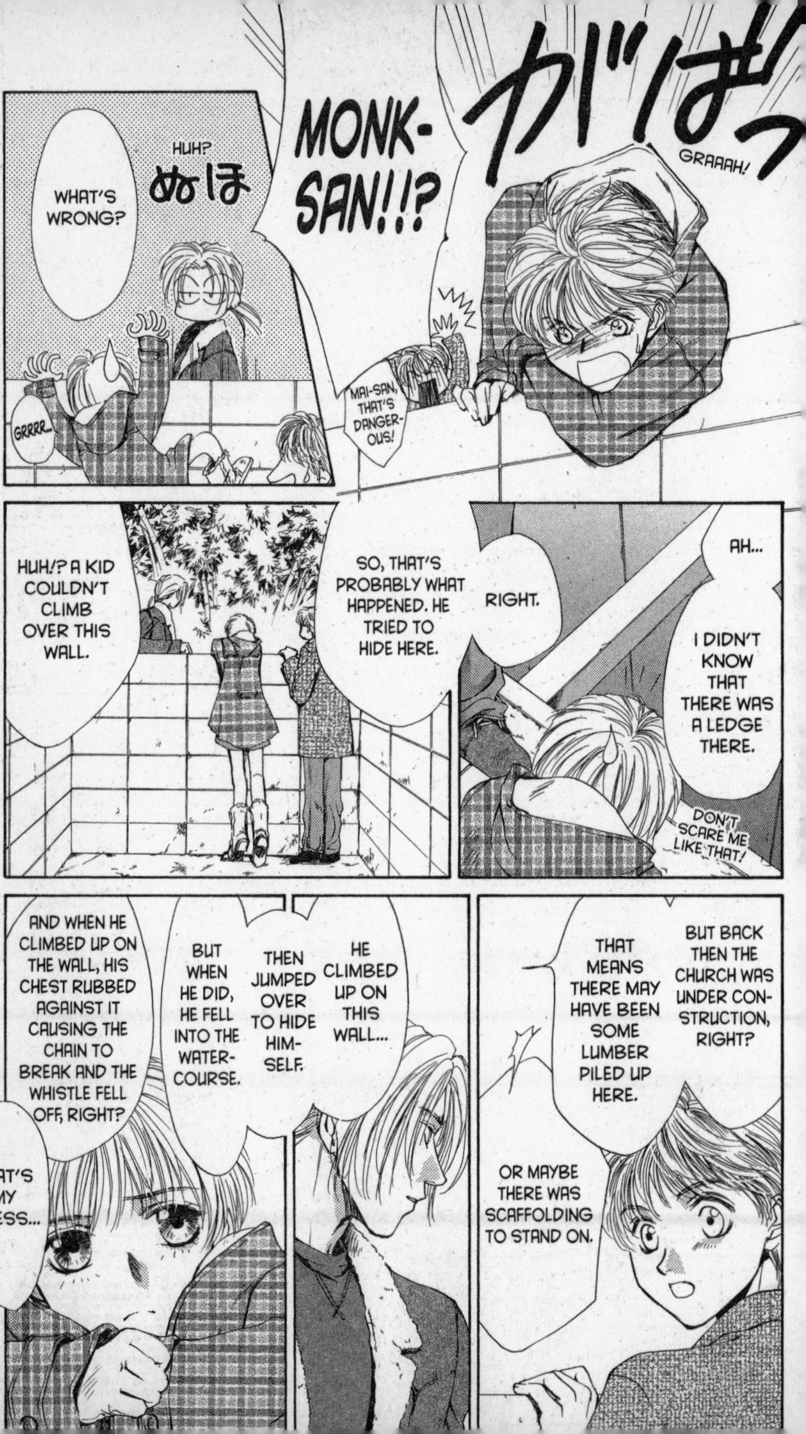
がばっ
GRAAAH!
MONK-SAN!!?
MAI-SAN, THAT'S DANGER-OUS!
HUH? ぬほ
WHAT'S WRONG?
GRRRR...
AH...
I DIDN'T KNOW THAT THERE WAS A LEDGE THERE.
RIGHT.
DON'T SCARE ME LIKE THAT!
SO, THAT'S PROBABLY WHAT HAPPENED. HE TRIED TO HIDE HERE.
HUH!? A KID COULDN'T CLIMB OVER THIS WALL.
BUT BACK THEN THE CHURCH WAS UNDER CON-STRUCTION, RIGHT?
THAT MEANS THERE MAY HAVE BEEN SOME LUMBER PILED UP HERE.
OR MAYBE THERE WAS SCAFFOLDING TO STAND ON.
HE CLIMBED UP ON THIS WALL...
THEN JUMPED OVER TO HIDE HIM-SELF.
BUT WHEN HE DID, HE FELL INTO THE WATER-COURSE.
AND WHEN HE CLIMBED UP ON THE WALL, HIS CHEST RUBBED AGAINST IT CAUSING THE CHAIN TO BREAK AND THE WHISTLE FELL OFF, RIGHT?
THAT'S MY GUESS...

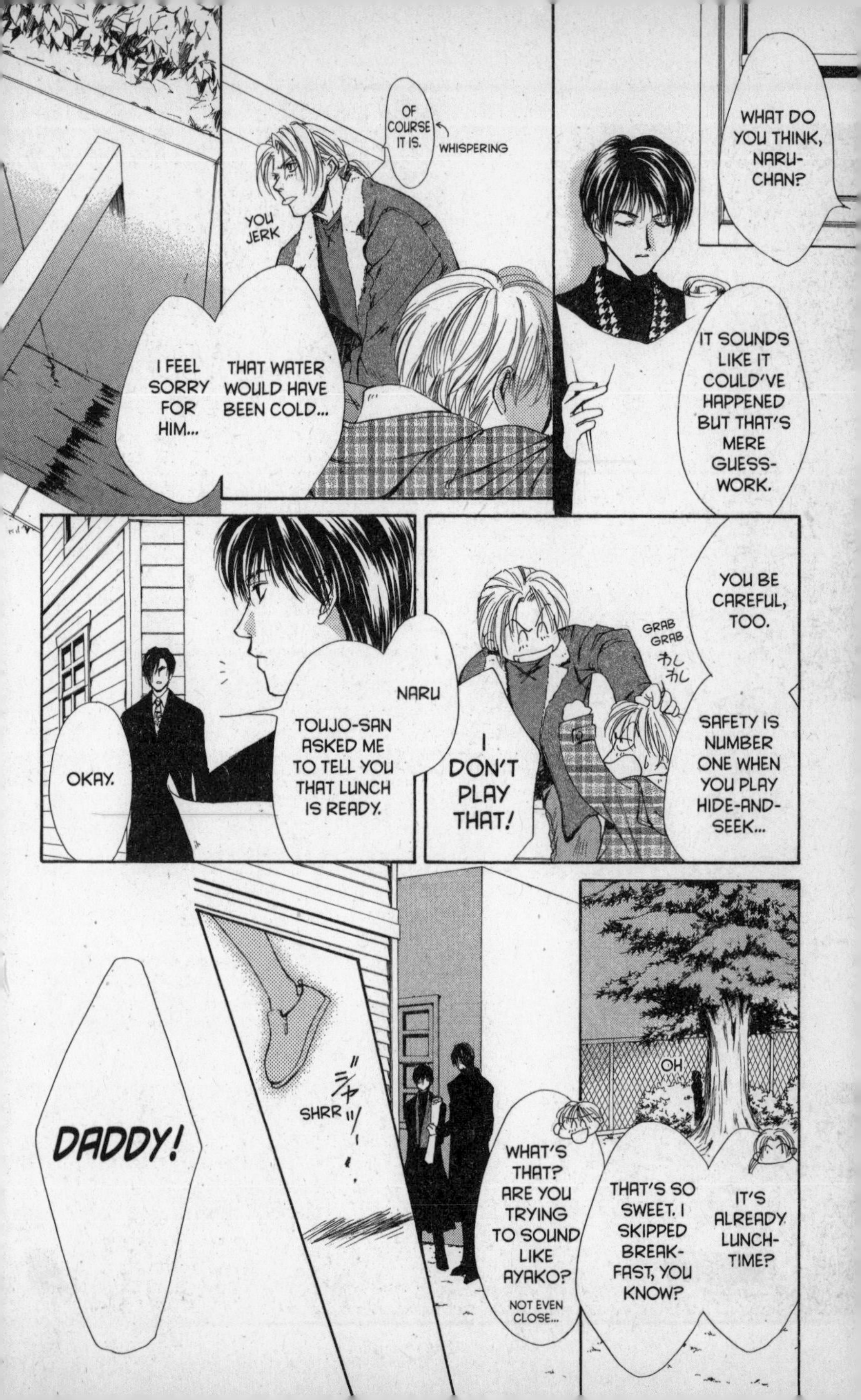
WHAT DO YOU THINK, NARU-CHAN?
IT SOUNDS LIKE IT COULD'VE HAPPENED BUT THAT'S MERE GUESS-WORK.
OF COURSE IT IS.
WHISPERING
YOU JERK
THAT WATER WOULD HAVE BEEN COLD...
I FEEL SORRY FOR HIM...
YOU BE CAREFUL, TOO.
GRAB GRAB
わしわし
SAFETY IS NUMBER ONE WHEN YOU PLAY HIDE-AND-SEEK...
I DON'T PLAY THAT!
NARU
TOUJO-SAN ASKED ME TO TELL YOU THAT LUNCH IS READY.
OKAY.
IT'S ALREADY LUNCH-TIME?
OH
THAT'S SO SWEET. I SKIPPED BREAK-FAST, YOU KNOW?
WHAT'S THAT? ARE YOU TRYING TO SOUND LIKE AYAKO?
NOT EVEN CLOSE...
シャッ
SHRR
DADDY!

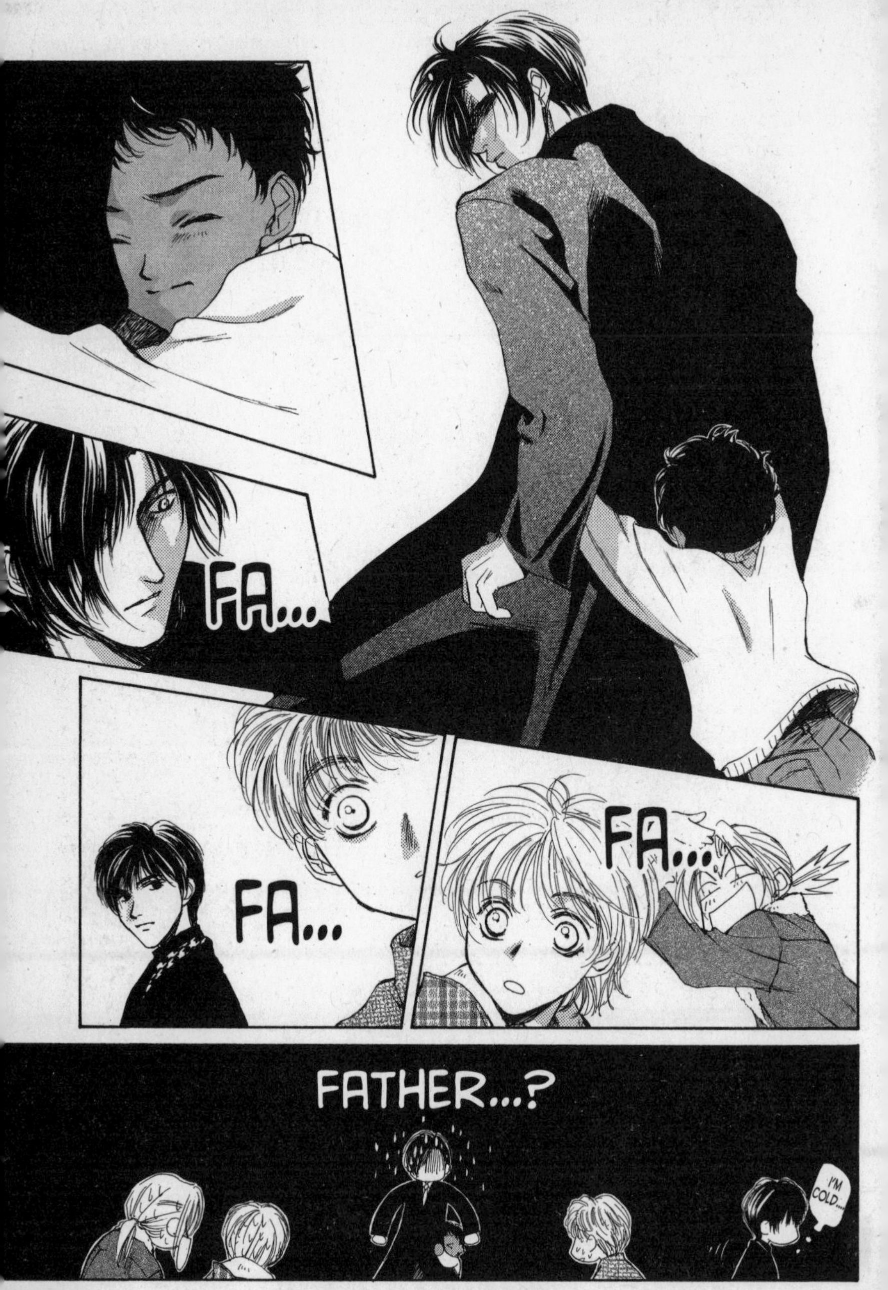
FA...
FA...
FA...
FATHER...?
I'M COLD...

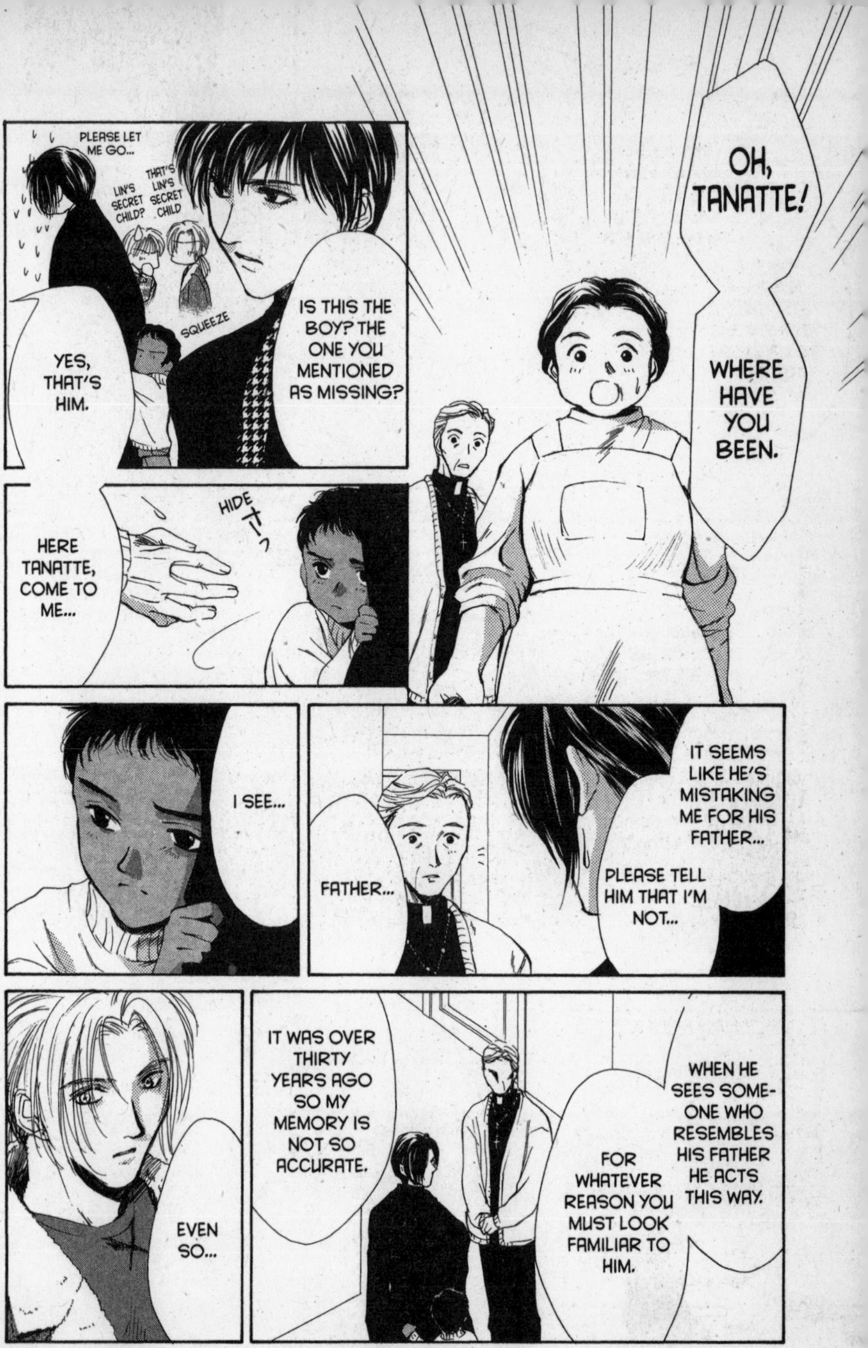
OH, TANATTE!
WHERE HAVE YOU BEEN.
IS THIS THE BOY? THE ONE YOU MENTIONED AS MISSING?
PLEASE LET ME GO...
THAT'S LIN'S SECRET CHILD
LIN'S SECRET CHILD?
SQUEEZE
YES, THAT'S HIM.
HIDE
HERE TANATTE, COME TO ME...
IT SEEMS LIKE HE'S MISTAKING ME FOR HIS FATHER...
PLEASE TELL HIM THAT I'M NOT...
FATHER...
I SEE...
WHEN HE SEES SOME-ONE WHO RESEMBLES HIS FATHER HE ACTS THIS WAY.
FOR WHATEVER REASON YOU MUST LOOK FAMILIAR TO HIM.
IT WAS OVER THIRTY YEARS AGO SO MY MEMORY IS NOT SO ACCURATE.
EVEN SO...

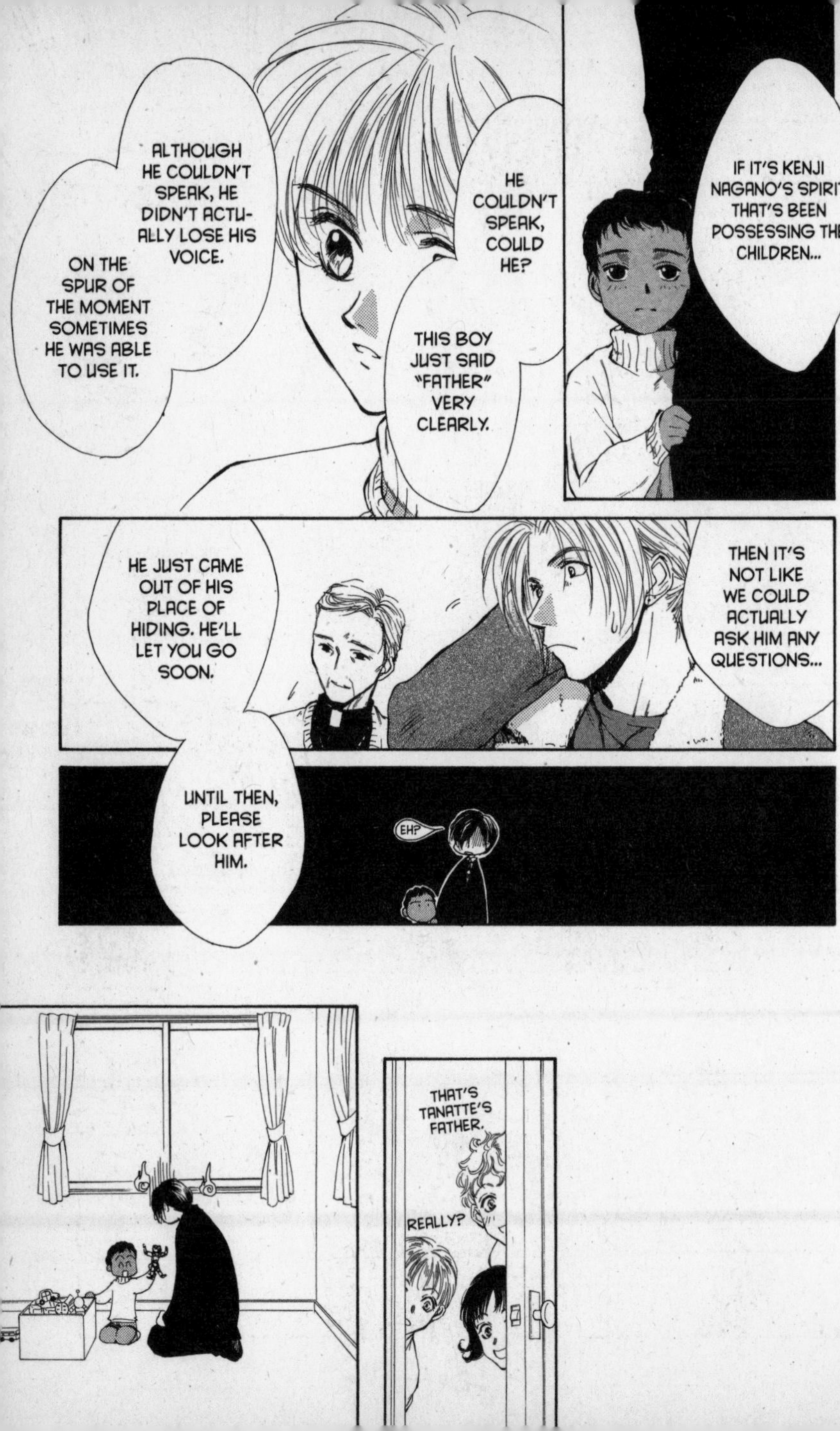
IF IT'S KENJI NAGANO'S SPIRIT THAT'S BEEN POSSESSING THE CHILDREN...
HE COULDN'T SPEAK, COULD HE?
THIS BOY JUST SAID "FATHER" VERY CLEARLY.
ALTHOUGH HE COULDN'T SPEAK, HE DIDN'T ACTU-ALLY LOSE HIS VOICE.
ON THE SPUR OF THE MOMENT SOMETIMES HE WAS ABLE TO USE IT.
THEN IT'S NOT LIKE WE COULD ACTUALLY ASK HIM ANY QUESTIONS...
HE JUST CAME OUT OF HIS PLACE OF HIDING. HE'LL LET YOU GO SOON.
EH?
UNTIL THEN, PLEASE LOOK AFTER HIM.
THAT'S TANATTE'S FATHER.
REALLY?

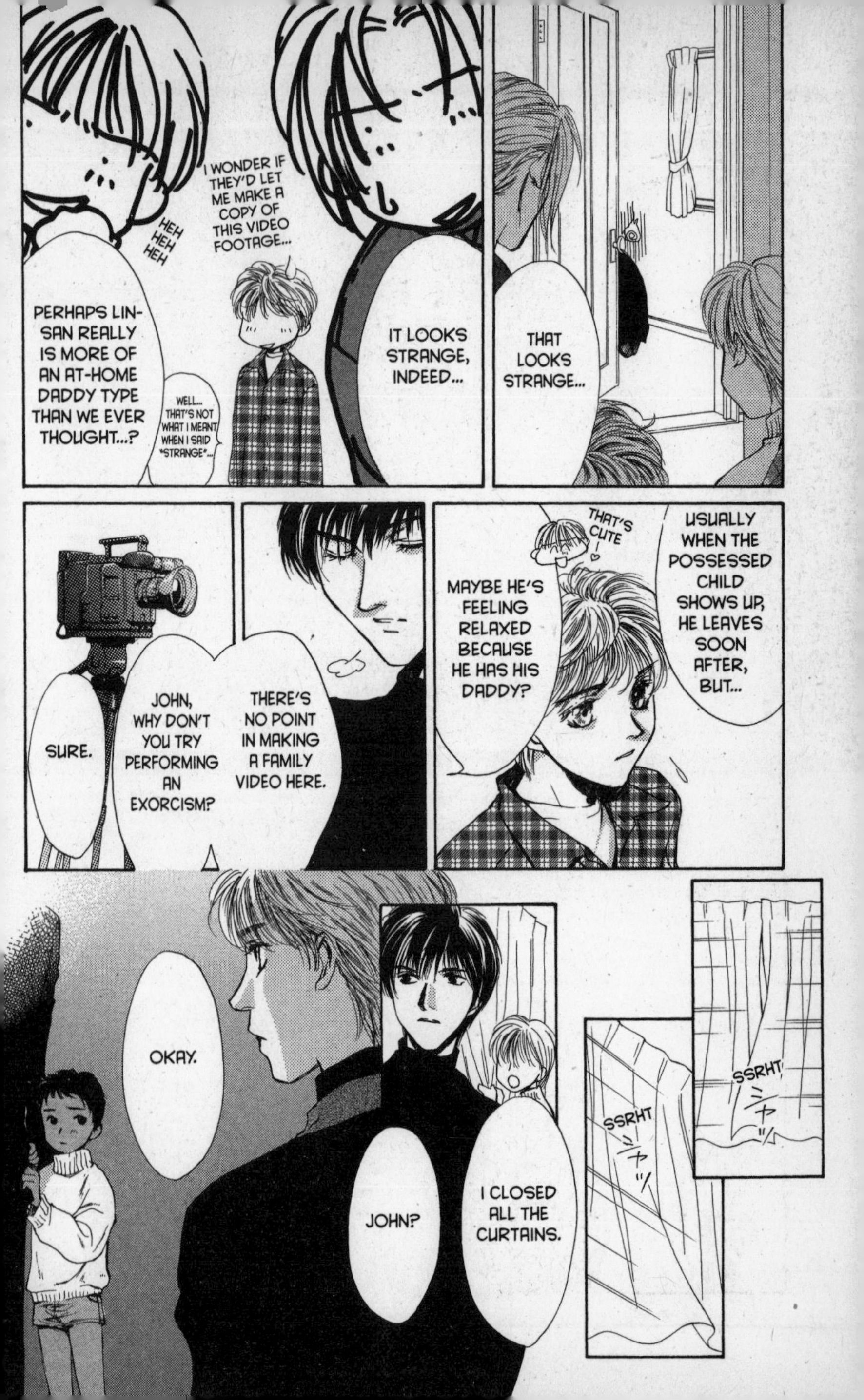
THAT LOOKS STRANGE...
IT LOOKS STRANGE, INDEED...
I WONDER IF THEY'D LET ME MAKE A COPY OF THIS VIDEO FOOTAGE...
HEH HEH HEH
PERHAPS LIN-SAN REALLY IS MORE OF AN AT-HOME DADDY TYPE THAN WE EVER THOUGHT...?
WELL... THAT'S NOT WHAT I MEANT WHEN I SAID "STRANGE"...
USUALLY WHEN THE POSSESSED CHILD SHOWS UP, HE LEAVES SOON AFTER, BUT...
THAT'S CUTE!
MAYBE HE'S FEELING RELAXED BECAUSE HE HAS HIS DADDY?
THERE'S NO POINT IN MAKING A FAMILY VIDEO HERE.
JOHN, WHY DON'T YOU TRY PERFORMING AN EXORCISM?
SURE.
SSRHT
SSRHT
I CLOSED ALL THE CURTAINS.
JOHN?
OKAY.

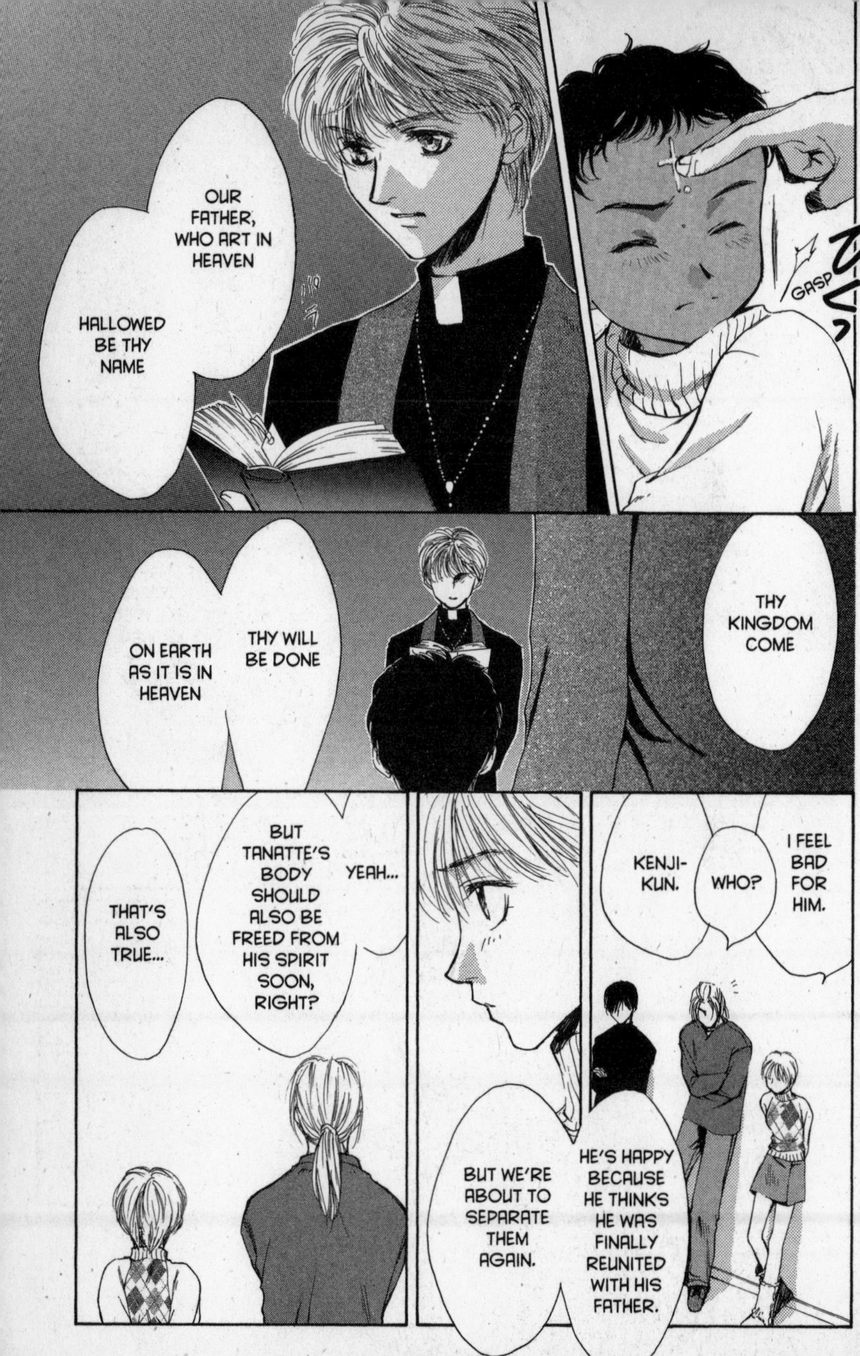
GASP
OUR FATHER, WHO ART IN HEAVEN
HALLOWED BE THY NAME
THY KINGDOM COME
THY WILL BE DONE
ON EARTH AS IT IS IN HEAVEN
I FEEL BAD FOR HIM.
WHO?
KENJI-KUN.
HE'S HAPPY BECAUSE HE THINKS HE WAS FINALLY REUNITED WITH HIS FATHER.
BUT WE'RE ABOUT TO SEPARATE THEM AGAIN.
YEAH...
BUT TANATTE'S BODY SHOULD ALSO BE FREED FROM HIS SPIRIT SOON, RIGHT?
THAT'S ALSO TRUE...

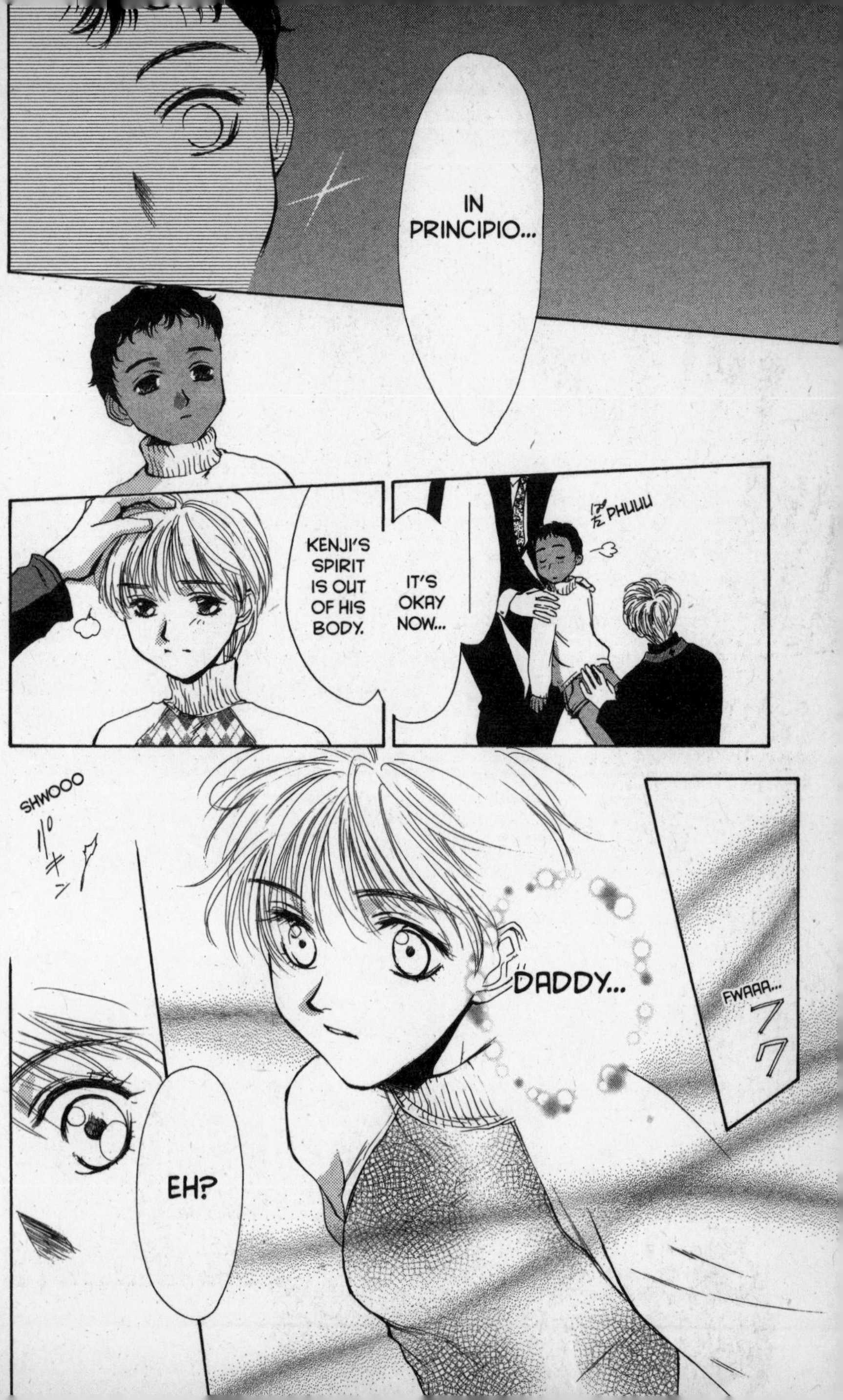
IN PRINCIPIO...
PHUUU
IT'S OKAY NOW...
KENJI'S SPIRIT IS OUT OF HIS BODY.
FWAAA...
DADDY...
SHWOOO
EH?

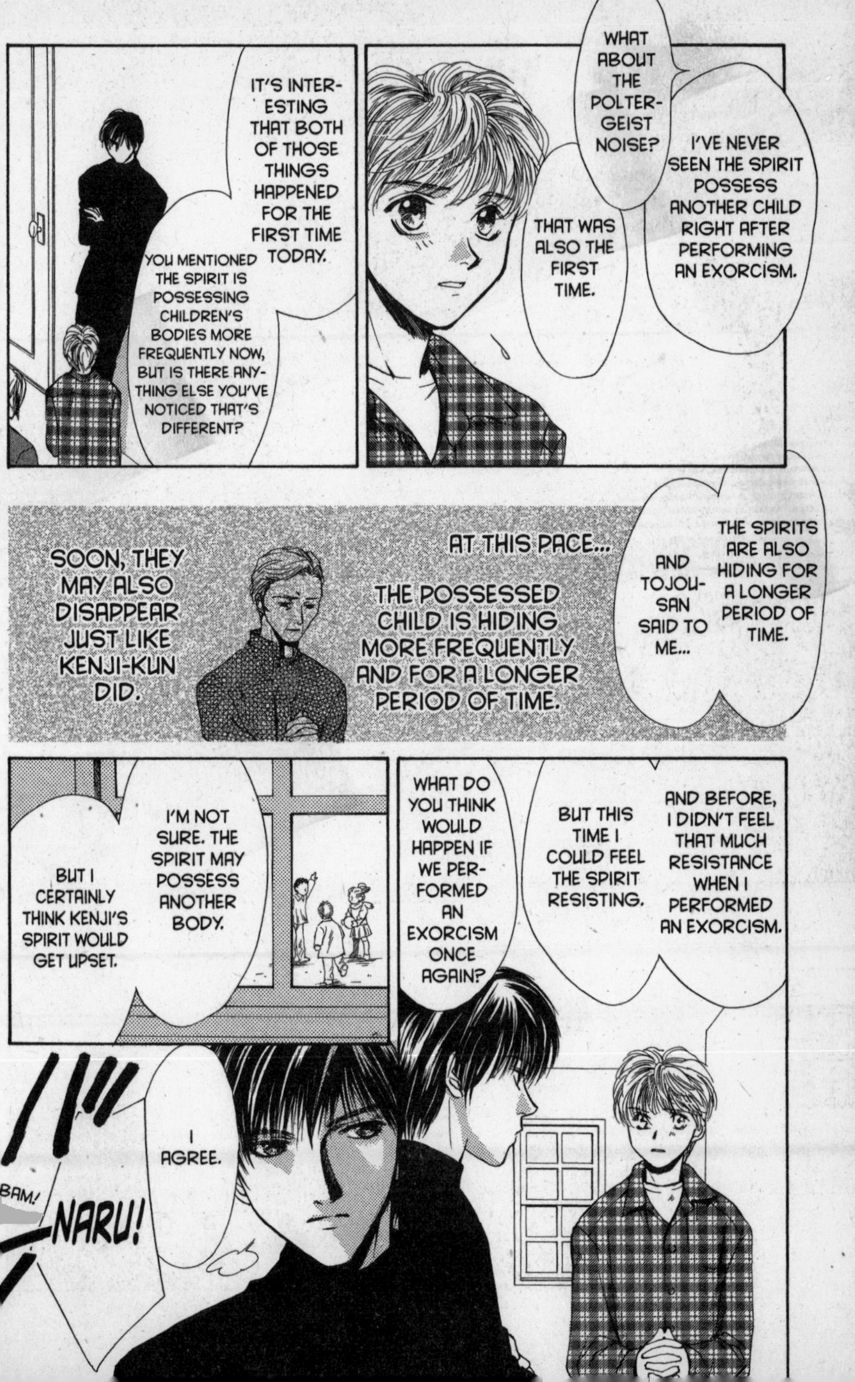
I'VE NEVER SEEN THE SPIRIT POSSESS ANOTHER CHILD RIGHT AFTER PERFORMING AN EXORCISM.
WHAT ABOUT THE POLTER-GEIST NOISE?
THAT WAS ALSO THE FIRST TIME.
IT'S INTER-ESTING THAT BOTH OF THOSE THINGS HAPPENED FOR THE FIRST TIME TODAY.
YOU MENTIONED THE SPIRIT IS POSSESSING CHILDREN'S BODIES MORE FREQUENTLY NOW, BUT IS THERE ANY-THING ELSE YOU'VE NOTICED THAT'S DIFFERENT?
THE SPIRITS ARE ALSO HIDING FOR A LONGER PERIOD OF TIME.
AND TOJOU-SAN SAID TO ME...
AT THIS PACE...
THE POSSESSED CHILD IS HIDING MORE FREQUENTLY AND FOR A LONGER PERIOD OF TIME.
SOON, THEY MAY ALSO DISAPPEAR JUST LIKE KENJI-KUN DID.
AND BEFORE, I DIDN'T FEEL THAT MUCH RESISTANCE WHEN I PERFORMED AN EXORCISM.
BUT THIS TIME I COULD FEEL THE SPIRIT RESISTING.
WHAT DO YOU THINK WOULD HAPPEN IF WE PER-FORMED AN EXORCISM ONCE AGAIN?
I'M NOT SURE. THE SPIRIT MAY POSSESS ANOTHER BODY.
BUT I CERTAINLY THINK KENJI'S SPIRIT WOULD GET UPSET.
I AGREE.
BAM!
NARU!

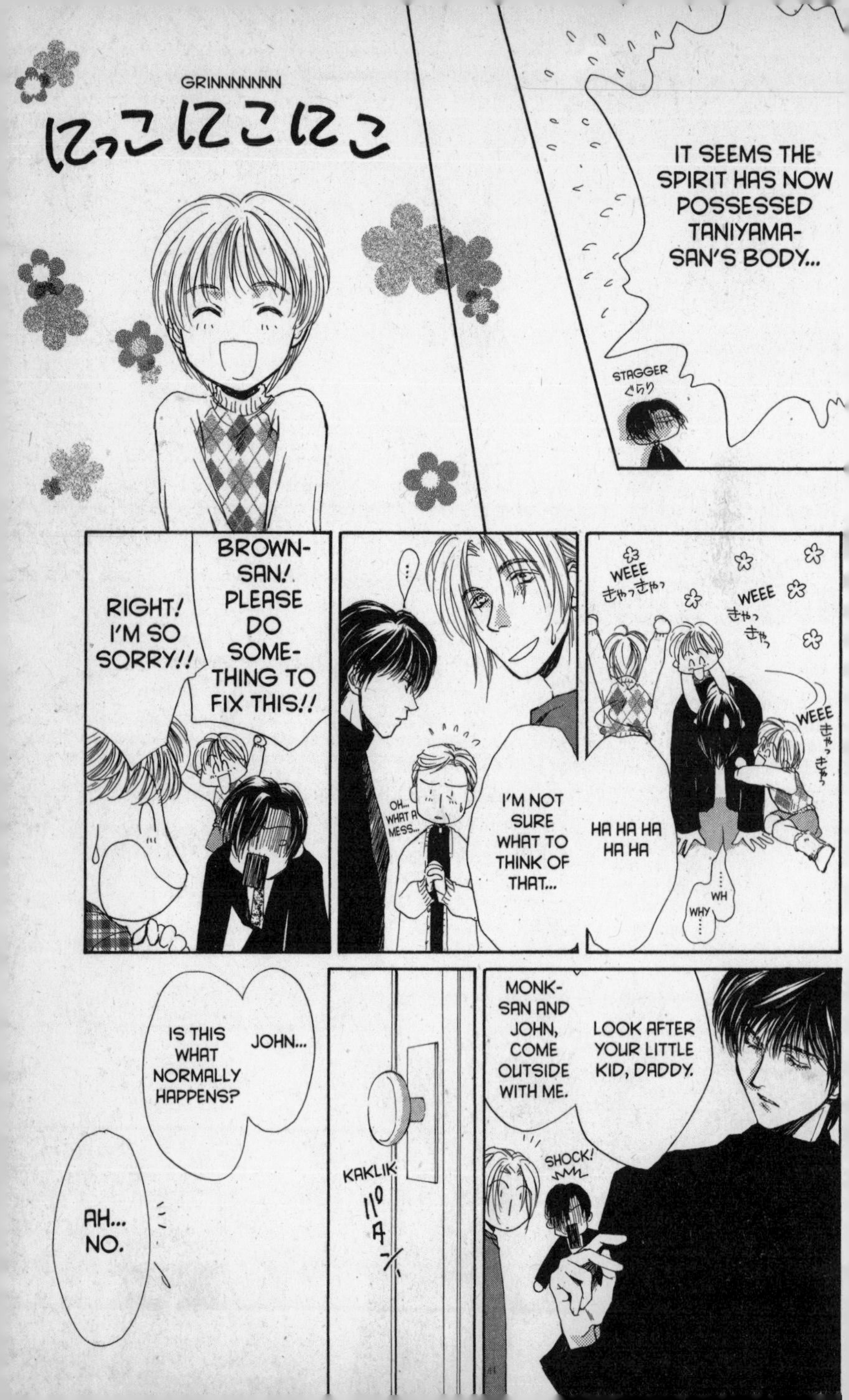
IT SEEMS THE SPIRIT HAS NOW POSSESSED TANIYAMA-SAN'S BODY...
STAGGER
ぐらり
GRINNNNNNN
にっこにこにこ
WEEE
きゃっきゃっ
WEEE
きゃっきゃっ
WEEE
きゃっきゃっ
HA HA HA HA HA
WH
WHY......
...
I'M NOT SURE WHAT TO THINK OF THAT...
OH... WHAT A MESS...
BROWN-SAN! PLEASE DO SOMETHING TO FIX THIS!!
RIGHT! I'M SO SORRY!!
LOOK AFTER YOUR LITTLE KID, DADDY.
MONK-SAN AND JOHN, COME OUTSIDE WITH ME.
SHOCK!
KAKLIK
パタン
JOHN...
IS THIS WHAT NORMALLY HAPPENS?
AH... NO.

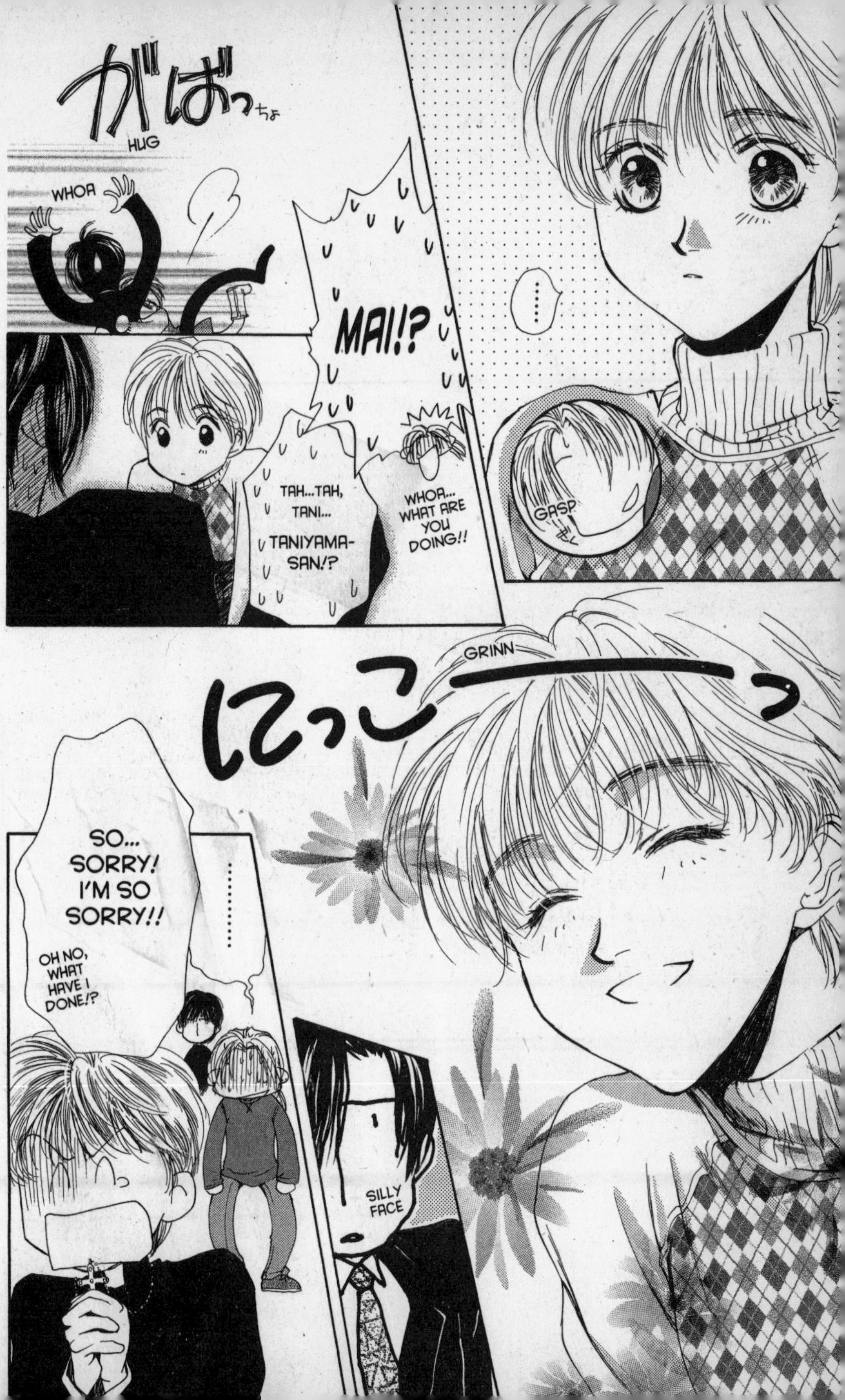
……
GASP
ぎく
がばっちょ
HUG
WHOA
MAI!?
WHOA... WHAT ARE YOU DOING!!
TAH...TAH, TANI...
TANIYAMA-SAN!?
にっこーーっ
GRINN
……
SO... SORRY! I'M SO SORRY!!
OH NO, WHAT HAVE I DONE!?
SILLY FACE

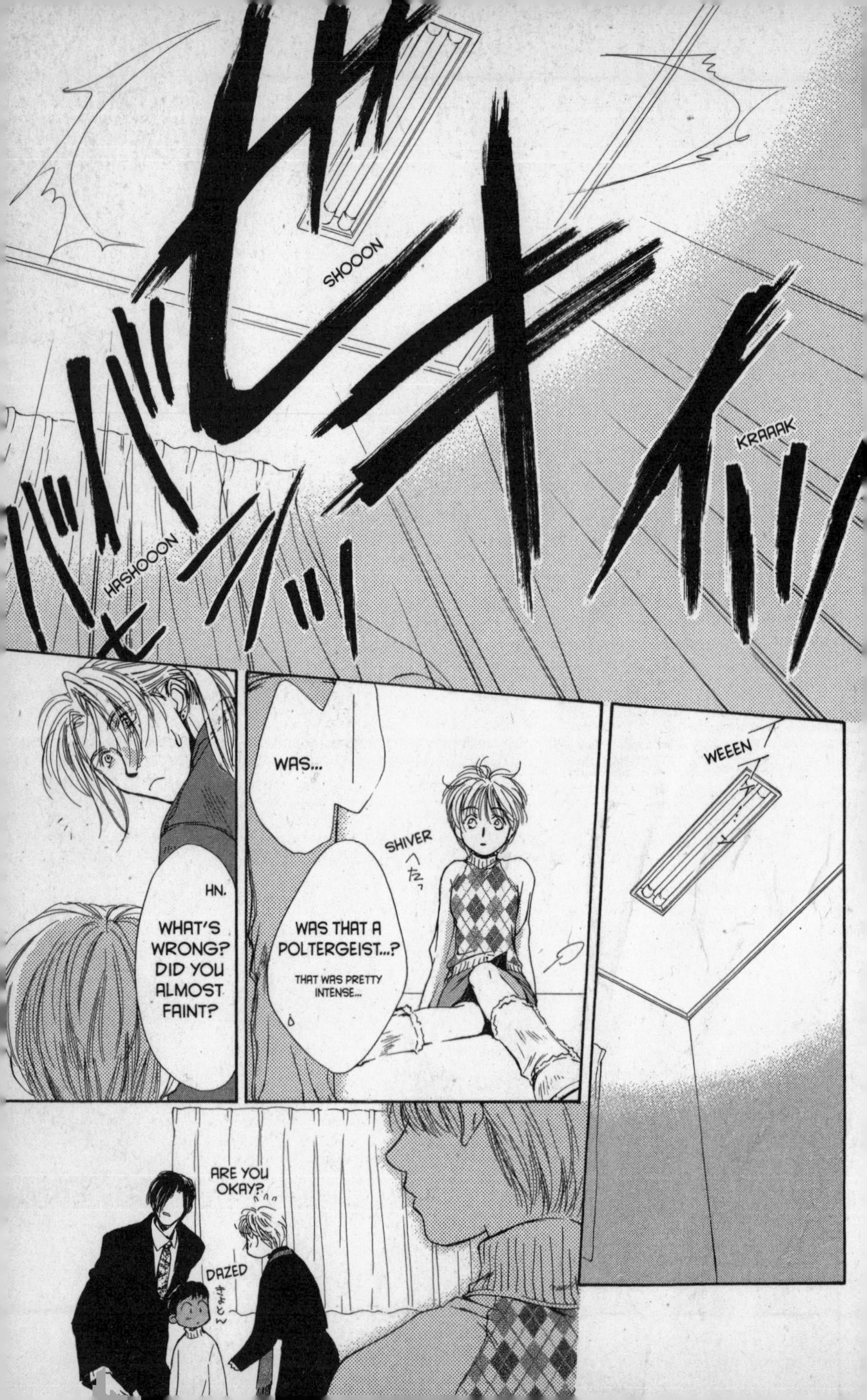
KRAAAK
SHOOON
HASHOOON
WEEEN
WAS...
SHIVER
WAS THAT A POLTERGEIST...?
THAT WAS PRETTY INTENSE...
HN.
WHAT'S WRONG? DID YOU ALMOST FAINT?
ARE YOU OKAY?
DAZED

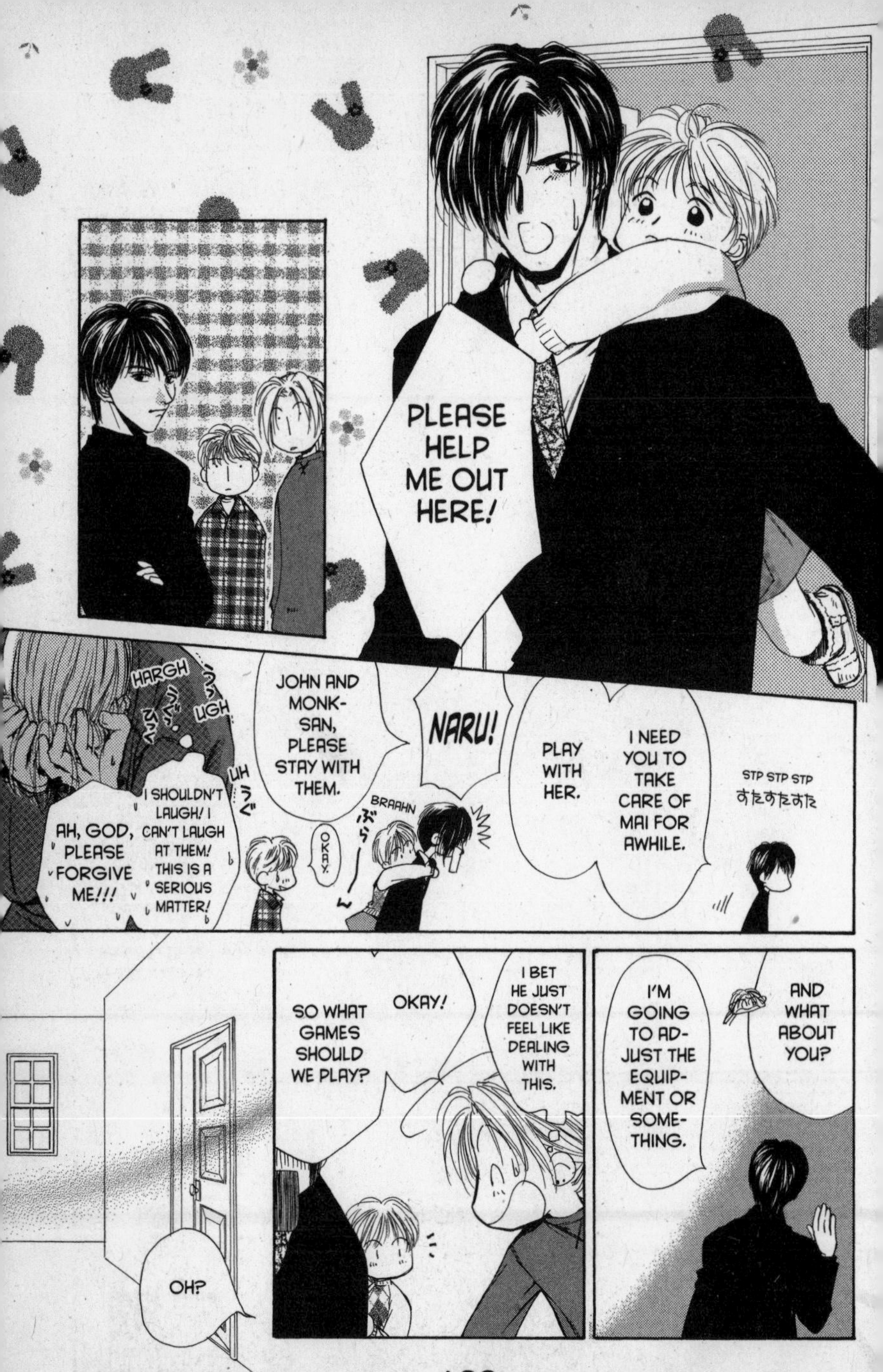
PLEASE HELP ME OUT HERE!
STP STP STP
すたすたすた
I NEED YOU TO TAKE CARE OF MAI FOR AWHILE.
PLAY WITH HER.
NARU!
JOHN AND MONK-SAN, PLEASE STAY WITH THEM.
BRAAHN
OKAY.
HARGH
UGH
UH
I SHOULDN'T LAUGH! I CAN'T LAUGH AT THEM! THIS IS A SERIOUS MATTER!
AH, GOD, PLEASE FORGIVE ME!!!
AND WHAT ABOUT YOU?
I'M GOING TO ADJUST THE EQUIPMENT OR SOMETHING.
I BET HE JUST DOESN'T FEEL LIKE DEALING WITH THIS.
OKAY!
SO WHAT GAMES SHOULD WE PLAY?
OH?

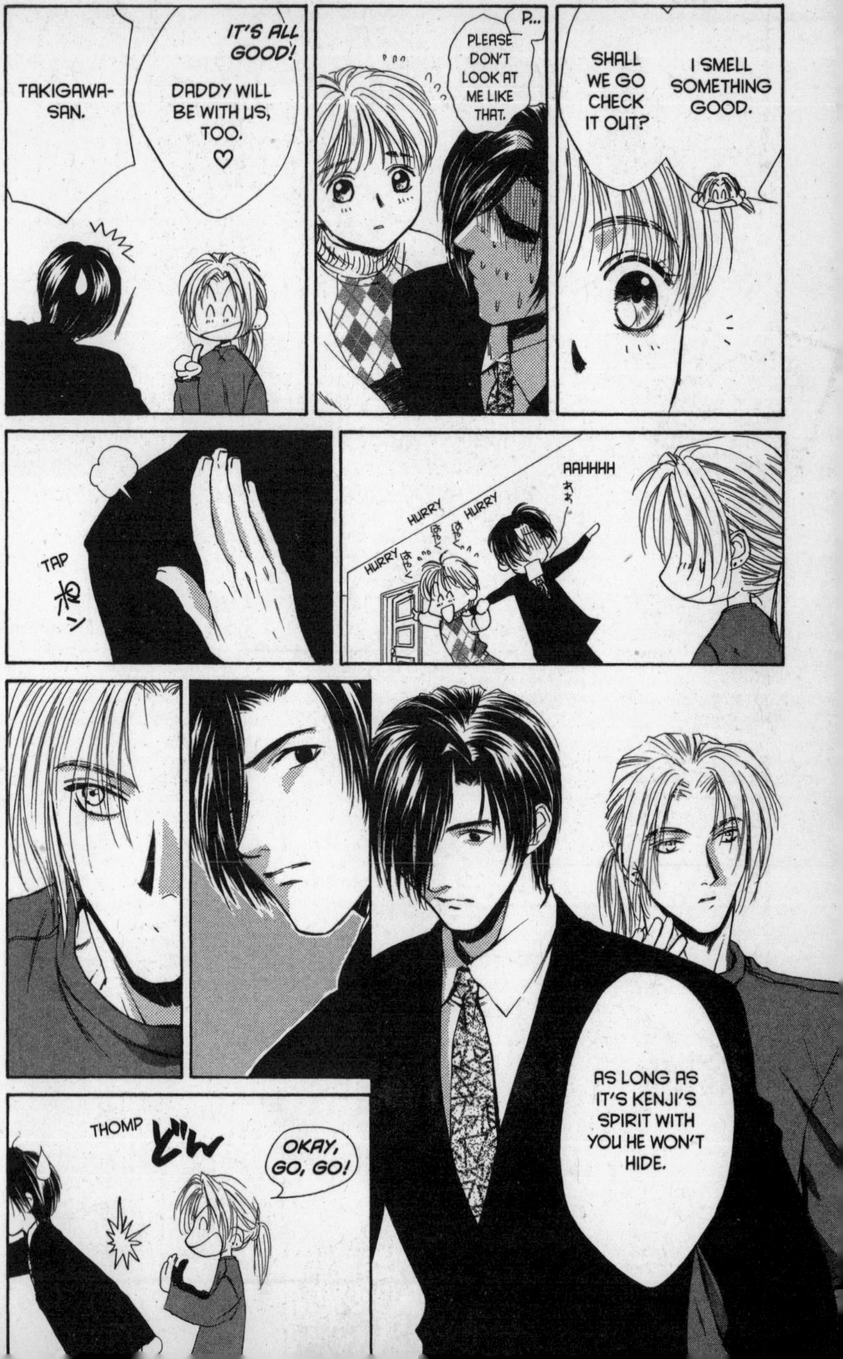
I SMELL SOMETHING GOOD.
SHALL WE GO CHECK IT OUT?
P...
PLEASE DON'T LOOK AT ME LIKE THAT.
IT'S ALL GOOD!
DADDY WILL BE WITH US, TOO. ♡
TAKIGAWA-SAN.
AAHHHH
HURRY
HURRY
HURRY
TAP
AS LONG AS IT'S KENJI'S SPIRIT WITH YOU HE WON'T HIDE.
THOMP
OKAY, GO, GO!

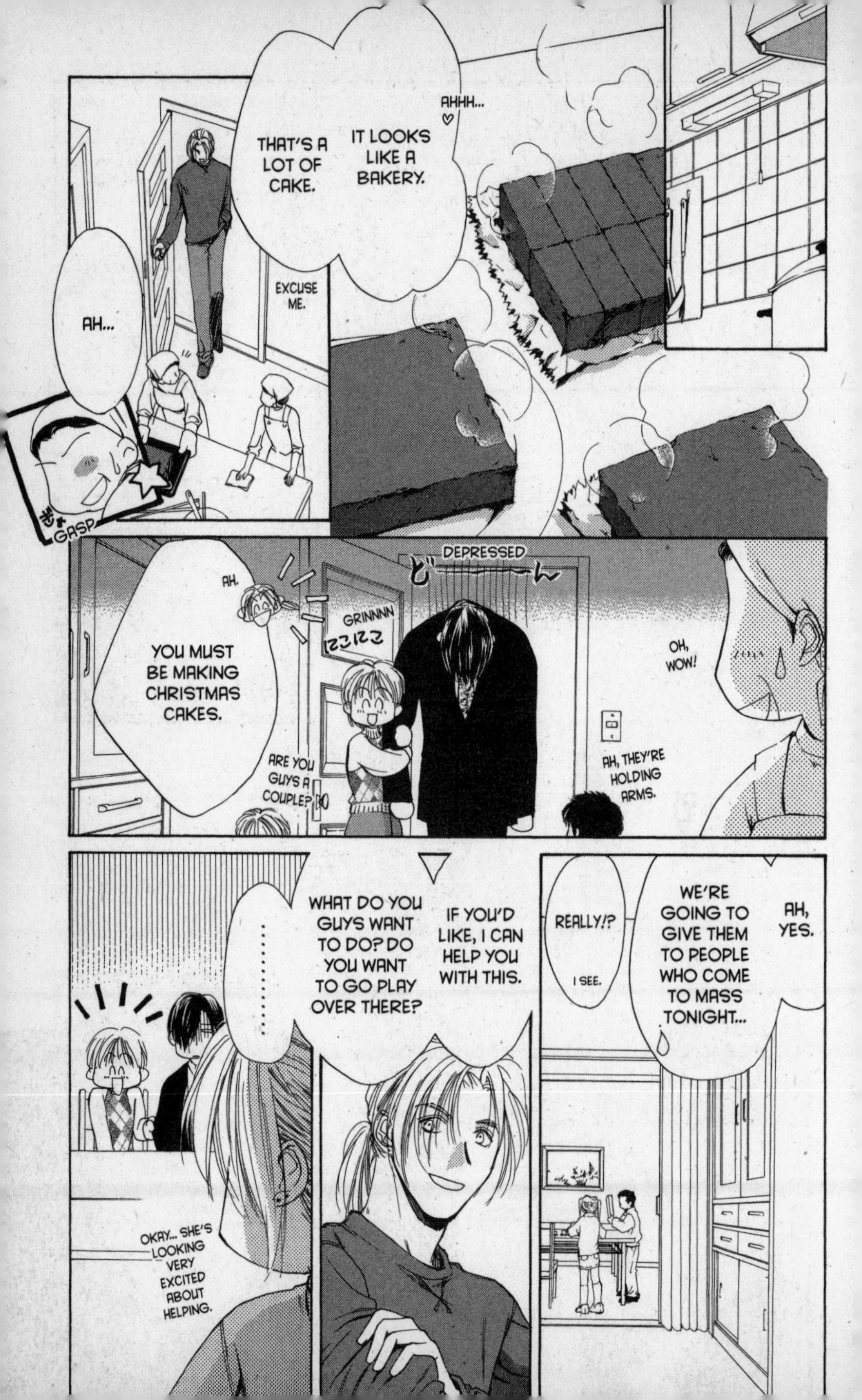
AHHH... ♡
IT LOOKS LIKE A BAKERY.
THAT'S A LOT OF CAKE.
EXCUSE ME.
AH...
GASP
OH, WOW!
AH, THEY'RE HOLDING ARMS.
DEPRESSED
どーーん
GRINNNN
にこにこ
AH.
YOU MUST BE MAKING CHRISTMAS CAKES.
ARE YOU GUYS A COUPLE?
AH, YES.
WE'RE GOING TO GIVE THEM TO PEOPLE WHO COME TO MASS TONIGHT...
REALLY!?
I SEE.
IF YOU'D LIKE, I CAN HELP YOU WITH THIS.
WHAT DO YOU GUYS WANT TO DO? DO YOU WANT TO GO PLAY OVER THERE?
......
OKAY... SHE'S LOOKING VERY EXCITED ABOUT HELPING.

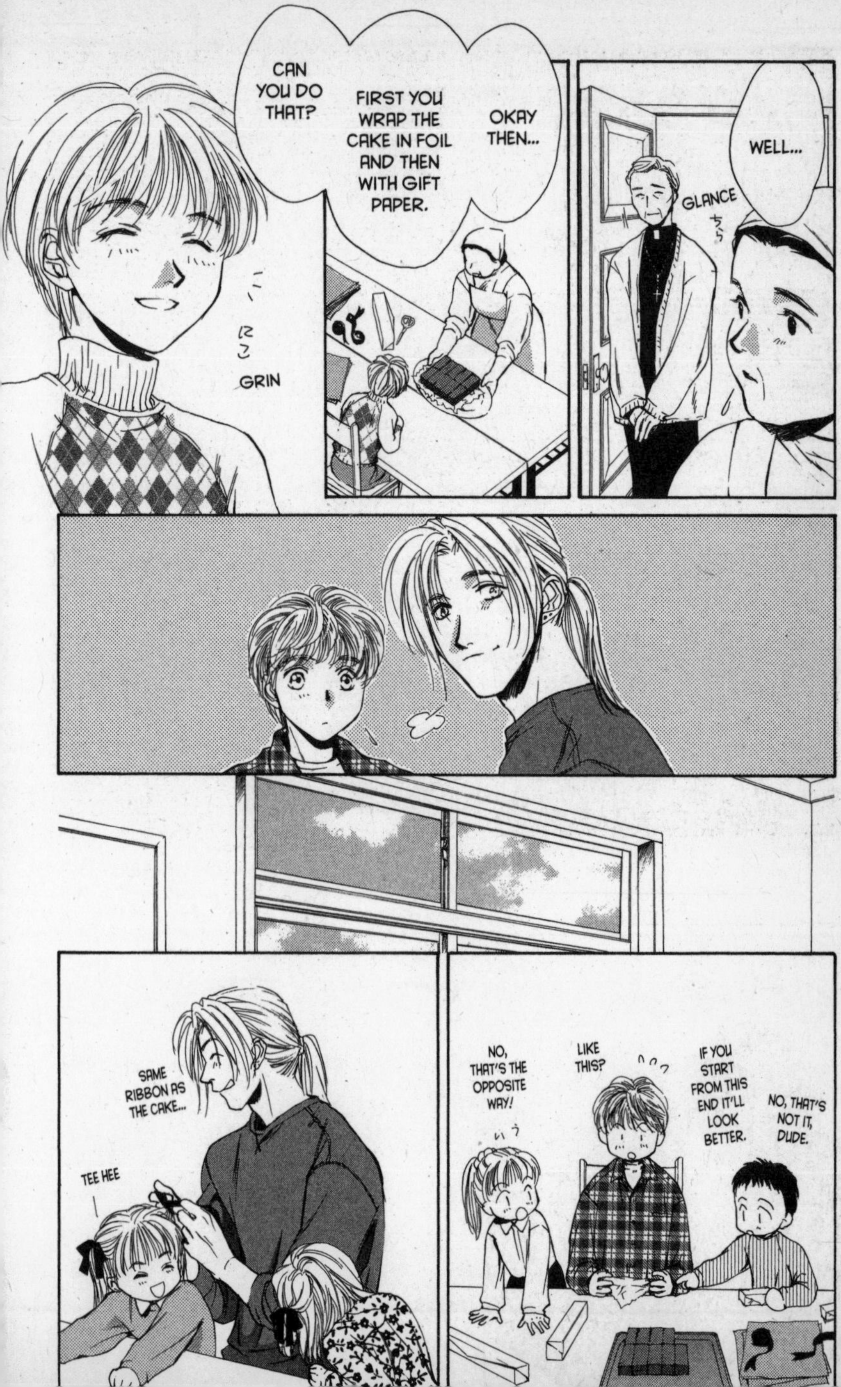
WELL...
GLANCE
ちら
OKAY THEN...
FIRST YOU WRAP THE CAKE IN FOIL AND THEN WITH GIFT PAPER.
CAN YOU DO THAT?
にこ
GRIN
NO, THAT'S NOT IT, DUDE.
IF YOU START FROM THIS END IT'LL LOOK BETTER.
LIKE THIS?
NO, THAT'S THE OPPOSITE WAY!
SAME RIBBON AS THE CAKE...
TEE HEE

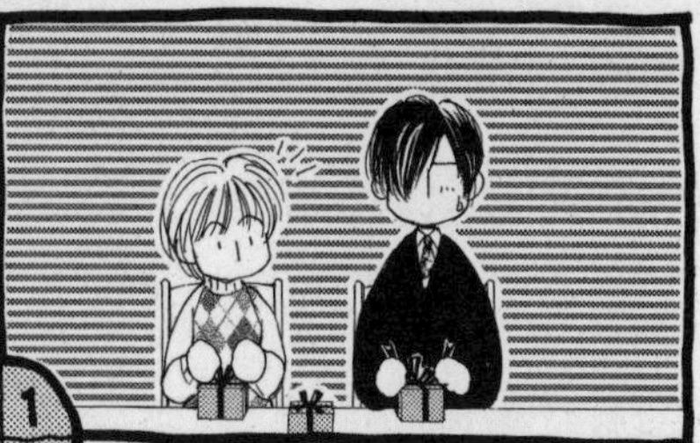

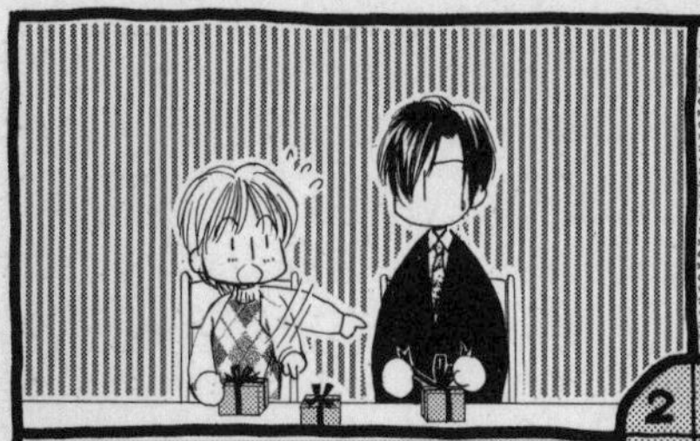

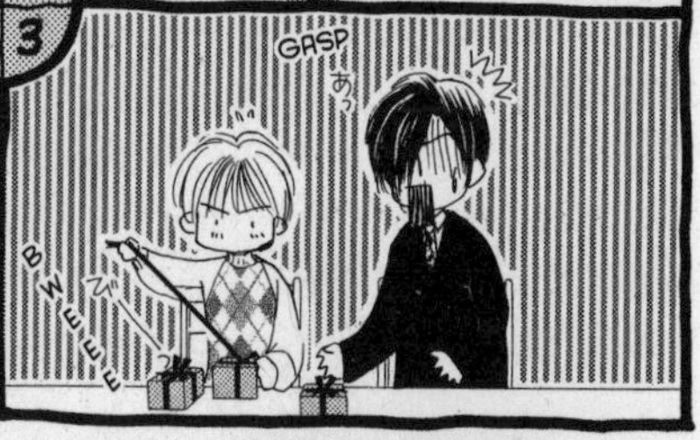
GASP
あっ
BWEEEE
ブ

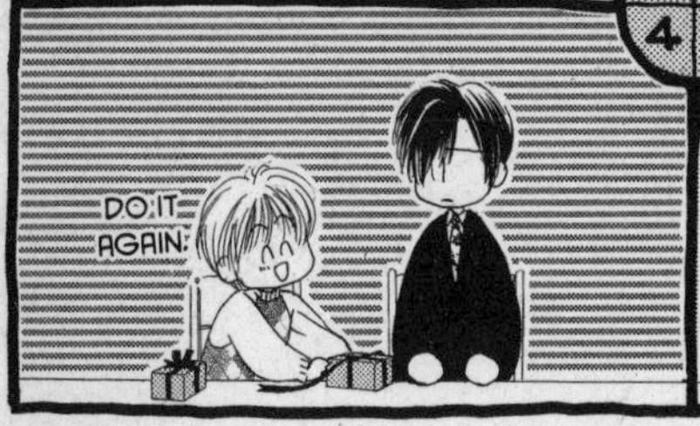
DO IT AGAIN

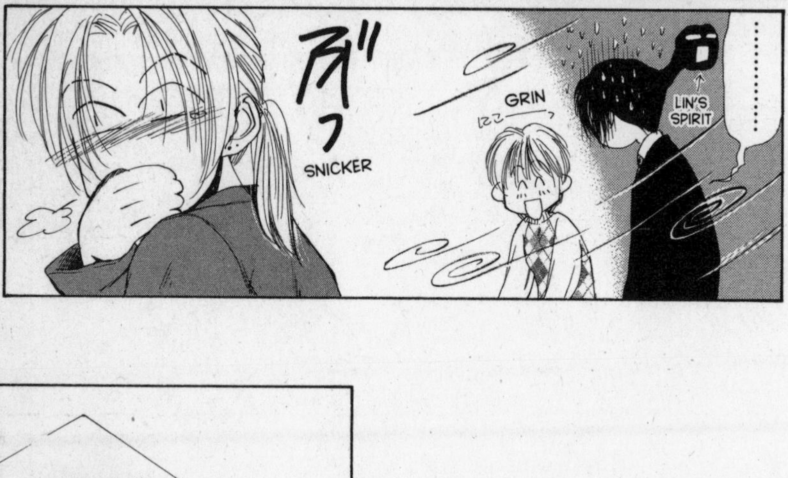
......
LIN'S SPIRIT
GRIN
にこー
ブッ
SNICKER

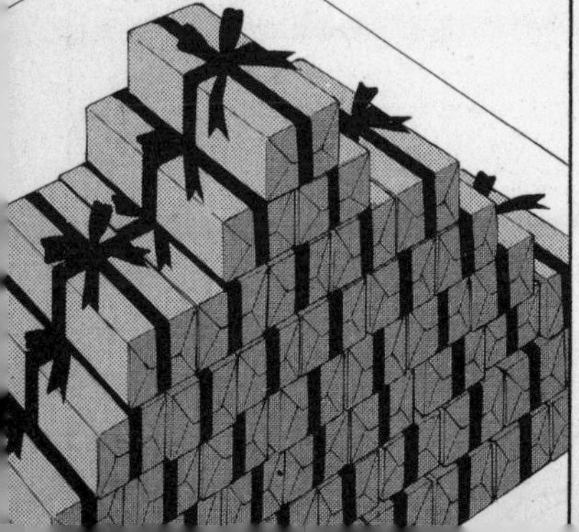

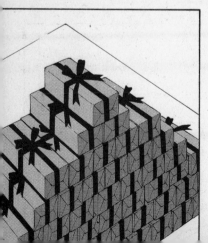

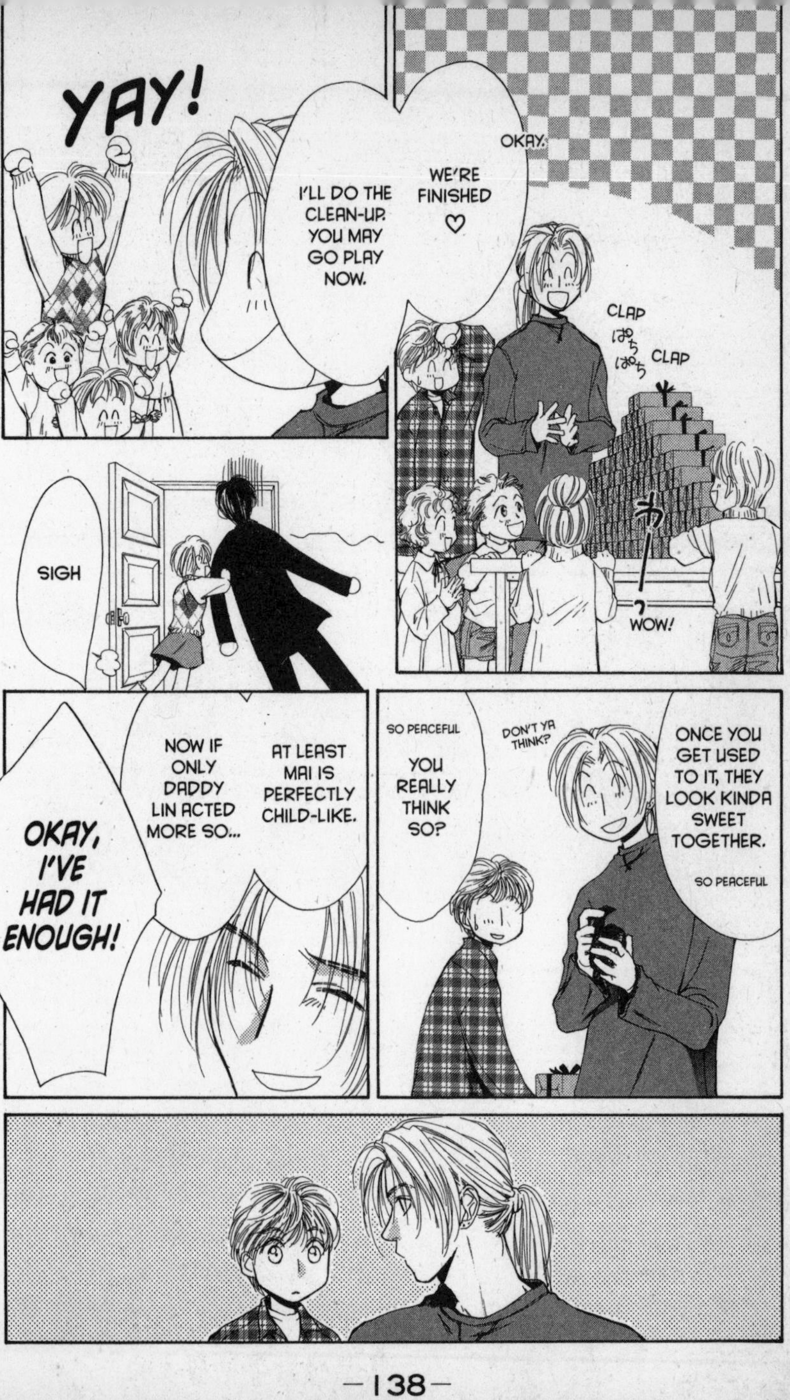
OKAY.
WE'RE FINISHED ♡
CLAP
ぱち ぱち
CLAP
わー
WOW!
I'LL DO THE CLEAN-UP. YOU MAY GO PLAY NOW.
YAY!
SIGH
ONCE YOU GET USED TO IT, THEY LOOK KINDA SWEET TOGETHER.
SO PEACEFUL
DON'T YA THINK?
SO PEACEFUL
YOU REALLY THINK SO?
AT LEAST MAI IS PERFECTLY CHILD-LIKE.
NOW IF ONLY DADDY LIN ACTED MORE SO...
OKAY, I'VE HAD IT ENOUGH!

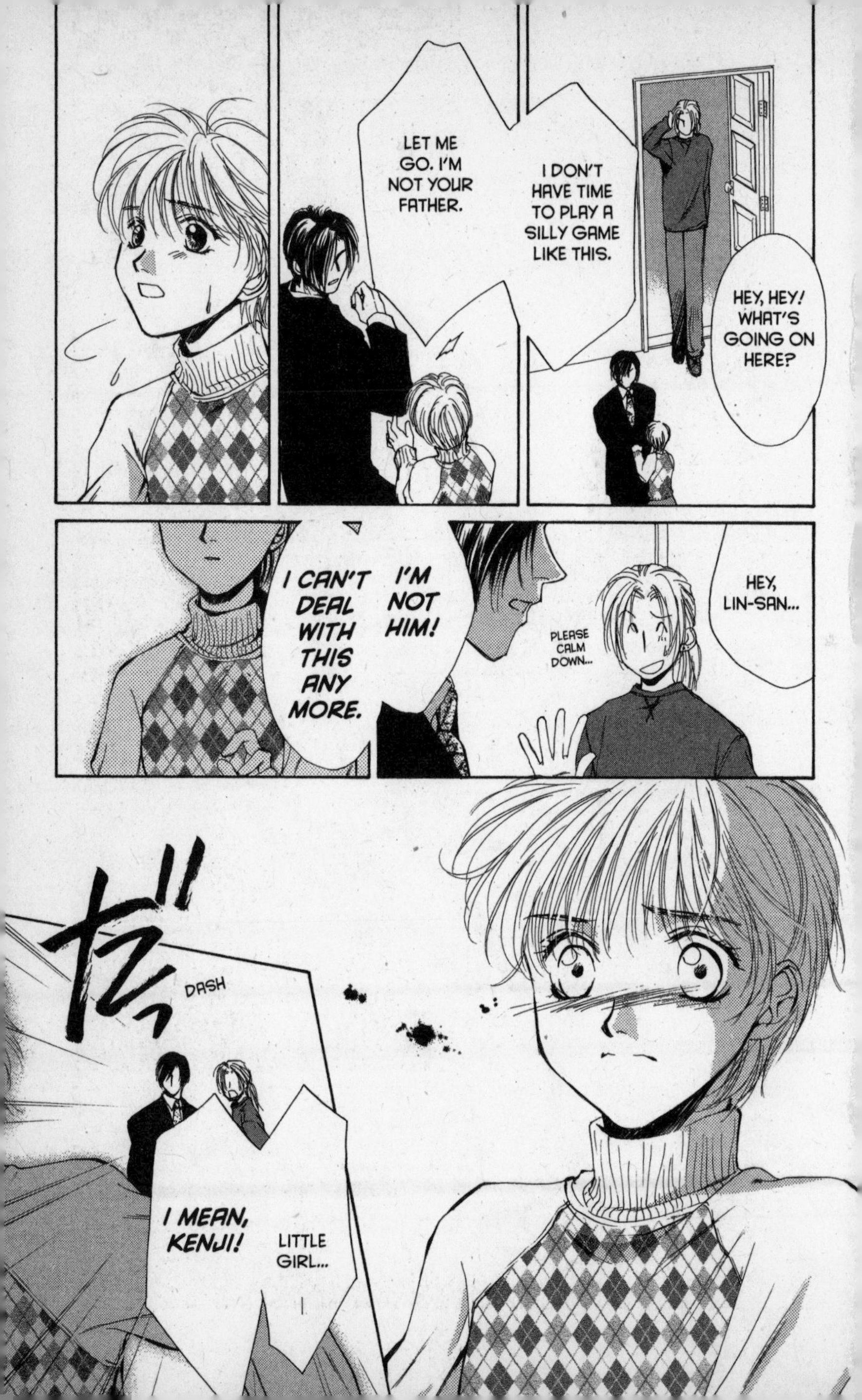
LET ME GO. I'M NOT YOUR FATHER.
I DON'T HAVE TIME TO PLAY A SILLY GAME LIKE THIS.
HEY, HEY! WHAT'S GOING ON HERE?
HEY, LIN-SAN...
PLEASE CALM DOWN...
I'M NOT HIM!
I CAN'T DEAL WITH THIS ANY MORE.
ダッ
DASH
LITTLE GIRL...
I MEAN, KENJI!

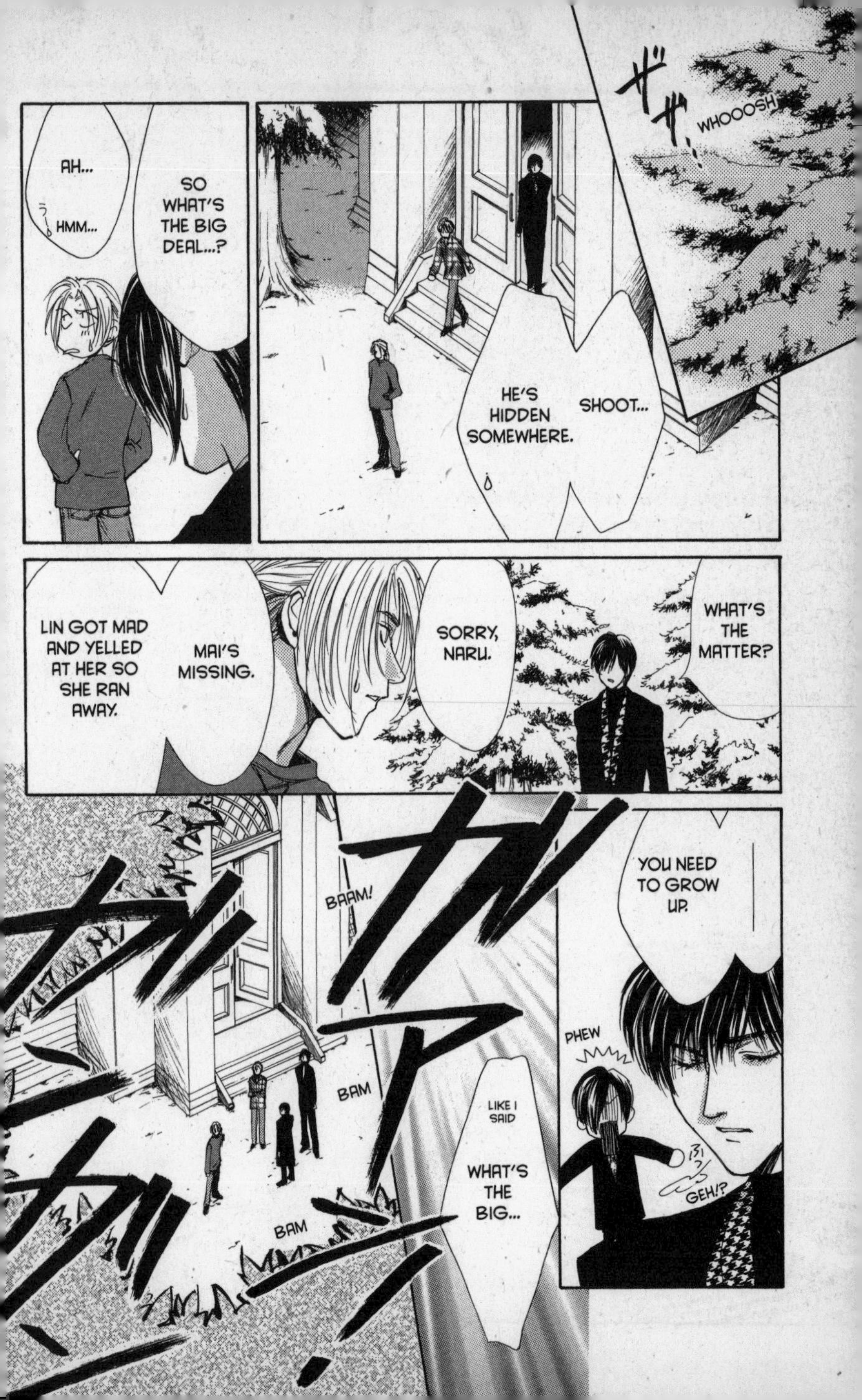
WHOOOSH
SHOOT...
HE'S HIDDEN SOMEWHERE.
SO WHAT'S THE BIG DEAL...?
AH...
HMM...
WHAT'S THE MATTER?
SORRY, NARU.
MAI'S MISSING.
LIN GOT MAD AND YELLED AT HER SO SHE RAN AWAY.
YOU NEED TO GROW UP.
PHEW
GEH!?
BAAM!
BAM
LIKE I SAID
WHAT'S THE BIG...
BAM

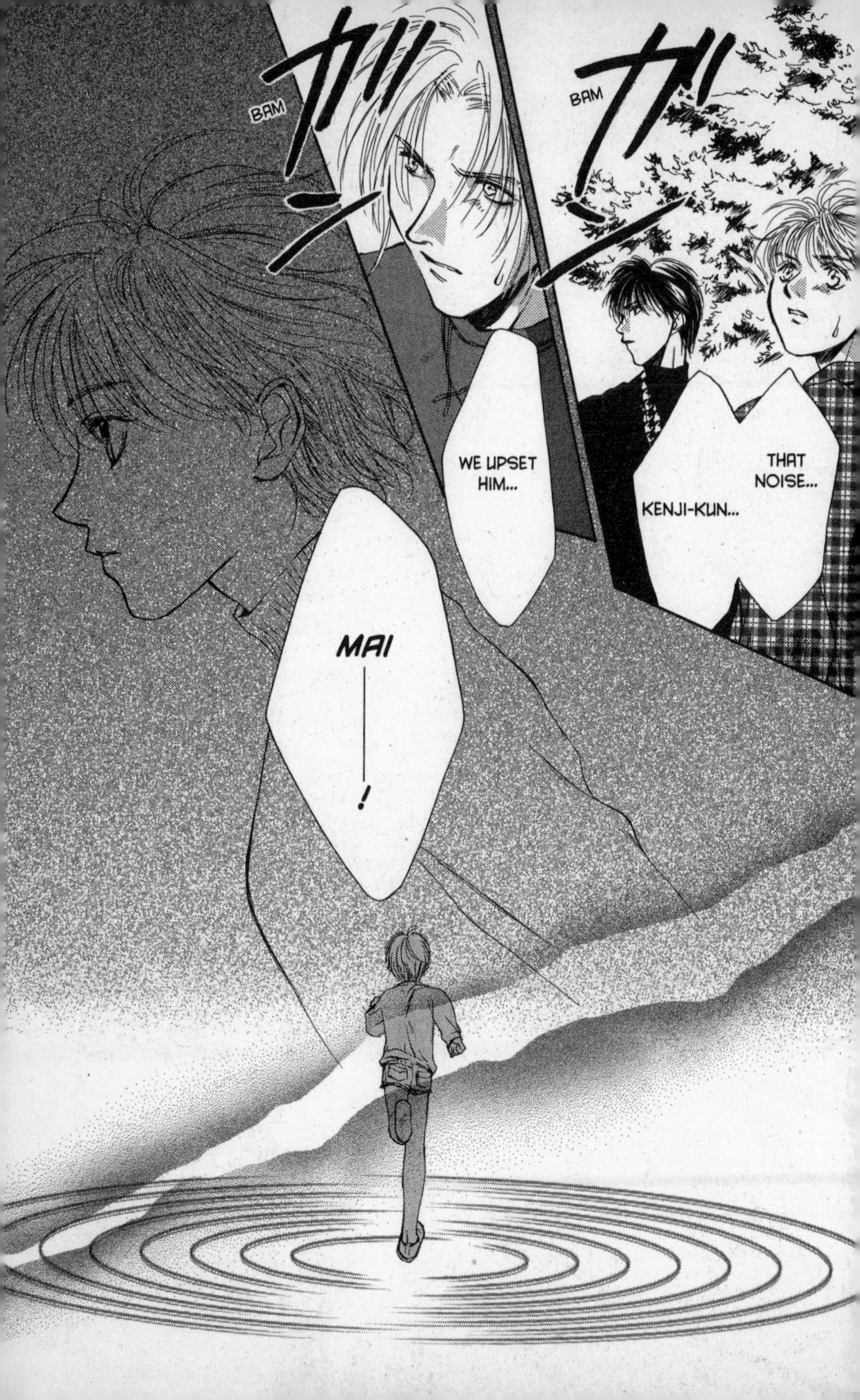
BAM
THAT NOISE...
KENJI-KUN...
BAM
WE UPSET HIM...
MAI—!

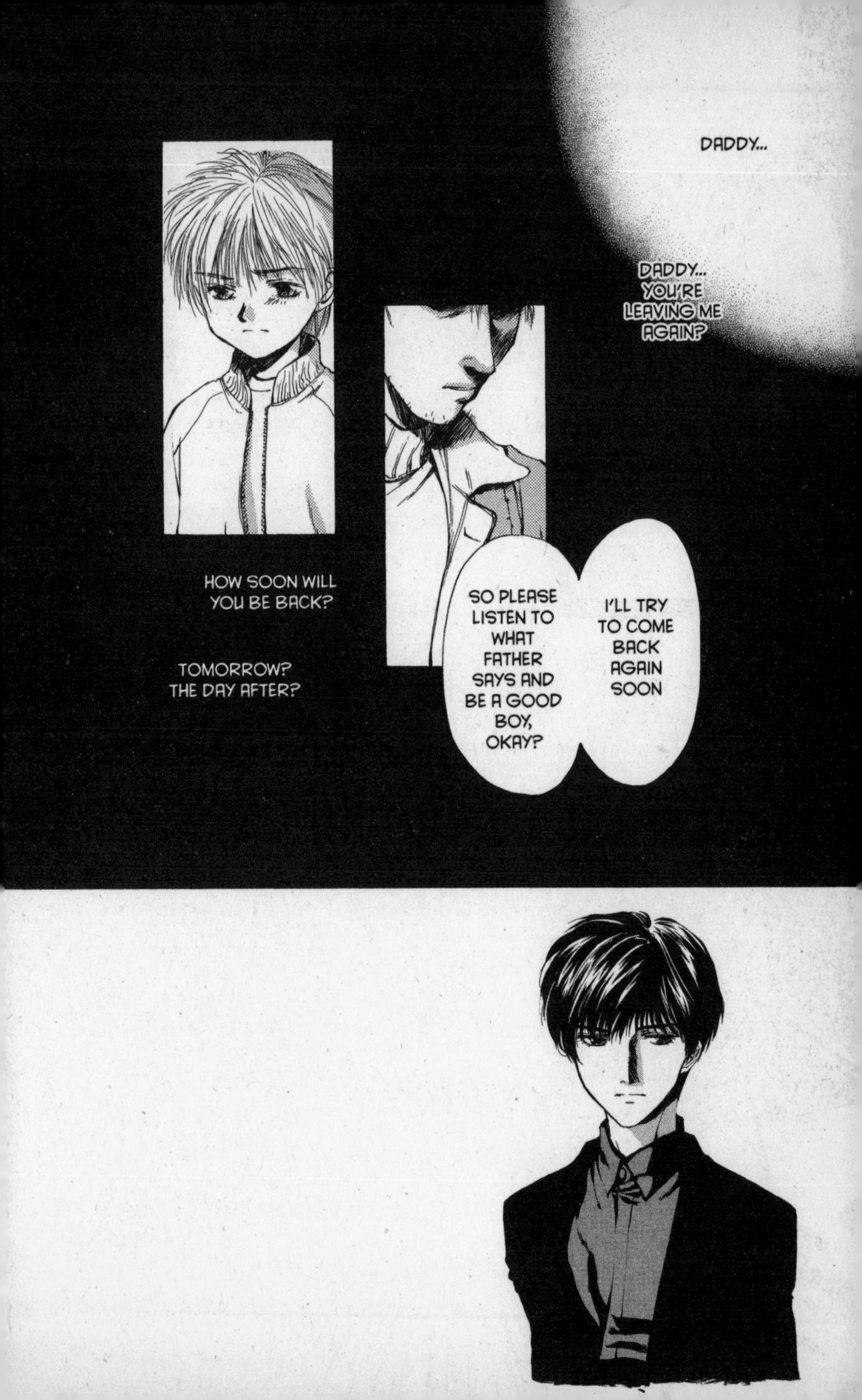
DADDY...
DADDY... YOU'RE LEAVING ME AGAIN?
I'LL TRY TO COME BACK AGAIN SOON
SO PLEASE LISTEN TO WHAT FATHER SAYS AND BE A GOOD BOY, OKAY?
HOW SOON WILL YOU BE BACK?
TOMORROW? THE DAY AFTER?

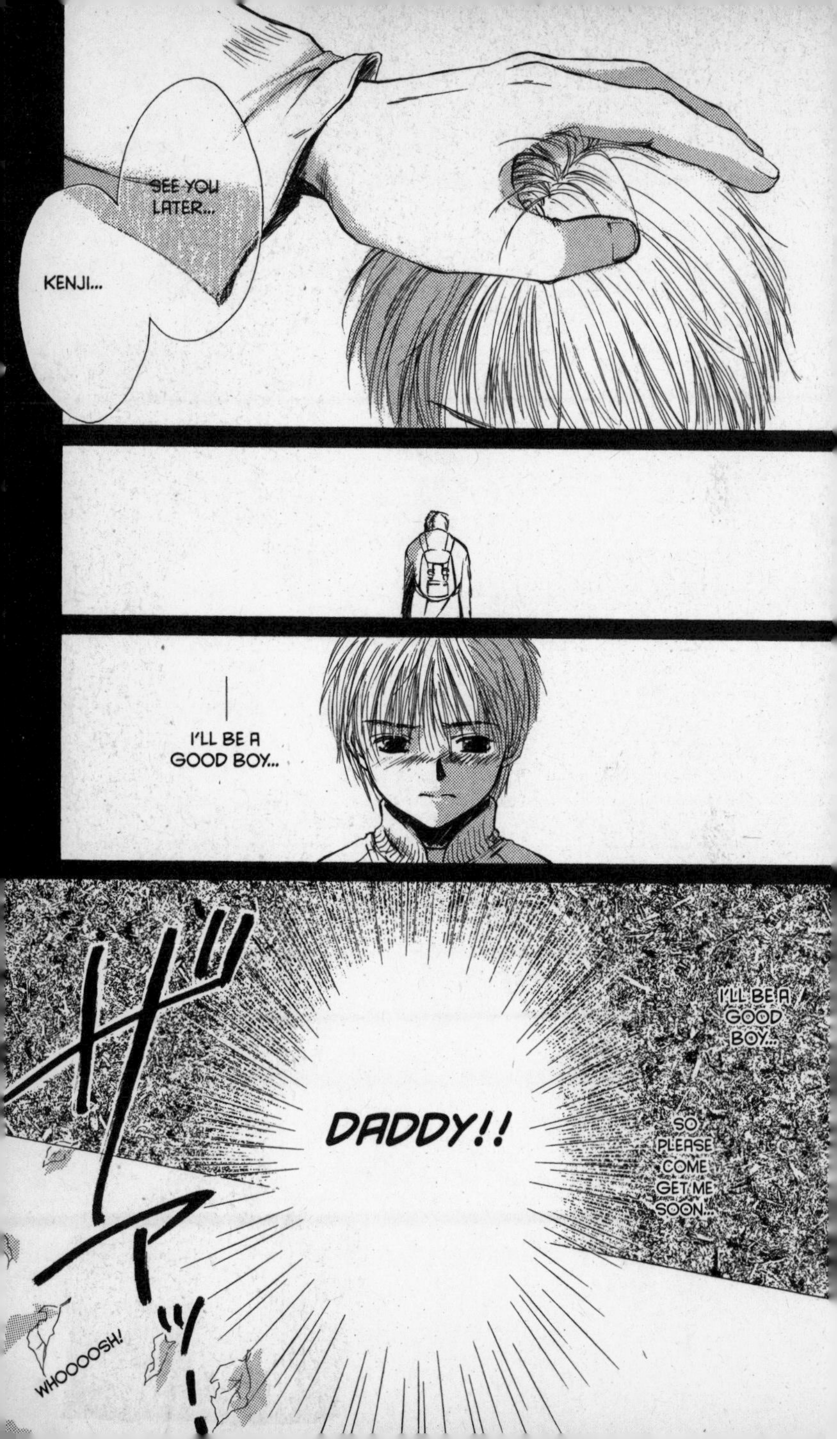
SEE YOU LATER...
KENJI...
I'LL BE A GOOD BOY...
I'LL BE A GOOD BOY...
SO PLEASE COME GET ME SOON...
DADDY!!
WHOOOOSH!

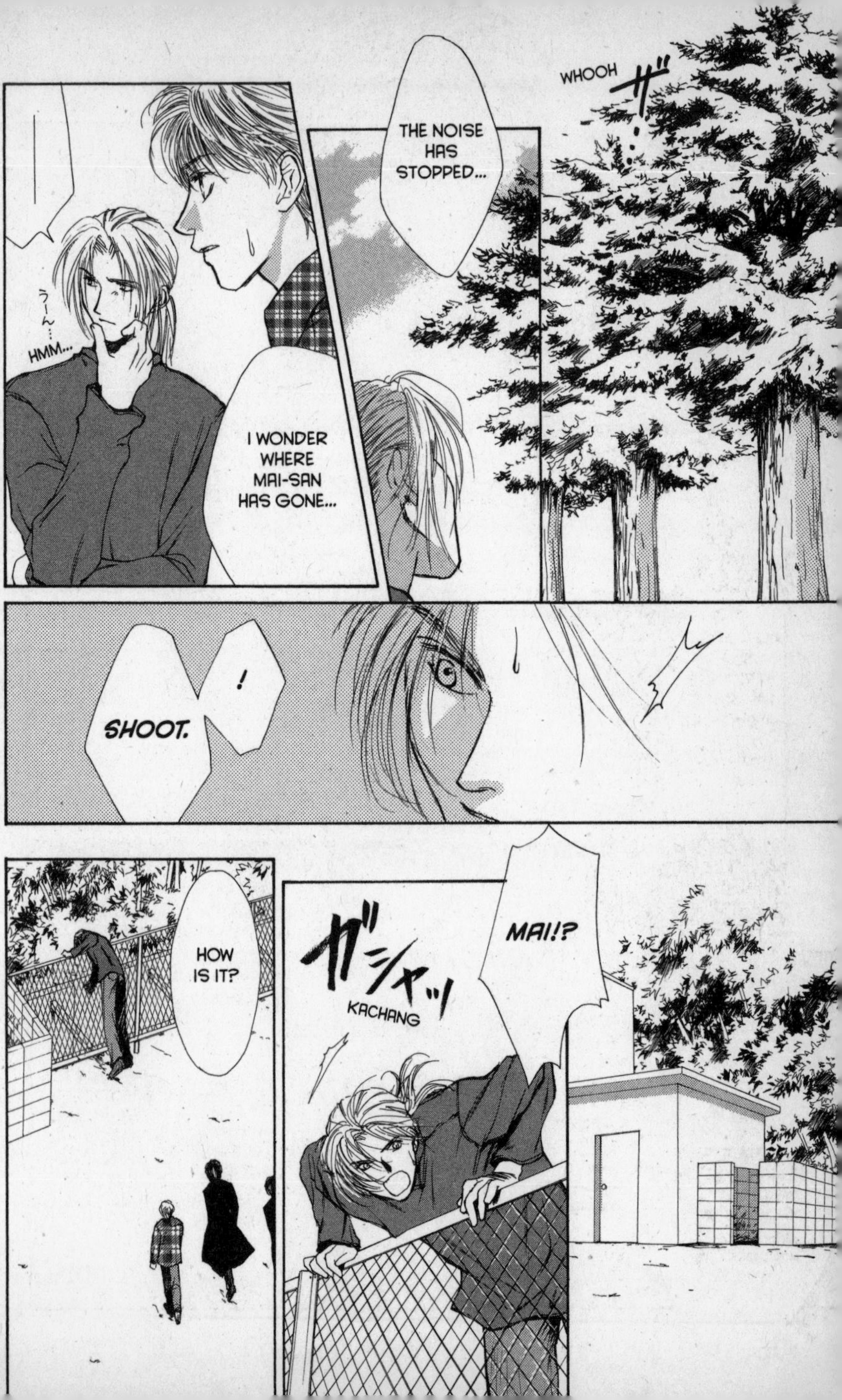
WHOOH
ザ
THE NOISE HAS STOPPED...
I WONDER WHERE MAI-SAN HAS GONE...
うーん…
HMM...
!
SHOOT.
MAI!?
ガシャッ
KACHANG
HOW IS IT?

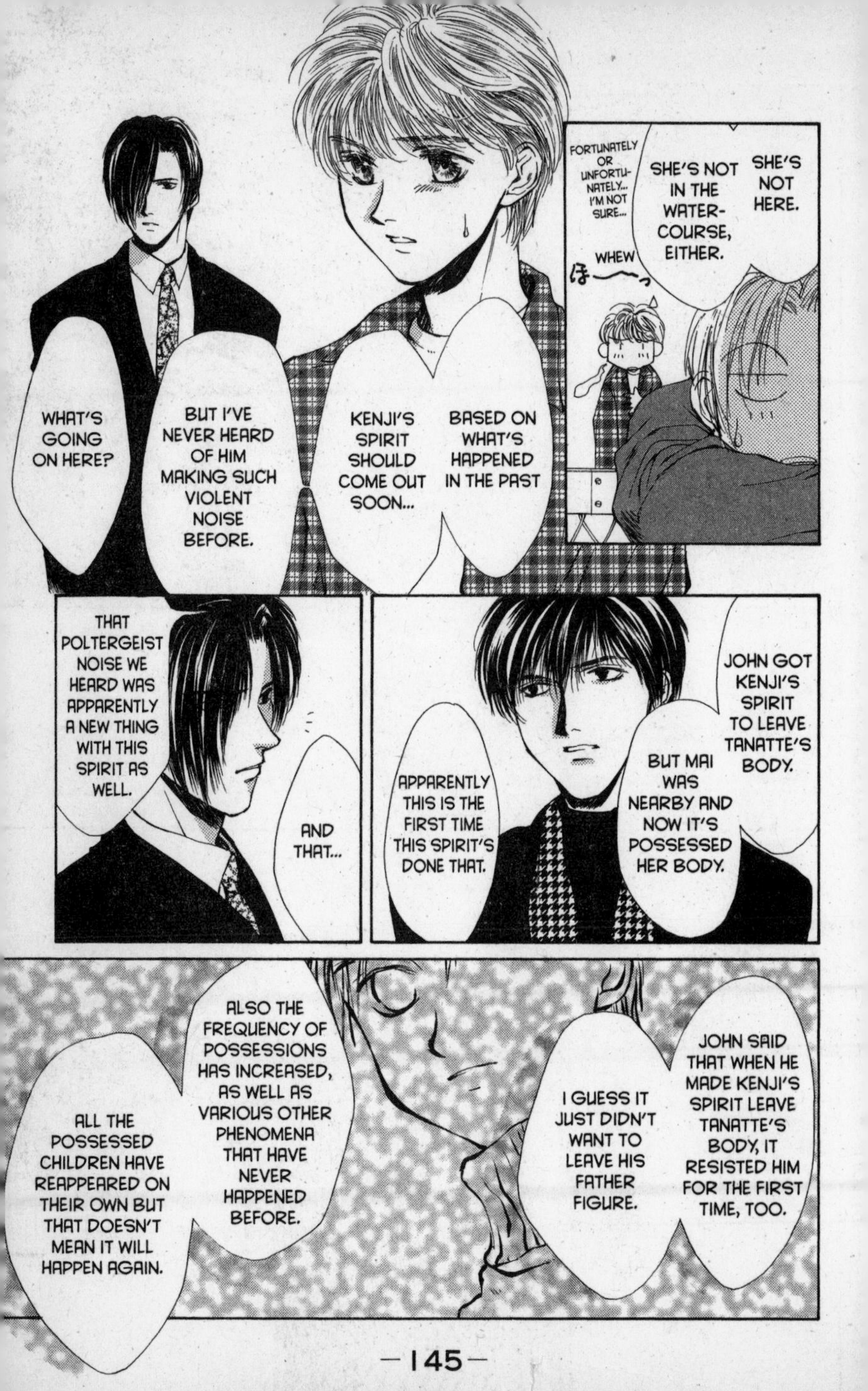
SHE'S NOT HERE.
SHE'S NOT IN THE WATER-COURSE, EITHER.
FORTUNATELY OR UNFORTUNATELY... I'M NOT SURE...
WHEW
ほ〜〜っ
BASED ON WHAT'S HAPPENED IN THE PAST
KENJI'S SPIRIT SHOULD COME OUT SOON...
BUT I'VE NEVER HEARD OF HIM MAKING SUCH VIOLENT NOISE BEFORE.
WHAT'S GOING ON HERE?
JOHN GOT KENJI'S SPIRIT TO LEAVE TANATTE'S BODY.
BUT MAI WAS NEARBY AND NOW IT'S POSSESSED HER BODY.
APPARENTLY THIS IS THE FIRST TIME THIS SPIRIT'S DONE THAT.
AND THAT...
THAT POLTERGEIST NOISE WE HEARD WAS APPARENTLY A NEW THING WITH THIS SPIRIT AS WELL.
JOHN SAID THAT WHEN HE MADE KENJI'S SPIRIT LEAVE TANATTE'S BODY, IT RESISTED HIM FOR THE FIRST TIME, TOO.
I GUESS IT JUST DIDN'T WANT TO LEAVE HIS FATHER FIGURE.
ALSO THE FREQUENCY OF POSSESSIONS HAS INCREASED, AS WELL AS VARIOUS OTHER PHENOMENA THAT HAVE NEVER HAPPENED BEFORE.
ALL THE POSSESSED CHILDREN HAVE REAPPEARED ON THEIR OWN BUT THAT DOESN'T MEAN IT WILL HAPPEN AGAIN.

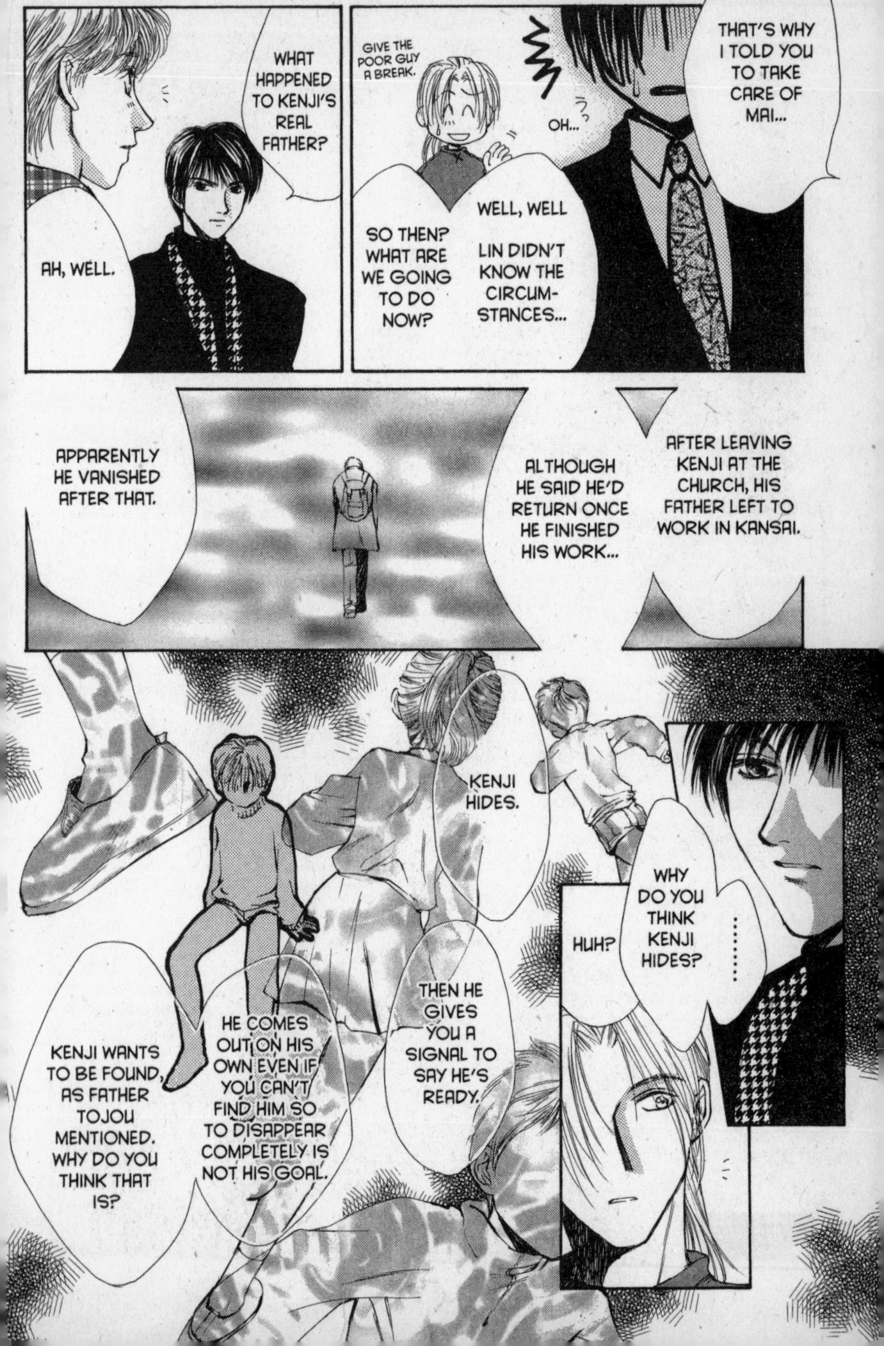
THAT'S WHY I TOLD YOU TO TAKE CARE OF MAI...
OH...
GIVE THE POOR GUY A BREAK.
WELL, WELL
LIN DIDN'T KNOW THE CIRCUMSTANCES...
SO THEN? WHAT ARE WE GOING TO DO NOW?
WHAT HAPPENED TO KENJI'S REAL FATHER?
AH, WELL.
AFTER LEAVING KENJI AT THE CHURCH, HIS FATHER LEFT TO WORK IN KANSAI.
ALTHOUGH HE SAID HE'D RETURN ONCE HE FINISHED HIS WORK...
APPARENTLY HE VANISHED AFTER THAT.
......
WHY DO YOU THINK KENJI HIDES?
HUH?
KENJI HIDES.
THEN HE GIVES YOU A SIGNAL TO SAY HE'S READY.
HE COMES OUT ON HIS OWN EVEN IF YOU CAN'T FIND HIM SO TO DISAPPEAR COMPLETELY IS NOT HIS GOAL.
KENJI WANTS TO BE FOUND, AS FATHER TOJOU MENTIONED. WHY DO YOU THINK THAT IS?

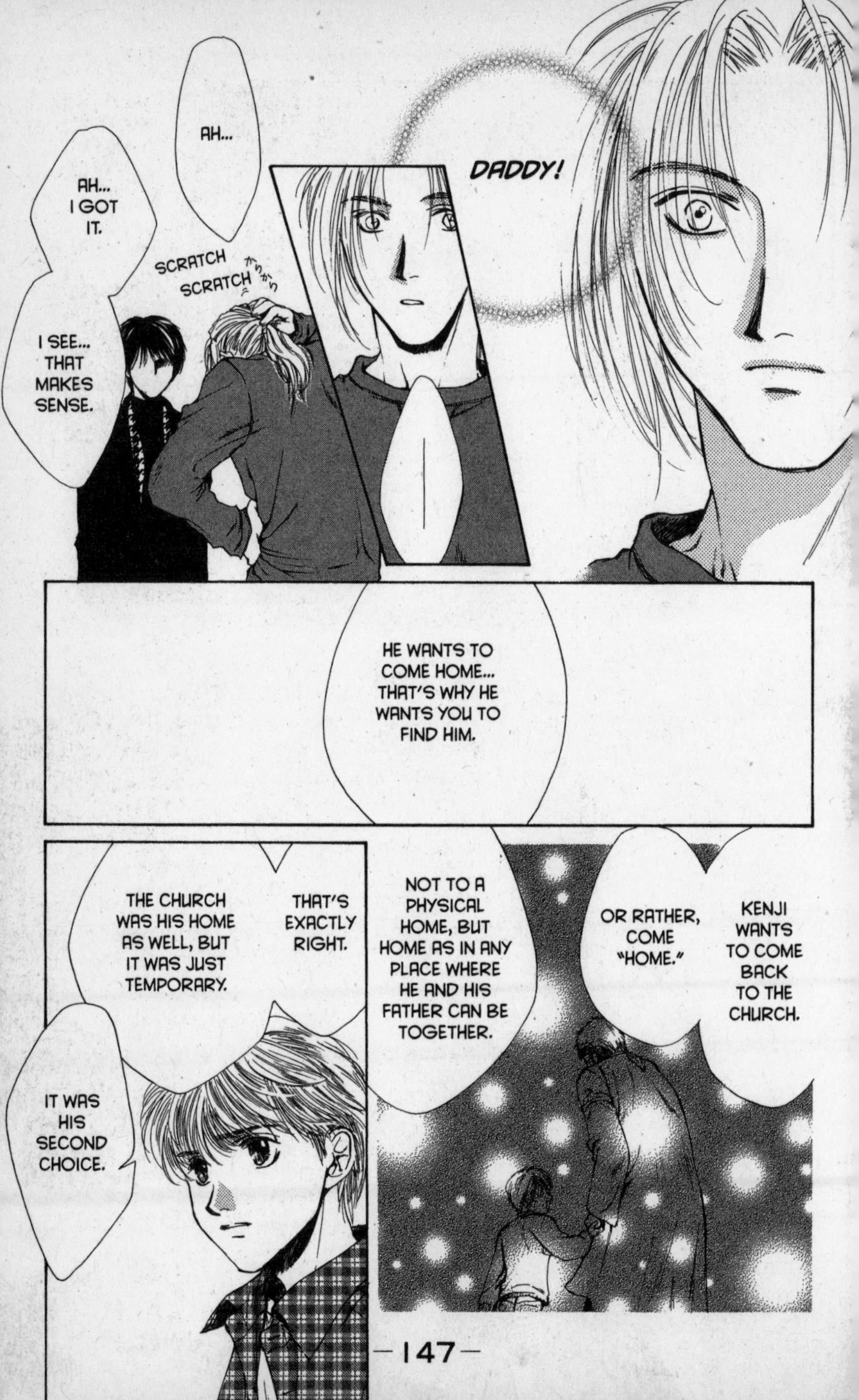
DADDY!
AH...
AH... I GOT IT.
SCRATCH SCRATCH
I SEE... THAT MAKES SENSE.
HE WANTS TO COME HOME... THAT'S WHY HE WANTS YOU TO FIND HIM.
KENJI WANTS TO COME BACK TO THE CHURCH.
OR RATHER, COME "HOME."
NOT TO A PHYSICAL HOME, BUT HOME AS IN ANY PLACE WHERE HE AND HIS FATHER CAN BE TOGETHER.
THAT'S EXACTLY RIGHT.
THE CHURCH WAS HIS HOME AS WELL, BUT IT WAS JUST TEMPORARY.
IT WAS HIS SECOND CHOICE.

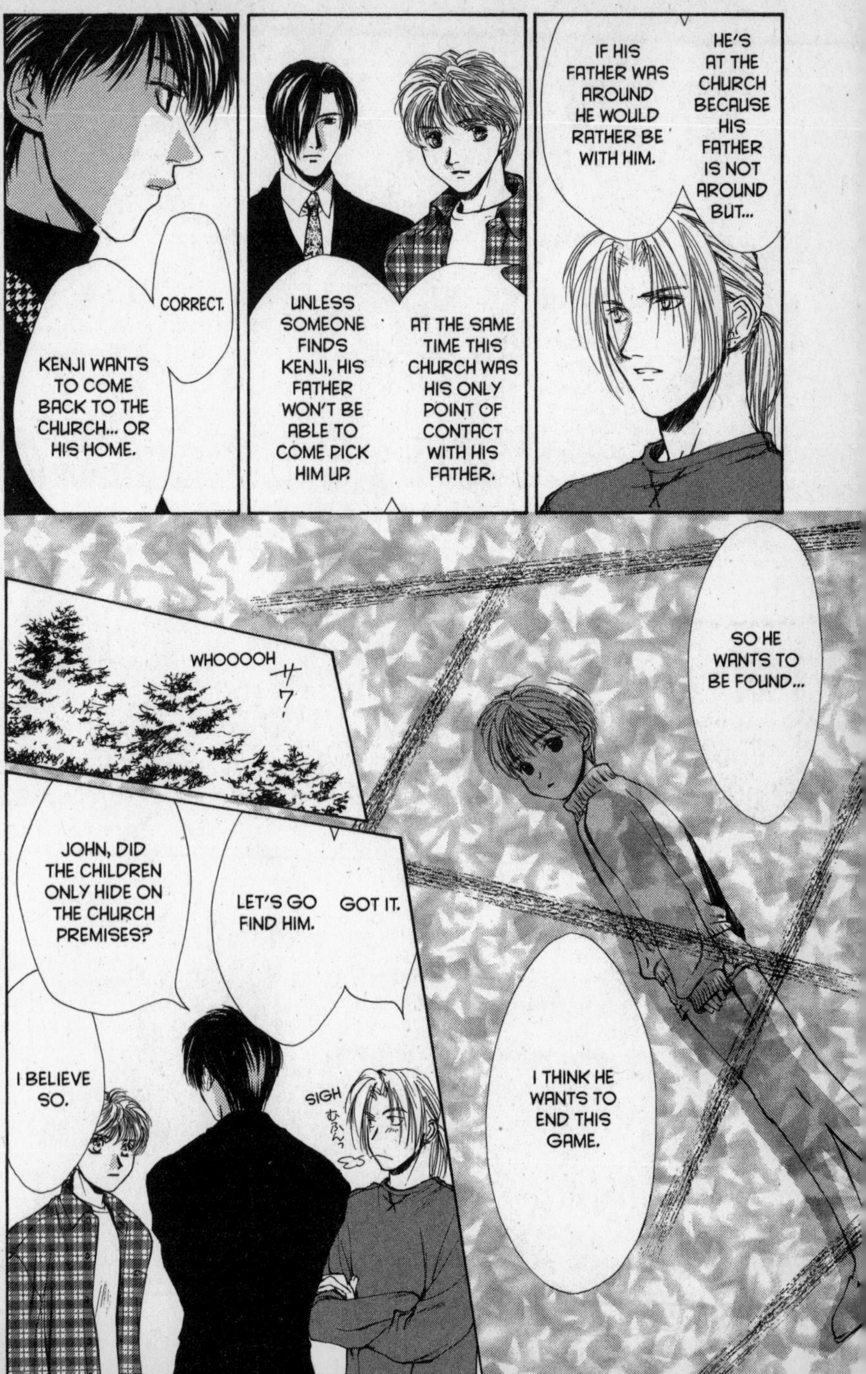
HE'S AT THE CHURCH BECAUSE HIS FATHER IS NOT AROUND BUT...
IF HIS FATHER WAS AROUND HE WOULD RATHER BE WITH HIM.
AT THE SAME TIME THIS CHURCH WAS HIS ONLY POINT OF CONTACT WITH HIS FATHER.
UNLESS SOMEONE FINDS KENJI, HIS FATHER WON'T BE ABLE TO COME PICK HIM UP.
CORRECT.
KENJI WANTS TO COME BACK TO THE CHURCH... OR HIS HOME.
SO HE WANTS TO BE FOUND...
I THINK HE WANTS TO END THIS GAME.
WHOOOOH
サワ
GOT IT.
LET'S GO FIND HIM.
JOHN, DID THE CHILDREN ONLY HIDE ON THE CHURCH PREMISES?
I BELIEVE SO.
SIGH

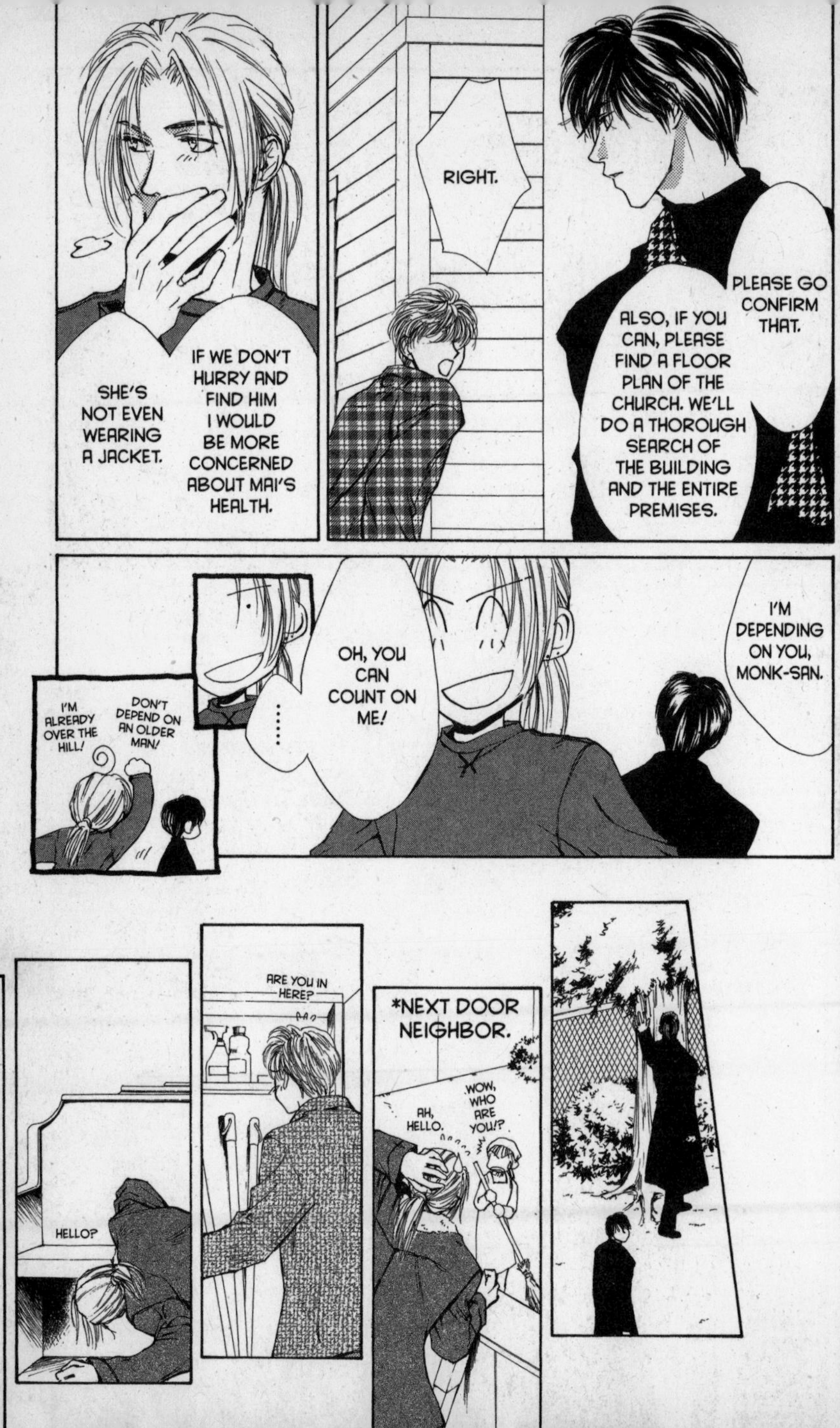
PLEASE GO CONFIRM THAT.
ALSO, IF YOU CAN, PLEASE FIND A FLOOR PLAN OF THE CHURCH. WE'LL DO A THOROUGH SEARCH OF THE BUILDING AND THE ENTIRE PREMISES.
RIGHT.
IF WE DON'T HURRY AND FIND HIM I WOULD BE MORE CONCERNED ABOUT MAI'S HEALTH.
SHE'S NOT EVEN WEARING A JACKET.
I'M DEPENDING ON YOU, MONK-SAN.
OH, YOU CAN COUNT ON ME!
......
DON'T DEPEND ON AN OLDER MAN!
I'M ALREADY OVER THE HILL!
*NEXT DOOR NEIGHBOR.
WOW, WHO ARE YOU!?
AH, HELLO.
ARE YOU IN HERE?
HELLO?

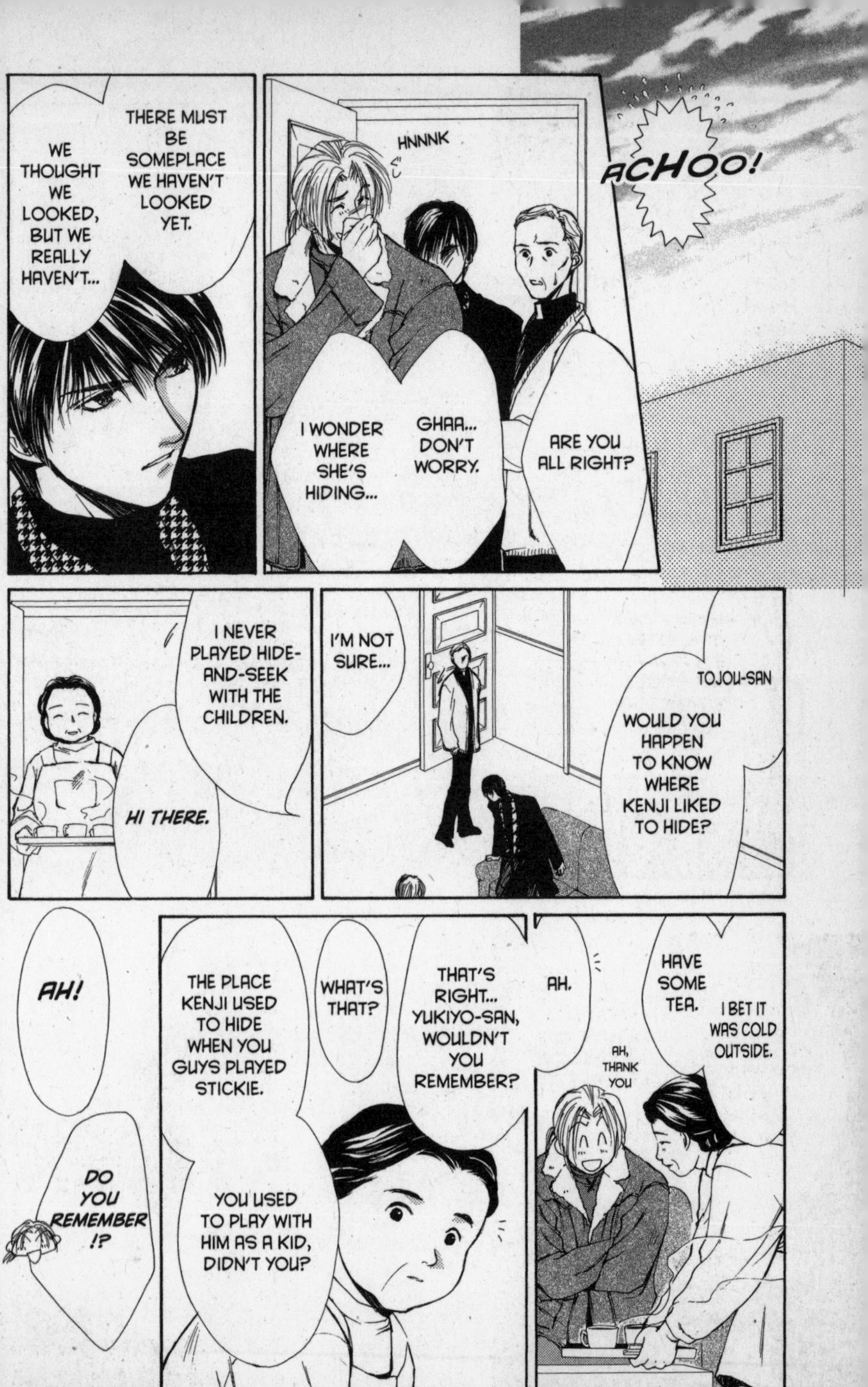

ACHOO!
HNNNK
ARE YOU ALL RIGHT?
GHAA... DON'T WORRY.
I WONDER WHERE SHE'S HIDING...
THERE MUST BE SOMEPLACE WE HAVEN'T LOOKED YET.
WE THOUGHT WE LOOKED, BUT WE REALLY HAVEN'T...
TOJOU-SAN
WOULD YOU HAPPEN TO KNOW WHERE KENJI LIKED TO HIDE?
I'M NOT SURE...
I NEVER PLAYED HIDE-AND-SEEK WITH THE CHILDREN.
HI THERE.
HAVE SOME TEA.
I BET IT WAS COLD OUTSIDE.
AH, THANK YOU
AH.
THAT'S RIGHT... YUKIYO-SAN, WOULDN'T YOU REMEMBER?
WHAT'S THAT?
THE PLACE KENJI USED TO HIDE WHEN YOU GUYS PLAYED STICKIE.
YOU USED TO PLAY WITH HIM AS A KID, DIDN'T YOU?
AH!
DO YOU REMEMBER!?

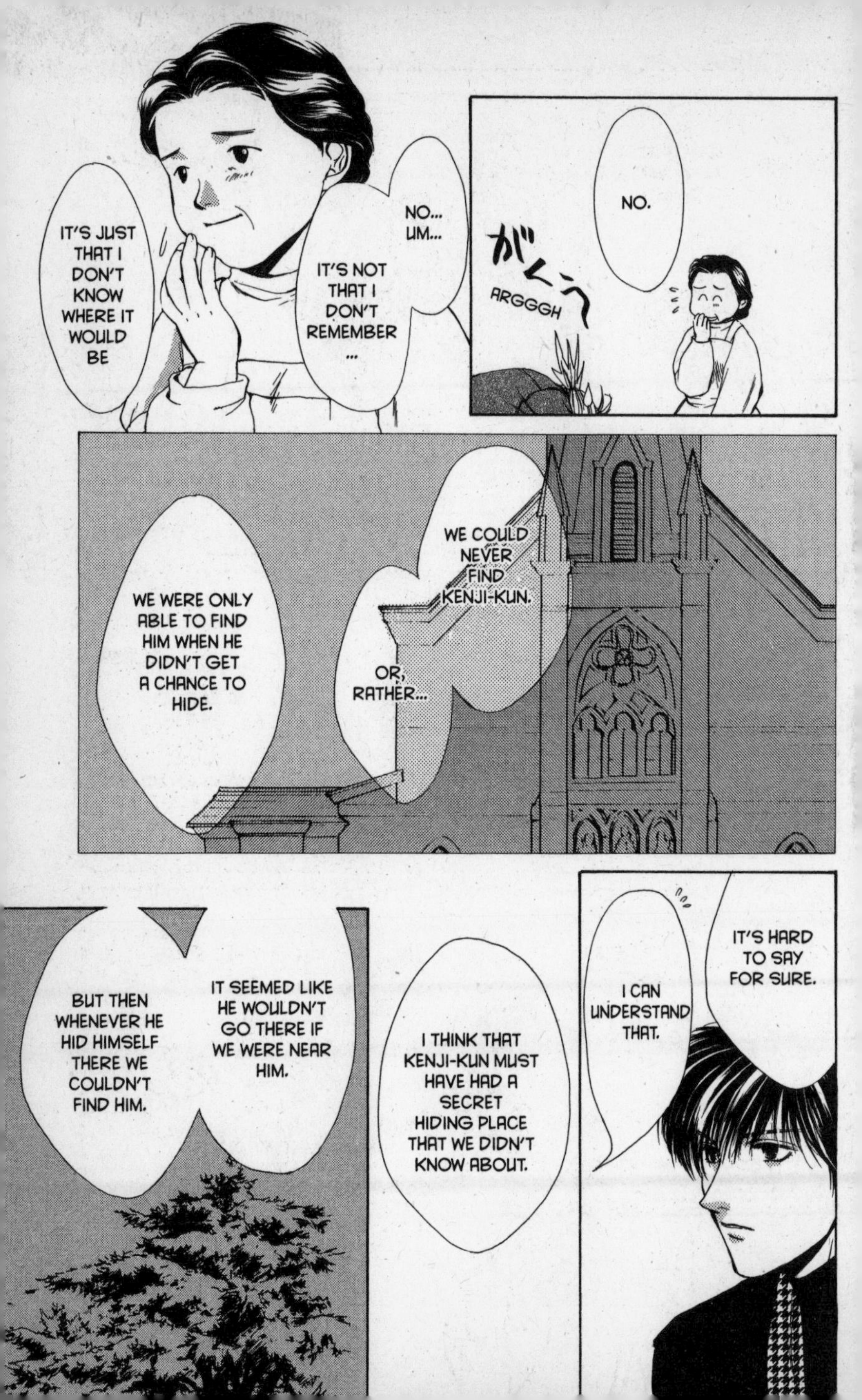
NO.
がくっ
ARGGGH
NO... UM...
IT'S NOT THAT I DON'T REMEMBER...
IT'S JUST THAT I DON'T KNOW WHERE IT WOULD BE
WE COULD NEVER FIND KENJI-KUN.
OR, RATHER...
WE WERE ONLY ABLE TO FIND HIM WHEN HE DIDN'T GET A CHANCE TO HIDE.
IT'S HARD TO SAY FOR SURE.
I CAN UNDERSTAND THAT.
I THINK THAT KENJI-KUN MUST HAVE HAD A SECRET HIDING PLACE THAT WE DIDN'T KNOW ABOUT.
IT SEEMED LIKE HE WOULDN'T GO THERE IF WE WERE NEAR HIM.
BUT THEN WHENEVER HE HID HIMSELF THERE WE COULDN'T FIND HIM.

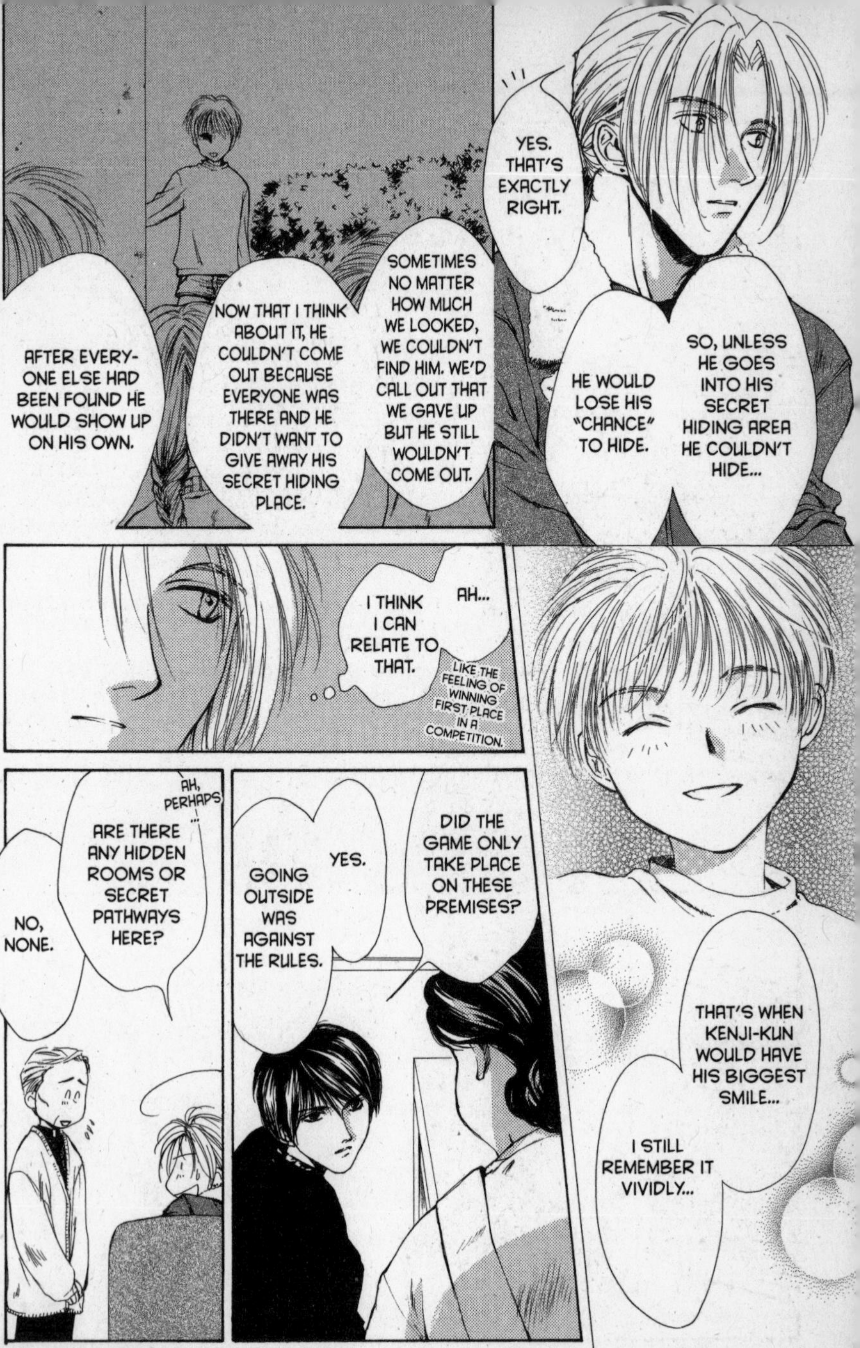
YES. THAT'S EXACTLY RIGHT.
SO, UNLESS HE GOES INTO HIS SECRET HIDING AREA HE COULDN'T HIDE...
HE WOULD LOSE HIS "CHANCE" TO HIDE.
SOMETIMES NO MATTER HOW MUCH WE LOOKED, WE COULDN'T FIND HIM. WE'D CALL OUT THAT WE GAVE UP BUT HE STILL WOULDN'T COME OUT.
NOW THAT I THINK ABOUT IT, HE COULDN'T COME OUT BECAUSE EVERYONE WAS THERE AND HE DIDN'T WANT TO GIVE AWAY HIS SECRET HIDING PLACE.
AFTER EVERY-ONE ELSE HAD BEEN FOUND HE WOULD SHOW UP ON HIS OWN.
THAT'S WHEN KENJI-KUN WOULD HAVE HIS BIGGEST SMILE...
I STILL REMEMBER IT VIVIDLY...
AH...
I THINK I CAN RELATE TO THAT.
LIKE THE FEELING OF WINNING FIRST PLACE IN A COMPETITION.
DID THE GAME ONLY TAKE PLACE ON THESE PREMISES?
YES.
GOING OUTSIDE WAS AGAINST THE RULES.
AH, PERHAPS...
ARE THERE ANY HIDDEN ROOMS OR SECRET PATHWAYS HERE?
NO, NONE.

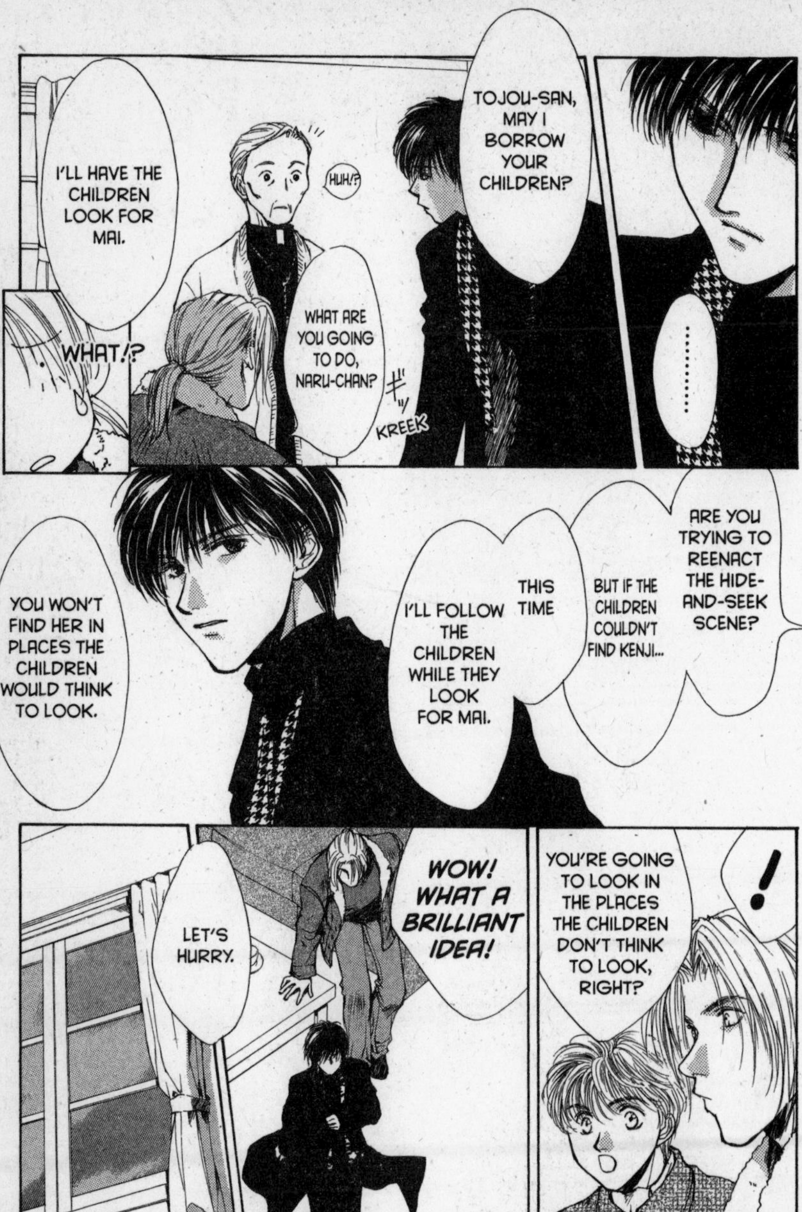
……
TOJOU-SAN, MAY I BORROW YOUR CHILDREN?
HUH!?
I'LL HAVE THE CHILDREN LOOK FOR MAI.
WHAT ARE YOU GOING TO DO, NARU-CHAN?
ギッ
KREEK
WHAT!?
ARE YOU TRYING TO REENACT THE HIDE-AND-SEEK SCENE?
BUT IF THE CHILDREN COULDN'T FIND KENJI...
THIS TIME
I'LL FOLLOW THE CHILDREN WHILE THEY LOOK FOR MAI.
YOU WON'T FIND HER IN PLACES THE CHILDREN WOULD THINK TO LOOK.
!
YOU'RE GOING TO LOOK IN THE PLACES THE CHILDREN DON'T THINK TO LOOK, RIGHT?
WOW! WHAT A BRILLIANT IDEA!
LET'S HURRY.

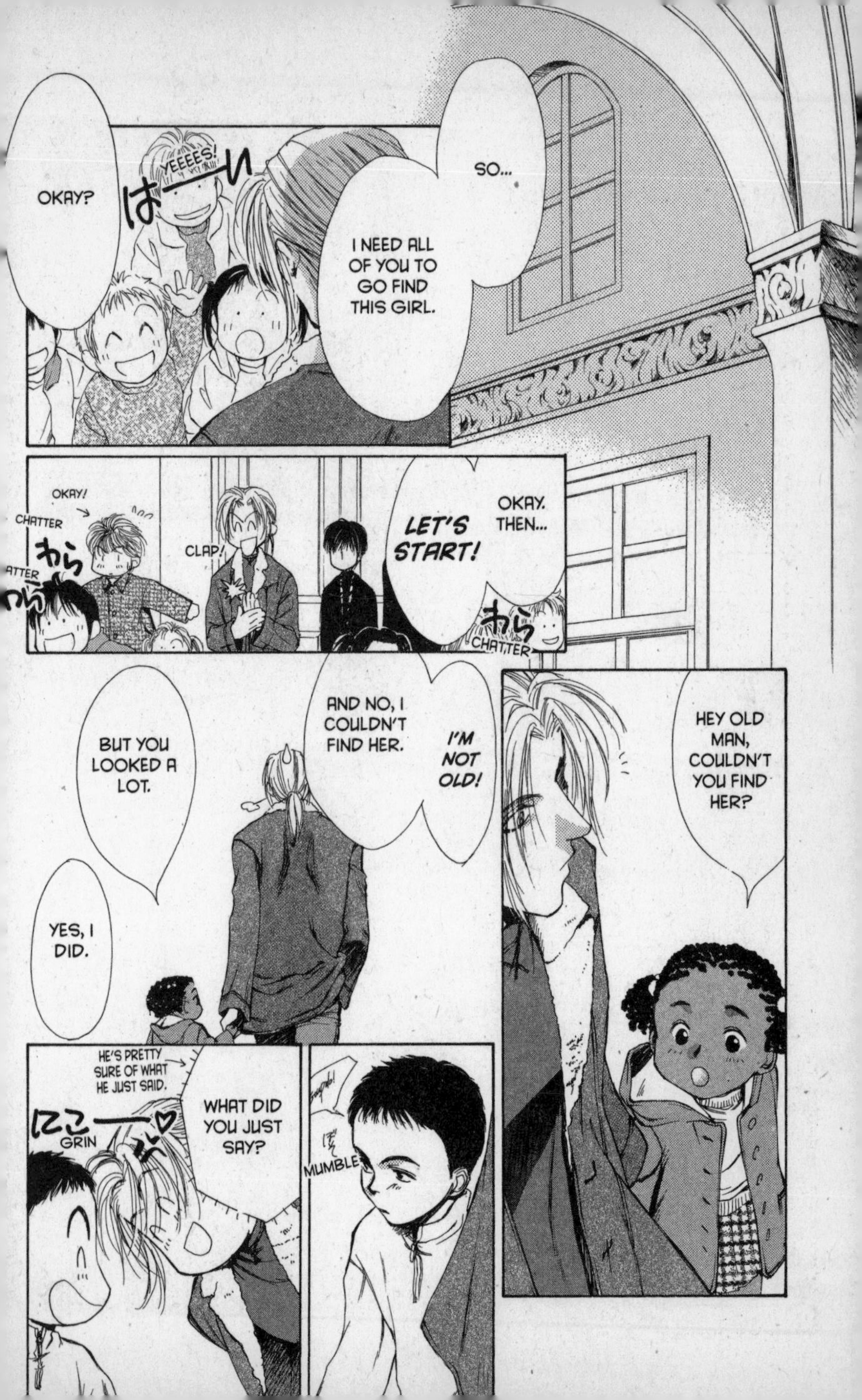
SO...
I NEED ALL OF YOU TO GO FIND THIS GIRL.
OKAY?
はーい
YEEEES!
OKAY. THEN...
LET'S START!
CLAP!
OKAY!
わら
CHATTER
わら
CHATTER
HEY OLD MAN, COULDN'T YOU FIND HER?
I'M NOT OLD!
AND NO, I COULDN'T FIND HER.
BUT YOU LOOKED A LOT.
YES, I DID.
MUMBLE
WHAT DID YOU JUST SAY?
HE'S PRETTY SURE OF WHAT HE JUST SAID.
にこー
GRIN

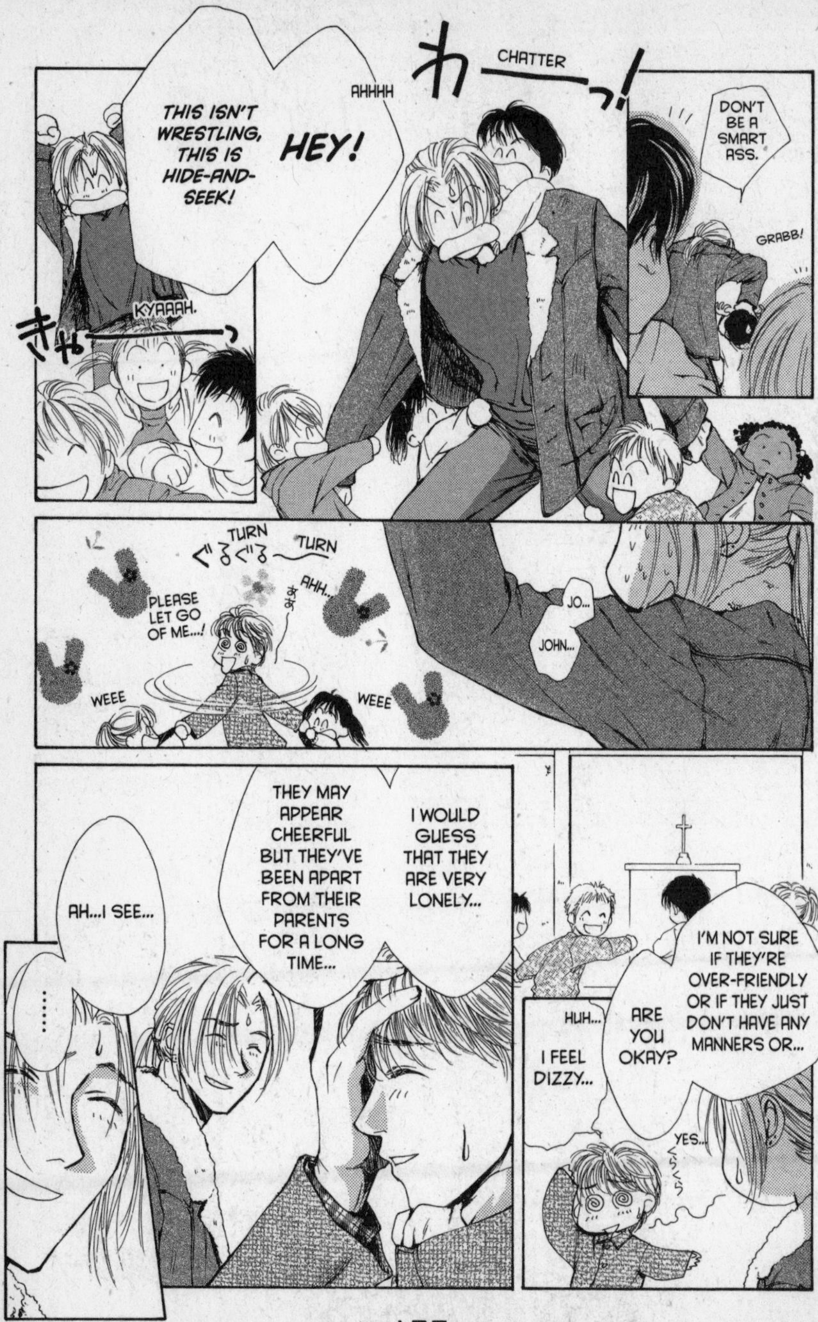
DON'T BE A SMART ASS.
GRABB!
わーっ!
CHATTER
AHHHH
HEY!
THIS ISN'T WRESTLING, THIS IS HIDE-AND-SEEK!
きゃーっ
KYAAAH.
JO...
JOHN...
ぐるぐる
TURN
TURN
ああ
AHH...
PLEASE LET GO OF ME...!
WEEE
WEEE
I'M NOT SURE IF THEY'RE OVER-FRIENDLY OR IF THEY JUST DON'T HAVE ANY MANNERS OR...
ARE YOU OKAY?
HUH...
I FEEL DIZZY...
YES...
くらくら
I WOULD GUESS THAT THEY ARE VERY LONELY...
THEY MAY APPEAR CHEERFUL BUT THEY'VE BEEN APART FROM THEIR PARENTS FOR A LONG TIME...
AH...I SEE...
......

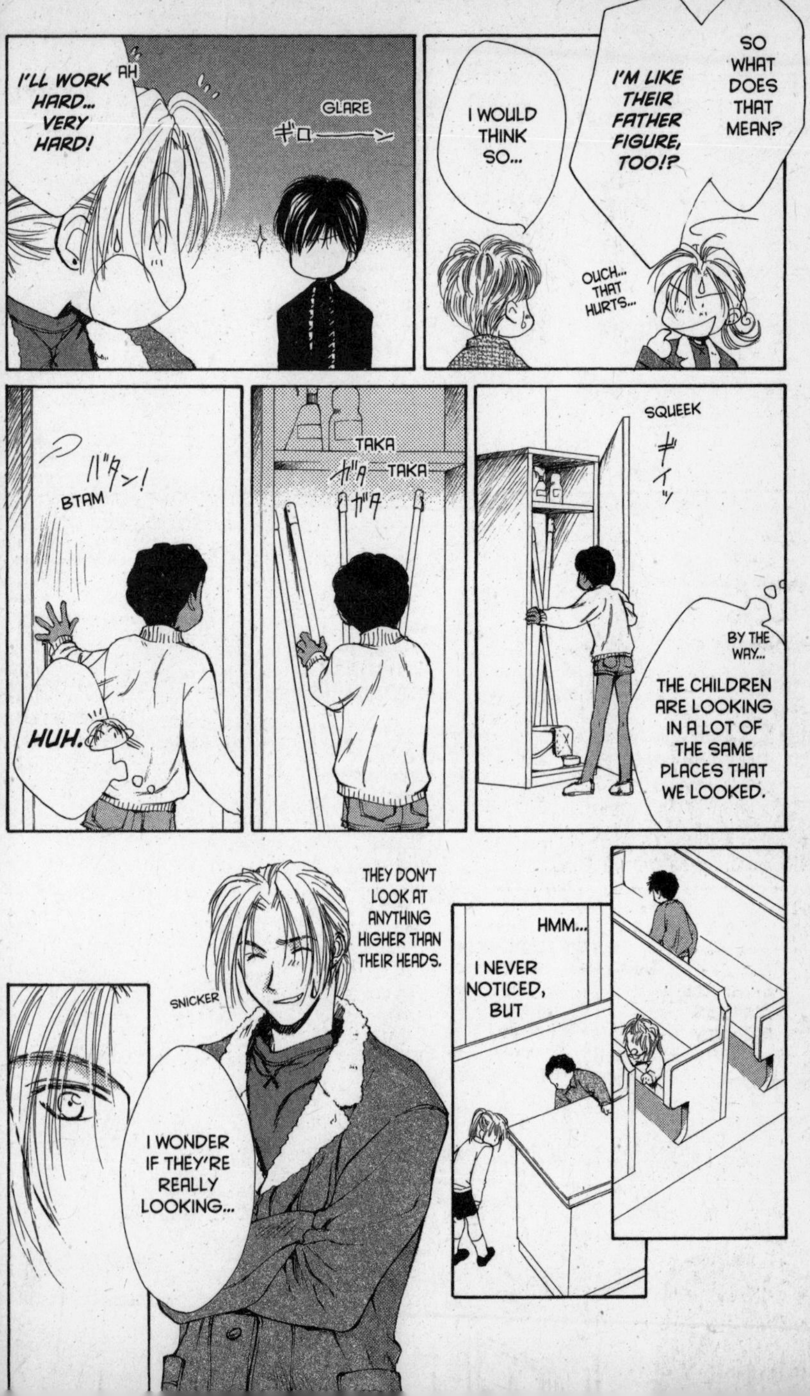
SO WHAT DOES THAT MEAN?
I'M LIKE THEIR FATHER FIGURE, TOO!?
I WOULD THINK SO...
OUCH... THAT HURTS...
GLARE
ギロ――ン
AH
I'LL WORK HARD... VERY HARD!
SQUEEK
ギィッ
BY THE WAY...
THE CHILDREN ARE LOOKING IN A LOT OF THE SAME PLACES THAT WE LOOKED.
TAKA
ガタ
TAKA
ガタ
バタン!
BTAM
HUH.
HMM...
I NEVER NOTICED, BUT
THEY DON'T LOOK AT ANYTHING HIGHER THAN THEIR HEADS.
SNICKER
I WONDER IF THEY'RE REALLY LOOKING...

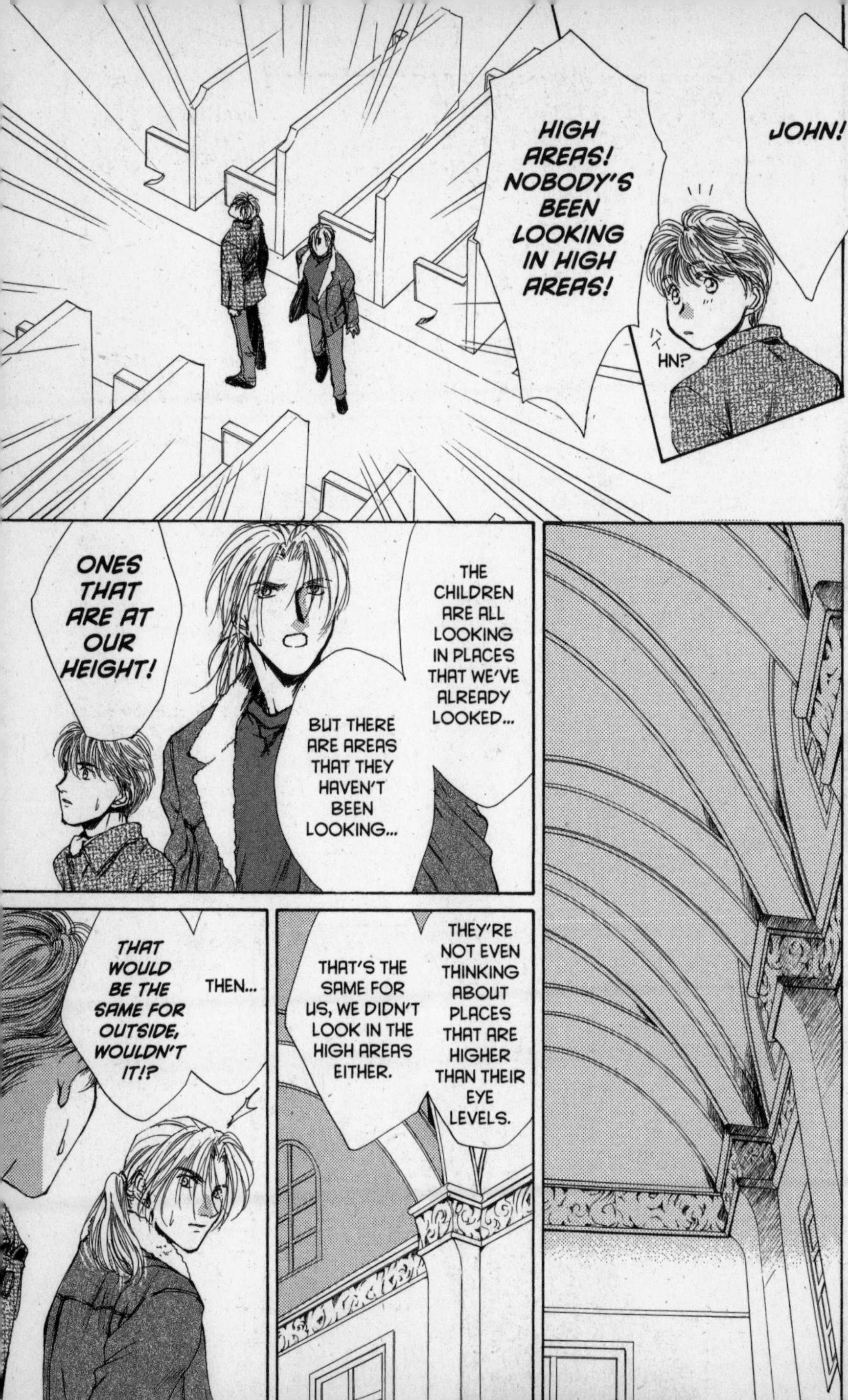
JOHN!
HN?
HIGH AREAS! NOBODY'S BEEN LOOKING IN HIGH AREAS!
THE CHILDREN ARE ALL LOOKING IN PLACES THAT WE'VE ALREADY LOOKED...
BUT THERE ARE AREAS THAT THEY HAVEN'T BEEN LOOKING...
ONES THAT ARE AT OUR HEIGHT!
THEY'RE NOT EVEN THINKING ABOUT PLACES THAT ARE HIGHER THAN THEIR EYE LEVELS.
THAT'S THE SAME FOR US, WE DIDN'T LOOK IN THE HIGH AREAS EITHER.
THEN...
THAT WOULD BE THE SAME FOR OUTSIDE, WOULDN'T IT!?

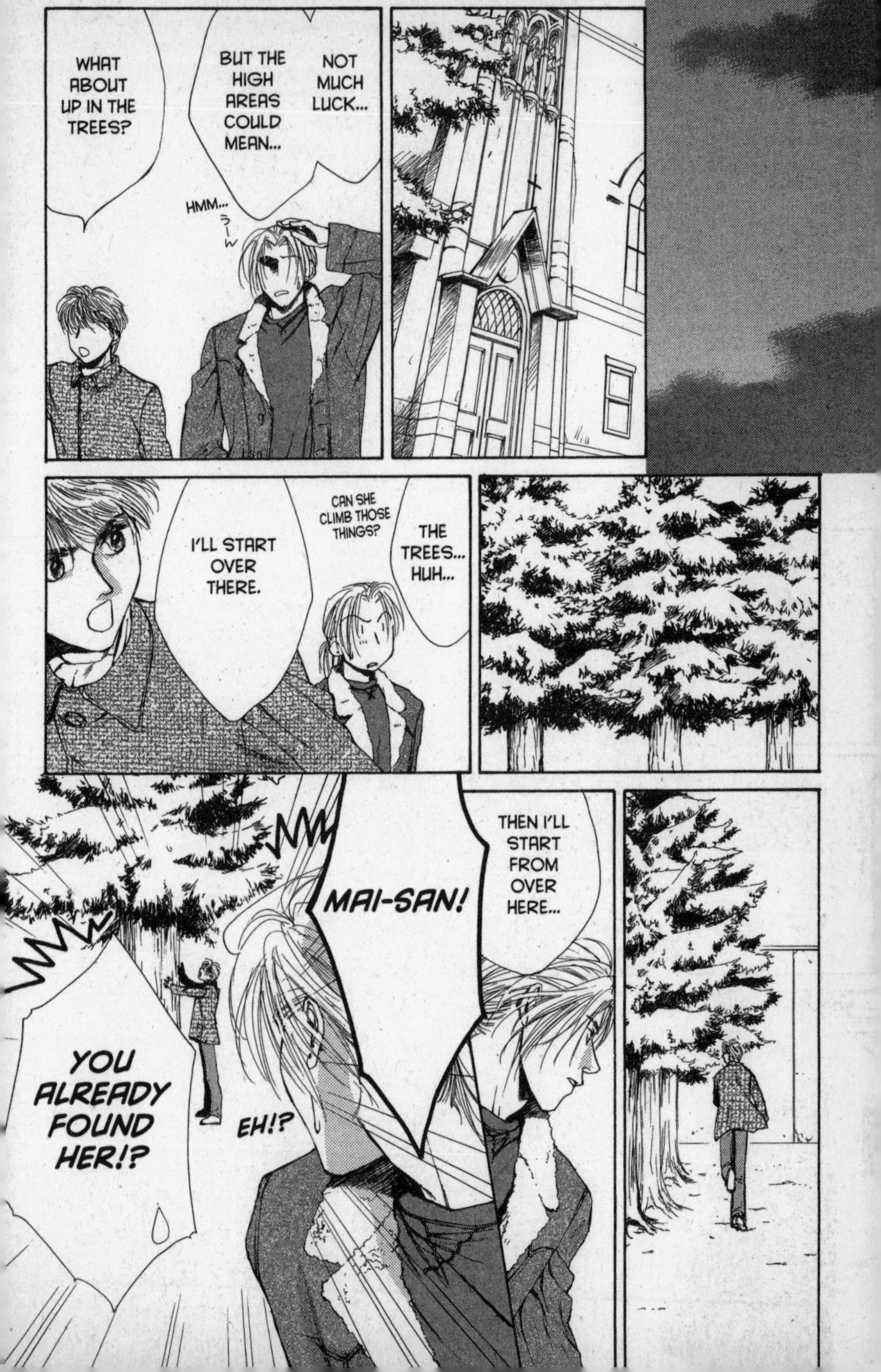
NOT MUCH LUCK...
BUT THE HIGH AREAS COULD MEAN...
HMM...
WHAT ABOUT UP IN THE TREES?
THE TREES... HUH...
CAN SHE CLIMB THOSE THINGS?
I'LL START OVER THERE.
THEN I'LL START FROM OVER HERE...
MAI-SAN!
EH!?
YOU ALREADY FOUND HER!?

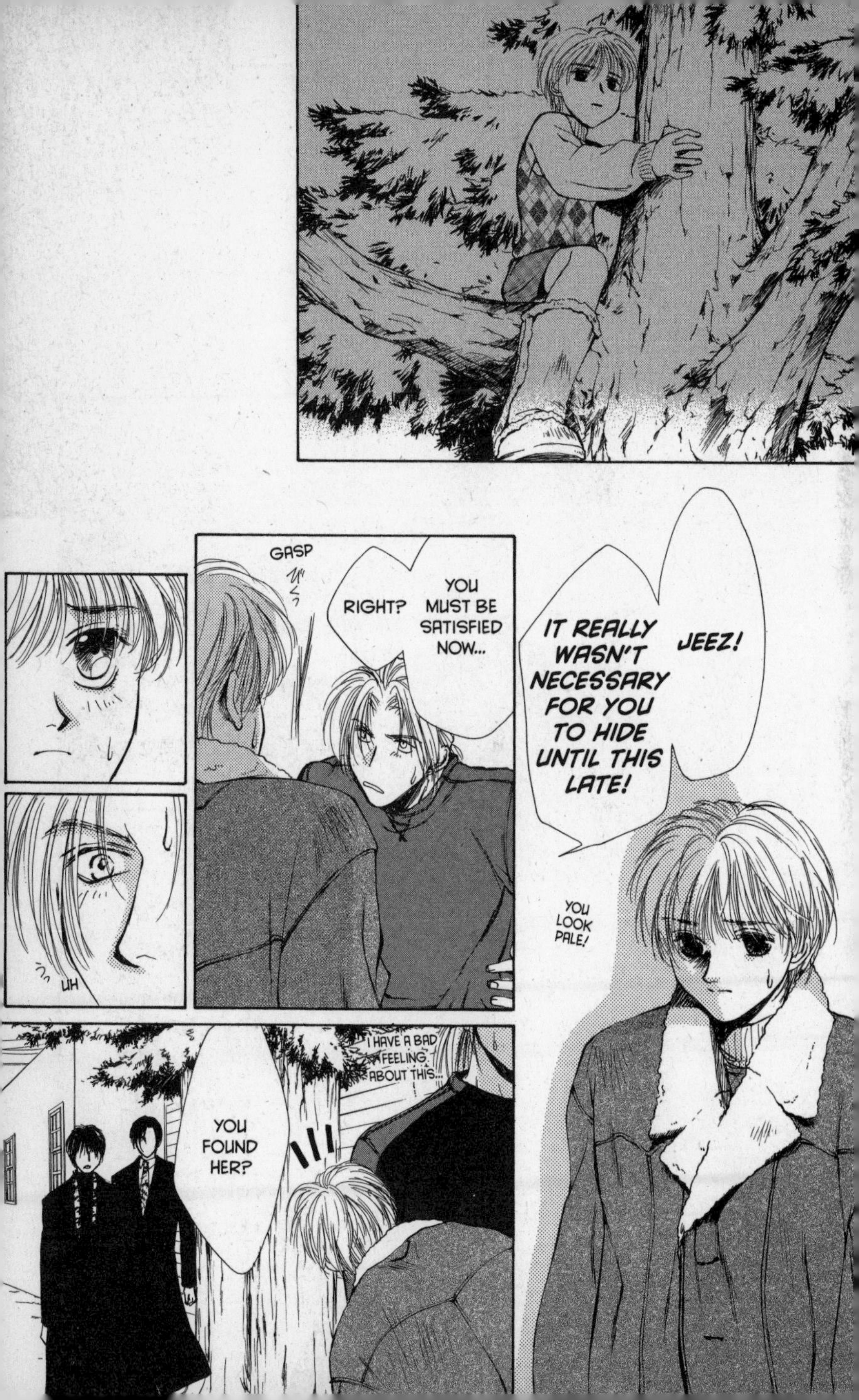
JEEZ!
IT REALLY WASN'T NECESSARY FOR YOU TO HIDE UNTIL THIS LATE!
YOU LOOK PALE!
GASP
YOU MUST BE SATISFIED NOW...
RIGHT?
UH
I HAVE A BAD FEELING ABOUT THIS...
YOU FOUND HER?

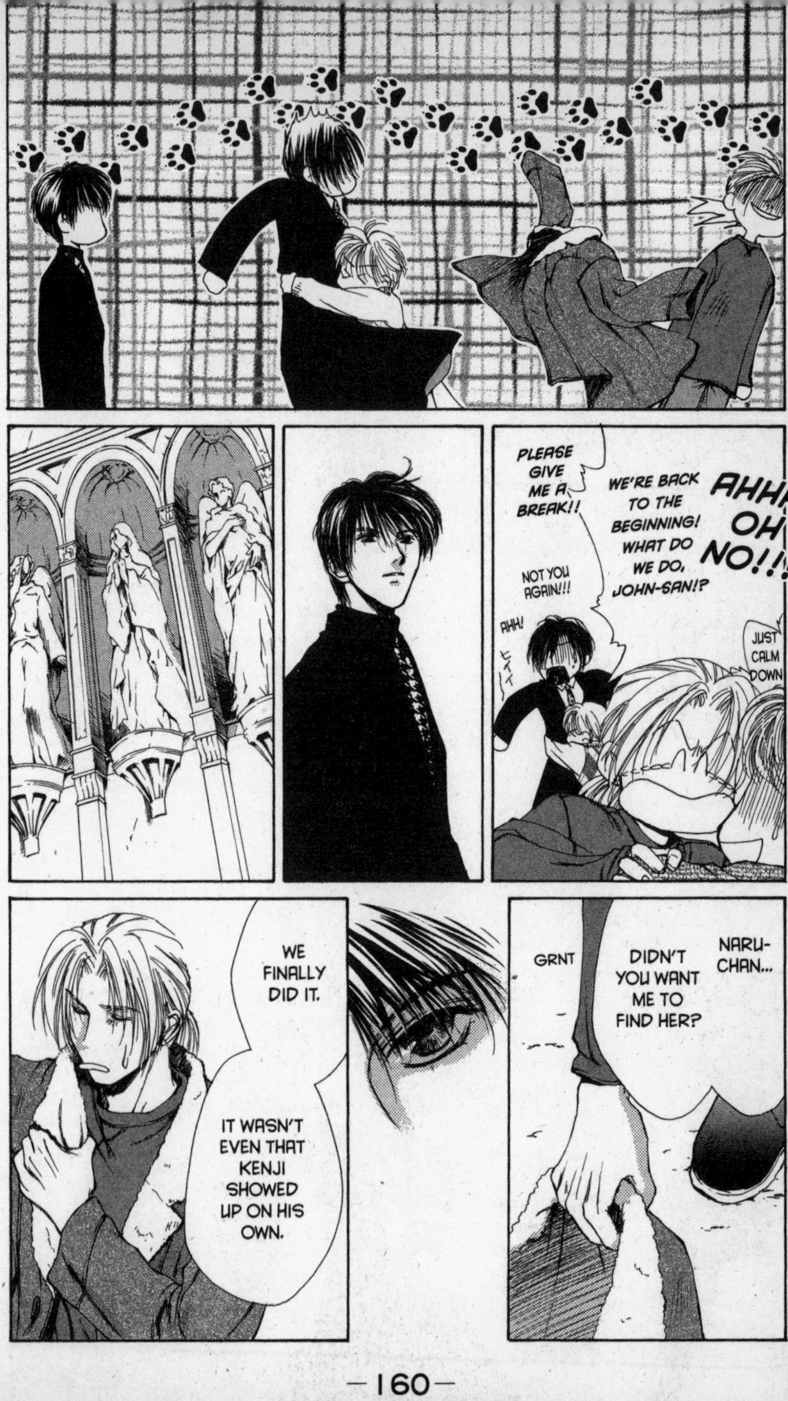
AHHH. OH NO!!!
WE'RE BACK TO THE BEGINNING! WHAT DO WE DO, JOHN-SAN!?
PLEASE GIVE ME A BREAK!!
JUST CALM DOWN
NOT YOU AGAIN!!!
AHH!
NARU-CHAN...
DIDN'T YOU WANT ME TO FIND HER?
GRNT
WE FINALLY DID IT.
IT WASN'T EVEN THAT KENJI SHOWED UP ON HIS OWN.

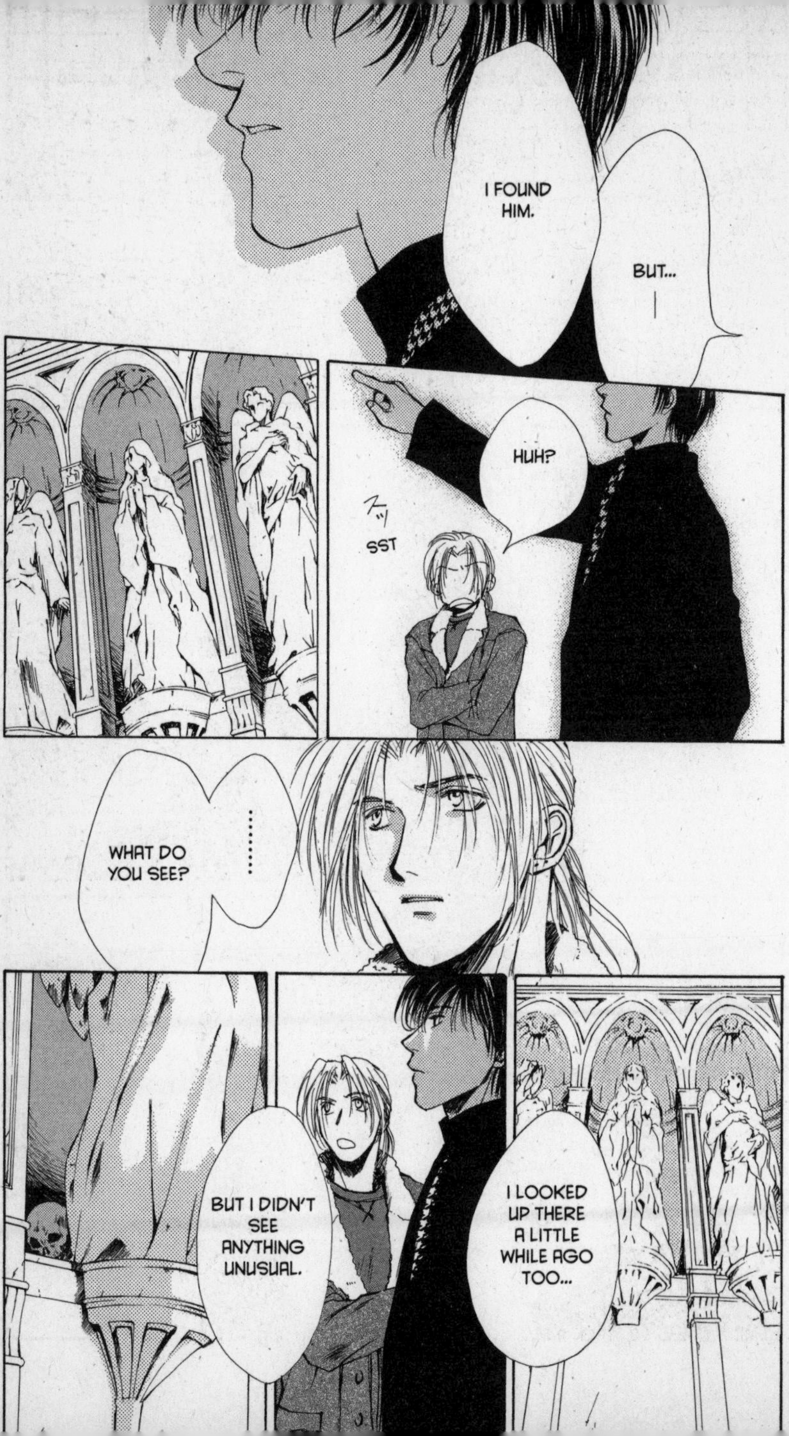
I FOUND HIM.
BUT...
HUH?
スッ
SST
......
WHAT DO YOU SEE?
I LOOKED UP THERE A LITTLE WHILE AGO TOO...
BUT I DIDN'T SEE ANYTHING UNUSUAL.

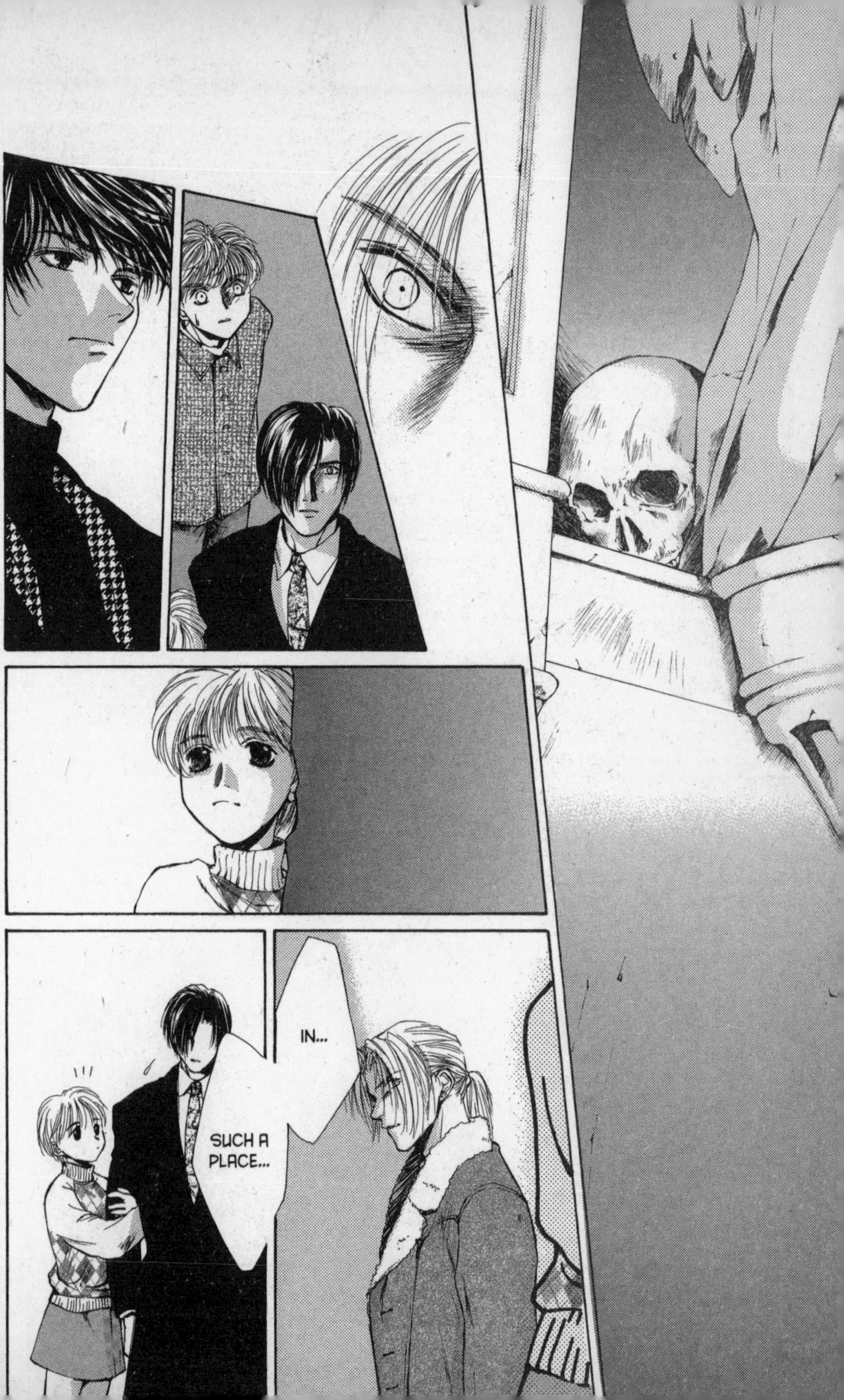
IN...
SUCH A PLACE...

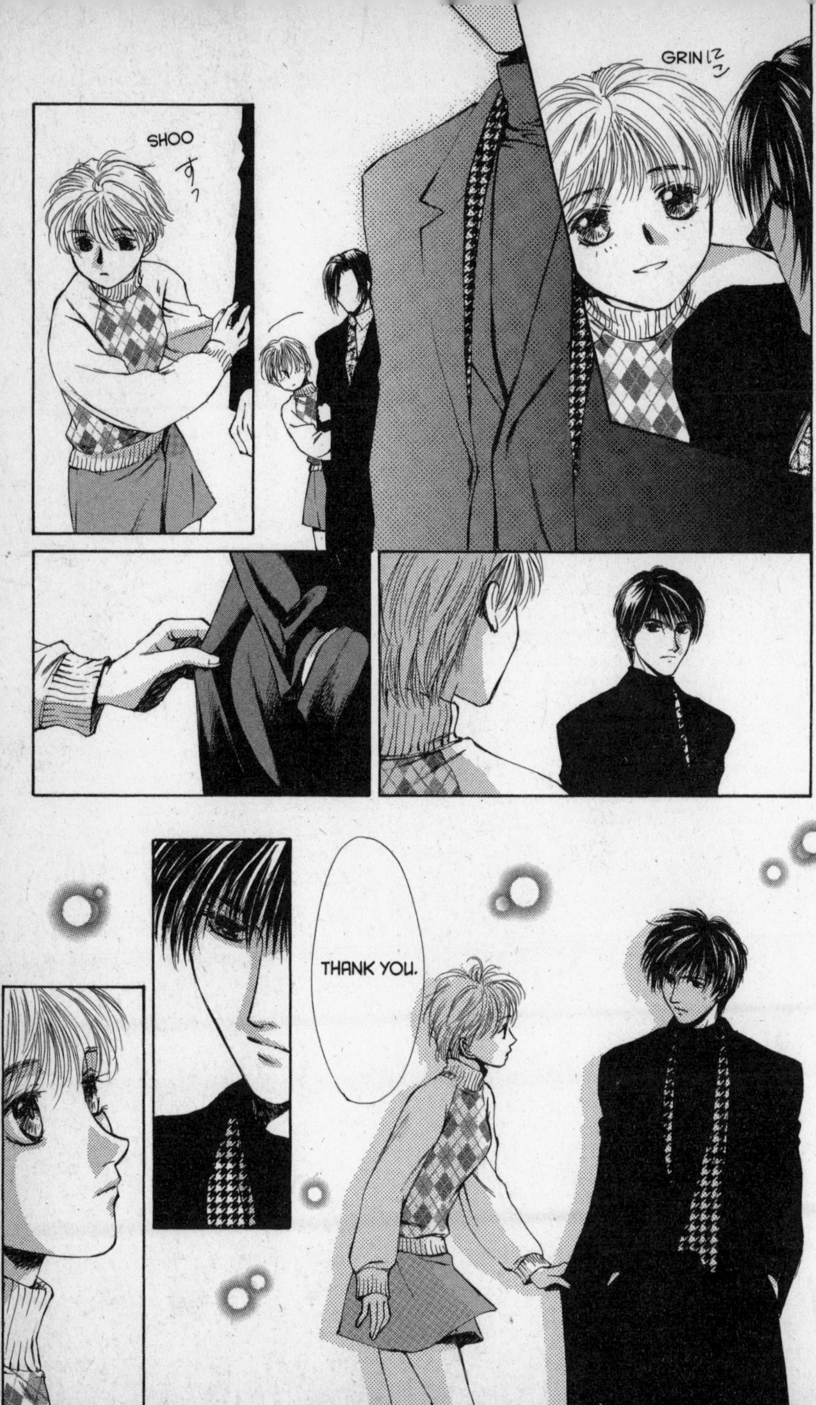
GRIN にこ
SHOO すっ
THANK YOU.

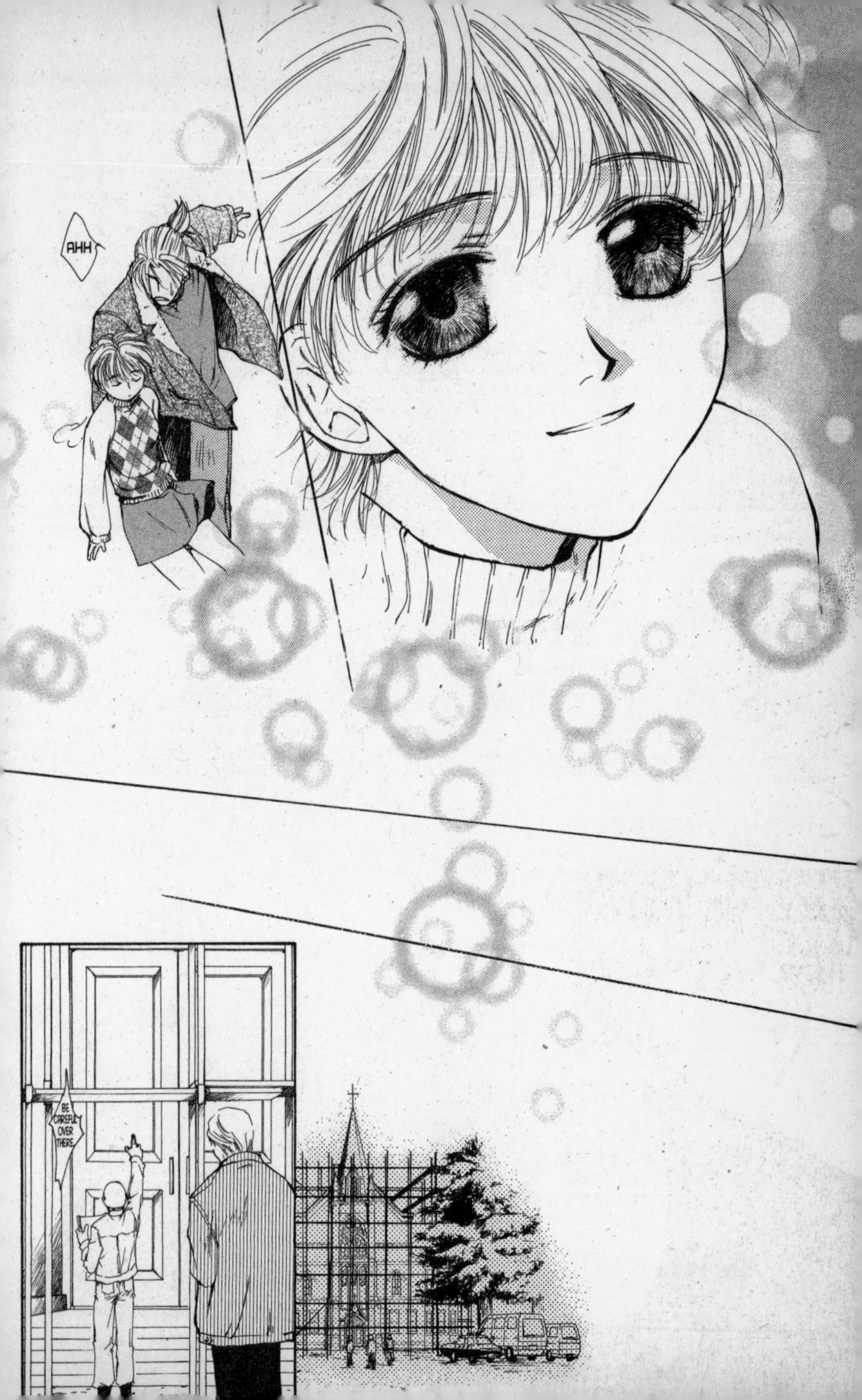
AHH
BE CAREFUL OVER THERE

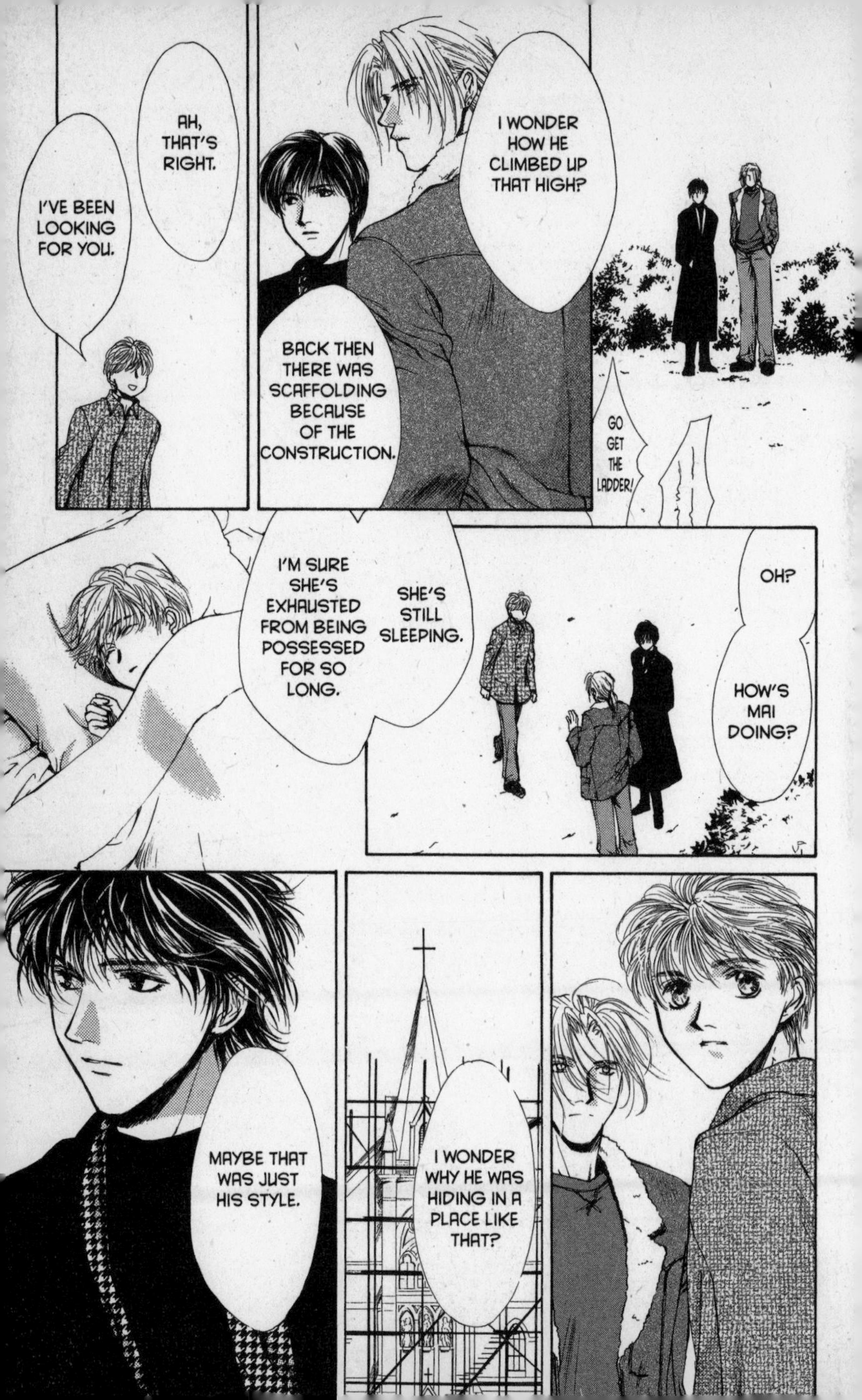
I WONDER HOW HE CLIMBED UP THAT HIGH?
BACK THEN THERE WAS SCAFFOLDING BECAUSE OF THE CONSTRUCTION.
AH, THAT'S RIGHT.
I'VE BEEN LOOKING FOR YOU.
GO GET THE LADDER!
OH?
HOW'S MAI DOING?
SHE'S STILL SLEEPING.
I'M SURE SHE'S EXHAUSTED FROM BEING POSSESSED FOR SO LONG.
I WONDER WHY HE WAS HIDING IN A PLACE LIKE THAT?
MAYBE THAT WAS JUST HIS STYLE.

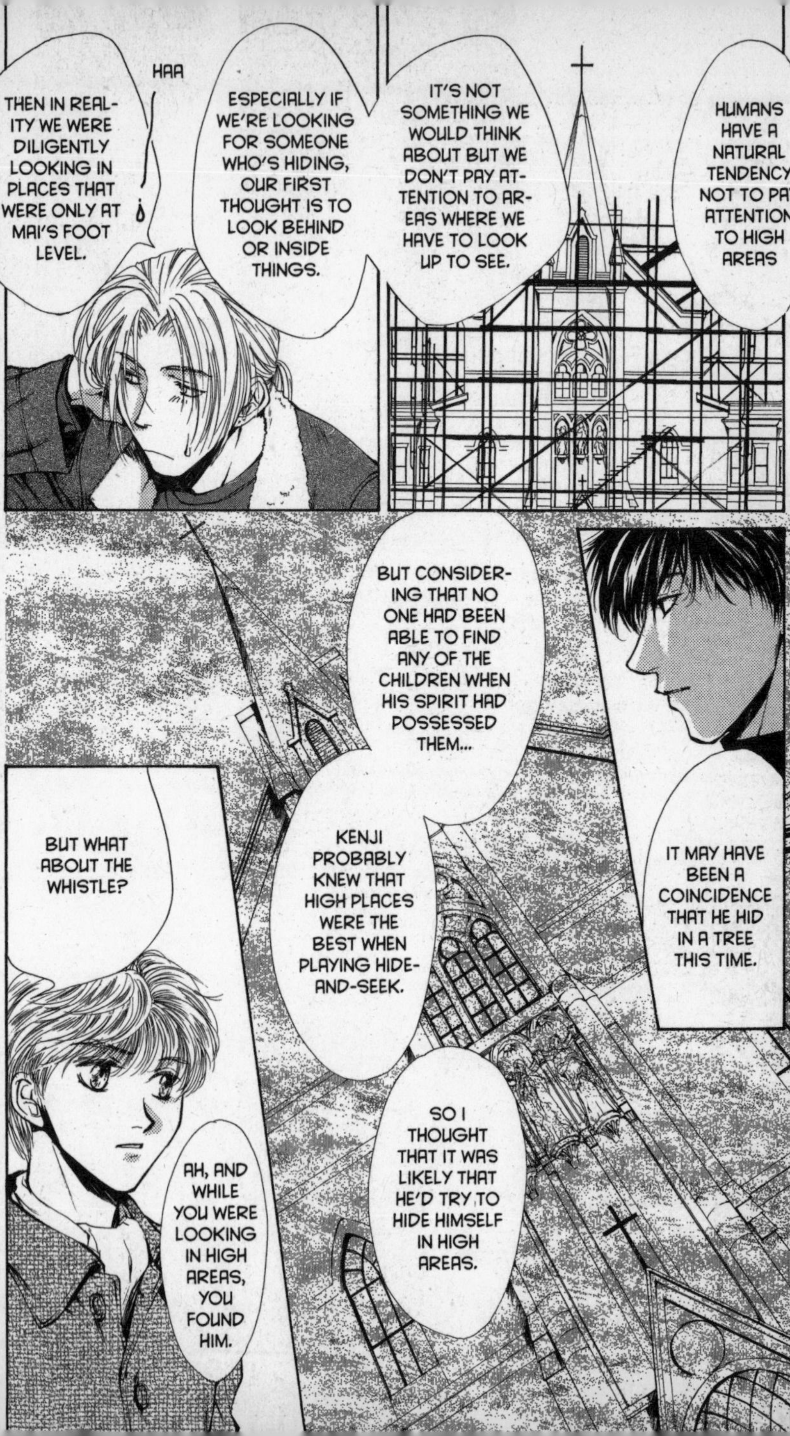
HUMANS HAVE A NATURAL TENDENCY NOT TO PAY ATTENTION TO HIGH AREAS
IT'S NOT SOMETHING WE WOULD THINK ABOUT BUT WE DON'T PAY ATTENTION TO AREAS WHERE WE HAVE TO LOOK UP TO SEE.
ESPECIALLY IF WE'RE LOOKING FOR SOMEONE WHO'S HIDING, OUR FIRST THOUGHT IS TO LOOK BEHIND OR INSIDE THINGS.
HAA
THEN IN REALITY WE WERE DILIGENTLY LOOKING IN PLACES THAT WERE ONLY AT MAI'S FOOT LEVEL.
IT MAY HAVE BEEN A COINCIDENCE THAT HE HID IN A TREE THIS TIME.
BUT CONSIDERING THAT NO ONE HAD BEEN ABLE TO FIND ANY OF THE CHILDREN WHEN HIS SPIRIT HAD POSSESSED THEM...
KENJI PROBABLY KNEW THAT HIGH PLACES WERE THE BEST WHEN PLAYING HIDE-AND-SEEK.
SO I THOUGHT THAT IT WAS LIKELY THAT HE'D TRY TO HIDE HIMSELF IN HIGH AREAS.
AH, AND WHILE YOU WERE LOOKING IN HIGH AREAS, YOU FOUND HIM.
BUT WHAT ABOUT THE WHISTLE?

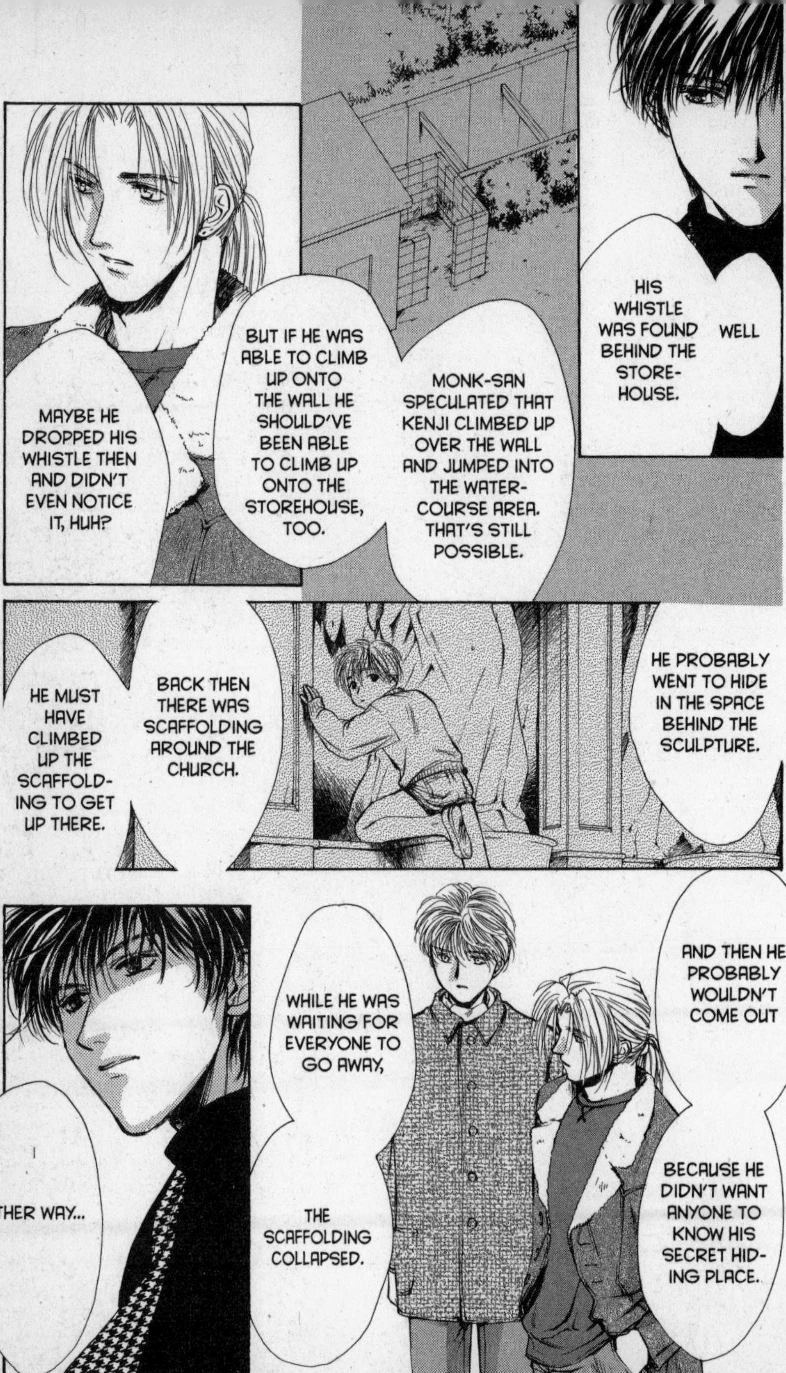
WELL
HIS WHISTLE WAS FOUND BEHIND THE STOREHOUSE.
MONK-SAN SPECULATED THAT KENJI CLIMBED UP OVER THE WALL AND JUMPED INTO THE WATERCOURSE AREA. THAT'S STILL POSSIBLE.
BUT IF HE WAS ABLE TO CLIMB UP ONTO THE WALL HE SHOULD'VE BEEN ABLE TO CLIMB UP ONTO THE STOREHOUSE, TOO.
MAYBE HE DROPPED HIS WHISTLE THEN AND DIDN'T EVEN NOTICE IT, HUH?
HE PROBABLY WENT TO HIDE IN THE SPACE BEHIND THE SCULPTURE.
BACK THEN THERE WAS SCAFFOLDING AROUND THE CHURCH.
HE MUST HAVE CLIMBED UP THE SCAFFOLDING TO GET UP THERE.
AND THEN HE PROBABLY WOULDN'T COME OUT
BECAUSE HE DIDN'T WANT ANYONE TO KNOW HIS SECRET HIDING PLACE.
WHILE HE WAS WAITING FOR EVERYONE TO GO AWAY,
THE SCAFFOLDING COLLAPSED.
EITHER WAY...

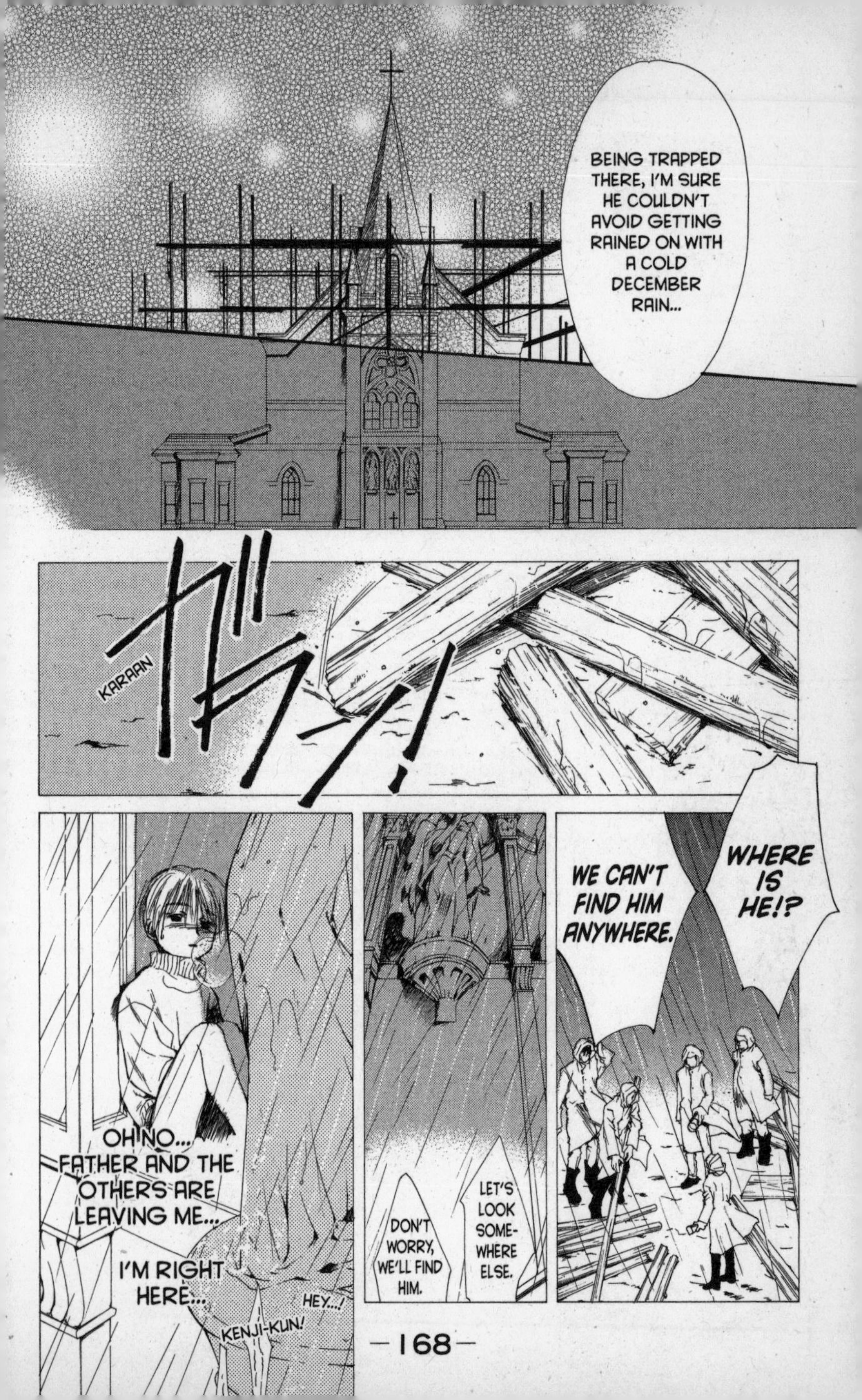
BEING TRAPPED THERE, I'M SURE HE COULDN'T AVOID GETTING RAINED ON WITH A COLD DECEMBER RAIN...
KARAAN
WHERE IS HE!?
WE CAN'T FIND HIM ANYWHERE.
LET'S LOOK SOME-WHERE ELSE.
DON'T WORRY, WE'LL FIND HIM.
OH NO... FATHER AND THE OTHERS ARE LEAVING ME...
I'M RIGHT HERE...
HEY...!
KENJI-KUN!

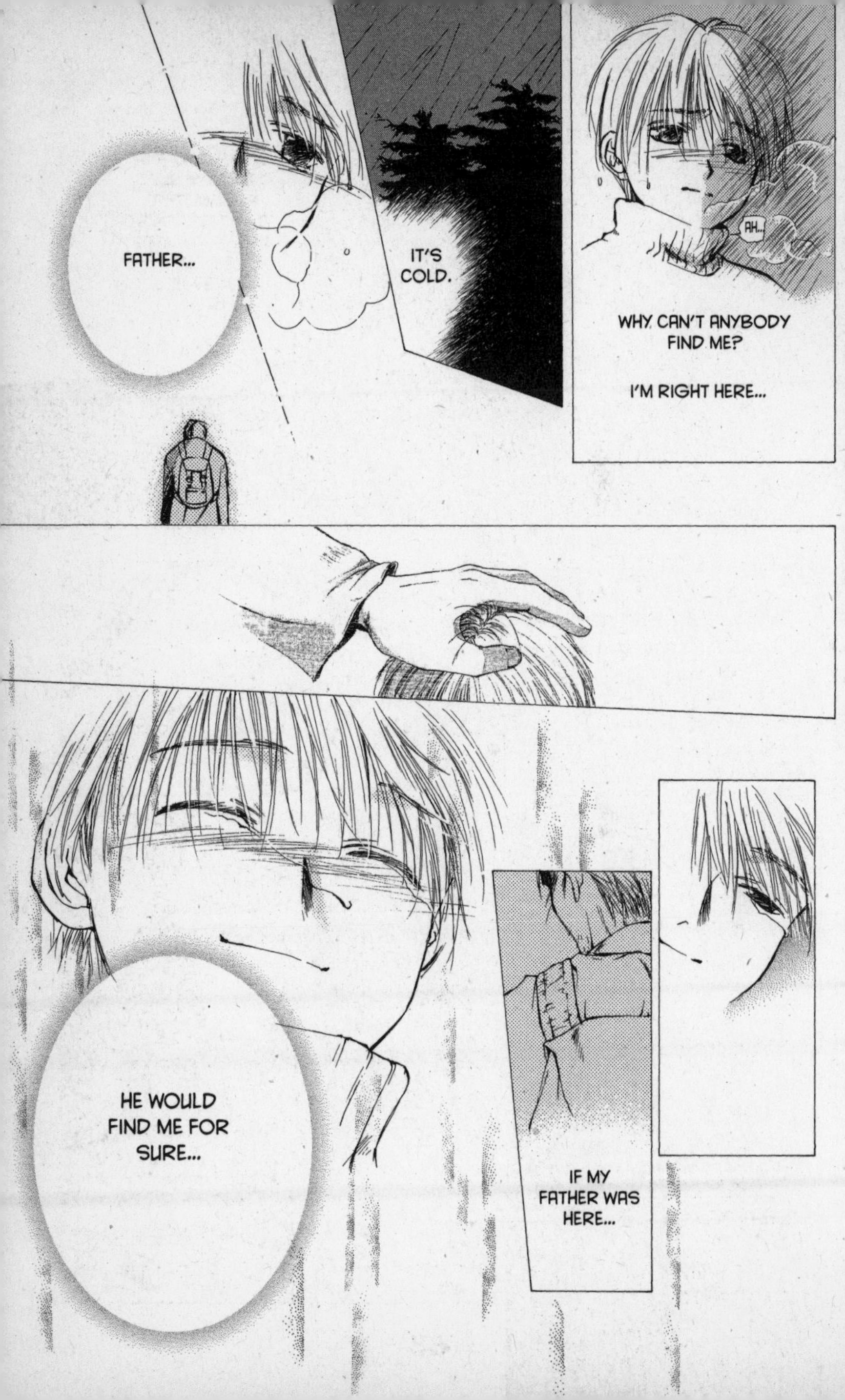
AH...
WHY CAN'T ANYBODY FIND ME?
I'M RIGHT HERE...
IT'S COLD.
FATHER...
IF MY FATHER WAS HERE...
HE WOULD FIND ME FOR SURE...

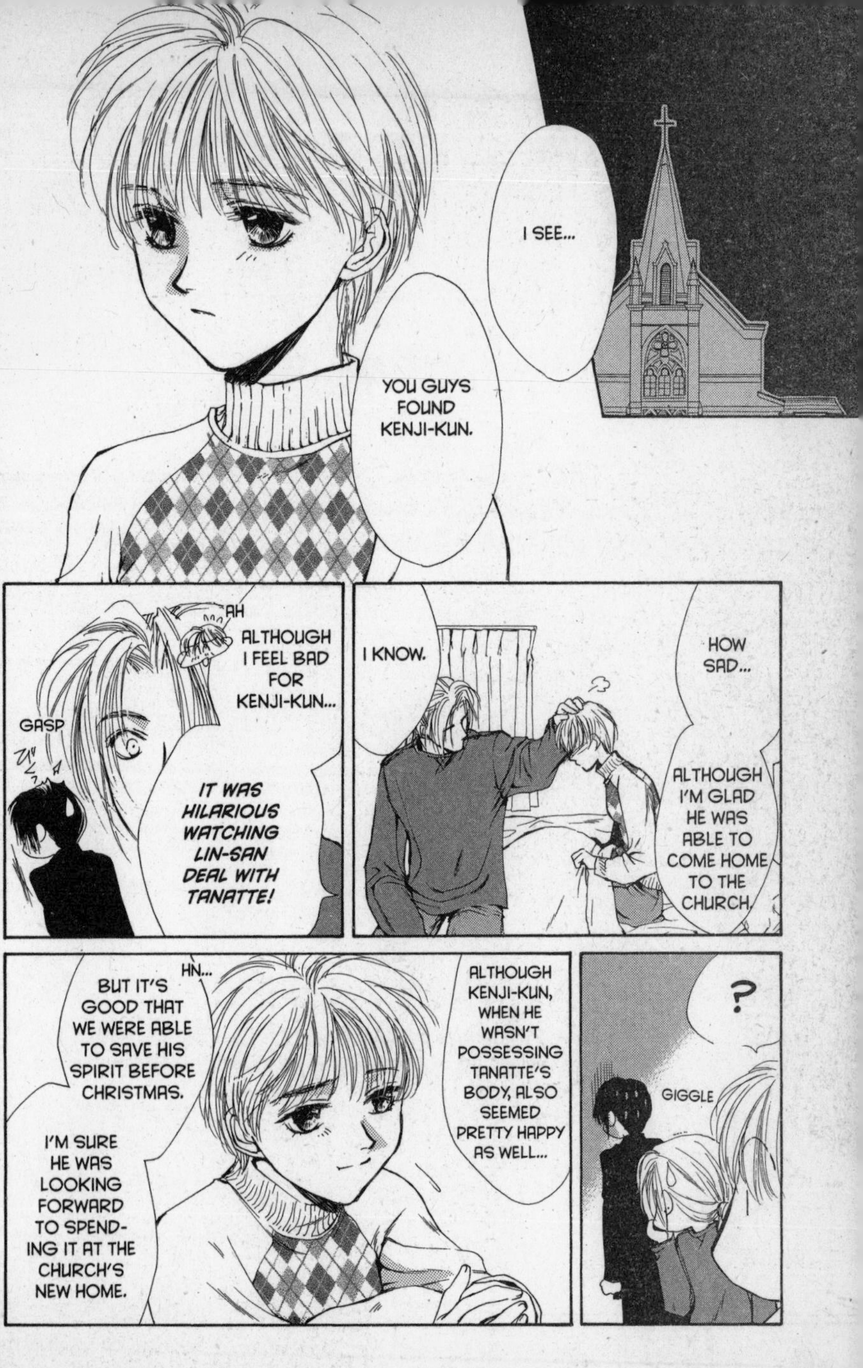
I SEE...
YOU GUYS FOUND KENJI-KUN.
HOW SAD...
ALTHOUGH I'M GLAD HE WAS ABLE TO COME HOME TO THE CHURCH.
I KNOW.
AH
ALTHOUGH I FEEL BAD FOR KENJI-KUN...
GASP
IT WAS HILARIOUS WATCHING LIN-SAN DEAL WITH TANATTE!
?
GIGGLE
ALTHOUGH KENJI-KUN, WHEN HE WASN'T POSSESSING TANATTE'S BODY, ALSO SEEMED PRETTY HAPPY AS WELL...
HN...
BUT IT'S GOOD THAT WE WERE ABLE TO SAVE HIS SPIRIT BEFORE CHRISTMAS.
I'M SURE HE WAS LOOKING FORWARD TO SPEND-ING IT AT THE CHURCH'S NEW HOME.

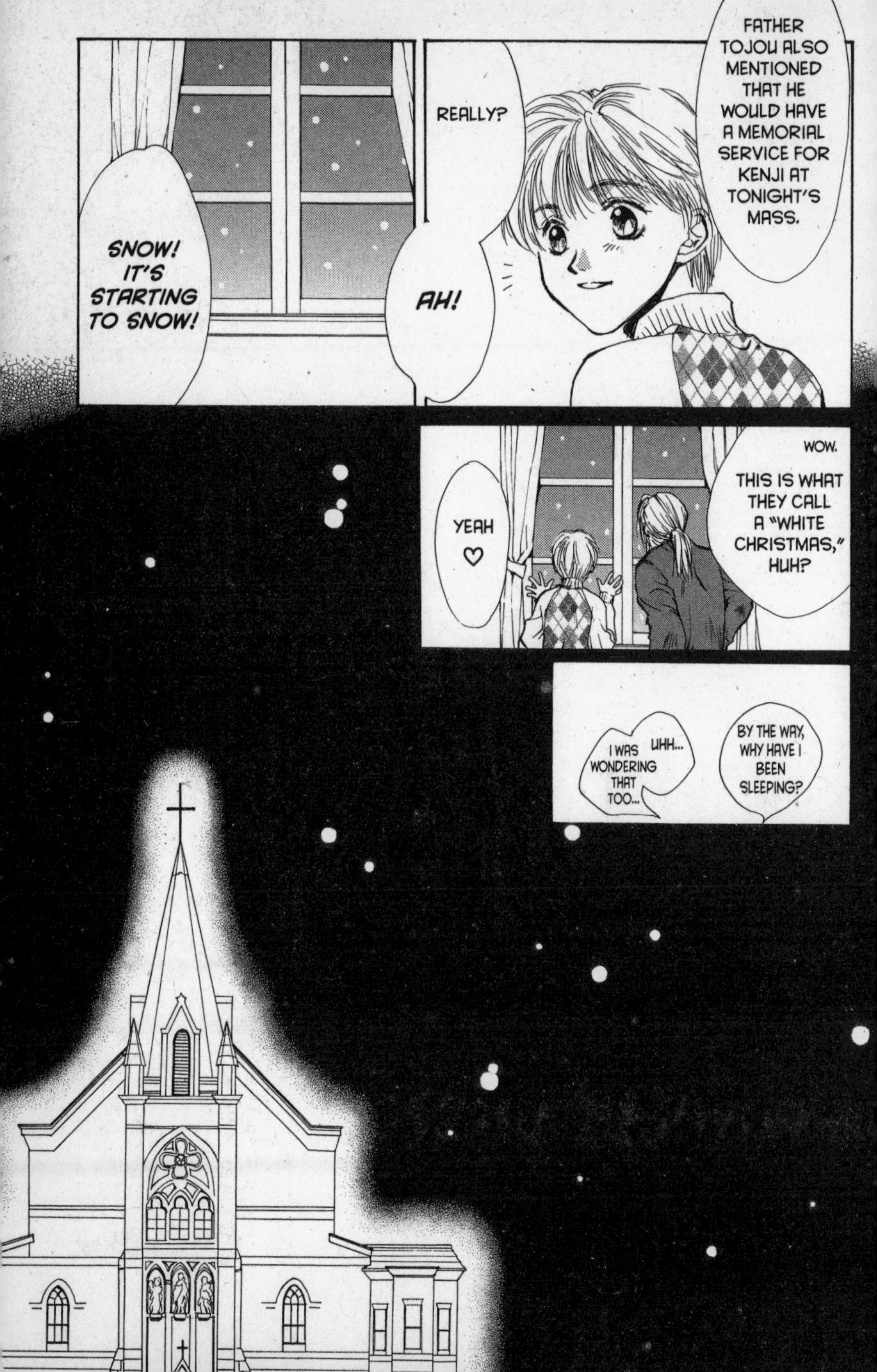
FATHER TOJOU ALSO MENTIONED THAT HE WOULD HAVE A MEMORIAL SERVICE FOR KENJI AT TONIGHT'S MASS.
REALLY?
AH!
SNOW! IT'S STARTING TO SNOW!
WOW.
THIS IS WHAT THEY CALL A "WHITE CHRISTMAS," HUH?
YEAH ♡
BY THE WAY, WHY HAVE I BEEN SLEEPING?
UHH...
I WAS WONDERING THAT TOO...

About the Creators of *Ghost Hunt*

ABOUT THE CREATOR

•

Shiho Inada

Born on October 17 in Kanagawa Prefecture.

Sign: Libra.

Blood type: B.

She made her debut with *Camouflage* in 1994.

Her best-known work is *Ghost Hunt*.

ABOUT THE WRITER

•

Fuyumi Ono

Born in Oita Prefecture.

She made her debut with *Teen's Heart,* published on Kodansha X Library.

Her most popular works: the *Evil Spirit* series and the *Twelve Kingdom* series.

Her works are widely read and although her novels are considered young adult fiction, her works are read by people from all walks of life.

Translation Notes

Japanese is a tricky language for most Westerners, and translation is often more art than science. For your edification and reading pleasure, here are notes on some of the places where we could have gone in a different direction in our translation of the work, or where a Japanese cultural reference is used.

PAGE 2, *KANSAI-BEN*

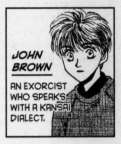

JOHN
BROWN
AN EXORCIST WHO SPEAKS WITH A KANSAI DIALECT.

The Japanese term for someone who speaks in a dialect used in the Kansai region of Japan is *Kansai-ben*. John Brown studied Japanese in Kansai and speaks Kansai dialect. Tokyo, on the other hand, is located in the Kanto region of Japan. Japanese spoken in Tokyo; however, is not known as Kanto dialect. It is simply called *hyojungo,* which literally translates as "standard Japanese."

PAGE 2, *MIKO*

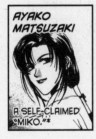

AYAKO
MATSUZAKI
A SELF-CLAIMED "MIKO."*

Miko means a priestess serving as an assistant at a shrine. In ancient times the *miko* served as a psychic medium. Today she mainly assists the priest in ceremonies and also performs ceremonial dances (*miko-mai*). Many people still believe that they regularly perform their ancient psychic duties.

PAGE 12, HEY, YOU!

WHAT!?
"HEY, YOU"!?

Omae (Hey you) is a rude way of calling someone you just met. Matsuyama is calling Naru "omae" and being disrespectful to him.

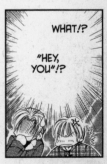

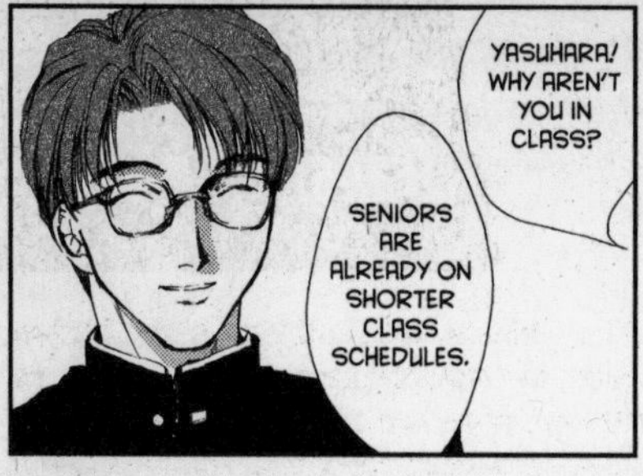
YASUHARA! WHY AREN'T YOU IN CLASS?
SENIORS ARE ALREADY ON SHORTER CLASS SCHEDULES.

PAGE 13, SHORTER CLASS SCHEDULE FOR HIGH SCHOOL SENIORS

In Japan most seniors in high school have a shorter class schedule by their third semester so that they can focus on studying for the university entrance exam. In general Japanese universities are hard to enter, and the competition to get into Japanese elite universities is extremely difficult. There's even a Japanese phrase *juken jigoku* which literally translates into "entrance exam hell."

PAGE 13, OUTSTANDING!

Takigawa and Mai are impressed with Osamu still being the student council president at their (senior) busiest time of the year, since most seniors are busy studying for the university entrance exam by this time of the year.

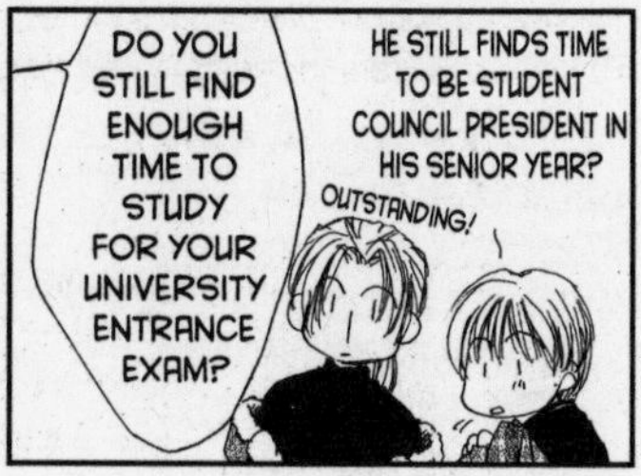
HE STILL FINDS TIME TO BE STUDENT COUNCIL PRESIDENT IN HIS SENIOR YEAR?
OUTSTANDING!
DO YOU STILL FIND ENOUGH TIME TO STUDY FOR YOUR UNIVERSITY ENTRANCE EXAM?

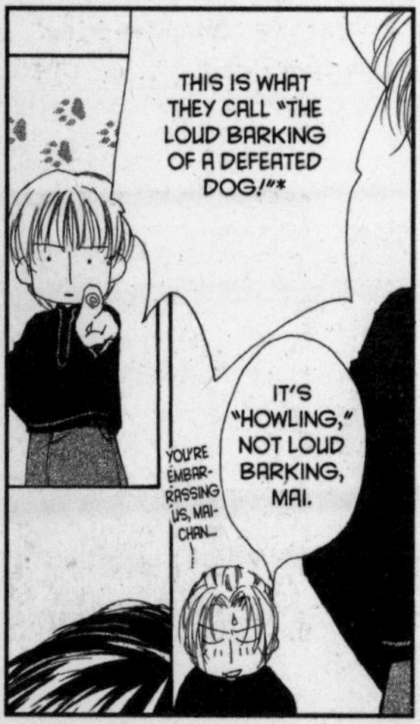
THIS IS WHAT THEY CALL "THE LOUD BARKING OF A DEFEATED DOG!"*
IT'S "HOWLING," NOT LOUD BARKING, MAI.
YOU'RE EMBARRASSING US, MAI-CHAN...

PAGE 16, HOWLING OF A DEFEATED DOG

Makeinu no touboe means "loser's howl," and is used to describe someone who complains after the decision is made. Here, Matsushima is being a jerk and doesn't know what he's talking about but he's still trying to argue with Naru so Mai is trying to make a point after he left the room... but she ended up using the wrong words...

PAGE 16, NAMU...

Takigawa is chanting because Mai made an embarrassing mistake and he has nothing else to say...

NAMU...

EH!?

THIS IS KOKKURI-SAN.*

PAGE 45, KOKKURI-SAN

Kokkuri-san is a type of fortune telling. It is sometimes believed that a fortune can be told by a fox spirit possessing someone's body. Generally performed by three people pressing one 10-yen coin [10 yen = approx.10 cent] on a piece of paper with multiple letters written on it and telling the fortune by seeing the letters that the coin points to. This is somewhat similar to a Ouija board, but the risk that you take by performing *kokkuri-san* is that someone in the room may become possessed by the spirit that is summoned during the session.

PAGE 53, JAPANESE-STYLE CLOSET

A Japanese-style closet, *oshi-ire,* is a built-in fixture for a Japanese style room and is about the size of one tatami mat (six feet long by three feet wide). *Oshi-ire* has a shelf in the middle that divides the closet into top and bottom storage spaces. Traditionally *oshi-ire* is used as a storage space for a futon when it is not in use.

MANY PEOPLE SAY THAT IF THE JAPANESE STYLE CLOSET DOOR OR EVEN A REGULAR DOOR IS A TINY BIT OPEN IT LOOKS CREEPY.

LIKE THIS.

PAGE 53, JAPANESE-STYLE ROOM

A Japanese-style room is called *washitsu*—the word *wa* means harmony (or peace) and *shitsu* means "room." *Washitsu* consists of *tatami* flooring as opposed to the wood or tile flooring of the rest of the house. The window and door fixtures of *washitsu* are sliding partitions called *shoji* and *fusuma*. *Shoji* is a light sliding screen consisting of a framework of wood covered with thin Japanese paper (*washi*). *Shoji* are mostly used as a partition between a porch-like area (or a garden) and a room. *Fusuma* are papered (or cloth) sliding doors for partitioning rooms.

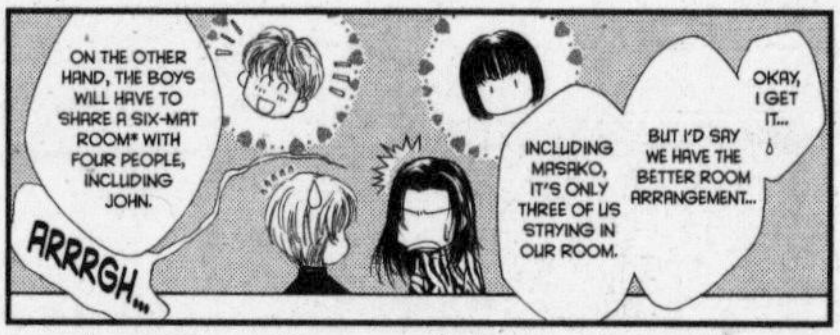
OKAY, I GET IT...
INCLUDING MASAKO, IT'S ONLY THREE OF US STAYING IN OUR ROOM.
BUT I'D SAY WE HAVE THE BETTER ROOM ARRANGEMENT...
ON THE OTHER HAND, THE BOYS WILL HAVE TO SHARE A SIX-MAT ROOM* WITH FOUR PEOPLE, INCLUDING JOHN.
ARRRGH...

PAGE 58, TATAMI MAT

A *tatami* is a straw mat about six feet long by three feet wide, with an average of 2.4 inches in thickness (a slight variation in size may be found in different regions of Japan). It is used for flooring Japanese rooms. Thanks to this tradition, the term *jo* (a unit, one mat in size) is still used today in Japan to describe the size of a room, even for Western-style rooms without *tatami* mats.

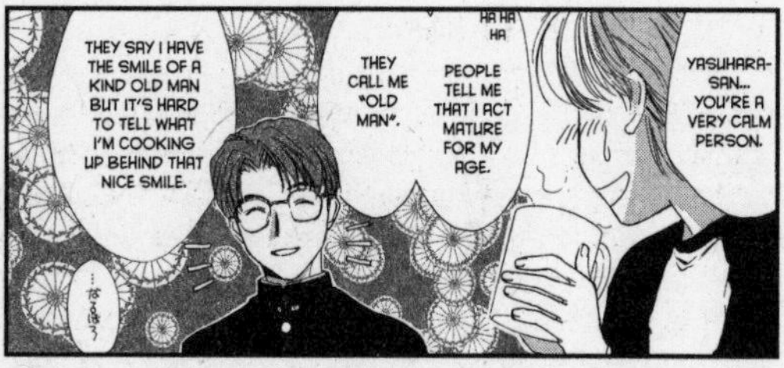
YASUHARA-SAN... YOU'RE A VERY CALM PERSON.
HA HA HA
PEOPLE TELL ME THAT I ACT MATURE FOR MY AGE.
THEY CALL ME "OLD MAN".
THEY SAY I HAVE THE SMILE OF A KIND OLD MAN BUT IT'S HARD TO TELL WHAT I'M COOKING UP BEHIND THAT NICE SMILE.

PAGE 95, ECHIGOYA

In the original Japanese, they don't call Osamu "old man"—they call him Echigoya. Echigoya was the most successful kimono fabric store during the feudal Edo period in Japan, and it was established in 1673 by Takatoshi Mitsui. It is the forerunner of the modern Mitsukoshi department store. By calling him Echigoya, they are saying he seems really old.

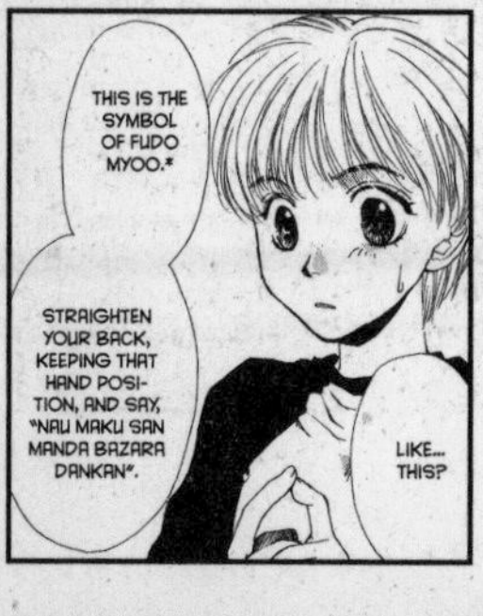
THIS IS THE SYMBOL OF FUDO MYOO.*
STRAIGHTEN YOUR BACK, KEEPING THAT HAND POSI-TION, AND SAY, "NAU MAKU SAN MANDA BAZARA DANKAN".
LIKE... THIS?

PAGE 99, FUDO MYOO

Fudo Myoo means immutable one, and he is the Buddhist god of fire. Fodo Myoo is the principal deity of the Five Angry Lords of Light and is known for his flaming sword and his rope. Here Takigawa is showing Mai how to perform an exorcism by instructing her how to make the symbolic signs of Fudo Myoo and chant mantra.

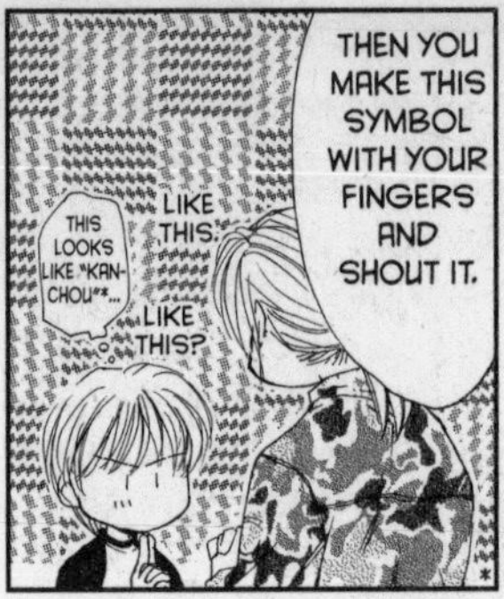
THEN YOU MAKE THIS SYMBOL WITH YOUR FINGERS AND SHOUT IT.
LIKE THIS.
THIS LOOKS LIKE "KAN-CHOU"*...
LIKE THIS?

PAGE 99, *KANCHOU*

The literal meaning of *Kanchou* is to give an enema, but sometimes Japanese children will kid around and point both index fingers and wrap the rest of their fingers to make the symbol of *kanchou*. They follow other kids with their hands in this formation as if they are about to give an enema to them, and the children will try to run away. Here, Mai is making the Fudo Myoo symbol but she can't help being reminded of *kanchou*.

PAGE 103, BUCKWHEAT CHAFF

Traditional Japanese pillows are filled with buckwheat chaff or red beans. Here Takigawa is handing over a pillow filled with buckwheat chaff, which is old-fashioned, but because of that it's meant to be a cute and funny scene in the story.

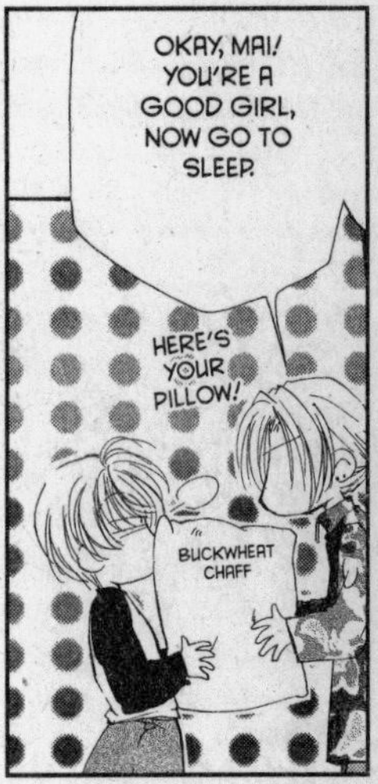
OKAY, MAI! YOU'RE A GOOD GIRL, NOW GO TO SLEEP.
HERE'S YOUR PILLOW!
BUCKWHEAT CHAFF

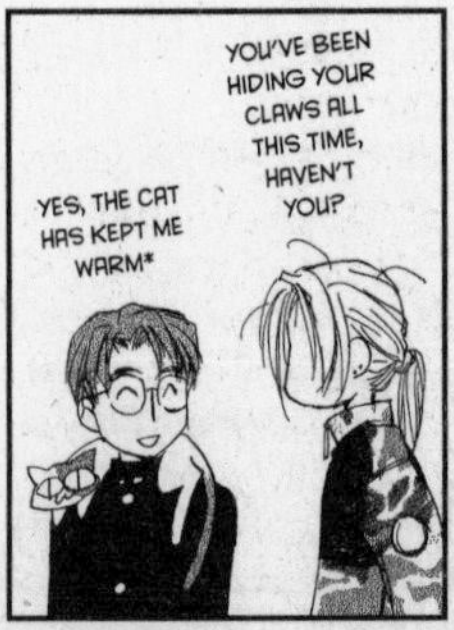
YOU'VE BEEN HIDING YOUR CLAWS ALL THIS TIME, HAVEN'T YOU?
YES, THE CAT HAS KEPT ME WARM*

PAGE 105, COVERING CAT

There are many Japanese sayings that reference cats. One of them is *neko-kaburi*, which literally means "covering yourself with cat." It indicates fake modesty, a put-on, or hiding one's claws. Osamu here was ordering Mai around and started to show his true character as president of his student council, and Takigawa is busting his chops in a friendly way, by telling him that Masao had been quiet all this time and now he is finally coming out.

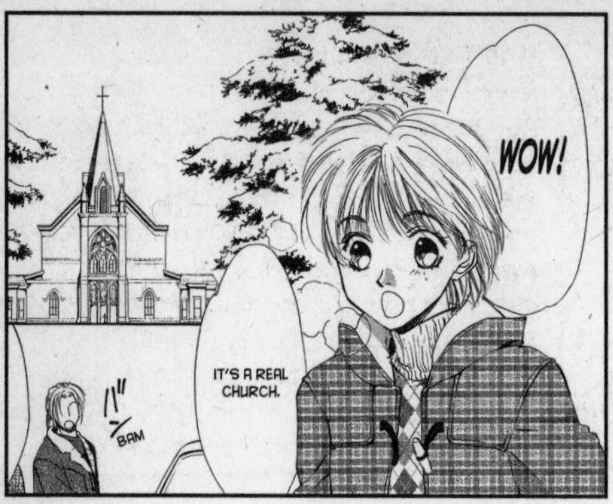
WOW!
IT'S A REAL CHURCH.
BAM

PAGE 108, CHURCHES IN JAPAN

There aren't as many churches in Japan as in the U.S. This is the first time Mai has ever seen a church in person and she's very excited about it.

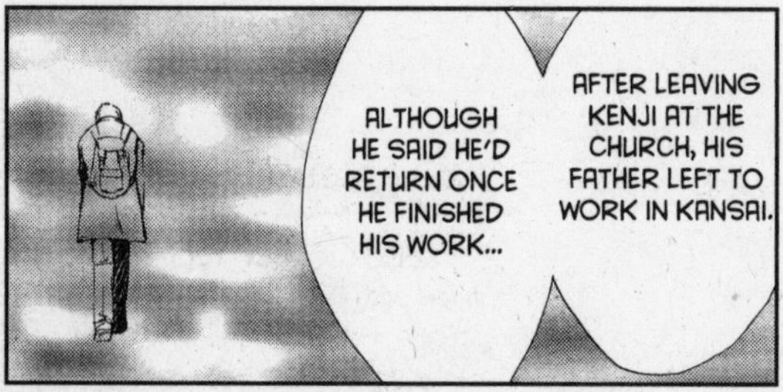
AFTER LEAVING KENJI AT THE CHURCH, HIS FATHER LEFT TO WORK IN KANSAI.
ALTHOUGH HE SAID HE'D RETURN ONCE HE FINISHED HIS WORK...

PAGE 146, KANSAI

Kansai is a region in Japan, which includes, Nara, Osaka, Kyoto, and Kobe. The dialect spoken in Kansai is called *Kansai-ben* (Kansai dialect).

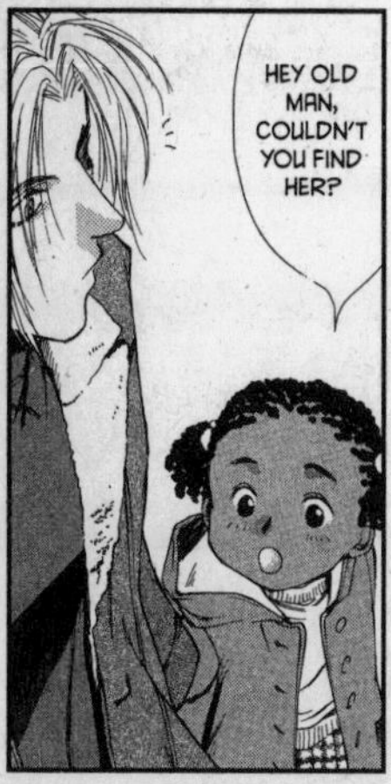
HEY OLD MAN, COULDN'T YOU FIND HER?

PAGE 154, *OJI-CHAN* AND *ONII-CHAN*

In the original Japanese, the little boy calls Takigawa *Oji-chan*. *Oji-chan* means an old man or an uncle and *onii-chan* means an older brother. *Onii-chan* can also be used to call a familiar man who is simply older than you. Here, the child is calling Takigawa *oji-chan* as an old man, but he's correcting her to call him *onii-chan* (an older brother-like man) because he doesn't want to be treated as an old man. [FYI: be careful not to get *oji-chan* mixed up with a similar word, *ojii-chan*, which means grandfather.]

GHOST HUNT

5

MANGA BY SHIHO INADA

STORY BY FUYUMI ONO

We're pleased to present you a preview from Volume 5. This volume will be available in English in September 2006, but for now you'll have to make do with Japanese!

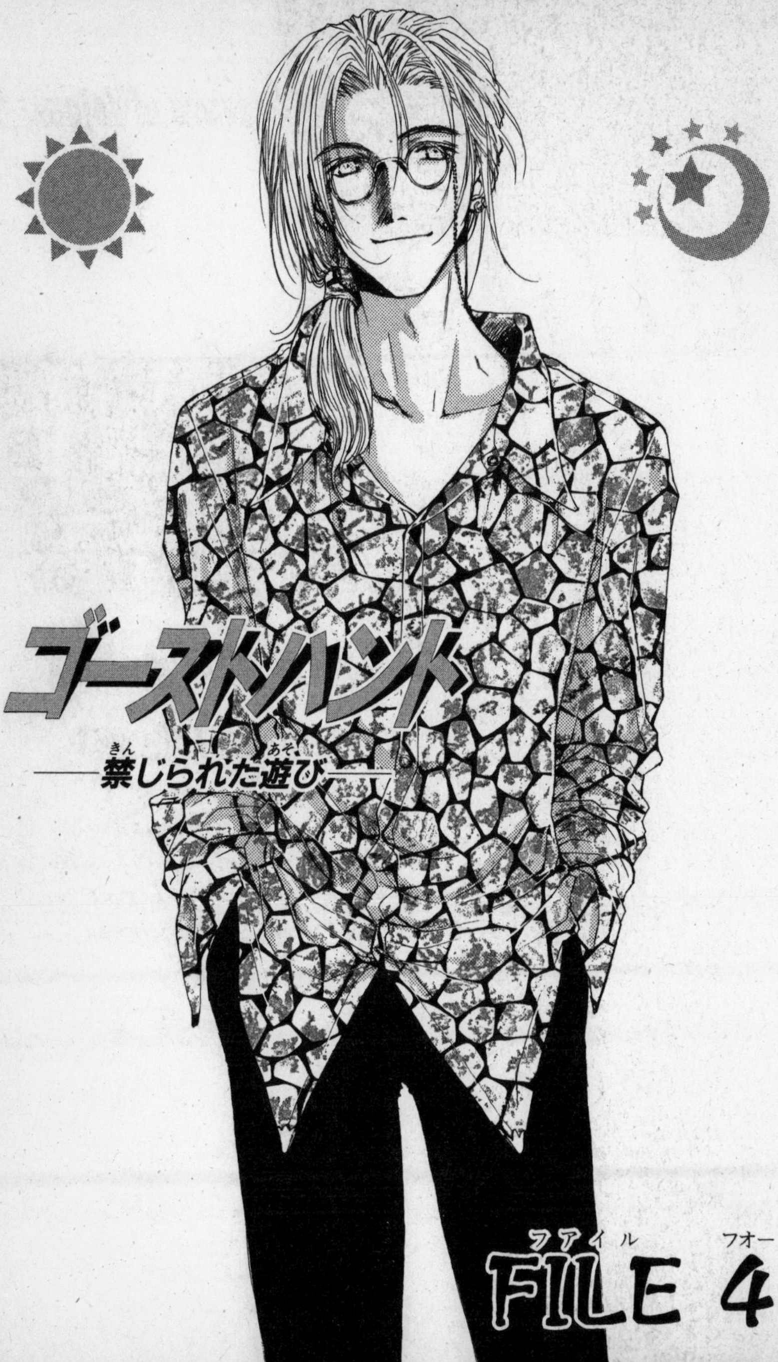
ゴーストハント
——禁じられた遊び——
FILE 4

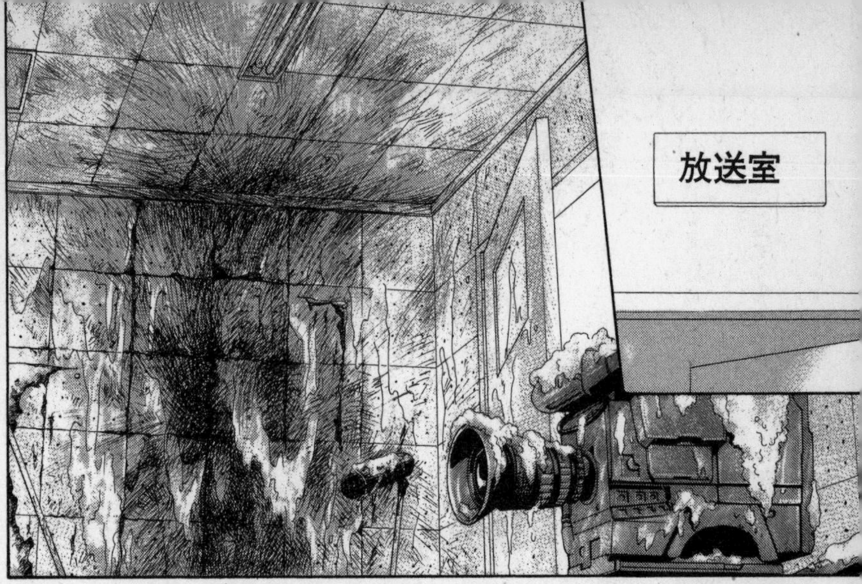
放送室

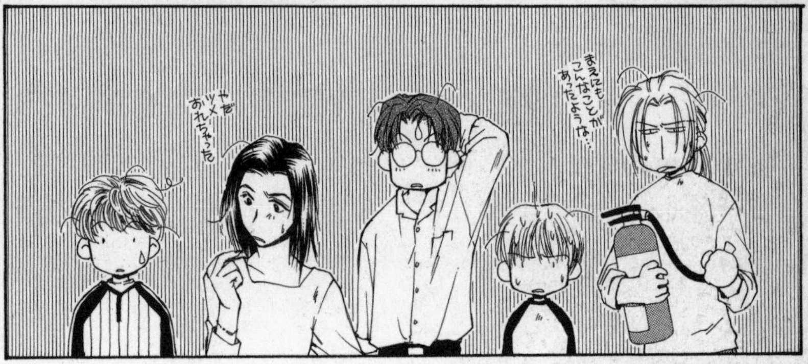
まえにも こんなことが あったような…
やだ ツメ おれちゃった

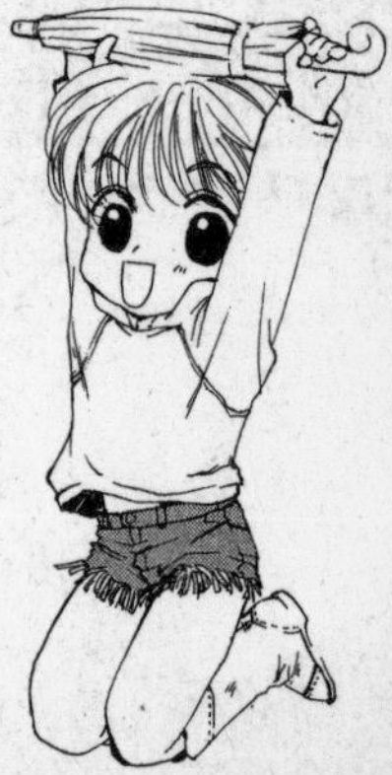

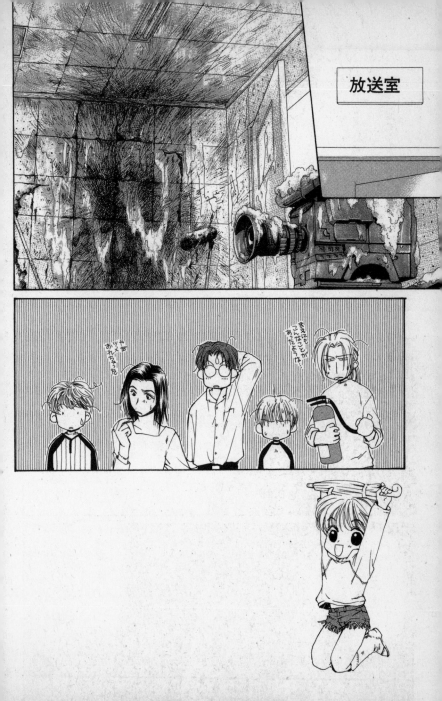

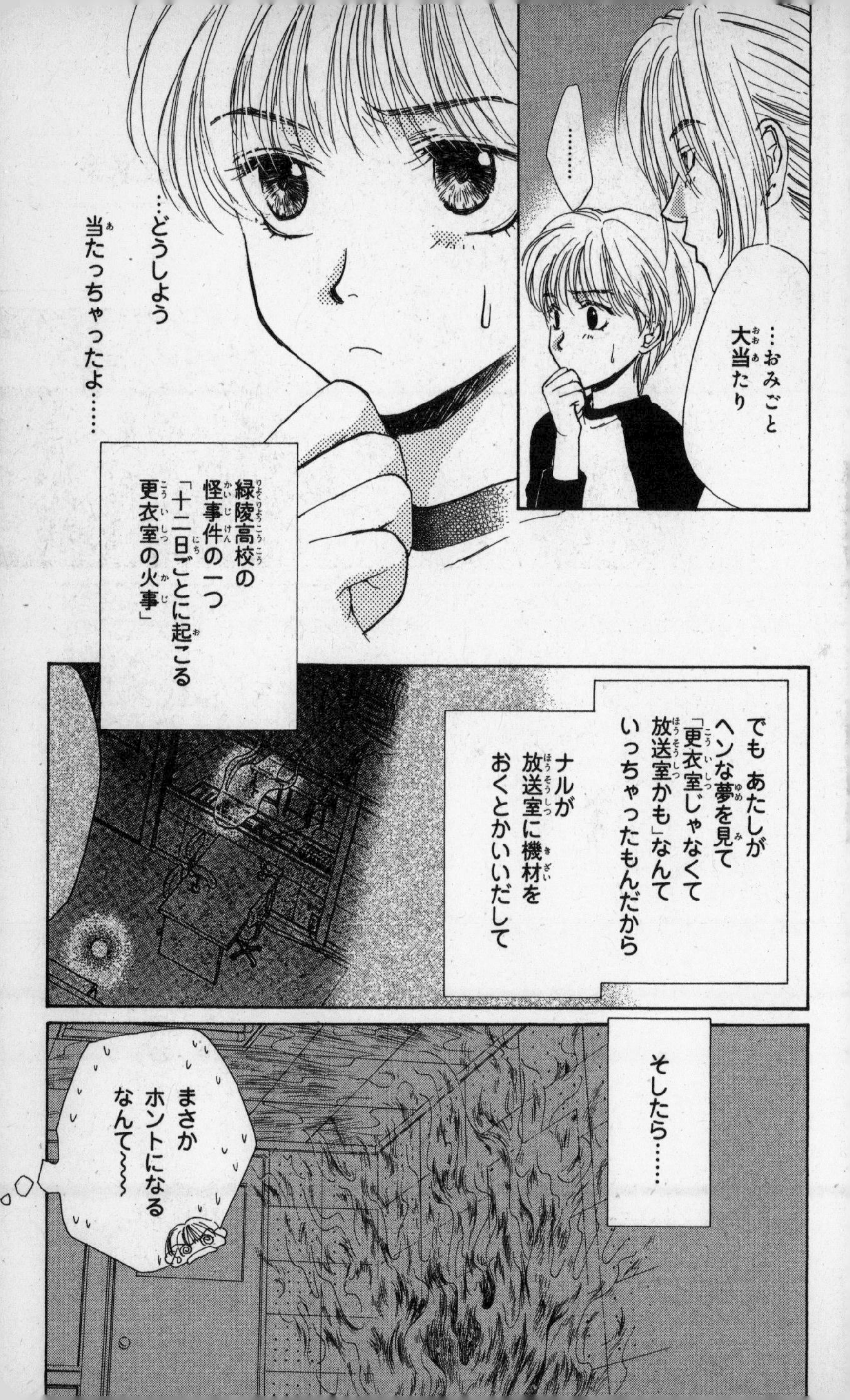
…おみごと 大当たり
……
…どうしよう
当たっちゃったよ……
緑陵高校の怪事件の一つ「十二日ごとに起こる更衣室の火事」
でも あたしが ヘンな夢を見て「更衣室じゃなくて放送室かも」なんていっちゃったもんだから
ナルが放送室に機材をおくとかいいだして
そしたら……
まさか ホントになる なんて~~~

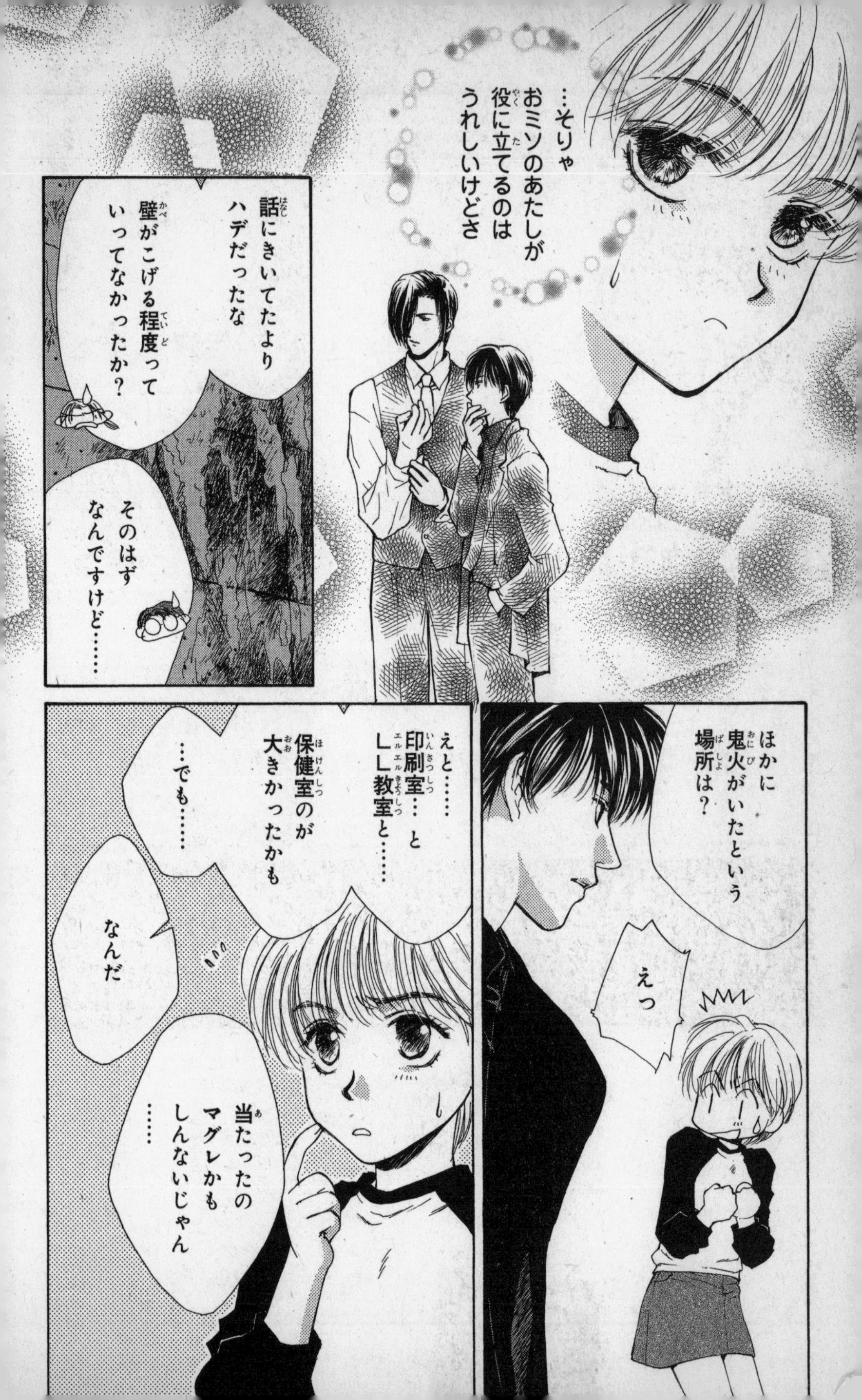
…そりゃ おミソのあたしが 役に立てるのは うれしいけどさ
話にきいてたより ハデだったな 壁がこげる程度って いってなかったか?
そのはず なんですけど……
ほかに 鬼火がいたという 場所は?
えっ
えと…… 印刷室…と LL教室と…… 保健室のが 大きかったかも
…でも……
なんだ
当たったの マグレかも しんないじゃん
……

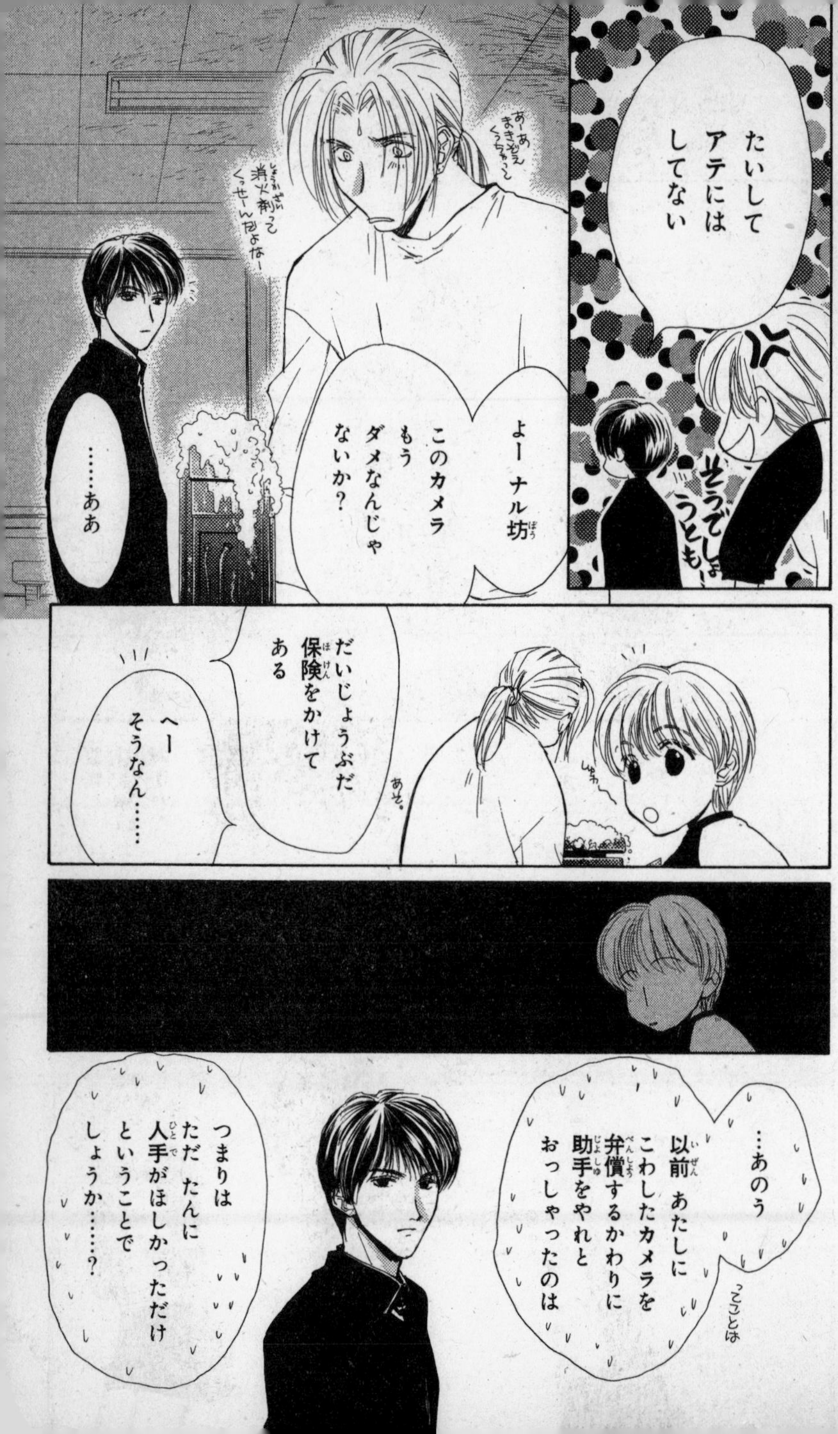
たいしてアテにはしてない
そうでしょうとも
よーナル坊
このカメラもうダメなんじゃないか?
あーあ まきぞえくっちゃって
消火剤ってくっせーんだよなー
……ああ
だいじょうぶだ保険をかけてある
あせ
へーそうなん……
…あのう 以前あたしにこわしたカメラを弁償するかわりに助手をやれとおっしゃったのは
ってことは
つまりはただ たんに人手がほしかっただけということでしょうか……?

TOMARE!

STOP!

YOU'RE GOING THE WRONG WAY!

MANGA IS A COMPLETELY DIFFERENT TYPE OF READING EXPERIENCE.

TO START AT THE **BEGINNING**, GO TO THE **END**!

THAT'S RIGHT!

AUTHENTIC MANGA IS READ THE TRADITIONAL JAPANESE WAY— FROM RIGHT TO LEFT. EXACTLY THE **OPPOSITE** OF HOW AMERICAN BOOKS ARE READ. IT'S EASY TO FOLLOW: JUST GO TO THE OTHER END OF THE BOOK, AND READ EACH PAGE—AND EACH PANEL—FROM RIGHT SIDE TO LEFT SIDE, STARTING AT THE TOP RIGHT. NOW YOU'RE EXPERIENCING MANGA AS IT WAS MEANT TO BE.